TREATY-BREAKERS OR "REALPOLITIKER"?
The Anglo-German Naval Agreement of June 1935

ÉVA H. HARASZTI

TREATY-BREAKERS OR "REALPOLITIKER"?

THE ANGLO-GERMAN NAVAL AGREEMENT
OF JUNE 1935

HARALD BOLDT VERLAG · BOPPARD AM RHEIN

Translated
by
Sándor Simon

Editorial Assistance
by
Prof. Eric Waldman

A joint edition published by Harald Boldt Verlag,
Boppard am Rhein and Akadémiai Kiadó, Budapest

ISBN 3 7646 1578 8

Printed in Hungary

"The policy of appeasement is not to be understood unless it is realized that it represented the acceptance by the British Government, at least in part, of Hitler's view of what British policy should be."

(A. Bullock: *Hitler, a Study in Tyranny*)

CONTENTS

FOREWORD

The subject of this study is the Anglo-German Naval Agreement concluded on June 18, 1935. The text of the agreement is accessible. Also the background leading up to its making is known more or less — at least to historians who have already studied the matter. The choice of the subject matter is nevertheless justified. The naval treaty concluded by the British and the Germans was evidently of greater advantage to the British side. The Germans, on the other hand, were given an equal chance to build up their fleet, including submarines. It remained, however, unexplained, why they entered into this agreement at all.

The agreement, already at the time when it was concluded, was full of contradictions. British foreign policy concerning the naval treaty was questioned — to say the least. It was opposed at home by the brightest minds in the Foreign Office, by the Permanent Under-Secretary of State for Foreign Affairs, Sir Robert Vansittart and by Anthony Eden, the future Foreign Secretary. Against the Agreement was also the most intelligent politician of the Opposition, Winston Churchill, the principal adviser to the Chancellor of the Exchequer, the Permanent Under-Secretary to the Treasury, Sir Warren Fisher, and Britain's best military expert, Sir Basil Liddell Hart. On the other side, in addition to defence and naval interests, certain regressive forces prevailed over these distinguished authorities, such as the vain hope of immediate advantages, the sterile and uninformed anti-Sovietism and conservatism of the Cliveden set, personal ambitions and vanity of some politicians, wrong appraisal of the bluffing dictator Hitler, a certain degree of misinformation and, last but not least, the traditional British balance-of-power policy which in the 1930's was already under revision from the point of view of the British Empire.

This writing is intended as a "case study," about an event which should not have occurred, and whose consequences were not only damaging but also fraught with inevitable dangers. Sensible and reasoning people in all parts of the world could see these dangers but they could not avert them because of the given situation.

This case study reflects a situation cross-section: an enlarged still from a motion picture of running events. It may be instructive to the contemporary observer because it shows also that a recognized, reasonable way is not always pursued, that decisions are interwoven with human vanities and inabilities, that occasionally even a clear-sighted, reasoning politician retreats as a result of clamorous activists, that appearances and calculated effects should not be underrated, or briefly summing up: how strongly the course and progress of history is burdened by man-made obstacles, by the limits characteristic of human nature and of human faculties. This complicated course of development can be found out only through a method which can evaluate the given objective socio-economic situation which in turn is determined by the behaviour and the attitude of people, and at the same time takes the variations of human nature into consideration. It confirms what Engels said eighty years ago: "History is made so that the end-result is always the product of many individual wills . . . for what every individual man wants is prevented by everybody else, and what came about nobody wanted."

In order to explore the historical process and its regular unfolding, we have to know what individual men wanted and why developments proceeded as they did. Research into details is therefore absolutely necessary in order to substantiate statements of principle. This cross-section is shown by a microscopic test which can present a basis for the diagnosis of pathological changes in the whole body.

"It is not merely treachery, it is folly."

(A French diplomat's spontaneous remark upon the Naval Agreement in June 1935)

INTRODUCTION

The Anglo-German Naval Agreement, concluded in the form of an exchange of notes on June 18, 1935, established a ratio of 35 to 100 between the German navy and the aggregate naval forces of the British Commonwealth countries. (In respect of submarines Britain declared parity, though Germany undertook, except for emergency, to abide by a ratio of 45 to 100.) Under the agreement Germany was entitled to expand her fleet actually by 420,000 tons, and thus to build up a naval force which was 15 per cent smaller, but much more up to date, than the French fleet.[1]

A competent British historian of diplomacy called the Anglo-German Naval Agreement one of the most bewildering events of the year 1935.[2] A considerable part of the writings and memoirs relating to the agreement described this momentous issue of the Anglo-German rapprochement as a turning point in Britain's foreign policy, or at least as the first concrete manifestation of the political line aimed at the appeasement of Hitler.[3] However, if we examine the events of the roughly two years which preceded the Naval Agreement in the light of diplomatic activities and reflected in the memoirs of the personages concerned, we may say that the conclusions of the Naval Agreement which undoubtedly expressed an Anglo-German rapprochement came neither as a

[1] The text of the Anglo-German Naval Agreement is published in Hungarian in Dénes Halmosy, *Nemzetközi szerződések 1918—1945* (International Treaties 1918—1945), Budapest, 1966, pp. 368—372.

[2] D. C. Watt, "The Anglo-German Naval Agreement of 1935: An Interim Judgment," *The Journal of Modern History*, June 1956, p. 155.

[3] The biographer of Under-Secretary Sir Robert Vansittart (1930—1938) explained it as follows: "Thus about the time that the great reign of King George V ended the Cabinet talk had turned from collective security to appeasement." *Cf.* I. Colvin, *Vansittart in Office*, London, 1965, p. 56.

surprise nor was it a turning point. Nevertheless, it was incontestably indicative of a success of the British policy of appeasement, and this is why it is worth to inquire into its origin, into the proceeding of its negotiation — also as a "novelty" of the Nazi methods of diplomacy and the first success scored by the "Ribbentrop Bureau" — and into its reception in Britain and abroad, as well as into its repercussions reaching as far as Munich and the outbreak of World War II.

— Nothing will content German opinion
but 'victory' and that they will treat the
Treaty of Versailles as an artichoke, pulling
it to pieces leaf by leaf."

(H. Nicolson: *Diaries and Letters 1930—39*
Collins, 1967, p. 157)

POLITICAL ANTECEDENTS TO THE NAVAL AGREEMENT

At the time of Weimar Germany the opinion prevailing in England was that
the Germans had been harshly and unjustly treated by the Versailles peace
arrangements following World War I. This was at that time the fashionable
view in Cambridge.[1] With Hitler's rise to power, however, British public
opinion, allergic to Nazi brutalities, temporarily became less interested in
remedying the German grievances, in recognizing or even considering the
justness of the German demands. Yet the winding path of British foreign policy
and its way of choosing the partners were usually charted, not by public senti-
ment or general desire, but by the traditional nineteenth-century policy of a
European balance of power that was thought to be in the "well-considered"
interest of the British Empire. It was in this spirit that members of the British
Cabinet, first of all the Secretary of State for Foreign Affairs and staff members
of his Office, chiefs and members of the Conservative Party, and conservative
lords of the press were — with few exceptions — brought up to become the
leaders of the United Kingdom. That is the reason why Hitler, right after his
coming to power could, at the Cabinet meeting of February 8, 1933, announce
his definite intention of rearming Germany. Thus it was possible that he steadily
increased the strength of the Reichswehr (from 96,000 men in the first half of
1933 to about 160,000 by the end of the same year). During the whole year
only two members of the British Parliament, Clement Richard Attlee for the
Labour Party and Winston Churchill for the Conservatives, raised the voice
of protest against the fact that Great Britain, ignoring the changes that had
occurred in Germany, continued the policy of appeasement towards the Germans.[2] Furthermore, on March 16, 1933, James Ramsay MacDonald, the

[1] E. Wiskemann, *The Europe I Saw*, London, 1968, p. 11. A good expression was
coined to qualify this: "Sentimental pro-Germanism." Miss Eleanor Rathborne
used it in the debate at Chatham House. *Cf.* M. Beloff, *The Foreign Policy of
Soviet Russia*, Oxford, 1947, vol. I, p. 109.
[2] Concerning this as well as the British and French Governments' policies in
1933—34, German rearmament, and MacDonald's disarmament proposal, *cf.*

13

former Labour Prime Minister, submitted to the League's Council in Geneva[3] a proposal which, on one hand, demonstrated to Hitler that "the Versailles powers were unable to take a united and strong line against him" and which, on the other hand, "could be expected to count upon appreciation only from Fascist Germany."[4] It was due to the particular British foreign policy based upon the European balance of power that the British Government was unable to fall into step with the French efforts regarding the questions of disarmament, or rather German rearmament, and the questions of security in general.

Britain's foreign policy was, in the first half of 1935, primarily influenced by the German question and, in the second half of the year, by the Italo-Ethiopian conflict. Developments in the Far East were temporarily eclipsed. At the beginning of the year, general attention was focussed on the Franco-Italian pact (the so-called Rome agreements) and the Saar plebiscite. The conventions signed on January 7, 1935, by Foreign Minister Pierre Laval of France and Premier Benito Mussolini of Italy were the result of the policy of a Franco-Italian rapprochement. By the terms of the pact, France made minor concessions to Italy in East Africa, while Italy agreed to conclude a Danubian pact guaranteeing the independence of Austria (the signatory states would have been Austria, Italy, Yugoslavia, Germany, Czechoslovakia and Hungary, with France, Poland and Rumania to be invited to accede to the pact). The two Governments recognized — in accordance with the Geneva declaration of December 11, 1932 — Germany's equality of rights in a system of security. They also came to an understanding that "no country should modify unilaterally its obligations concerning armaments, and agreed to take concerted action in case this principle would not be recognized."[5]

What did Paris and Rome expect and what did they receive from their agreement, and how did London and Berlin react to it?

France tried hard to win over Italy to her own side against growing German revanchism. Laval shrewdly exploited the German—Italian controversy over the Austrian question, and with the Rome pact he lent obvious support to Italy's war against Ethiopia and, for the duration of that war, he even received some safeguards against Germany (in the form of a Franco-German accommodation and in that of Italian collaboration in blocking the German aspirations). Laval's further aim was to increase the strength of Italy's and France's Mediterranean fleets so that — as was vaguely intimated by an Italian historian — the Italian fleet in the Mediterranean should cease to be "a tool of British

Mária Sz. Ormos, "A fegyverkezés kérdése az európai diplomáciában Hitler hatalomra jutása után (1933—34)" [The Armaments Issue in European Diplomacy after Hitler's Access to Power (1933—34)], *Századok*, 2—3/1966, pp. 400—448.

[3] J. R. MacDonald's second so-called National Cabinet was formed in November 1931 and lasted until June 1935. Some of its best known members were: Neville Chamberlain, Chancellor of the Exchequer; Sir Herbert Samuel, Home Secretary; Sir John Simon, Secretary of State for Foreign Affairs; and the Marquess of Londonderry, Secretary of State for Air.

[4] *Cf.* Ormos, *loc. cit.*, pp. 403, 408.

[5] Quoted by Halmosy (*op. cit.*, p. 355) in connection with the Rome agreements. — As to the substance, discussion and failure of the Danubian pact, see M. Sz. Ormos, "Sur les causes de l'échec du pacte danubien (1934—35)," *Acta Historica*, 1—2/1968, pp. 21—83.

policy.''[6] At the same time Laval wished to prevail upon Britain to accept his conception for a solution of the disarmament question. (Britain willingly supported the Franco-Italian declaration opposing the unilateral repudiation of Part V of the Treaty of Versailles.)

Italy, on the other hand, wanted to enlist the support of France, and consequently of Britain, for her war against Ethiopia. According to Hans Georg von Mackensen, the German Minister in Budapest, the agreement arrived at between Italy and France was ascribed by Berlin mainly to Mussolini's effort "to prevent by all means a Franco-German rapprochement which would seem feasible after the final settlement of the Saar question."[7]

The Rome agreements made it possible for the German leaders to stress again in confidential circles their firm refusal of an Eastern pact, and although they raised no objection in principle to the Danubian pact at the time, they found a practical loophole just in the Rome agreements' clauses concerning Central Europe. The German argument against the Franco-Italian pact of January 7, 1935, was the following: "There is no objection in principle to a Danubian pact, but first some not quite clear points of the Protocol should be precisely defined. To Germany the main difficulty is that, by virtue of the Rome agreements, this pact ought to be concluded under the auspices of the League of Nations. Berlin is *not* inclined to this and will reject any attempt made to bring Germany back into the League."[8]

In order to clear up this problem, the following notorious facts should be remembered: Germany was admitted to the League of Nations on September 8, 1926, and, as one of the great powers, she was made a permanent member of the Council of the League. She resigned from the League on October 19, 1933, and definitively withdrew from the Disarmament Conference, giving as a reason that the disarmament proposals failed to guarantee in practice Germany's equality of rights in respect of armaments — or rather her open rearming which at the time already assumed immense proportions. Germany's withdrawal from the League of Nations in 1933 gave a new impetus to the efforts at the creation of a system of collective security. The plan of the Eastern pact was proposed by Louis Barthou, Foreign Minister of France, in 1934. His idea was to complement the Locarno Treaty with a so-called Eastern Locarno pact and, by organizing in this way a system of collective security, to check Germany's threatening expansion. Germany was against the Eastern Locarno plan, against French guarantees in Eastern Europe, and still more against Soviet guarantees in Western Europe. In its memorandum of September 8, 1934, the German Government refused to accede to the pact on the grounds that Germany still preferred the system of bilateral treaties of non-aggression

[6] G. Salvemini, *Prelude to World War II*, London, 1953, p. 219.

[7] Conversation between Foreign Minister Kálmán Kánya of Hungary and the German Minister in Budapest, Hans Georg von Mackensen. Daily report, January 23, 1935. OL Küm. Pol. 1935—2/16—290.

[8] Quoted from Halmosy, *op. cit.*, p. 355. As concerns the German objections, see the aforementioned conversation with Mackensen. — With respect to the plan and the story of the Eastern pact, *cf.* Halmosy, *op. cit.*, pp. 347—351. As to its more recent scientific evaluation in Hungarian, *cf.* Mária Ormos, *Franciaország és a keleti biztonság 1931—1936* [France and Eastern Security 1931—1936], Budapest, 1969, p. 453.

with the neighbouring countries, and furthermore that she could not participate in any new international security systems as long as the powers deny her claim to equality in respect to armaments. But the making of an Eastern pact was actually prevented by Poland. The talks aiming at such a pact were definitively abandoned as a result of the Italo-Ethiopian war which started in the autumn of 1935.

The British standpoint in connection with the Rome agreements underwent a positive development as a consequence of complementary, interacting diplomatic events in Europe. As we read in a comprehensive report of the Czechoslovak Chargé d'Affaires in London: "The Rome pact arrived at between Laval and Mussolini was received in England with great sympathy. The press here stresses that for long years this is the first time that the ex-allies have again come closer together. Also it expresses the hope that this will furnish a basis for further negotiations and strengthen co-operation between the two countries and even lead to a détente in Central Europe and to a definitive settlement of the questions concerning the Danube area. At the time of the January talks, Foreign Secretary Sir John Simon and Mr. Anthony Eden called on Laval, who spent two hours informing them in detail of the purpose and significance of the Rome agreements. The British ministers thanked Laval for this information and wished him much success in his efforts exerted in the interest of consolidation in Europe."[9]

During these talks those essential problems arose which came to light barely a month later in the Franco-British declaration. The British Cabinet discussed in a lenghty meeting on January 9 the Franco-Italian accord, expressed its satisfaction concerning the result, and emphasized the great significance of the pact for the British Government. It constituted a promise for the possibility of Germany's return to Geneva and for the conclusion of a disarmament convention. The Rumanian Chargé d'Affaires in London informed his Minister of Foreign Affairs, Nicolae Titulescu, accordingly and mentioned the busy preparations being made, between London and Paris, for a forthcoming visit to London by French Premier Pierre-Étienne Flandin and M. Pierre Laval. It was at this British Cabinet meeting of January 9 that the question of a British guarantee to be offered to France was raised.[10]

Before the Saar plebiscite of January 13 the British Government still cherished faint hopes of wooing Germany to rejoin the League of Nations. On January 10 the British Ambassador in Berlin, on instructions from London (and in agreement with the French Government), saw Foreign Minister Baron Konstantin von Neurath about this issue. He received a negative response because of the old argument that Germany would have nothing in common

[9] See the relevant passage in the comprehensive report for 1935 by the Czechoslovak Chargé d'Affaires in London, Dr. Černý, "Francouzsko-italská dohoda v Rimě," London, December 1935. AMZV P. Z. Conf. No. 125. — The documentary material of the Czechoslovak Legation in London dating from this period is very ample and informative.

[10] M. Radu Florescu, Rumanian Chargé d'Affaires in London, to Foreign Minister Nicolae Titulescu of Rumania, London, January 10, 1935. OL Küm. Pol. 417. Miscellaneous political papers. Coloured telegrams (foreign diplomatic telegrams passing through and decoded in Hungary, assorted by countries on different coloured paper) R. XI.

with the League until her equality of rights in respect of armaments was recognized. In the view of some observers the British step was only a gesture and the British Government would have been most surprised had its initiative led to any practical political result.[11] The League of Nations arranged for a plebiscite in the Saar under international control on January 13, 1935 after the 15 years, stipulated by the Treaty of Versailles, had expired. (By virtue of Article 39 of Section IV of Part III of the Treaty of Versailles, upon expiry of fifteen years, the population of the territory shall be called upon to make its choice of the sovereignty under which it will wish to be placed.) The population could vote either to join Germany or France, or to continue under the existing international regime. The vast majority (90.05 per cent) of about 500,000 valid votes were cast for the return of the territory to Germany, and barely 9 per cent was in favour of the status under the League of Nations. The Saar Territory was reunited to Germany on March 1, 1935. After that Hitler declared on several occasions that Germany had no further territorial claim in the West. A foreign policy chronicler and analyst of the events, György Ottlik, an alternate member of the Hungarian delegation to the League of Nations (1927—34) and editor-in-chief of the daily *Budapesti Hírlap* (1934—35) and later of the monthly *Nouvelle Revue de Hongrie* (1935—39), evaluated the Saar vote as follows: "The brilliant result of the Saar plebiscite signified the further enormous strengthening of German national consciousness: the triumph of the 'we are for Germany' idea. The course of historic events which led to the German edict of March 16, to the unilateral repudiation of the military provisions of the Treaty of Versailles, was probably set into motion by this succes, by the inconceivable growth of the Führer's prestige."[12] The "peaceful occupation" of the Saar Territory was really a big success for Hitler. The man-in-the-street in Germany saw — or he was made to see — that Germans wanted to return home from everywhere.

Her claim to the Saar Territory having been satisfied, Germany reasserted her claim to equal rights in armaments. France persisted in demanding the organization of a security arrangement, while Britain tried to mediate between them by linking the two issues, by making them interdependent and seeking their simultaneous solution.

Describing the general European constellation at the time, an English peer made a rather revealing statement in *The Hungarian Quarterly*, a liberal-looking Hungarian revisionist mouthpiece published in English: "In England, it may be stated, a feeling of sympathy for Germany has been steadily growing, and if Hitler had shown sufficient foresight to cease from persecuting the Jews and to restrain the brutalities of his followers, British opinion, whatever may be the case elsewhere, would have been almost unanimously united in his favour. He has a remarkably strong case, although he has done much to damage it. He can show that Germany has not been treated fairly since the war, that the Allied Powers have not fulfilled their engagements, that the treaty which he has broken was forced upon Germany . . . There are plenty of other justifi-

[11] Černý's quoted report; communication from Nicolae Petrescu-Comnen, the Rumanian Minister in Berlin. January 11, 1935. OL Küm. Pol. 417. R. XI.

[12] György Ottlik, "Külpolitikai szemle" [Foreign Political Review], *Magyar Szemle*, May 1935.

cations for Hitler's periodical outbreaks, but in spite of his reiterated assertions that Germany only desires peace, his actions do not correspond with his words. It is now clear to the world that Germany, secretly at first, but now openly, is making war preparations on a gigantic scale and that a war mentality is being steadily inculcated throughout the country. The answer is of course that all this means nothing but defensive action. But in fact, who is likely to attack Germany? . . . One thing ought to be made clear, and that is that England's liability is confined to Locarno and the British public will never consent to be dragged into war in order to prevent the Germans from doing as they please in their own territory, or in opposing the *Anschluss* by force if it is really desired by Austria."[13]

The peculiar British attitude towards Germany was based on tradition. At that time the peculiarity followed rather from British adherence to tradition even though having cognizance of Hitler's obvious intentions and actions. The plan to divert Germany from Western towards Eastern Europe had been conceived as early as 1927 in the mind of Lord D'Abernon, then British Ambassador to Germany, who could already rely on a similar conception expressed by Lord Salisbury during the nineteenth century. A revival of this tradition was hinted at by David Lloyd George, former Prime Minister of Great Britain (1916—1922), in his speech to the House of Commons on November 28, 1934, when he made this prediction: "In a very short time, perhaps in a year or two, the Conservative elements in this country will be looking to Germany as the bulwark against Communism in Europe . . . two or three years ago a very distinguished German statesman said to me: 'I am not afraid of Nazism, but of Communism' — and if Germany is seized by the Communists, Europe will follow . . . Do not let us be in a hurry to condemn Germany. We shall be welcoming Germany as our friend."[14] At about the same time Hermann Göring, then Minister of the Air Forces in the German Cabinet, stated at a reception given to diplomats and foreign correspondents that, "concentration camps are a necessary instrument in the fight against Communism."[15] Lloyd George's words were vindicated before long. Soon Hitler was called on by the first appeasers, non-official diplomats, who visited Nazi Germany and her Chancellor as private individuals. Hitler's talks with such unofficial persons were followed up by visits of British statesmen to Berlin.

The first "non-official appeaser" calling on Hitler was Lord Allen of Hurtwood (Clifford Allen), a well-known pacifist and Labour politician, one of MacDonald's oldest followers and trusted friends, one-time chairman of the Independent Labour Party. He was introduced by Bernhard von Bülow, Secretary of State at the German Foreign Office, in these terms: "He (Lord Allen) is coming, as the representative of a group in process of formation of well-known English personalities which has as its aim an understanding with Germany, in order

[13] Lord Newton, "The Present European Situation," *The Hungarian Quarterly.* Summer 1936. Vol. I, No. 2, pp. 212—213.

[14] Salvemini, *op, cit.*, p. 220. — As to Lloyd George's sympathy for Germany, his visit to Hitler and his dissappointment, see my study entitled "Békéltetők" [Appeasers], with documentation, in *Történelmi Szemle*, 3—4/1969, pp. 231—283.

[15] *Cf. The Times*, December 12, 1934, report on Göring's speech. Published in M. Gilbert, *Plough My Own Furrow*, London, 1965, p. 356.

to acquaint himself with the situation in Germany. We are making efforts to put him in touch with a number of influential people in Berlin. Lord Allen, however, has also expressed the wish to be received by the Führer and Chancellor . . . Precisely because Lord Allen is a prominent representative of British Labour circles, I regard this as a chance to influence the attitude of these circles, which have so far been openly hostile and with which we shall certainly have to reckon if, as is to be expected after the approaching British General Election at the end of this or the beginning of next year, the Labour Party acquires a considerably stronger influence in the shaping of British policy than it has at present. An additional factor is the significance of Lord Allen himself as a personal friend of MacDonald's and as a representative of the above-mentioned group interested in promoting Anglo-German understanding."[16] Lord Allen had explained to his friends as early as April 1934 that it would be a mistake to appear to be on the side of France concerning the secret rearming of Germany and it also would be a mistake to justify the "wicked treaty" and the policies of France which had hindered for ten years world reconciliation: "God knows, the danger from Germany is bad enough, but the dangers from France during the last few years have been equally grave. Therefore, during the next six months, the key issue of world peace is not so much to expose the wickedness of this or that country as to make one last desperate effort to get a disarmament treaty signed, based on the idea of collective security. If that could be done we could very quickly deal with the menace from Germany. But to discuss this danger directly with France in her present mood, would simply fan the flames of an early war."[17]

Lord Allen arrived in Berlin on January 8, 1935. He met Foreign Minister Neurath, Minister of Justice Wilhelm Frick (who was to be Protector of Bohemia and Moravia from 1943 to 1945), as well as Rudolf Hess, deputy chief of the Nazi Party, and Hitler. In his notes made for himself he described details of his meeting with Hitler at the Chancellery such as Hitler's surroundings and behaviour, the impression the Führer made on his visitor, Hitler's vitality and fanaticism. He wrote: "This man looks upon politics as a kind of religion . . . he too will persecute for his religion, kill for it and die for it . . . Hitler sat there, not an explosive demagogue, but a man of volcanic energy and perfectly clear about his case. We discussed the whole European situation in technical detail. We estimated alternative lines of foreign policy. We examined the motives and intentions of all the major countries in Europe. Whether it is the effect of two years of power, or whether it be that he has been subject to caricature I cannot say, but this was not a man to allow a moment of time to be lost or a word to be wasted. The argument was precise, the sequence quick and logical: nor was the conversation one-sided."[18] Lord Allen's discussion with Hitler was confidential in nature. In an interview to the *Daily Telegraph*, however, he intimated that Hitler had unlimited influence in Germany; that the keynote of Germany's attitude was her desire to have equal status with other great powers; that if other countries persisted in their humiliating policies towards Germany, there would again grow up a warlike spirit, which

[16] *Ibid.*
[17] *Ibid.*, pp. 354—355.
[18] *Ibid.*, pp. 357—358.

would prompt her to spread destruction for a second time, even though she was aware that all the odds were against her: "Germany will ... always be a tactless nation ... Her present desire for peace, if it is not met with genuine understanding, will change so that she becomes ready to fight for her rights, even if she is again defeated."[19] According to German records of the conversation, Hitler broached the possibility of a general accord regarding armaments between Germany and England (including a naval pact as part of the agreement), which might later be acceded to by Italy and several small states.[20] On the other hand, Baron von Freyberg Eisenberg-Allmendingen, a retired Vice-Admiral, when speaking of his long talk with Lord Allen, told Szilárd Masirevich, then Hungarian Minister in Berlin, that Lord Allen, who was a trusted man of MacDonald's, came to Berlin upon the latter's instruction to inquire along three lines: (1) On what conditions would Germany return to Geneva. (2) On what conditions would Germany be a party to a convention on the reduction of armaments. (3) What would Germany's wishes be in respect of land and air armaments. The question of naval armaments was not raised.[21]

According to information gathered in London by László Széchenyi, Hungary's Minister to Great Britain, MacDonald had sent out Lord Allen, in view of the forthcoming visit to London by P.-É. Flandin, the French Premier, "to sound out Berlin. This is surprising," he wrote, "for the British Government does not usually charge private persons with diplomatic missions."[22]

The visit to Berlin by the next private individual evidently did not suprise Széchenyi. A British personality, no less influential than Lord Allen, paid his respects to Hitler still in January 1935. He was Lord Lothian (Philip H. Kerr), formerly private secretary to Lloyd George, a leading figure of the British Conservatives (the Cliveden set) who were bent on appeasing Hitler in the mid-30's, and a trusted servant of every British Government in power.[23] He was received at the Foreign Office in Berlin by Neurath and Bülow. He discussed disarmament with Werner von Blomberg, Minister of War of the Reich, with Rudolf Hess, and with Joachim von Ribbentrop, then Germany's representative to the Disarmament Conference. "Lord Lothian inquired mainly about Germany's disposition to the League of Nations and pointed out that in the question of security Germany had to take into consideration the infinite sensitiveness of the French."[24] His conversation with Hitler, in the presence of Hess, Ribbentrop, and an interpreter, lasted two hours and a half. The talk was in essence about the armament race, the feasibility of a convention for

[19] Ibid., pp. 358—359.
[20] Cf. F. Berber (ed.), Deutschland—England 1933—39: die Dokumente des deutschen Friedenswillens, Essen, 1940. Quoted vaguely regarding the navy by Watt, loc. cit.
[21] Masirevich's report from Berlin, January 29, 1935. OL Küm. Pol. 1935—2/25—377.
[22] Széchenyi's report from London, January 25, 1935. OL Küm. Pol. 1935—2—253.
[23] See his life history in J. R. M. Butler, Lord Lothian (Philip Kerr), 1882—1940, London, 1960. — Incidentally, at the time of Munich, both he and Lord Allen turned against the policy of appeasement, which they had earlier advocated.
[24] Masirevich's report, February 3, 1935. OL Küm. Pol. 1935—2/25—517.

the reduction of armaments as a basis for a political agreement with regard to Eastern Europe. Finally the conversation became rather one-sided, being confined to Hitler's anti-Communist and anti-Soviet tirades and his arguments in support of Germany's claim to equal rights. It was in the course of this oratorical performance of interesting logic that Hitler concretely suggested that, as a start for an Anglo-German understanding, three important issues should be considered, namely the fleet, the land army and the air force:

"(1) The fleet is a vital necessity for England. Germany does not feel threatened by British superiority at sea. So long as Russia does not become a sea power, we are prepared to accept the ratio, so far as the fleet is concerned, 35 : 100. (2) Army. Just as we Germans recognize England's vital necessity of being supreme at sea, so England should realize that Germany must have a strong army. Germany is the most vulnerable country in the world. It has to face a coalition of alarming strength, France and Russia. It must be capable of meeting this threat. But it is quite indifferent to us how powerful the British Army is. It was the greatest psychological failure in German history when German politicians before the War challenged the historical rights of the British people, that is their naval supremacy. It is absurd to think that the tradition, which has grown up within Germany for a thousand years — that military tradition later exemplified in Russia — resulting from the vital necessities of the German peoples situated in the heart of Europe, it is absurd to think that this tradition can be removed by a treaty. England's superiority at sea is based on the traditional qualities of the British people. In the same way the qualities of the German soldier have been formed. (3) Air. This is a new arm, and we ask here for parity with England. But England's air force should reach a certain strength, otherwise, if Germany only has parity with England, it would be greatly inferior to the French, and parity would be dangerous, for Germany would not be in a position to meet attacks from France and Russia. He would not object to a bilateral agreement. A *bilateral agreement* is better than none."

At this point Lothian asked Hitler: "Would the Führer then welcome a discussion between London and Berlin which would have as its objective the working out of a plan designed to stabilize Europe for ten years?" Upon Hitler's positive answer Lord Lothian stated: "Best thing I can do is to inform the P. M., Simon and Baldwin of this talk and to emphasize that Anglo-German conversations can be conducted with a view to a plan designed to stabilize Europe for ten years."

Hitler agreed. "If he now could speak not as Chancellor, but as a student of history, he would say that the best means of preserving peace would be for England and Germany to make a common declaration that anybody who breaks the peace shall be punished by these two Powers."

Lord Lothian of course imparted his impressions to Baldwin and Foreign Secretary Simon. Also he stated his views in an article and a letter to *The Times* (February 1 and March 11, 1935). In the next few weeks he was busy mediating between Whitehall and Wilhelmstrasse.[25]

[25] For the text of the Lothian-Hitler conversation, see Butler, *op. cit.*, pp. 330—337. It is briefly mentioned in DGFP Ser. C. Vol. III. — The complete text is published in Hungarian in my aforementioned study (see Note 14 above).

Was this mediation of non-official appeasers in agreement with official British foreign policy?

After Louis Barthou's death Sir Robert Vansittart, Permanent Under-Secretary of State for Foreign Affairs, found it problematical to carry on the policy of collective security. Step by step, Vansittart came into conflict with Foreign Secretary Simon. While Vansittart laboured for co-operation with the Soviet Union, Sir John Simon was the first to formulate in clear terms and in official form the policy of appeasement. Before Lord Lothian's visit to Berlin, on January 19, 1935, Sir John wrote this to King George V: "The practical choice is between a Germany which continues to rearm without any regulation or agreement and a Germany which, through getting a recognition of its rights and some modification of the Peace Treaties, enters into the comity of nations and contributes in this or other ways to European stability. As between these two courses, there can be no doubt which is the wiser."[26] It was in these weeks that — most probably as a result of the propaganda spread in England by the "Ribbentrop Bureau," a semi-official agency of the Nazi Foreign Office — it was rumoured in London clubs and city circles, as well as in country houses of Conservative politicians, that England and Germany had actually come to terms: Germany would rule on land and England would be sovereign at sea. It was then that Lothian came home with Hitler's promises in his briefcase. Lothian's report was discussed at Cabinet meetings, and it evidently confirmed the opinion of the ministers, whose majority anyway had an inclination towards appeasement. That is how things stood in early February 1935, when Prime Minister Flandin and Foreign Minister Laval of France went to London for a three-day visit to discuss the possibility of a general agreement between Germany and other nations, an arrangement which — as was indicated in the communiqué on the London talks — might be a substitute for the Versailles provisions regarding Germany. These talks resulted in the London Protocol which proposed an air pact to be concluded among the signatories to the Locarno Treaty and a somewhat milder Eastern pact intended to secure the peace of Eastern Europe.[27] In working out the London proposal of February 3, the British Government managed to exert restraint on the French. For example, it categorically rejected the French demand that the air pact should be concluded even if no agreement came about with Germany. The proposed text of the pact was kept in a conciliatory tone. The British and French Ambassadors to Germany, Sir Eric Phipps and André François-Poncet, presented the final text to Hitler, who received the diplomats in the company of Foreign Minister Neurath, and declared immediately that he disclaimed the allegation that Germany was rearming unilaterally, and he pointed to the speed of French and Soviet rearmament. Then François-Poncet pointed out that as early as 1934 Hitler had already demanded an army of 300,000 men,

[26] V. H. Nicolson, *King George V*, p. 522. Quoted by Colvin, *op. cit.*, p. 40.

[27] The proposal of the air pact was practically for an extension of the obligations undertaken in the Locarno Treaty, that is, the further development of the treaty provisions and their application in case of sudden air attack. *Cf.* in this respect Széchenyi's report from London, February 15, 1935. OL Küm. Pol. 1935—2/5—577.

admitting thereby that France had the right to rearm further. Hitler interrupted him saying that circumstances had changed in the meantime.[28]

The official German reply aroused no general enthusiasm in France, because the German Government agreed to direct talks with England only with respect to the air pact, failing to state its view on other points raised in the London proposal. The possibility of Germany's re-entry into the League of Nations was referred to only as a final contingency. The German note asserted that it was not Germany who had prevented the Disarmament Conference from resuming in April 1934. Consequently, Germany should not be expected to make new proposals. Since rearmament was taking place on a large scale all over Europe, Germany's demands had also increased with regard to "defensive armament." Afterwards Neurath still added that Germany had no intention to drive a wedge between England and France, but "for reasons of principle she had to propose bilateral German-British conversations."[29] On the whole the German reply met the expectations of London, though — as was summed up by L. Széchenyi, Hungary's Minister in London — "some deception can be observed in England on account of the enthusiasm with which Berlin has received the plan of an air pact implying the legalization of Germany's air armaments and has thereby indirectly stressed its evident indifference towards the rest of the proposal."[30]

Although the German note of reply caused disappointment in France, the French Government through its Ambassador in London informed the British Government that Paris did not object to the British entering into such talks with Germany, nor — should London so decide — to the Foreign Secretary making a trip to Berlin. But the situation created by the reply note required that an agreement should be worked out through the usual diplomatic channels between London and Paris with a view to establishing the common procedure to be followed before Sir John's visit to Berlin.[31]

The Italian Government welcomed the London arrangements, because it regarded them as favourable for "a possible accommodation with Germany". The Belgian Government also let London know of its approval of the idea of simultaneous negotiations about questions of equal rights and security. The Soviet Government informed the British and French Governments of its agreement with the London plan, if the proposed system were to include all regional treaties, first of all the Eastern pact. The Soviet Union's concern was manifested by its Ambassador in London, Ivan Mikhailovich Maisky, who expressed the conviction that Britain and France still were holding the Locarno front in the West but had entirely given up the Eastern pact. Under-Secretary Vansittart understood the reality of the Soviet standpoint on the whole but asked for patience. When the Czechoslovak Ambassador to Great Britain, Jan

[28] This half-hour episode is related in more detail by Dr. Vojtěch Mastný, Czechoslovak Minister to Germany, in his secret report on the German repercussions of the London talks. Berlin, February 5, 1935. AMZV P. Z. 1935, No. 11.

[29] Masirevich's confidential report from Berlin on February 18, 1935 and his cipher telogram of February 22, 1935. OL Küm. Pol. 1935—2/19—670 and 686.

[30] February 21, 1935. OL Küm. Pol. 1935—2/19—731.

[31] Cf. the aforecited comprehensive report for 1935 by Dr. Černý, Czechoslovak Chargé d'Affaires in London (see Note 9 above).

23

Masaryk, called on him and his deputy, Sir Orme Sargent, at the Foreign Office to find out what the situation was after the French statesmen's visit, Vansittart made an optimistic statement in these terms: "We have done the bulk of work, and this certainly is some progress. I think the most important fact in all Europe is that we do not know what Germany does, not only as concerns her position regarding the London arrangements, but for the time being we cannot know either in what direction her policy is going to turn. I hope I need not emphasize particularly that we do not have much confidence in Hitler. As long as we do not clearly know the position of Germany, it is needless to prepare any definitive plan for improving the situation in Eastern Europe, and this is why I think the fear voiced by Litvinov [Maksim Maksimovich Litvinov, People's Commissar for Foreign Affairs of the Soviet Union] is excessive."[32] A few days later Vansittart wrote in his private notes the following remark: "So far as in me lies, I am doing all that is possible to further the policy of helping Russia — by friendly response — out of the dangerous, indeed, fatal path that would lead to Berlin . . . We must help M. Litvinov to the utmost of our power."[33] Vansittart's deputy, Sir Orme Sargent, however, was not dedicated to this policy. He was counted as a foe of the Soviet Union. Masaryk gained the impression in talks with him that Sargent would be very glad to see the failure of Litvinov's policy.[34]

The Soviet press commented vividly upon the foreseeable consequences of the London talks and analyzed the causes and the tactical ground of the British attitude. An *Izvestia* editorial of February 5 stated the view that while England was ready to aid France if Germany threatened French territory, yet it was not known what action England would take in case German expansionism would be directed towards Eastern or Southern Europe, i.e. against one of France's allies. Another article in the February 18 issue of the same newspaper stated that if "Germany today is given freedom of action in Eastern Europe, tomorrow she will achieve it in the West." Since Soviet foreign policy clearly realized the dangers involved in Germany's Eastern policy, Moscow tried to make leading British quarters understand its own position and at the same time Litvinov's idea of an "indivisible peace." The Soviet Government also placed orders amounting to £1 million, still before the London visit by the French statesmen, in order to gain the favour of British financiers and industrial circles. As far as the deeper political reasons for the British orientation towards the Soviet Union are concerned, let us examine the train of thought of a contemporary Hungarian legation report written with incontestable analytical skill: "After the French visit to London it has become certain (1) that England will hardly sign the Eastern pact or any other treaty on the security of Eastern Europe; (2) that she has achieved that France will not

[32] The Czechoslovak Minister to Great Britain, Jan Masaryk, on his visit to Vansittart and Sargent. London, February 6, 1935. AMZV P. Z. 1935, No. 33. — As to this and the further policies of the British Government, *cf.* I. M. Maisky's colourful, valuable *Memoirs of a Soviet Ambassador* (In Russian), Moscow, 1964, published in Hungarian (abridged) under the title *Utazás a múltba* [Journey into the Past], Budapest, 1967, p.676.

[33] Colvin, *op. cit.*, p. 42.

[34] See Note 32.

insist on a previous draft of the Eastern pact. England has also expressed the desire that the Eastern pact be confined to the Eastern European states, that is Russia, Germany, the Baltic States, Poland and Rumania (without the participation of France and Czechoslovakia). Thus England has declined to agree to the direct or indirect realization of a Russo-French defensive pact (either with or without Czechoslovakia). This makes it easy to understand why Russia is dissatisfied with the London decisions which left her out, and in which England declared her readiness *to defend French territory in Europe, but not to support France's position in Europe by protecting Czechoslovakia, one of her Eastern allies.* The Soviet Government clearly sees also England's attitude towards the Danubian pact: she consents to the Franco-Italian pact which guarantees the independence of Austria, but she is in no way interested in the treaties between successor states of former Austria-Hungary."[35]

The Soviet note of reply concerning the London talks was presented by the Soviet Ambassadors in Paris and London on February 19. But this reply was of no practical interest to the British Foreign Office and did not effect its policies. In vain did Vansittart try to make the Soviet foreign policy understood in England. This Soviet note of February 19 proposed among other things an alliance of four European great powers — the Soviet Union, France, Great Britain and Italy — against the aggressor preparing for war. This alliance might be joined by the Little and the Balkan Entente, so that this coalition would cover 365 million people, amounting to 70 per cent of the European population.[36]

Instead, however, plans were being made in Whitehall as to how and by whom the parley with Hitler should be continued. On February 25, Foreign Secretary Simon announced to the House of Commons that on March 8 he and the Lord Privy Seal, Mr. Eden, would go to Berlin, while the invitations to Moscow, Warsaw and Prague were still under consideration. A special Cabinet meeting approved of the trip of Simon and Eden, and since Sir John did not wish to go farther than Berlin, Eden alone had to respond to the other invitations. By that time Eden, aged 38, having a wide intellectual horizon and enjoying the confidence of influential Conservative circles, had accumulated considerable diplomatic experience, in contrast to Foreign Secretary Simon, who was 25 years his senior and whose conduct of foreign policies appealed neither to the Opposition nor to the intellectual élite of the Conservative Party. In the meantime, however, the White Paper on the British armament programme was made public on March 4, 1935 — deliberately or unintentionally — at a rather inappropriate moment (See also Appendix I, p. 163).[37]

[35] Report by Sándor Kiss, Hungarian Minister in Helsinki, March 5, 1935. OL. Küm. Pol. 1935—2/28—920. (My italics. — É. H. H.)

[36] Report by the same, February 24, 1935. OL Küm. Pol. 1935—2/19—811.

[37] As was stated in the comprehensive report for 1935 by Dr. Černý, Czechoslovak Chargé d'Affaires in London, "the circumstance that the White Paper was made public at the very time when the British Ministers' visit abroad was under discussion, does not mean that there should be any connection between the two issues. The date of publication of the memorandum was simply adjusted to the debate in the House of Commons, which is known to be put through according to a prearranged schedule, which in this case was all the more strict as the debate had to be closed before the end of the current fiscal year, March 31. The White Paper

It is worth while dwelling at some length on the circumstances of the formulation of this armament programme, since they allow us an insight into the mechanism of British foreign and home policies. The White Paper covered the 1935 budget of three defence portfolios (War, Admiralty and Air) and was designed to provide the public at home and abroad with some of the reasons or explanations for the nearly 10 per cent increase in the expenditures of national defence. The fact that the document proved to be a poor success was due to the irreconcilable contradiction of Britain's armament and appeasement policy, to the difference of Conservative and Labour policies on rearmament, to a number of economic factors and interdepartmental disputes as well as personal and professional problems. The authors of the draft White Paper — three leading civil servants — Sir Warren Fisher (Permanent Under-Secretary to the Treasury and head of H. M. Civil Service from 1919 to 1939), Sir Maurice Hankey (Secretary of the Committee of Imperial Defence and the Cabinet, 1912—1938 and 1918—1939 respectively), and Sir Robert Vansittart (Permanent Under-Secretary of State for Foreign Affairs) — wanted this document to promote a revolution in British foreign policy, to call attention to the danger of German militarism, and the need for greater defence efforts. But the politicians — as A. J. P. Taylor[38] put it — emasculated the plan.

---

had been prepared long before the plan of the Berlin visit was brought up. The only controversial point raised at the Cabinet meeting deciding the publication of the document was whether to publish it before or after the Berlin negotiations. The conclusion was reached that it was better to abide by the original scheme, namely the earlier publication."

The Hungarian Minister to London, L. Széchenyi, in his report of March 9, 1935, pointed to the fact that the White Paper had been compiled, not by the Foreign Office, but by Sir Maurice Hankey as Secretary of the Committee of Imperial Defence, long before the fixing of the trip to Berlin. And the Foreign Office took the view that it was wiser to make the document public before than after the Berlin conversations, because in the latter case everyone would have regarded it as an admission of the fiasco of the negotiations. The report of Hungary's Minister to Germany, Masirevich, reflects the German opinion: With the publication of the White Paper Great Britain could, as always before, find the way back to France and give the Germans to understand that for their sake she was not disposed to give up Franco-British collaboration.

[38] In the second half of 1934 Sir Maurice Hankey was touring the British dominions for months. The official character of his tour was denied, but part of the Australian and the British press disclosed that Hankey and the Australian Government had not only discussed questions of imperial defence, but worked out a detailed memorandum on the introduction of compulsory military service, the fortification of major industrial centres and seaports, the development of the Australian air force, etc. All this made it clear that the Dominion Governments and Hankey had discussed problems concerning co-ordination of the defensive rearmament policies of Great Britain and her dominions. The newspapers mentioned also that Hankey had made it clear to the Dominion Governments that they must partake of the burdens of imperial defence to which the London Government contributed by building and maintaining the naval base at Singapore. *Cf.* Széchenyi's report from London, January 10, 1935. OL Küm. Pol. 1935—2/5—252. —As is known, British foreign policy prior to the Munich crisis was influenced by the position taken up by the Foreign Ministers of the Dominions, who could not conceive of

In the political atmosphere of 1934-35 the British Prime Minister still had to be careful about raising the question of armaments.

In the year of the 1935 General Election, the Government, formally a coalition but in practice a Conservative formation (the truth of this qualification appears also from the fact that real political power was in the hands of the Conservative Stanley Baldwin and not in those of Prime Minister J. R. MacDonald), was of the opinion that the indication of increased armaments in the budget might imperil the election prospects of the Conservative Party. Actually, under the direction of the official leader of the Parliamentary Labour Party, George Lansbury, one of the best known representatives of pacifism, the vast majority of the British trade unions still persisted in opposing the development of the British Army, Navy and Air Force. (As was evidenced by the result of the Peace Ballot published in 1935. Of 11,627,765 votes 10,533,826 demanded adherence to the League of Nations principle. The change did not take place until September, when in view of the Italo-Ethiopian conflict a good portion of the same large sections of population, relying equally upon the League of Nations idea, voted to apply collective — if need be, military — sanctions against Italy by the armed forces which they did not wish to strengthen.)[39]

The possibilities of British rearmament in the spring of 1935 were determined, in addition to factors of domestic policy, by a number of omissions which had been committed in armament policy during the preceding years, and which at this time were recognized but not easy to rectify. At about that time British Staff Officer Whiteford explained to Major Álgya-Papp, Hungarian Military Attaché in London, that it would be most desirable — not only from the British but from the general European point of view — if Germany got entangled in a war with Russia without interference from other powers. In this way both would become weaker, and "Europe may possibly get rid of the constantly threatening peril of Bolshevism for another fifty years."[40] This eventuality, looking so propitious to England, did not come to pass either at that time or at any later date, and British leading quarters knew full well — also the anti-Hitler and anti-appeasement Vansittart thought so — that it was much too late for them not to appreciate "their erstwhile enemies' desire for military equality. What they object to in the case of Germany is not the fact of her rearming, but the methods and especially the proportions of her rearmament which had made it rather difficult to establish a system of parity."[41]

a German attack on Czechoslovakia as an acceptable casus belli, especially when Chamberlain himself, as seen from London, regarded Czechoslovakia as "a faraway country." Cf M. Gilbert, The Roots of Appeasement, London, 1966, p. 181. — Concerning Taylor's opinion, see his criticism of the article by D. C. Watt, "Sir Warren Fisher and British Rearmament against Germany," The English Historical Review, January 1967, pp. 201—202.

[39] Hungarian Chargé d'Affaires György Királdy-Lukács' report from London, September 9, 1935 and January 15, 1936. OL Küm. Pol. 1935—2/1—2833 and 1936—2—293.

[40] Major László Álgya-Papp's report No. 79/15 1935 forwarded home by courier on May 8. OL Küm. Pol. 1935—2/7—1760.

[41] Széchenyi's conversation with Vansittart. Széchenyi's strictly confidential report from London, May 30, 1935. OL Küm. Pol. 1935—2/7—1923.

In the fifteen years following Versailles, Britain had failed to provide for a general development of her armed forces. Until 1934, a yearly average of at most 14 per cent of the public expenditures had been devoted to the development of the Army and the Navy.[42] By the time of Hitler's access to power, when the London Government came to see its own inability to protect the British interests in the Far East and elsewhere because of the insufficiency of naval and air forces, Britain already had considerably fallen behind.

During the world economic crisis, which had shaken the London City and the whole of Britain's business life, there could be no question of any strengthening of the country's defences. The issue of British armaments could be realistically raised after 1933 only by those who saw the need for it and were also in a position to act within the bounds of possibility.

The armament effort was vigorously supported by Sir Warren Fisher, the Permanent Under-Secretary to the Treasury, who was a man of enormous dynamic energy, quick to make up his mind, fearless and dictatorial in disposition and rather impatient, a leading civil servant who bothered little about formalities (he was said to have ruined the Civil Service by being on Christian name terms with everyone) and was as decidedly anti-Nazi as Vansittart himself. He did not at all believe in a *modus vivendi* with the Germans in the long run.[43] He insisted resolutely that Britain had one really threatening enemy: Germany. The reason for fear, in the stage of technological development of the time, was German air power, in face of which England was vulnerable to a degree unprecedented in her history. For this very reason he was in disagreement, then and later, with the Air Ministry's more optimistic view and the data adduced in its support.[44] He also was convinced of the extreme importance that the leadership of the country should be comprised of men of great experience. In his opinion, England of the 1930's suffered under a definite lack of military and civil experts as well as of competent and highly qualified advisers. Therefore, he worked hard to keep his hands in the British armament efforts. He controlled the financial aspect of armaments and took care that his conceptions did not get distorted in the wrangle among the defence portfolios. As early as 1924 the Committee of Imperial Defence (CID) set up a subcommittee composed of leading officers of the Army, Navy and Air Force. Sir Warren Fisher said at the time, "We converted ourselves to military impotence.

---

[42] Miklós Major, "Az angol fegyverkezés gazdasági vonatkozása" [Economic Aspects of British Rearmament], *Magyar Katonai Szemle*, 10/1938, pp. 184—201. Especially illustrative of the proportions, organizational conception and implementation of the British armament programme launched in 1935.

[43] Sir Warren Fisher — just like his successor, Sir Horace Wilson, chief adviser to Chamberlain — had so much widened his scope of authority (by controlling all information issued to the ministries and the Cabinet, by witholding important reports he did not like, by preventing promotions if he was antagonized, etc.) that he exerted considerable influence upon British foreign policy, rearmament questions and Cabinet decisions. His role has not yet been definitively clarified. An important contribution to his characterization is the article entitled "Sir Warren Fisher and British Rearmament" in D. C. Watt, *Personalities and Policies*, London, 1965, pp. 100—116.

[44] The issue of the air forces will be discussed in more detail in connection with Simon's and Eden's trip to Berlin.

To have disarmed so drastically in the two or three years after the war was not unnatural though possibly not wise. But the Government of 1924 to 1929 had no excuse for further reducing our armed forces to a skeleton, as by then it was known that the Weimar Republic (so called) was in process of reconstructing a disguised army on a truly formidable scale. This British Government's tragic action formed unfortunately a model for subsequent Governments; and though in 1936 a façade of rearmament was announced by the then Government, it was ludicrously insubstantial . . ."[45]

Sir Warren Fisher did all in his power to get the British Government to take the German challenge seriously, and he managed to do much behind the backs of the ministers to overcome the orthodox views. The CID even established another special subcommittee, the Defence Requirements Subcommittee (DRC). At a meeting of the DRC in November 1933, Vansittart and Fisher succeeded in convincing their colleagues that the ultimate potential enemy, "certain to become within a few years a serious menace to Britain," was Germany. In that period, however, it was impossible, in the DRC meetings, to drive home to the Chief of Air Staff, Sir Adrian Ellington, that Britain's ability to improve her poor defences in the air was quite incommensurate with the scope of the danger. Sir Warren thought that the Army was altogether outdated in equipment, training and composition. The combined programme to repair Britain's deficiencies amounted to about £71 million, spread over five years, of which about 50 per cent was to be spent on the Army. In 1934 the Cabinet cut the total figure by one-third, halved the Army's proposed figure, agreed to postpone for several years the replacement of Britain's obsolescent capital ships and while allotting a vastly increased sum to the build-up of the air defence of Great Britain. The Chiefs of Staff were far from happy about this report, refusing to accept that Britain and her Empire could be made "safe and secure" by the unilateral rearmament of only one of the three services. As a result of their protests the DRC was reconstituted and told to report on the full measures needed to increase the country's defences in all three armed services without regard to their financial requirements. Thus there came about the lengthy White Paper which, on account of the approaching General Election, was made public with cautious polishings by Baldwin, but which nonetheless showed signs of the anti-German attitude of Vansittart and Fisher. (So much so that the document bearing the signature of the head of the British Government publicly criticized even the spirit of the education of German youth.)

The White Paper represented a major innovation in British constitutional practice, as for the first time defence policy was to be reviewed and debated as a whole in the British Parliament.[46] Hungarian Minister Széchenyi even called the attention of his Foreign Minister, Kálmán Kánya, to the significance of the White Paper: "It purports a lot more than the motivation of the defence budget," he wrote on March 9. "This document specifies the British Government's objectives with regard to the problems of particular concern to world

[45] Sir Warren Fisher, *The Beginnings of Civil Defence*, Public Administration XXVI, Winter 1948. Quoted by Watt, *op. cit.* (1965), p. 105.
[46] *Ibid*, pp. 107—108.

peace, and for this very reason general interest is manifested for its discussion in the Commons scheduled for early next week."[47]

The aggregate increase of about £ 10,500,000 (that constituted a 10 per cent rise) in the defence expenditures, as motivated in the White Paper, eventually came as no surprise. The raise in the Air Force budget was a natural consequence of previous debates and Sir Warren's efforts. The increase in the expenditures of the Navy and the Army was intended not so much for the establishment of new military units, as was the case with the Air Force, but rather for the replacement of obsolete war materials with more modern equipment. As a matter of course, the authors of the White Paper made references in the text to the basically peaceful goals of British foreign policy, to international treaties to be concluded in the interest of collective security under the auspices of the League of Nations, to the Locarno agreements, to several proposals concerning security in Eastern Europe, etc. They quoted British manifestations and suggestions relating to the situation before and after the Disarmament Conference and also described the mood of the British public urging disarmament. In this connection they kept explaining the Government's increased peace efforts, while stressing the fact that the security requirements could not be overlooked. The document stated that Britain's unilateral disarmament and her desire to have this example followed by other countries had failed. The result of this policy was that Britain lacked the proper means of self-defence against an aggressor. The Disarmament Conference had practically come to an impasse, and Germany, in defiance of the provisions of Part V of the Treaty of Versailles, was not only rearming openly and on a large scale, but had withdrawn from the League of Nations, too. Inquiries had borne out that if the British defence forces should not be modernized, the level of defence would be insufficient in case of aggression, and it would be impossible to secure the sea routes, the supply of the population, the protection of major cities and their inhabitants from air attacks.

Furthermore, the White Paper stated that the build-up of defences against possible dangers had been started and the programmes of the defence forces co-ordinated. With regard to the Navy and to the Army, the technical lag was to be eliminated. Those services were to be gradually supplied with modern equipment. Appropriate human and material resources had to be secured. These prerequisites were indispensable for the protection of Britain's substantial interests against aggression and for her co-operation in any collective security system. Only in the case of the Royal Air Foce was it considered necessary to raise the number of units. In the future, however, it would be inevitable to develop also the anti-aircraft equipment of the Army. If rearmament was to go on under the actual circumstances, the anxieties of Germany's neighbours would increase even further. This in turn would create a situation threatening the peace. This is the reason, the White Paper stated, that Britain was concerned not only about the state of preparedness of the armed forces but also about the spirit in which the entire German population, especially the youth, was being educated and organized. Of course, not only Germany, but the whole world, too, was rearming. England could not afford to look on with folded arms.

[47] OL Küm. Pol. 1935−2/1−947.

Therefore, she had to repair the deficiencies of her defensive installations. In case of war the safety of the fleet was to be ensured in the first place, in order to be able to maintain communications by sea. This should be the basis of the British imperial defence system. Any other military arrangement would be of little use when the fleet would not be effective. More cruisers should be built. The battleship would continue to be an important element of the system of British naval strategy, but the outdated battleships should be replaced as soon as possible, and the newly constructed ones would be put into operation in pursuance of the future naval pact. The White Paper specified the most essential tasks of defence for the three armed services. For the event of aerial warfare it envisaged that owing to air force development Britain might become exposed to attacks coming from great distances. Therefore it ascribed prime importance to the area of the North Sea, which had been for centuries one of Britain's main spheres of interest and had remained so up to the present. At the same time with the development of the military defences of the country, preparations began for the protection of the public utility services and the civilian population. Finally, the White Paper repeatedly referred to the aims of the British Government, to its belief in the efficiency of peaceful means, emphasizing at the same time that the postponement of Britain's rearmament as an indication of her policy of peace would be blunder. The international situation and world-wide rearmament made it necessary to continue developing the three defensive arms, and this could not be delayed any further without having to incur great danger.[48]

On March 11 the British Parliament voted for the nearly 10 per cent increase in the defence budget.

The questions raised by the White Paper in March 1935, were, of course, of great concern to the best theoretical and practical military expert of Britain, Captain Liddell Hart, and to Jack Dill, a leading functionary of the War Office, who was the most excellent strategic mind of the British Army of the interwar period. In March 1935, Liddell Hart joined the editorial staff of *The Times*, in which his opening article appeared on March 14, dealing with the White Paper. He stated that because of England's state of vulnerability the policy of isolation was strategically untenable, while a policy of collective security was, as he called it, "an adequate standard of defence." He wrote: "The most 'forceful' argument for pursuing the method of collective security is the strategic; and it is a pity that this has been so much obscured by less practical considerations. The more one reflects upon the inevitable strategic conditions of to-day, the more is one driven to see that the de velopment of the collective security is not only a moral ideal but a British interest from the most practical point of view." And in a leading article also on March 14, he kept explaining that, "to attain a level of armament in all three spheres [Army, Navy, Air Force] which would give us back our old security is impossible, technically or financially. Contemplation of these hard facts drives us, willynilly, towards admitting the wisdom of the policy of collective security . . ."[49]

[48] Statement Relating to Defense issued in Connection with the House of Commons Debate on March 11, 1935, London, 1935.
[49] *The Memoirs of Captain Liddell Hart*, London, 1965, Vol. 1, pp. 285—286.

In those days Jack Dill asked him to come to the War Office for a talk about current and perspective defence problems. They discussed the world situation over a large map. Dill disliked the idea that Britain might be on the side of Russia in a French-Italian-Soviet alliance against the probably emerging German-Japanese bloc, and he suggested: "Could we not let Germany expand eastwards at Russia's expense?" Liddell Hart pointed to the danger of "feeding the tiger that might turn on you," saying that Germany now as before regarded Britain as the ultimate obstacle to her ambition. Dill asked Liddell Hart if he could suggest any good reasons for coming to an arrangement with Russia. Hart's reply pointed out: (1) Russia was the only effective counterpoise to a Japanese threat to Britain's position in the Far East, and (2) France would not let go of Russia, and Britain could hardly let go of France.

To the question into which direction they should let Germany expand, the two men found no answer. Jokingly they mentioned India, pointing out that it was anyway becoming a burden to Great Britain. Liddell Hart was convinced in the spring of 1935, that a thoughtful soldier like Jack Dill, just like himself, "saw no way of meeting from Britain's limited resources the ominous contingencies that were developing simultaneously in the Far East, Middle East and Europe."[50]

Sir John Simon's and Anthony Eden's visit to Berlin scheduled for March 8 was, as a result of the White Paper, put off. Reading this document apparently made Hitler "sick." Officially it was announced that during his tour of the Saar Territory the Chancellor had caught cold and was in need of a rest of convalescence for about two weeks. The British statesmen's visit therefore, might not take place before the end of March. On March 7, Foreign Secretary Simon told the Commons that after Berlin Mr. Eden would go on to Moscow and Warsaw. Thereafter Sir John went to Paris and talked with Pierre Laval. Hitler, in response to the White Paper, not only made a show of political illness, but also gave Europe the so-called "Saturday surprises." On March 9, the first Saturday "surprise," Hermann Göring announced that the *Luftwaffe* was in existence. On the second Saturday, March 16, Berlin promulgated a law reintroducing conscription and the build-up of a peace-time army of thirty-six divisions with a numerical strength of five hundred and fifty thousand men. The German Government unilaterally repudiated with this decision the provisions of Part V of the Treaty of Versailles providing for the disarmament of Germany. Hitler was said to have given three reasons for this step in a conversation with the Italian Minister to Berlin:

(1) Russia's existing 101 divisions;

(2) the White Paper (that is the adoption on March 11 by the British Parliament of a 10 per cent increase in the defence budget);

(3) the decision of the French Chamber of Deputies on the extension of the period of military service.

The Chancellor of the Reich remarked also that he had the relevant Bill in his desk for a long time. He waited only for a suitable occasion to make it public. Moreover, Bülow said to Hungary's Minister in Berlin, Masirevich, that the proclamation of universal conscription did not alter the *de facto* existing situation — and in this he was right. Notice should be taken also of a com-

---

[50] Liddell Hart, *op. cit.*, Vol. I, pp. 291—292.

ment made by Frigyes Villani, the Hungarian Minister to Italy, who said that Hitler had intended with the proclamation to confront the powers with an accomplished fact before the Berlin visit of the British statesmen.[51]

Hitler's "March 16 surprise" caused great consternation among the great powers concerned. They had been aware of the fact of German rearmament, but they were shocked by the violation of the rules of the diplomatic game, by the timing of the announcement and by the general impression that according to the official German statement, Germany's armed forces amounted to nearly twice as much as the number used as the basis of negotiations of a year before. The news allegedly took the British Government completely by surprise. Cabinet members were called home from their week-end holiday. A ministerial conference was held on Sunday, and then the French Ambassador presented to the Foreign Office an aide-mémoire listing France's wishes and requesting Anglo-Franco Italian consultations and the calling of a special session of the Council of the League of Nations. The Monday Cabinet meeting approved the draft note of Sunday by which the British Government protested against the establishment of the *Wehrmacht*, but indicated that before the visit to Berlin it did not intend to enter into three-power consultations. French Ambassador Charles Corbin was not informed of the content of that note until after it had been forwarded to Berlin. It was hardly imaginable to make a golden bridge more convenient for Hitler than this *fait accompli*. Opposition leader Lansbury explained in sharp words in the House of Commons that at no time since August 1914 had England been so close to a war than during these days.

Foreign Secretary Simon did not at all wish to give up the trip to Berlin. On one hand, he expected to strengthen thereby his personal position, and, and on the other hand, he as well as several other Cabinet members "hoped to get assurances at the given moment that the German Government would not expand its navy to such an extent as it did its land forces."[52] Simon evidently had drawn this conclusion from what he had heard from Germany's Ambassador to London, Leopold von Hoesch. Shortly after the promulgation of the law of March 16, Hoesch was instructed by his Government to work out, on the basis of the London talks of February 3, the programme for the new negotiations, especially for an agreement concerning the ratio of naval strength between Germany and Britain.[53]

After a certain period of suspense, Hitler agreed to receive on March 24 Foreign Secretary Sir John Simon in the company of Lord Privy Seal Anthony Eden. Prior to that date, the British Government had sent Eden to Paris with the task of assuring the French Government that in Berlin there would be no departure from the line of the February 3 Anglo French consultations.[54]

[51] Masirevich's cipher telegram from Berlin, March 18, 1935. OL Küm. Pol. 1935—21/5—968 and 1011, as well as Frigyes Villani's cipher telegram from Rome, March 16, 1935. OL Küm. Pol. 1935—21/5—954.

[52] Chargé d'Affaires Királdy-Lukács' report from London, March 23, 1935. OL Küm. Pol. 1935—2—1120.

[53] W. Malanowski "Das deutsch—englische Flottenabkommen vom Juni 1935," *Wehrwissenschaftliche Rundschau*, July 1955, pp. 408—420.

[54] Report by Gábor Apor, Hungarian Minister to Austria, Vienna, March 8, 1935. OL Küm. Pol. 1935—2/11—869.

Regarding the impending British visit, Secretary of State Bülow of Germany was of the opinion — as he stated to the Hungarian Minister in Berlin, Masirevich, too — that, nevertheless, there was no unity among London, Paris and Rome. He indicated that the British came to Berlin as if nothing had happened in the meantime; that the Berlin talks took place without preparation, and that Simon still laboured under the delusion that in exchange for military concessions, Germany would be willing to enter into compromises on the question of Central Europe and with respect to the Eastern pacts.[55]

The negotiations took place in Berlin on March 25 and 26 with the participation of Chancellor Hitler, Foreign Minister Neurath, and Ribbentrop, the German plenipotentiary on disarmament issues, as well as Sir Eric Phipps, the British Ambassador to Berlin. According to the official communiqués the British and German statesmen discussed the questions touched upon during the London talks of February 3, the question of Locarno, the conditions of Germany's re-entry into the League, and many other issues which we shall describe in detail in connection with Sir John Simon's report to Parliament. It is interesting to note that in Berlin the British Foreign Secretary avoided the subject of the demilitarized Rhineland zone, though Vansittart had advised him to bring up this issue. Hitler may have noticed the avoidance of this subject.[56] (See Appendix II, p. 171.) The issue of the ex-German colonies was brought up, and Simon inquired about the present air strength of Germany. Hitler answered quietly: "We have reached parity with Great Britain."

This statement made a greater impression on Eden than on Simon, although Eden all the while seemed to be more sceptical than Simon. Back in London, Sir John prepared a twenty-page secret memorandum for the Cabinet, and at first — as he also mentioned in the House of Commons — he deemed it undesirable to make a full statement, since the whole journey was intended to serve the purpose of mutual information and of fact-finding. The diplomatic correspondent of the *Daily Telegraph*, however, learned of some of the information in Berlin and on March 29 the newspaper referred to "the strong appeal which Herr Hitler undoubtedly made to Sir John Simon for an Anglo-German alliance." Meanwhile Vansittart had read the secret memorandum and decided that Hitler's remarks on air parity should be made public. Consequently, towards the end of March, the great London newspapers published the big news: "Herr Hitler is said to have admitted that the German Air Force is already as large or slightly larger than the Royal Air Force." Strictly speaking, this was a hoax. The Germans protested immediately that Hitler had never said "or slightly larger." The BBC was also ready with an answer: "It is now learned, however, that actually there is good reason to believe that the German Air Force has now attained equality with our own." Sir John Simon had to be frank to the Commons and admitted the accuracy of the report that Hitler had claimed to have achieved air parity with Britain.[57]

[55] Masirevich's strictly confidential report, Berlin, March 22, 1935. OL Küm. Pol. 1935—21—1087.

[56] Colvin, *op. cit.*, p. 43.

[57] *Ibid.*, p. 45. The British Minister to Vienna, Sir Walford Selby, told Austrian Foreign Minister Berger-Waldenegg that Simon's visit to Berlin was "the last though sincere effort on Britain's part to draw Germany, on the basis agreed with

According to Eden, an important result of the Berlin talks was that it stirred up anew a controversy that had been raging since 1933 between the Air Ministry and the Foreign Office. The fact is that these two ministries had contradictory information about Germany's air preparedness. The British Air Ministry saw no immediate danger, while the Foreign Office formed a more accurate estimate of the size of the German Air Force.[58] The situation was further complicated by the fact that both opinions had supporters in both departments.

Churchill saw clearly, then and later, that it would have been possible in 1933 or even in 1934 for Britain to have created an air power which could have imposed the necessary restraints upon Hitler's ambition.[59] In June 1934 the Air Ministry sent the Foreign Office a memorandum on data concerning the build-up of the German air force within the next fifteen months. This paper, in the view of Foreign Office experts, underrated Germany's air strength, yet the Cabinet accepted its estimate. When Parliament's winter session opened on November 28, 1934, Churchill in the name of some of his friends declared to a full House of Commons that ". . . Germany already, at this moment, has a military Air Force . . . which only awaits an order to assemble in full open combination; and . . . this illegal Air Force is rapidly approaching equality with our own." He predicted that according to the German and British programmes the two air forces in 1935 would be equal in strength and "by the end of 1936 the German military Air Force will be nearly 50 per cent stronger."

In his speech on the same day — already referred to in a different context — Baldwin immediately refuted Churchill's estimate. According to Baldwin's view Germany's air force was only half of the Royal Air Force stationed in Europe.[60] The Prime Minister's words (because of MacDonald's advanced

Laval in London, into the club of the great powers for joint, peaceful co-operation. If this does not work, Britain will, in common with France and Italy, immediately set about rearming against Germany and then the Germans shall face the consequences. He openly alluded to an impending war. (The British diplomat is believed to have acted upon instructions.)" Gábor Apor's report of March 8, 1935. OL Küm. Pol. 1935—2/11—869.

[58] *The Eden Memoirs: Facing the Dictators*, London, 1962, p. 182.

[59] W. S. Churchill *The Second World War*, Vol. I: "The Gathering Storm," London, 1955 (5th ed.), p. 106.

[60] *Ibid.*, pp. 106—107. — It should be noted here that the British Ambassador to Germany, who had been called home to London, returned to Berlin on November 26, 1934. Upon his return to Berlin he was received, at his request, by Hitler. He informed the Führer in advance about what would happen in Parliament on November 28. He disclosed that it would be announced that Germany possessed 300,000 troops and many airplanes, even bombers. Hitler said the figures were false. In fact, he said, they did have bombers, but this was due to the failure to convene the international conference which would have imposed an international ban on the construction of bombers. And even if now the Reich could count upon a friendly neighbour in the East (Poland), it must still meet the vast army and technically most advanced air power of the Soviet Union. Considering Britain's and France's air fleets and that they were of equal strength, Germany would, even if she kept up an air force equalling the aggregate strength of the French and British air forces, be unable to attack both countries, for she would have to use part of her air fleet against the Soviets whose air strength was equal to that of the two

age and weakening eyesight Baldwin was already considered to be the actual head of MacDonald's second, National Cabinet) reassured many sceptics until, on March 9, 1935, Göring announced the establishment of the *Luftwaffe*. Churchill, in a letter to Baldwin on March 17, 1935, and in the House of Commons debate on the development of the RAF and related investments on March 19, again explained his position and reminded Baldwin of the wrongness of his refutation of November 28, 1934.

Then followed Hitler's protest to Simon concerning the parity of the *Luftwaffe* with the RAF, and the Foreign Secretary willy-nilly reported this to Parliament on April 3. But this was still not the end of the story. The extremely important issue of air preparedness came up for discussion in April and May of the same year and in subsequent years up to the time of Munich.[61]

Western powers. *Cf.* the report by Italian Ambassador Vittorio Cerruti from Berlin, November 28, 1943. OL Küm. Pol. 417. Miscellaneous political papers No. 681. (Hitler, as usual, was bluffing here as well; according to 1937 estimates, the number of aircraft was 1,125+546 in Britain, 5,400 in France, 3,000 in Germany, 4,325 in the Soviet Union. *Cf.* Lajos Németh, "A világ fegyverkezési versenye" [The World's Armament Race], *Külügyi Szemle*, July 1937, pp. 252—253.) — Incidentally, Britain in 1934 appropriated only £ 20 million for her air budget, including £ 9 million for aircraft and air defence installations. At the end of 1934, according to Simon's statement to the British Parliament, the British estimated the strength of the German Air Force at 600 to 1,000 airplanes. *Cf.* Cerruti's report, December 1, 1934. OL Küm. Pol. 417. Miscellaneous political papers No. 207.

[61] When Hitler claimed that Germany had reached air parity with Great Britain, he showed Simon a diagram putting British air strength at 2,100 machines. Simon at once questioned this estimate, saying that Britain's first-line strength was only 690. On April 10 Simon wrote a letter to MacDonald, asking that the whole question of German air strength should be urgently investigated by the Committee of Imperial Defence. Simon in this letter strongly emphasized the standpoint of the Foreign Office (Vansittart and others) that the German superiority with regard to all first-line machines stationed in Britain, was some 30 per cent. There was proof that the Germans had 1,375 machines of military type and a total of 3,000 machines of all types. Still more alarming than the number of German planes was the speed at which Germany was manufacturing those machines. The actual rate of production of 200 aeroplanes a month was likely to double Germany's first-line strength within a very short time. The number of men employed in the German aircraft industry had doubled between the autumn of 1933 and the autumn of 1934 and since then had increased by a further 83 per cent. Simon stated that it was to be feared that in respect of air strength Britain would no more be able to catch up with Germany. The final conclusion of his letter boiled down to this: " . . . this country is seriously open to the threat of sudden attack by a Continental Power in a degree to which it has not been exposed for hundreds of years." *Cf. The Eden Memoirs*, pp. 183—184.

Also on April 10, the Secretary of State for Air, Lord Londonderry, circulated to his colleagues a special memorandum. In it — alone in Europe — he took the view that there was no reason for fear, because the number of Germany's first-line planes would not reach 1,300 before October 1936: " . . . there is no ground for alarm at the existing situation. Whatever first-rate strength Germany may claim, we remain today substantially stronger *if all relevant factors are taken into account*. But the future . . . must cause grave concern." He recommended a programme which would give Britain a total of about 1,500 first-line aircraft by 1937, approximately corresponding to the German figure for the same year. Looking back

In this context we wish to deal with this issue only in order to understand the reason why Hitler brought up the question of air parity at the Berlin talks and to what extent it affected the wishes for an Anglo-German Naval Agreement. Eden thought the Chancellor was not in error about the figures and that he

---

upon that period, Londonderry in 1939 confirmed that Germany in 1935 had not possessed 1,000 first-line aeroplanes; but he maintained that in spite of this, he had suggested to Baldwin that, regardless of financial difficulties, the 52 squadrons requested by the Air Staff should be organized. However, the Cabinet, afraid of financial troubles at pre-election times, declined. Londonderry, therefore, thought there was no other alternative but to restore amity with the Germans. *Cf.* E. Haraszti, "Two Secret Reports from the Hungarian Archives," *The New Hungarian Quarterly,* No. 27, 1967, pp. 107—137.

As early as May, Prime Minister MacDonald, in an article published by *The Newsletter*, admitted that Germany's air preparedness was greater than it had been believed to be in November 1934. On May 22 Baldwin made the open admission that in 1934 he had been misled entirely with regard to the future, yet the whole Government had to shoulder the responsibility. Still, a single man was sacrificed. As Jan Masaryk, the Czechoslovak Minister to London, wrote in May 1935: "He had obviously to sacrifice someone because of Britain's fiasco due to his having claimed that Germany had far from as many aircraft as Britain and I would not be surprised at all if Londonderry should be the one to be sacrificed, who is said to have refused a few months ago, together with the greedy Neville Chamberlain, the money offered for air armaments." Masaryk's report, May 16, 1935. AMZV P. Z. 1935, No. 17. — Indeed, Londonderry was forced to resign. From 1931 to 1935 he had been at the head of the Air Ministry which in those years grew into one of the most important imperial offices. In the period of the policy of disarmament Londonderry and his ministry tried to wheedle as much as possible out of the stingy Treasury. Before 1935, until Simon had returned from Berlin, the money Londonderry asked for was found too much. Later the trouble was he did not ask for enough money. By the way, early in May the Hungarian Minister to Great Britain was present at a conversation between Londonderry and an M. P. of the Government party. On this occasion Londonderry said that Hitler in Berlin had proposed air parity in the German-British-French relation on a basis of 1,900 first-line machines. In Londonderry's view Hitler had been bluffing deliberately when announcing Germany's parity with Britain. He could demonstrate the parity only by allowing also for second-line and reserve aircraft and by comparing this strength to the heavily sifted British first-line air fleet. *Cf.* Széchenyi's top-secret report from London, May 6, 1935. OL Küm. Pol. 1935—21/5—1581.

Aside from this, the Air Ministry, which was called to decide an all-important issue of national interest, needed a politician of greater abilities to head it. Furthermore, in such times, the Air Minister must be in the House of Commons. Thus the choice fell on Sir Philip Cunliffe-Lister (later Lord Swinton), then Secretary of State for the Colonies, a man of more forceful dynamism than Londonderry. The great achievement of Cunliffe-Lister's period in office was the designing and promotion of the ever-famous Hurricane and Spitfire fighters. The first prototypes of these models flew in November 1935 and March 1936 respectively. *Cf.* Churchill, *op. cit.* Vol. I, pp. 114—114. — Let us add for the sake of completeness that the *Luftwaffe* could not be developed further at the same rate as it was at the time of the announcement of air parity. Of course, the Hitler team tried to maintain their leading position in the air and to make use of it in their diplomacy. Between 1935 and 1939 the British Government made serious efforts to develop aviation and achieved qualitatively first-rate results. However, even at the time of

37

was lying in order to impress Simon. Later Hitler told the Austrian Foreign Minister that he had claimed air parity only to compel Britain to conclude the Naval Agreement. But Eden was of the opinion that the two questions were unrelated. He believed that Hitler was determined to enter the Rhineland and, therefore, it could have served his purpose to make the British believe that the striking power of the *Luftwaffe* was stronger than it actually was. However, Hitler lost no time in making his figures become truly comparable with those of the British.[62] Lord Londonderry held the view that the German Chancellor had made statements of this kind in order to strengthen his position and enhance his popularity at home.[63] In his memoirs Harold Macmillan disagreed with Eden. According to him, Hitler had attained his aim already by announcing the fact of air parity: "It led the Government to accept with almost indecent haste the Führer's offer in May, limiting German naval strength to 35 per cent of the British."[64] Succeeding events — the Anglo-German Naval Agreement of June — confirmed the opinion of Macmillan in this respect.

It also appears from the memoirs that British Government circles, as well as those who initiated policies in and outside the Government, were very much preoccupied with the visit of Simon and Eden to Berlin and with the subsequent airing of the air parity issue. Foreign Secretary Sir John Simon had to make a detailed statement to the House of Commons. He said there on April 9, 1935 — as has been mentioned briefly before — that the German Government was unwilling to accede to the proposed Eastern Locarno pact, a set of treaties on mutual assistance, because it considered those instruments both contrary to German interests and dangerous to Germany. Hitler saw the interests of the Reich and of Eastern Europe secured by simple bilateral non-aggression pacts and the formula by which the contracting parties undertook to deny the aggressor every kind of assistance. Hitler declared himself disposed to conclude such non-aggression pacts with all neighbouring countries, except Lithuania. He was not in principle against the Danubian pact, but he did not find it necessary. With regard to Austria he deemed it hard to define non-aggression. But if the other powers should agree to a draft treaty, Germany would be ready to take it into consideration. Hitler said he insisted on possessing all kinds of arms already in existence in other countries. Over and above his "mild" remark pointing to Germany's full equality, he raised the demand for full parity with the French or the British air fleet, whichever of the two was larger; however, he added, he had to make reservations regarding the Soviet air force, to which, should it turn out to be larger than the air fleet of any of the two great powers concerned, the German Reich's defensive sys-

---

the outbreak of war, production only reached half that of the Germans. In April 1935 the French allegedly built one bomber a day. The speed of this aircraft was identical with that of the German aeroplanes, but the French engines were made of better material. France did not allow herself to be surpassed by Germany in this respect. *Cf.* Cerny's aforecited report, April 3, 1935. — According to the above estimate of 1937, France's air strength numbered 5,400 machines.

[62] *The Eden Memoirs.* p. 186.

[63] Széchenyi's report from London, May 6, 1935. OL Küm. Pol. 1935—21/5—1581.

[64] Harold Macmillan, *Winds of Change*, 1914—1939, London, 1966, p. 404.

tem would have to adapt itself. In his quite long-winded lecture, Hitler pointed emphatically — as Simon said — to the Russian peril, against which the only defence was provided by the German people and Germany. He even offered England the benefits of this defence.[65] Furthermore, Hitler declared that Germany was in need of a fleet equal in tonnage to 35 per cent of the British navy.[66] And Germany's return to the League might be topical only if her equality of rights as a great power was recognized in every respect, together with her title to colonial mandates, that is, to the possession of colonies.[67]

Sir John Simon admitted that the German Chancellor's stand on this question was a great disappointment to him. Besides, in diplomatic quarters it had become generally known that Simon and Eden were disappointed in their entire conversation with Hitler and that the Chancellor's lecture imbued with self-assurance made no reassuring impression on them.

According to Simon "the Berlin talks disclosed tremendous differences of opinion."[68] Czechoslovak diplomats gathered the information that the impressions gained by Simon in Berlin were more unpleasant than those aired in the press. As a matter of fact, the Foreign Secretary had convinced himself

[65] Černý's report from London, April 1, 1935. In this connection he related his confidential informant's communication. Accordingly Hitler really believed he did and would protect the world from Bolshevism. Eden then asked Hitler indiscreetly how it happened that for so many years the *Reichswehr* had been able to co-operate closely with the Bolsheviks, to supply them with arms and moral support. Hitler gave no reply. *Cf.* AMZV P. Z. 1935, No. 13. — According to Eden's diary notes, when describing his experience of the Berlin talks, he found Hitler's "whole tone and temper very different to a year ago, rearmed and rearming with the old Prussian spirit very much in evidence. Russia is now the bogey." *The Eden Memoirs*, p. 138. — This was confirmed also by Leopold von Hoesch, German Ambassador to London, who believed that "Mr. Eden had gained the impression that the Reich Government was indeed much concerned with the Russian problem." DGFP Ser. C. Vol. IV, No. 12.

[66] The naval proposal is interpreted by Eden in these terms: "Simon then referred to a proposal . . . that Germany should have a fleet equal in tonnage to 35 per cent of the British. Hitler had apparently thought that this would give him a navy equal to that of France. The Foreign Secretary pointed out that the French Navy was in fact more than half the size of the British. He added that the figure of 35 per cent appeared to the British Government to be so large as to make general agreement almost impossible. Hitler, however, declared that he did not see any heavenly or earthly authority which could force Germany to recognize the superiority of the French or Italian fleet. This was tough talking, but Simon, in view of the forthcoming discussions in London, preferred not to probe the naval question further." *The Eden Memoirs*, p 139. — Pertinax, a prominent French journalist of the time, also pointed out that Hitler really wanted his fleet to be equal to the French Navy. Simon rectified stating that the 35 per cent claim meant that the German naval force would be 15 per cent smaller than the French fleet. *Cf.* A. Géraud (Pertinax), "France and the Anglo-German Naval Treaty,". *Foreign Affairs*, Oct. 1935, pp. 51—61.

[67] According to Széchenyi, the Hungarian Minister to London, it was a novelty that Germany made her return to Geneva subject to new conditions — to equality of rights being interpreted to mean recognition of Germany's *"Mandatsfähigkeit."* April 9, 1935. OL Küm. Pol. 1935—2 1274.

[68] Ottlik, *loc. cit.*

that the whole German nation was in arms. The two British politicians had left Berlin down-heartedly under the general impression that there was no chance of agreement, the policy of Versailles had failed, and "the conditions created there can no longer be restored."[69]

On the other hand, German Foreign Minister Neurath was of the view, or at least he wished to give the impression, that the British had not only been agreeably impressed by the Chancellor, but that even Simon — who had been in Berlin for the first time — had taken home with him "a certain measure of understanding for the German point of view."[70] He compared the British guests with businessmen of the motion-picture industry who purchased a good film together with a lot of bad ones.[71] Hitler was disappointed with the fact that his British "audience" was not quite convincingly impressed by his references to the Soviet "peril" and to the joint interests of Britain and Germany on this account. This was confirmed also by Eden's journey to Moscow. Eden being a more dashing personality and a more clever political figure than Simon, the report on the Berlin results which he wired home from Moscow was not only formally better and more elaborate than Simon's account, but it gave a more realistic analytical evaluation of the situation. Let us quote a few passages:

"During the thirty-six hours train journey there has been opportunity to think over results of our Berlin conversations . . .

"The essential question seems to be does a basis now exist for a general European settlement? A year ago I believe there was such a basis, but it is exceedingly difficult to maintain that it exists now. An important purpose of our visit to Berlin was to learn whether the German Government was willing to take her place at Geneva. We now know she will not do so, except at a price which includes return of her colonies and probably other unspecified conditions as well. It would seem in principle that, quite apart from the merits of this demand, it is highly undesirable to establish a precedent that a bribe should be offered to any nation in any circumstances . . .

"Apart altogether from the question of Germany's return to the League, is there elsewhere any basis of agreement? Germany's demands on land and at sea, in respect of neither of which is there any sign of abatement, seem to make an agreement impossible, while her attitude to the Eastern Pact and the Danubian Pact makes any security agreement extremely doubtful, to say the least.

"If, as it would seem from this analysis, there is in fact no basis for a general settlement, what should be the policy of His Majesty's Government? . . . In such conditions it remains to be considered whether there may not be only one course of action open to us: to join with those powers who are members

---

[69] Széchenyi's report of April 9, 1935, and Ottlik, *loc. cit.*

[70] Neurath to Hassell, Berlin, April 4, 1935. DGFP Ser. C. Vol. IV, No. 9.

[71] Czechoslovakia's Minister to Germany, V. Mastný, on the visit of Simon and Eden. Secret. Berlin, March 29, 1935. AMZV P. Z. 1935, No. 26. Mastný got his information from Sir Eric Phipps, the British Ambassador to Germany. Sir Eric did not at all conceal his disappointment, "and as far as further development is concerned, he can see little hope of saving Poland, though he has little relevant information himself." This statement is interesting because it was made in 1935.

40

of the League of Nations in re-affirming our faith in that institution . . . It may be that the spectacle of the Great Powers of the League re-affirming their intention to collaborate more closely than ever, is not only the means of bringing home to Germany that the inevitable effect of persisting in her present policy will be to consolidate against her all those nations which believe in a collective system, but will also tend to give confidence to those less powerful nations which through fear of Germany's growing strength might otherwise be drawn into her orbit."

Sir Robert Vansittart's response to this telegram was: "These views seem very sound." But the British Cabinet did not think so and took a course different from Eden's view.[72] It should be noted here that Eden's point of view began just at the time of the 1935 Berlin talks to indicate that he would have liked to seek more effective forms of defence against Germany, and were not as unambiguous as he later claimed in his memoirs.

After Simon went back to London, Eden continued his exploratory mission. His next stop was Moscow, where he had conversations with leaders of the Communist Party and of the Soviet Union. He exchanged information with them about the European and Far Eastern policies of their two Governments. In the afternoon of the very first day, March 28, Eden was received at the Soviet Foreign Office by the People's Commissar for Foreign Affairs, Maksim Maksimovich Litvinov. The meeting was attended by the two Ambassadors concerned (Maisky and Lord Chilston). Eden then gave Litvinov a full account of their Berlin talks, a fuller one than that which Sir John Simon had given to the French and other Western Ambassadors in Berlin.

---

[72] *The Eden Memoirs*, pp. 142—143. — We must know that British and American politicians opposed to Nazism were aware of Simon's incompetence and limited abilities in foreign affairs and they made several attempts to get him to resign. A personal friend and adviser of President Roosevelt's, Supreme Court Justice F. Frankfurter — who in 1934, while staying in England, advised Roosevelt of the declining prestige of the British National Government — attributed this, besides home policy factors, to the widely accepted view (admitted even in Government circles) that Simon had been a failure at the Foreign Office. "Simon's policy is unpopular both with the P. M. and the advanced Tories in the Cabinet," Frankfurter wrote to Roosevelt on January 11, 1934. MacDonald would have liked for a second time to rid himself gently of Simon. (Halifax was chosen to succeed him.) *Cf. Roosevelt and Frankfurter: Their Correspondence, 1928—45*, London, 1968, pp. 186—188. — Churchill wrote about Simon essentially the same thing: "Sir John Simon's conduct of foreign affairs was not in 1935 viewed with favour either by the opposition or in influential circles of the Conservative Party. Eden with all his knowledge and exceptional gifts began therefore to acquire prominence. For this reason, after becoming Lord Privy Seal at the end of 1934, he had retained by the desire of the Cabinet an informal but close association with the Foreign Office and thus had been invited to accompany his former Chief, Sir John Simon, on the inopportune but not unfruitful visit to Berlin." Churchill, *op. cit.* Vol. I, p. 119. — It was Eden's view that Simon would certainly try his hardest, but Sir John once complained that he never knew what people were thinking. So Eden wrote of him: "In fact his antennae were weak." *The Eden Memoirs*, p. 175. And in another place: "I fear that J. S. is uncertain which way to turn. Vansittart drives him his way, but J. S. is reluctant to travel. Yet he clings to the F. O. It is an unhappy situation for us all." *Ibid.*, p. 187.

During the conversation Litvinov asked Eden whether the possibility of Germany's return to Geneva was related to the issue of the demilitarized zone in the Rhineland. Eden thought Litvinov meant that Hitler wanted to reoccupy that territory. Eden told Litvinov that Hitler regarded the Soviet Union as a serious menace both from the point of view of world revolution and of military aggression, and that the Chancellor considered Germany in the role of a barrier against this double danger. In 1934 it had been France that Hitler had in mind, now it was the Soviet Union. Litvinov related in detail the development of Soviet-German relations, from Rapallo up to Franz von Papen's proposal for a secret agreement with France aimed at the Soviet Union, and to the Hugenberg memorandum clamouring for *Lebensraum*. He told Eden about the story of the Soviet offer of a Baltic pact with Germany. This would have included a reciprocal guarantee by Germany and by the Soviet Union of the integrity of the Baltic States. The Soviet Union had made the offer first to Poland and then to Germany, but both Governments declined. Litvinov said that the fact of mutual guarantee envisaged with France would also be ineffective, since the French Government was unwilling to give any guarantee to the Baltic States.

As it appears from this conversation, Litvinov saw that the principle of mutual assistance in itself was no real guarantee of defence, therefore, he wished to extend that concept and to make it more concrete. In his view (and in Stalin's too) mutual assistance ought to have been guaranteed by means of military pacts. Litvinov also said that the reason why Hitler had the affront to explain in so many words that he had his eye upon expansion in the East, was that he thought that this policy was acceptable to Great Britain and to the other powers. Hitler was building on the assumption of continued Anglo-Soviet antagonism. The *Reichswehr*, according to Litvinov, would rather make a bargain with Moscow. Litvinov pointed out that he was absolutely certain that Germany intended to attack somewhere. Germany first was bent upon revenge and afterwards upon domination.[73] Litvinov explained to Eden that the Soviet Union was concerned not merely about its own frontiers, but also about the peace in Europe. The Soviet people had a great deal to catch up with the rest of the world in technical development and standard of life. Should a war break out in Europe, it would affect, even though indirectly the Soviet Union as well. For this reason the Soviet Government strongly supported the idea of collective security and approved of the Central European pact and the Eastern pact alike. Britain might try in helping to win Poland over to this idea, since the Polish statesmen attached great importance to London's opinions particularly in view of the Franco-Polish quarrel. The alternative to this was a pact without the participation of Germany and Poland, however, this arrangement would lose half of its value. Litvinov attributed great importance to Britain's attitude and asked Eden whether there was any possibility of a British guarantee of integrity for the Baltic States. Eden's answer was very sceptical, or rather pessimistic, as far as Germany was concerned. In 1934 he had thought that there was a basis for a general settlement with Germany and that France had been unwise to turn

[73] Regarding this and the whole journey to Moscow, see *ibid.*, pp. 144—163.

down the German offer. He did not believe that Great Britain would guarantee the integrity of the Baltic States, since the interest of the British Government in those states was not like its interest in Belgium or the Netherlands.

During the second conversation between Litvinov and Eden the Soviet statesman observed that there was a difference between the two Governments in their evaluation of the nature of the German policy, because British politicians refused to believe in the aggressiv character of German policy. Eden said that it would be fairer to say that they were not as convinced of it as the Soviet Government was. Litvinov outlined the Soviet view of German aggressiveness and British meekness: "The Soviet public cannot be expected to understand the play of internal politics and public opinion which influences British policy." Eden then began to explain that "the British public is not anti-German at present . . ," and not pro-French. "A great many people in England think that French rigidity has helped Hitler's rise . . . If they were finally convinced that Germany intended to break the peace, they would align themselves accordingly."

The most important event of Eden's visit to Moscow was, of course, the call he paid to Stalin. This meeting was the first occasion for Stalin to receive a politician from Western Europe. Stalin's personality made a strong impression on Eden, who was never to change his opinion of Stalin's remarkable qualities. Though he "knew the man to be without mercy", he respected "the quality of his mind and even felt a sympathy" which he had never "been able entirely to analyse. Perhaps this was because of Stalin's pragmatic approach" to things. Eden could not easily forget that he was talking to a Party man, and concluded that "certainly no one could have been less doctrinaire" than Stalin. Even in later times, during the war, Eden found his encounters with Stalin stimulating. In his opinion Stalin was a man who handled himself well in conference and was "well-informed on all points that were of concern to him. Stalin was prudent, but not slow. Seldom raising his voice, a good listener, prone to doodling, he was the quietest dictator I have ever known . . . Yet the strength was there, unmistakably."[74]

Their discussion lasted about an hour. Stalin thought that the European situation in 1935 was fundamentally worse than the situation in 1913: "In 1913 there was only one potential aggressor, Germany. Today there are two, Germany and Japan." Eden got the impression that Stalin had more understanding for the German point of view than Litvinov. Stalin admitted that the Germans were a great and capable people with exceptional powers of organization and great industrial strength. They thought the Treaty of Versailles was unjust to them, and therefore it prompted them to revenge. Stalin saw a solution in the pacts: Germany must be given to understand that in case of her attacking any nation, the whole of Europe would be against her. Stalin was of the view that the League of Nations in its actual state was unsuitable for the purpose. He emphasized the importance of the British point of view: ". . . much must depend upon the part which His Majesty's Government was willing to play in a collective system under present conditions. It would be fatal to let events drift, since there was no time to loose if a check were to

[74] *Ibid.*, p. 153.

be placed on a potential aggressor. That should be in our power now, when actual war was probably some little time away. A check at the last moment might fail."

Eden stated in his telegram to London after his talk with Stalin, among other things: "Stalin showed in the course of this conversation a remarkable knowledge and understanding of international affairs."[75]

What he had seen in the Soviet Union convinced Eden that the signs of growing Soviet military power could be a helpful restraint upon Hitler's ambitions. The joint statement on the results of the Moscow talks dealt with the international situation, the idea of the Eastern pact and other questions raised in the British and French declaration of February 3, as well as the improvement and development of Anglo-Soviet relations. The two parties were of the opinion that it was necessary, even more necessary now than ever before, to work for the creation of a universal system of European security. It was pointed out in the joint statement that the organization of security in Eastern Europe and the draft of the mutual assistance pact are in no way intended to isolate or to encircle any state, but they should create equal security for all states which are parties to such conventions.

Under these conditions, the participation in the pacts of Germany and Poland would mean the best solution of the question. The negotiating parties had been confirmed in their belief that friendship and collaboration between the two countries, the Soviet Union and Great Britain, were of utmost international importance of the universal promotion of peace and security.

What mattered most to Eden was the passage in the statement issued on the Moscow talks that "there was at present no conflict of interest between the two Governments on any of the main issues of international policy . . ."[76]

During the talks at Moscow there was general agreement between the two parties regarding the *way* of preserving peace; the best solution was thus seen *substantially* in the strengthening of the system of collective security and *formally* in the conclusion of regional pacts of mutual assistance. Britain was primarily interested in a Western regional pact (proposed on February 3), and the Soviet Union in an Eastern regional pact, the two being complementary as they were designed to "organize" peace in two different parts of Europe. And the Soviet Government took a stand openly in favour of the Western pact, as did the British Government in favour of the Eastern pact. Eden specially emphasized this by reaffirming that the British point of view was unchanged also after his trip to Berlin. In essence, however, this agreement had already become formal by that time. On the part of the Soviet Union it represented a tactical move, for the pacts in question had no longer any significance at the time. The Soviet Government, however, did not reject them, because, for want of something better, these pacts might be a useful starting point, but in themselves, they were unsuitable to safeguard the peace. The main goal of Soviet foreign policy, however, was to conclude the Franco-Soviet treaty.

The usually well informed Hungarian diplomat, Mihály Jungerth-Arnóthy, when analyzing the repercussions of Eden's stay in Moscow, pointed out in

[75] *Ibid.*, pp. 156—157, 160.
[76] *Ibid.*, p. 162.

44

his cipher telegram from Moscow that the Lord Privy Seal had informed the Soviet Government of his Berlin talks without reservations, and that the Russians had gained the impression that the British did not want to pursue a policy against Russia either through the Germans or through the Japanese. This knowledge gave Moscow great satisfaction.[77] A Hungarian foreign policy analyst also pointed out that Eden must have been given a reassuring picture of the Soviet intentions in the Far East and of the military strength of the Soviet Union, because London was beginning to steer an increasingly anti-Japanese course.[78]

It was confidentially rumoured by informed Italian sources that the most important result of the Moscow talks was Britain's future stand against German expansionism in the East. Allegedly Eden had been told that, since the idea of the Eastern pact was to be considered as definitively dead because of Germany's opposition, the Soviet Union intended to enter into compacts with France and Czechoslovakia.[79] Several sources said that Eden had been disillusioned when leaving Moscow, that it had been his impression that the Soviet Union as a military power was no serious factor, and so England would not profit much from the rapprochement with the Soviet Union.

On the other hand, in a commentary to the Anglo-Soviet conversations a columnist of *The Times* wrote on March 31, 1935, that the British had been given an alarming picture of Germany's warlike mood, while in Moscow they found Russia had no intention to make war. The writer saw the quick change-over of British public opinion in the fact that Britain's new orientation was fully vindicated by the belief that the danger of war from Germany was greater than the danger of a world revolution from Russia.

According to the Rumanian unofficial paper *L'Indépendance Roumaine* (Apr. 2) Anglo-Soviet collaboration was "sealed" by Hitler.[80]

Our reason for describing at length Eden's journey to Moscow has been that the details point out that some (unfortunately very few) insiders of leading British political circles, who were educated, enlightened, and well informed about international politics, had both the possibility and the inclination to co-operate with the Soviet Union in restraining — and not appeasing — Hitler. It is regrettable that owing to the given power relationships under the prevailing circumstances those few British statesmen who were of a broader mental vision though never departing from the British imperial conception — like Vansittart, Eden, and Churchill — were unable to get their ideas across, and that only after Munich did Britain learn to understand the fact, which had been seen outside Britain long before, that the policy of appeasement pursued by Neville Chamberlain, who had been Prime Minister since 1937 and by the Cliveden set which backed him, was dangerous and would lead to disaster.

[77] Mihály Jungerth-Arnóthy's cipher telegram from Moscow, April 9, 1935. OL Küm. Pol. 1935—2/28—1230.

[78] Ottlik, *loc. cit.*

[79] Cipher telegrams from Rome, April 2, 1935. OL. Küm. Pol. 1935—2/28—1163 and 1131.

[80] For a summary of these views, *cf.* the report of the Hungarian Minister in Helsinki, April 9, 1935. OL Küm. Pol. 1935—2/28—1295.

When after his cordial reception at Moscow, Eden arrived in Warsaw, he expected that Marshal Józef Pilsudski and Colonel Józef Beck, the Polish Minister for Foreign Affairs, would abide by their original policy, that they would denounce neither the 1934 German–Polish nor the Soviet–Polish agreement, and that they would not agree to the Eastern pact but would prefer to keep both neighbours at arm's length. Eden began his talks with Foreign Minister Beck on April 2. He informed the Polish statesman of his conversations in Berlin and Moscow. Beck kept asking him questions about the intensity of the relations between Berlin and Moscow. Eden told him of his Moscow impressions: the Soviet Government was convinced that Germany was preparing to attack somewhere, and Litvinov held the view that the Eastern pact should be concluded even without Germany and Poland participating. Eden, in turn, ascertained in his conversations with Beck that Warsaw would not join the Eastern pact even in spite of Litvinov's offer that in a given case the Soviet Union would render assistance only at Poland's request.[81] Beck drew up a clever and convincing array of arguments which, in his opinion, made it inadmissible for Poland to accede to the Eastern pact. According to diplomatic sources the main points of his reasoning were the following:

(1) Poland cannot afford to become a theatre of war. (2) She cannot allow Soviet armed forces even innocent passage through her territory nor Soviet airplanes the flight over Polish territory. (3) Poland cannot jeopardize the results obtained through bilateral treaties. (4) She cannot permit German troops to march across her territory. (5) Poland wishes to do her utmost to hold the line of balance between Moscow and Berlin. (6) All this does not preclude the possibility of Poland participating in some other appropriate and broader-based conception aimed at safeguarding peace in Eastern Europe.[82]

In spite of Eden's warnings, Colonel Beck did not take the facts of German rearmament seriously enough. Beck was "not a bit afraid of German rearmament," Eden said to Lord Cranborne who was one of his party, "there was plenty of time."[83]

At the same time Colonel Beck let the German Ambassador in Warsaw, Hans Adolf von Moltke, inform the Berlin Foreign Office of his conversation with Eden, in the course of which the conclusion had been drawn that the Eastern pact no longer existed. In Beck's view the British underestimated the Russian threat. The Polish Foreign Minister disclosed to Moltke that it had been found also that Britain, just like Italy, was opposed to the Franco-Czecho-Russian military alliance.[84] This subject really must have come up in some form, because also Eden, who in his memoirs likes to embellish embarrassing issues which might reveal the occasional wrongness of his own point of view, makes mention of this case. He says that he put the question to Beck

[81] *The Eden Memoirs*, p. 167.

[82] In addition to other known memoirs (Colonel Józef Beck; Count Jan Szembek, Polish Under-Secretary for Foreign Affairs), cf. also the strictly confidential report by Péter Matuska, Hungarian Minister to Warsaw, April 7, 1935. OL Küm. Pol. 1935—2/19—1225.

[83] *The Eden Memoirs*, p. 170.

[84] Urgent telegram to the German Foreign Minister from Hans Adolf von Moltke, Germany's Minister in Warsaw, April 5, 1935. DGFP Ser. C. Vol. IV, No. 11, pp. 12—15.

as to what the position of the Polish Government would be if France and Russia should agree to a pact of mutual assistance. But he omits to record what he said of the British position.[85] Incidentally, Eden had the impression that Colonel Beck was over-confident of his country's position. This over-confidence might have been justified if Poland had been as powerful a country as her two neighbours. We are of the opinion that Beck, being in sympathy with Germany, failed to see the difference between expansionist, power-hungry Germany and the Soviet Union, which had given proof of its readiness to promote the realization of indivisible peace. Eden found that Beck disliked the French, which was a great misfortune for Poland. Beck was not level-headed and experienced enough, nor was he wise enough for the position he held. Eden later came to the conclusion that Poland ought to have accepted the plan of an Eastern Locarno as proposed by Litvinov. This step would have determined or at least influenced Hitler's policy towards Czechoslovakia.

Eden, the memoirist, gave a correct interpretation of the Polish question. It is not without interest, however, to look into the conclusions he had drawn from the situation in 1935. According to the facts and to some sources, he stated the following: The Eastern pact did not exist any longer, and to guarantee the security of Poland and of Eastern Europe in general was impossible by relying on the Soviet Union, considering that the Polish Government refused to allow Soviet troops to enter Polish territory. This almost inevitable conclusion had a great effect later.

The fourth stop of Eden's journey was Prague. It had been considered for long in the London Foreign Office whether to include the Czechoslovak capital in the itinerary, probably because the British had wished to avoid to create the impression in Berlin that Britain pursued a policy of encirclement with regard to Germany.[86] The British Minister to Czechoslovakia, Sir Joseph Addison, claimed that it was at his request that Eden included in his programme a visit to Eduard Beneš, even though that it was not expected to bring any concrete results. It seemed needless to "annoy" Prague.[87] In Eden's judgment, "Beneš was eager and dexterous, perhaps a little too dexterous. His active mind was forever scheming new plans and projects, they were so numerous that they could not all be good." Of course, Eden informed also him of his conversations in Berlin, Moscow and Warsaw. Beneš thought that German opposition to the Eastern pact was not based on fear of the Soviet Union but arose out of the Polish question. Beneš warned Eden not to isolate the Soviet Union: should this be done, Moscow might come to an agreement with Germany at the expense of Western Europe. This view was shared by Mussolini, too. To a question from Eden, Beneš explained that Poland did not take the German peril seriously because she considered herself a great power and she thought her help to Western Europe was indispensable. At the

[85] *The Eden Memoirs*, p. 166.
[86] Černý's report from London, March 9, 1935. AMZV P. Z. 1935, No. 10.
[87] Strictly confidential report by the Hungarian Minister to Czechoslovakia, János Wettstein, Prague, April 11, 1935. OL Küm. Pol. 1935—2/16—1255. — According to the head of the British Foreign Office Southern Department the purpose of the trip to Prague was, "just to please Mr. Beneš, no big business is done in Prague." Confidential report by Királdy-Lukács from London. OL Küm. Pol. 1935—2/16—1118.

same time Poland resented the emergence of Russia as a European power. Eden was surprised at Beneš's ebullient optimism about his country's relationship with Germany. It was Beneš's optimism that led him to say that, if Germany knew that the three Western powers were agreed on a general line and the Little Entente was with them, the *Anschluss* with Austria would not come to pass. A case characteristic of Beneš's flexibility was noted down by Eden in his memoirs. When preparing to leave Prague and driving with Beneš to the airport, Eden related to his host the view of the British Military Attaché in Berlin who believed that it would take five to eight years until Germany was ready for aggressive action. To Eden's surprise Beneš agreed, "if only we hold firm." Eden remarked in his memoirs: "Germany, he was sure, could attempt no tricks just yet and in five years many things could happen, mortality played its part."[88]

Commenting upon the Beneš—Eden talks, diplomatic circles pointed to Beneš's statement that Eden's tour concerned vital interests of Czechoslovakia. This rather strong expression is extremely interesting, because Beneš in 1935 actually admitted thereby that the existence of Czechoslovakia depended on the German question.[89]

On April 4, 1935, while Eden was making his tour, *The Times*, which was generally considered in Europe to be the official organ of the British Government, carried a pro-German editorial written in a conciliatory tone, which strongly criticized Eden and reminded the Government that its policy followed in the current months might certainly determine the trend of European affairs for many years to come.

After Eden's return home, one of his most noteworthy political performances was his speech at Fulham. Giving account of his journey, he stated in that speech that in Berlin they had been unable to attain any result in any single important aspect concerning the security and armament issues of the Anglo-French accord of February 3, 1935, a most essential event of international life. Eden said then that "the possibility of an aggression by Russia upon Germany — since the recreation of the great Polish state —has become a geographical anachronism. The British are not 'anti' any nation in Europe . . . We are not 'anti' any nation, but we should be, we must be 'anti' any who might seek by force to break the peace."

The Czechoslovak Chargé d'Affaires in London wrote in a confidential report: "The foreign policy of the British Government has not even after Eden's return from his trip to Eastern Europe changed in favour of a more resolute and firmer trend. The viewpoints regarding the European problems are essentially different not only from those held by the general public but also by some officials within the Government. The group that not too long ago was working hard for an understanding between England and Germany — and we have to count to them first of all the Prime Minister — now begins to see that for the sake of safeguarding the peace, it is absolutely necessary to co-operate with the other great powers, for otherwise it is impossible to organize peace in Europe. . . . it can be inferred that, psychologically, MacDonald sees the

[88] *The Eden Memoirs*, p. 173.
[89] *Cf.* Wettstein's report from Prague, April 5, 1935. OL Küm. Pol. 1935—2/16—1199.

48

relations with Germany in a different light now than a few months earlier. But he still must be regarded as a man who, also at the decisive moments, will be inclined to settle things so as to make arrangements which threaten any agreement or negotiation."[90]

These lines, which were written one day before the opening on April 11 of the tripartite conference in Stresa, North Italy, described the conditions in Britain rather realistically. Stresa was a deliberate reaction upon the promulgation on March 16 of the law on universal conscription in Germany, and it could have been one that could have changed essentially the situation in Europe. The meeting had been urged persistently by France and Italy. Conditions in England had also become ripe for such a conference. Paris had hoped that after Simon's and Eden's trips abroad, Britain would be willing to join an anti-German bloc. At the same time also in France "there is growing confidence in the Duce, a good deal is expected of his presence at Stresa, although it is resented that Mussolini is rattling not only his own but also France's sabre".[91] In the opinion of some, the diplomatic initiative was then taken in hand by Mussolini. After the German proclamation of March 16, he was most impatient to call immediately a conference of the three powers (Britain, France, Italy). He became resolutely dedicated to the plan, which had been maturing in his mind between July 1934 and April 1935, which was to guarantee Austria's independence. The conclusion of an Anglo-Franco-Italian pact was not without interest for Italy.[92] Today, however, we know for certain that in March 1935 the question of "vital interest" to Mussolini was not Austria but Ethiopia. The three powers' Stresa front of unity was realized in order to oppose German expansion. Its price was: keeping silent about Ethiopia.[93] Mussolini wanted in Stresa to obtain freedom of action in Ethiopia. This was the important issue for him at the time.

Thus on April 11 the representatives of the three powers met at the Borromeo Palace on Isola Bella near Stresa, North Italy, and carried on discussions for three days. The British delegation was composed of fairly distinguished personages: Prime Minister MacDonald, Foreign Secretary Simon and Under-

---

[90] Černý's confidential report from London, April 10, 1935. AMZV P. Z. 1935, No. 14.

[91] Report by the Hungarian Minister to France, Sándor Khuen-Héderváry, Paris, April 11, 1935. OL. Küm. Pol. 1935—2/19—1261.

[92] As is well known, Hitler and Mussolini met in Venice on June 14—15, 1934. Mussolini thought he received assurance that Hitler would abandon his efforts to annex Austria. But when on July 25, 1934, a Nazi *coup d'état* was attempted in Vienna and Chancellor Dollfuss was assassinated (it was in Dollfuss that Mussolini had seen the guarantee of the Austrian *status quo*), the Duce at once dispatched two Alpine infantry divisions to the Italo-Austrian border to warn Hitler that if a single German soldier set foot on Austrian soil, Italy would go to war against Germany. Mussolini wired also Vienna to make known his determination. In the German proclamation of March 16, too, he saw a similar threat to Italy. *Cf.* F. Chabod, *L' Italia contemporanea (1918—1948)*, Torino, 1961; Colvin, *op. cit.*, p. 62. — The German Ambassador to Rome, von Hassell, often referred in his reports to Italy's fear and to Austrian independence being a certain key question of Italian diplomacy. DGFP Ser. C Vol. IV, p. 3. Quoted also by Colvin, *op. cit.*, pp. 61—62.

[93] *Ibid.*, p. 61.

Secretary Vansittart heading a host of experts. This composition alone, even invited many comments. The Hungarian Minister to Great Britain explained the unusual, simultaneous absence from Whitehall of the head of the Foreign Office and of the Permanent Under-Secretary "only by the discord that now can be clearly observed between the ministers and the Foreign Office." The Czechoslovak Chargé d'Affaires in London stated that it was a pity that Eden was prevented by illness from taking part in the negotiations. He saw in Vansittart the only counterpoise to the vacillating policy of MacDonald and Simon.[94]

In fact Eden should have gone to Stresa, however, as a result of his plane having run into a severe storm on his homeward journey from Berlin, he suffered a heart attack. His doctors forbade him to do any work for six weeks. Some viewed this heart attack as a political sickness, saying that Eden did not like to join in undertakings of dubious consequence. But Eden did not regard the coming Stresa talks in this light. He believed that the very task of the British should be to try to impose "a superstructure of mutual assistance above a general non-aggression pact," so if Germany should decline to participate, her intentions would become clear to the whole world. The real difficulties should be faced. At the all-important high-level negotiations in Stresa it was essential to have experience and aptitude, to explore and fathom the intentions and purposes.[95] Vansittart had persuaded MacDonald to go to Stresa himself if Eden did not go. Like Sir John Simon, Ramsay MacDonald was a meek person, one who was unable to decide and face the realities. Great Britain was therefore weakly represented at this momentous meeting, which Prime Minister Flandin and Foreign Minister Laval attended on behalf of France, and at which Italy was represented by Mussolini in the company of the Under-Secretary at the Italian Foreign Ministry, Fulvio Suvich.[96]

Eden in his sick-bed reminded MacDonald and Simon separately that Stresa might provide a particular opportunity to pump Mussolini for information since his designs aimed at Ethiopia were already evident. Both promised Eden to talk over the question with the Duce; moreover, Simon even took with him an Ethiopia expert in the person of Mr. Thompson. As a matter of course, colonial experts attended on behalf of Italy, too. With regard to the antecedents to the Italo-Ethiopian conflict in respect to Britain, all we wish to note here is that the Italian Ambassador in London, Dino Grandi, at the end of February, has asked the British Government whether it would be ready to discuss certain spheres of interest related to Ethiopia. Prior to this, early in 1935, Laval and Mussolini had arrived at an agreement in the African question, the contents of which is known though not proved by documentary evidence. The only thing certain is, namely, that Laval had ceded economic interests to Italy. The British Government then called a conference of representatives of the Foreign Office, the Colonial Office, and other competent officials to consider the issue, while at the same time seeking information from the Governments of the Sudan and the other adjoining colonies. Meanwhile,

[94] Confidential cipher telegram by the Hungarian Minister in Great Britain, L. Széchenyi. London, April 10, 1935. OL Küm. Pol. 1935—2/1—1239. — Černý's confidential report, April 10, 1935. AMZV P. Z. 1935. Conf. No. 14.

[95] *The Eden Memoirs*, pp. 176, 177.

[96] Colvin, *op. cit.*, p. 129; Churchill, *op. cit.*, p. 119.

following the Anglo-French talks of February 3, Italy had begun military preparations for war on Ethiopia. At that time London, to say nothing of Paris, was bearing serious responsibility for having failed to try to discuss the problem in time, before the military position of the Fascist power grew so strong that Rome could hardly afford to retreat. Stresa could have provided the last chance for this.

From most of the memoirs looking back upon this period, it can be concluded that Mussolini reckoned that Britain was not interested in Ethiopia, or — as appears from the secret Italian paper dated December 1934 which contains the principles for the action in Ethiopia — that if she should display interest, the Italian Government would yield. Therefore he thought it was politically and tactically advisable if he refrained from raising at Stresa the question of the Ethiopian situation which then seemed to take a favourable turn from his point of view. The British statesmen at the conference of the Big Three, against their own intention or will, also found no occasion to discuss the situation relating to Ethiopia. But Vansittart and the British Ambassador to Rome, Sir Eric Drummond, did not insist on bringing up this issue at the conference meetings. One day, a British technical adviser in Stresa brought Vansittart the surprise news that to his knowledge high-ranking officials of the Italian Foreign Ministry were prepared for the contingency that the question of Ethiopia might be raised at the conference.[97] Certain indirect remarks seem to confirm the assumption that the question was being discussed also by Vansittart and the British colonial expert interested in the matter. The British gave the Italians cautious and by no means specific warnings on this subject. These warnings did not give an indication of the vehement protest which Britain was to raise later, starting in about June. The abundant literature on this issue does not verify the information which the Hungarian Minister to Italy, György Barcza, received in the following November from the British Chargé d'Affaires. It is mentioned here because it indicated that in Stresa the British Foreign Secretary asked Mussolini confidentially but pointedly about the Italian Government's designs regarding Africa. On this occasion Mussolini gave Simon the categorical reply that "Italy has no designs of conquest in Africa, and the task of the military reinforcements dispatched to her colonies is solely to protect the frontiers of Eritrea and Somalia from the continual Ethiopian border skirmishes. Italy is contemplating no aggressive moves. Thus the head of the Italian Government has deliberately misled the British about his designs . . . and though the British Government has not for a moment given credit to this assurance from Signor Mussolini, it has to protest emphatically against the charge that the British Government . . . has deceived the Italian Government."[98] According to the British Chargé d'Affaires, Simon had put the big question to the Fascist dictator.

What Eden says about Stresa in this respect is still more interesting. He affirms that a very good opportunity to bring up the Ethiopian problem arose when Mussolini said that the League of Nations, while being effective in European affairs, was incapable of influencing the settlement of crises in

[97] Colvin, op. cit., p. 60.
[98] Strictly confidential report by Hungary's Minister to Italy, G. Barcza. Rome, November 10, 1935. OL Küm. Pol. 1935—2/7—3488.

Asia and Latin America. The Memel question and the issue of the remilitariza-
tion of the Rhineland also came up at Stresa, but any mention of Ethiopia
was strangely suppressed. This happened in the reading of the final draft, after
the resolutions of the Stresa conference had been drawn up. It contained the
sentence which stated that the three powers "find themselves in complete
agreement in opposing, by all practicable means, any unilateral repudiation
of treaties, which may endanger the peace, and will act in close and cordial
collaboration for this purpose." Just before the last clause was read, Mussolini interrupted, proposing: "Let us say here 'which endanger the peace of
Europe'." There followed an awkward silence. MacDonald turned to Simon;
Vansittart looked quickly at him; Simon between them sat immobile and said
not a word in objection. Afterwards, Grandi reproached Vansittart and Ralph
Wigram, head of the Central Department at the Foreign Office: Mussolini
would no longer believe his (Grandi's) warnings, since the British had made
no objection on account of Ethiopia ![99] According to Eden, the responsibility
for what happened rested in the first place with Simon, because he had a
better knowledge of the situation than MacDonald.

What was the essence of the Stresa front? What were the decisions arrived
at after three day's discussions, during boat excursions and in unofficial talks?
We wish to add details to some points on the basis of the confidential information supplied by Suvich to the Hungarian Minister in Rome. Therefore, we
quote here the six points of the joint resolution in full:

1. They agreed upon a common line of conduct to be pursued in the course
of the discussion of the request presented to the Council of the League of Nations by the French Government.

2. The information which they have received has confirmed their view that
the negotiations should be pursued in favour of the development needed for
the security of Eastern Europe.

3. The Representatives of the three Governments examined afresh the Austrian situation.

They confirmed the Anglo-Franco-Italian declarations of February 17
and September 27, 1934, in which the three Governments recognized that the
necessity of maintaining the independence and integrity of Austria would
continue to inspire their common policy.

Referring to the Franco-Italian protocol of January 7, 1935, and to the
Anglo-French declarations of February 3, 1935, in which the decision was
reaffirmed to consult together as to the measures to be taken in the case of
threats to the integrity and independence of Austria, they agreed to recommend
that representatives of all the Governments enumerated in the protocol of
Rome should meet at a very early date with a view to concluding the Central
European agreement.

4. As regards the proposed Air Pact for Western Europe, the Representatives
of the three Governments confirmed the principles and procedure that should
be followed as envisaged in the London communiqué of February 3, and agreed
to continue actively the study of the question with a view to the drafting of a
pact between the five Powers mentioned in the London communiqué and of
any bilateral agreements which might accompany it.

[99] Colvin, *op. cit.*, p. 61.

5. In approaching the problem of armaments, the Representatives of the three Powers recalled that the London communiqué envisaged an agreement to be freely negotiated with Germany to take the place of the relevant clauses of Part V of the Treaty of Versailles, and took into careful consideration moti vated by anxiety, the recent action of the German Government and the report furnished by Sir John Simon of his conversations with the German Chancellor on this subject.

It was regretfully recognized that the method of unilateral repudiation adopted by the German Government, at a moment when steps were being taken to promote a freely-negotiated settlement of the question of armaments, had undermined public confidence in the security of a peaceful order. Moreover, the magnitude of the declared programme of German rearmament, already well in process of execution, had invalidated the quantitative assumptions upon which efforts for disarmament had hitherto been based, and shaken the hopes by which those efforts were inspired.

The Representatives of the three Powers, nevertheless, reaffirm their earnest desire to sustain peace by establishing a sense of security, and declare for themselves that they remain anxious to join on every practicable effort for promoting international agreement on the limitation of armaments.

6. The Representatives of the three Governments took into consideration the desire expressed by the States, whose military status was respectively determined by the Treaties of Saint-Germain, Trianon, and Neuilly, to obtain the revision of this status.

They decided that the other States concerned should be informed of this desire through the diplomatic channel.

They agreed to recommend to the other States concerned to examine this question with a view to its settlement by mutual agreement within the framework of general and regional guarantees of security.[100]

The information which Suvich supplied was the following:

"Re 2. — The negotiations for the Eastern pact will continue.

"Re 4. — The air pact will be entered into by Britain, Belgium, France, Italy and Germany, but it would have to be preceded by the conclusion of a bilateral air agreement between Great Britain and France.

"Re 5. — The reason why Hitler's March 16 breach of treaty had to be censured so severly was that it was feared that the Council of the League would not accede to the request presented by France and would fail to condemn the German action. The last sentence in this point, which deals with the limitation of armaments, should not be taken so seriously, because no one really has disarmament in view and the powers see their security in the further development of their armed forces."[101]

The results of Stresa are not difficult to size up. At the time Hitler found himself confronted with the coalition of three great powers. More than one responsible official of the diplomatic service of the German Reich — among them Hoosch, Germany's Ambassador in London — was of the opinion that

[100] *Documents on International Affairs 1935*. Vol. I, pp. 80—82.
[101] Strictly confidential report by F. Villani. Rome, April 17, 1935. OL Küm, Pol. 1935—21/5—1363.

"now there is but a single way out: to put an end to unilateral treaty-breaking and return to the only possible and sensible policy, to normal negotiations, to the conventional rules of the diplomatic game".[102]

The Western great powers in Stresa had the chance to keep Hitler in check. But there was only one way to do so. This was hinted at also by Churchill and formulated by the British Minister to Prague, Sir Joseph Addison, who otherwise was of no particularly sparkling wit. He expressed his view on April 11, 1935, as follows: "Against German rearmament it is possible to take a stand in one of two ways: either resign to it or apply military sanctions against Germany. Since the latter way is ruled out, whoever insists on it, is talking claptrap. Hence neither the Stresa conference nor the French move initiated in the League of Nations could be expected to yield any positive result."[103] Vansittart's biographer today refers to Stresa as a typical example of missed opportunities and of the resulting dangers. In Eden's view, diplomacy has to face the difficulties of checking the rot once discovered under the rug. Stresa could have shaped and influenced history, but the way it happened, Stresa remained only a landmark. A momentary recoil before Hitler and the scene following the conference changed at once. "The Stresa front had the shortest life of any diplomatic experiment since the war," wrote an eminent British historian, G. P. Gooch. And according to Munich researchers, Stresa gave only the appearance of a united front, and ". . . nothing could in fact be further from the truth."[104]

Mussolini's conquest of Ethiopia — decided upon as early as 1933, and finalized in December 1934 — dispelled even the appearance of the Stresa front. His new rapprochement with Germany made an end of Germany's isolation. At that time Mussolini was also afraid that Germany and Britain might work out a rapprochement between them at his expense. He constantly followed with attention the pro-British and anti-Italian currents. He appointed to Berlin a new, pro-Nazi Ambassador, Bernardo Attolico, and recalled Vittorio Cerruti, a notorious anti-Hitlerite. On the other side, Hitler had not the slightest intention of pursuing a policy against Mussolini. He said, for example, to the Polish Ambassador that the Duce was taking a great risk in Ethiopia and although Mussolini displayed hostility to Germany, he (Hitler) would regard an Italian defeat as a big disaster in view of their common cause and their common ideological platform. As early as May, or perhaps even earlier, Mussolini was already seeking better relations with Germany. Hitler manifested benevolent neutrality in regard to the Ethiopian affair and sent his chief of military intelligence, Vice-Admiral Wilhelm Canaris, to Gardone near Verona to talk over the German–Italian problems with his Italian counterpart, Colonel Mario Roatta. (They conferred at length on September 16 and 17,

[102] W. G. Edler Herr zu Putlitz, *Németországból Németországba: Egy volt német diplomata emlékezései* [From Germany to Germany: Memoirs of a Former German Diplomat], Budapest, 1958, p. 144. (New ed. in German: *Unterwegs nach Deutschland*, Berlin, 1972.)

[103] Strictly confidential report by J. Wettstein, Prague, April 11, 1935. OL Küm. Pol. 1935—2/16—1255.

[104] G. P. Gooch, "The Grouping of the Powers," *The Hungarian Quarterly*, Vol. 3, No. 1, p. 15. — J. W. Wheeler-Bennett, *Munich: Prologue to Tragedy*, London, 1966. p. 278.

1935.) The two intelligence chiefs explained the Western relationships of their respective countries and concluded their talks with a promise to exchange naval intelligence concerning fleet movements in the Far East. Colonel Roatta proposed an agreement with the Gestapo "for the common struggle against the communist danger."[105]

After Stresa, also France indulged in a smart game of political masquerading. On May 2, 1935, in the course of organizing the system of collective security, that is, her anti-German coalition, she signed the Franco-Soviet treaty of mutual assistance which had been prepared by Barthou. Two weeks later (May 16) Czechoslovakia, under French influence, concluded a similar pact with the Soviet Union.[106] But the Franco-Soviet treaty, the ratification of which was being delayed by the French, was not an unambiguous act. A detailed discussion of this policy is beyond the scope of this book. Suffice it to say that Laval was not a firm believer in Franco-Soviet friendship, an attitude he had inherited from the late Barthou.

Among French and British historians it is still disputed today whether or not Hitler immediately after Stresa was on the point of capitulating . . . And then came the British with their readiness to enter naval discussions, the French say. And then came Laval with his German orientation, the British might say. And then came Mussolini, we might say, and Hitler regained his composure. Albeit we are convinced that Hitler was not frightened by the Stresa front. Foaming with rage, he dressed down his Ambassador in London, Hoesch, who had suggested a return to the conventional rules of diplomacy and re-entry into the League of Nations. In response to Stresa, Hitler announced on April 25 that Germany would set afloat twelve submarines within six months.[107] Hitler calculated well. His statement on the construction of the German Navy — still before the opening of the negotiations with Britain for a Naval Agreement, as had been agreed in Berlin between Hitler and Simon at the time — did not discourage British Government circles from the negotiation. The preparation of the naval discussions — which Ribbentrop called, without any reason whatever, "the great and historic German contribution" — started in April—May 1935. This marked the beginning of the active British policy of appeasement, which was to lead to Munich, and from there inevitably to the outbreak of World War II.

[105] Sir Ivone Kirkpatrick, *Mussolini: Study of a Demagogue*, London, 1964. — R. H. Whealey, "Mussolini's Ideological Diplomacy: An Unpublished Document," *The Journal of Modern History*, Dec. 1967, pp. 432—434.

[106] On April 5 the Hungarian Minister to Prague, J. Wettstein, already reported that Czechoslovakia and the Soviet Union had allegedly made a provisional military air defence agreement, providing to the Soviet air fleet two bases in Czechoslovakia, one at Žilina, the other at Olomouc. Supposedly considering the uncertainty of developments regarding Germany, Czechoslovakia had for long been reluctant to conclude an agreement of this kind, although the French Government was said to have pushed her in this direction. The final impetus to the decision was believed to have been given by the open admission of German rearmament. OL Küm. Pol. 1935—2/16—1199.

[107] Regarding this train of thought, *cf.* A. J. P. Taylor, *The Origins of the Second World War*, New York, 1962, p. 118. According to the author it seems likely that Hitler was content to wait for the Stresa front to break up. As to Hitler's raging on account of Hoesch, *cf.* Putlitz, *op. cit.*, p. 144.

"We consider it to be a cardinal requirement of our national and imperial security that our foreign policy should be so conducted as to avoid the possible development of a situation in which we might be confronted simultaneously with the hostility, open or veiled, of Japan in the Far East, Germany in the West, and any Power on the main line of communication between the two."

(*Third Report of the Defence Requirements Sub-Committee*. D. P. R. 52, 21 Nov. 1935, P. R. O. Cab. 24/259)

POSITION AND STRATEGY
OF THE GERMAN AND BRITISH FLEETS

To give a pertinent evaluation of the Anglo-German Naval Agreement of June 18, 1935, we have to concentrate on the question of submarines. A German naval expert had reason to assess the ultimate worth of this naval pact for Germany in these words: "*abrogation* of all naval clauses of the Treaty of Versailles, e.g. of the prohibition of submarines, aeroplanes, coastal fortifications."[1] Admiral Erich Raeder, Commander in Chief of the German Navy in 1935, a trusted man of Hitler's and his principal naval adviser since 1933 (moreover, a famous expert on cruisers), had good reason to insist that in case of war, similarly to World War I, in view of British superiority at sea and of a probable blockade, Germany had first of all to construct a fleet of submarines.[2]

---

[1] IMT 1949, Vol. 34, p. 175: Doc. C.—017. Table des Matières d'un Travail Historique du Colonel Scheff sur la Marine Allemande de 1919 à 1939, sous les amiraux von Trotha, Behnke, Zenker et Raeder.

[2] As for Admiral Raeder, *cf.* D. M. Kelley, *22 Cells in Nuremberg*, London, 1947 p. 109; and the strictly confidential report by Masirevich on what Raeder said of Hitler before the Hungarian Minister to Germany. February 18, 1935. OL Küm-Pol. 1935—21—663. — See also E. K. Chatterton, *Leaders of Britain*, London, n. d., p. 93 — At the start of World War I it already had become evident that ships of immense worth could be sunk by a mine or by a single torpedo discharged from a submarine. In September 1914, for example, a 300-ton German submarine (U-9) sank three British cruisers in a couple of hours, sending about 36,000 tons of shipping to the bottom of the sea. In 1918 on an average 150 German submarines operated successfully despite the nearly 4,000 submarine chasers and escort boats and 2,000 airplanes of the Entente. *Cf.* G. Lévay, "A haditechnika a tengereken" [The Technique of War on the Seas], *Hadtudományi Közlöny*, 3/1967, p. 176. — And an example from World War II: On October 4, 1939, a German submarine sank the giant battleship *Royal Oak* lying at anchor in Scapa Flow and damaged the battle-cruiser *Repulse*. Churchill analyzed the singular event in a statement to the House of Commons. *Cf.* Lajos Csürös: *Tengerek, hajók, háborúk* [Seas, Ships, Wars], Budapest, 1942.

Hitler, on the other hand, had reason to "put all his satanic energy into the rehabilitation of the German Army, expending such resources as he could spare for sea-warfare upon a new submarine fleet. In this respect he showed foresight. A race in capital ships could not be won at any rate for many years, and he probably did not think it worth the winning."[3] Therefore, Churchill was justified to state that, "the only thing that ever really frightened me during the war was the submarine peril . . . The Admiralty, with whom I lived in the closest amity and contact, shared these fears."[4]

According to records of the secret rearming of Germany, the first submarine was put into service on June 29, 1935, three and a half months after the announcement of universal conscription in Germany on March 16, 1935. After that new submarines were floated at intervals of about eight days. Thus at the beginning of October, 12 German submarines with fully trained personnel were already in service. On March 7, 1936, during the critical moment of the occupation of the demilitarized zone on the West, 18 submarines were available, 17 of which had already passed the test period, and in case of emergency they could have been employed without difficulties on the French coast up to the Gironde.[5]

[3] M. Lewis, *The History of the British Navy*, London, 1957, p. 255.

[4] K. Dönitz, *Zehn Jahre und zwanzig Tage*, Bonn, 1958, pp. 501—502. The book contains a collection of what Churchill, in his work *The Second World War*, wrote about the German submarine peril.

[5] CWT, Vol. X, pp. 455—460. Navy Manual No. 352. Secret. Extracts from the Fight of the Navy against Versailles 1919—35, dealing principally with concealed rearmament. Ed. by Cap. Schüssler. Published by the High Command of the German Navy. Berlin, 1937. — As to precise data, see also the secret copy sent on November 4, 1935, by Hoesch to Craigie. P.R.O Adm. 116—3368. This document contained information on the completion of German submarines in pursuance of the Naval Agreement of June 18, 1935. The dates of completion were the following: U—1 June 29, 1935; U—2 July 25, 1935; U—3 August 6, 1935; U—4 August 17, 1935; U—5 August 31, 1935; U—6 September 7, 1935; U—7 July 18, 1935; U—8 August 13, 1935; U—9 August 21, 1935; U—10 September 11, 1935; U—11 September 21, 1935; U—12 September 30, 1935; U—13 to U—20 from the end of November 1935 to the middle of May 1936. "On September 28, 1935, with three further vessels, U—7, U—8 and U—9, the first operational flotilla, the Weddigen Flotilla, was put into commission" with Doenitz, a captain, as flotilla commander. "During the next few months, further nine U-boats of the same type, U—10 to U—18, joined the flotilla." Grand Admiral Karl Doenitz as Commander in Chief of the German Navy was the architect of the submarine weapon with which the Germans hoped to defeat the Allies. Immediately after Hitler's death, on April 30, 1945, Doenitz became head of the German State and functioned for 20 days as successor to the "Führer." Doenitz quoted an officer who had been one of his original submarine commanders in the Weddigen Flotilla, for the following description of that first training year, 1935—36: "The knowledge acquired during this single year of intensive training, in which the crews were tested to the limits of human endeavour, was the foundation in so far as choice of types, armament and training are concerned, upon which the future structure of the U-boat arm was built . . . The salient feature of this training year, 1935—36, was the fact that it eradicated from the minds of all the commanders and their crews the inferiority complex . . . ." K. Doenitz, *Ten Years and Twenty Days*, Cleveland—New York, 1959, pp. 12—13, 16—17.

How was Hitler capable of accomplishing this in two years? Can we suppose that he alone violated the military, naval and air clauses of the Treaty of Versailles? (Articles 181 to 198 in Part V restricted the German Navy to 6 battleships of the *Deutschland* or *Lothringen* type, not in excess of 10,000 tons each, to 6 light cruisers of at most 6,000 tons, 12 destroyers of 800 tons, and 12 torpedo boats of 200 tons, or the same number of vessels to be built for replacement. Submarines were forbidden. The treaty provisions prohibited Germany from maintaining any military and naval air forces.)[6]

The truth is that the Germans violated or circumvented these provisions of the Versailles Treaty practically from the time the Peace Treaty came into force (January 10, 1920). The Germania and Vulkan shipbuilding yards sold the blueprints of German submarine cruisers to Japan as early as 1920. The first submarines were constructed in the Kawasiki shipyard under the supervision of German submarine builders in order to keep them in practice. In 1922, with the approval of the German Admiralty, a German submarine construction office was founded as a Dutch firm, called *"Ingenieurskantoor voor Scheepsbouw"* (I.v.S.), in The Hague. The purpose was to keep together a German submarine construction staff which, by doing practical work for foreign navies, could be kept in continuous practice and on top of technical development.

The same happened in the case of the German naval bases and fortifications on the coast. Even prior to Hitler's rise to power, the naval bases on the North Sea and Baltic coast (Kiel, Swinemunde, Pillau, Wilhelmshaven, Cuxhaven, Emden, Heligoland, etc.), which should have been demolished or restored to peace-time functions, were practically all fortified again, and new submarine bases were built.[7] How was all this done? In part, the Germans purposefully and consistently repurchased from England German vessels "for commercial purposes" out of the regular naval budgetary allocations and in part, the Chief of the Maritime Traffic Office of the Admiralty, Captain Lohmann, founded and financed foreign enterprises like the afore-mentioned I. v. S. and other factories, which also brought in large profits. The building of coastal fortifications and submarines was covered mainly out of secret or "black" funds.[8] Between 1933 and 1935, I. v. S. constructed the submarines U—1 to

[6] Halmosy, *op. cit.*, p. 67. As to the characteristics of the various types of ships, see Csürös, *op. cit.*

[7] Regarding the history of German naval bases since 1853, *cf.* E. C. Talbot-Booth, *All the World's Fighting Fleets*, London, n. d., pp. 421—422.

[8] An additional important connection which can be traced back to the year 1925 was taken up with Spain. At the instigation of Captain Lohmann and Lt. Comdr. Canaris, the Spanish King and Primo de Rivera in 1925 gave the order to Echevarieta, a Spanish industrialist, to set up a torpedo factory under German supervision. Under the contract 1,000 torpedoes were made simultaneously with the collaboration of German engineers. German credits made it possible also to establish contacts between the factory and I. v. S. Incidentally the I. v. S. technical director was Dr. Techel, a former chief submarine constructor of the Germania shipbuilding yard. In 1925 I. v. S. managed to obtain an order for the construction of two 500-ton submarines. Captain Lohmann, as Chief of the Maritime Traffic Office of the Admiralty, contributed one million marks to this deal in order to beat the considerably lower prices of the foreign competition, especially the French and Italian. Lieutenant-Commander Bartenbach in 1924 had assumed a position

U—24. U—25 and U—26 were also built, but in secrecy and piecemeal and their parts were kept in storage in Kiel. Submarine construction in Finland, Spain and Turkey (since German submarines were built by I.v.S. in these countries too) gave German officers and seamen the opportunity to be trained for this service. In 1933—34 a 250-ton submarine built in Finland was the training ship for officers who had served on the first submarines launched after World War I. The fact is that this 250-ton submarine gave a start to the speedy development of the German Submarine fleet. The above facts may explain the short time it took Hitler to "surface" the German submarines, to announce their completion, and to make political capital out of their existence.

Let us take a closer look at the German and British strategic conceptions which determined the development of the German fleet, including the submarines, and whose roots also went back to World War I. They were linked with the provisions of the Naval Treaties worked out at the 1922 Washington Conference and at the 1930 London Naval Conference, and also had a bearing on the race for naval bases and for territories rich in raw materials.

This conception was primarily and decisively influenced by the armament policy and geographical position of the greatest maritime power, Great Britain. Britain's geographical situation implies three essential facts: (1) Britain is an island country; (2) she is separated from the European continent by a narrow sea channel; (3) this island is the center of a vast and powerful Empire whose different parts are connected by arteries of sea communication.

Britain has no land boundaries and since the Hundred Years' War she has had no expansionist ambitions on the European continent. The sea is her natural defence and advantage as well. This was the reason why she was jealously guarding her supremacy at sea with a mighty fleet while at the same time she could afford to keep her land armies at a low level.

The naval race had begun already during World War I. Strictly speaking, naval rearmament was a competition of economic, not military, factors. It was a struggle for territories with raw materials. In the 1920's and 1930's about 70 per cent of the world's crude oil production was in the hands of the United States of America, and another 10 to 12 per cent fell to Latin America. Europe was in need of huge imports from overseas in addition to the full exploitation of the European resources which amounted to nearly 6 to 8 per cent. The output of the Persian oilfields yielded about 2 to 3 per cent. Sixty

---

as naval adviser in Finland. First of all he succeeded there in having three 500-ton and one 100-ton submarines built in Finnish shipyards according to I. v. S. projects for the German Navy. The naval officers first received practical training here. In 1925 a Yacht School was started in Neustadt, where the young people were trained for motor-boat driving, radio communication, etc. Lohmann was aware of the prime importance of oil for the development of the German fleet. In 1925 he founded the Bremen Oil Transport, an enterprise on the model of the Anglo-Persian Oil Co. As early as 1923, German naval quarters had contacted several foreign maritime offices with the view of the further improvement of the electrical torpedo. In 1927 a Swedish contract made it possible to create an accumulator plant at Karlskrone (Sweden), which improved the use of torpedoes. *Cf.* CWT, Vol. X, pp. 455—460. No. 352.

five per cent of the caoutchouc needed for the manufacturing of rubber was supplied by Indochina and 30 per cent by the Dutch East Indies. Nearly 90 per cent of all copper, a base material indispensable for the electrical industry, also came from overseas territories. Sixty per cent of the world's cotton production was grown in America. The British colonies supplied the world market with 35 to 40 per cent of the output of unmanufactured wool. The unhampered flow of shipping and undisturbed sea communication in times of peace is a matter of economic development. In times of war, it is a matter of life and death.

In respect of food supplies, Britain was dependent on imports for nine months of the year. Her domestic industry's requirements of raw material and crude oil presupposed free maritime communication. She had only coal in surplus and for export, but also this required sea transportation. Britain's power had been linked with the seas for many centuries. From the late 1930's onwards, however, modern strategic interests required also a powerful air force in addition the fleet. Of the British Empire's total population of about 460 million at that time, nearly 350 million were Asiatics and 50 million lived in Africa. However, only about 40 per cent of Britain's external trade was transacted between the metropolitan country and the colonies. The security of the Empire and the freedom of maritime traffic were based on considerations of naval strategy. The most essential naval and air bases for the traffic through the Mediterranean towards India, Australia and New Zealand, were Gibraltar, Malta, Cyprus, Aden and Singapore. In order to secure the supply of crude oil, the Iraqi oil concern was established. In part this was done jointly with France. Oil could be conveyed with the aid of special pipelines from Iraq to the Mediterranean Sea. The dangers of aerial attack, in view of the above considerations, made the submarines issue an extremely important question in the eyes of Britain. The experience of World War I had shown that this combat arm constituted the greatest danger to the British Empire's seaborne food and trade. This was correctly pointed out by Churchill, as will be seen below in detail. The question was carefully analyzed by British naval strategists.[9] Britain, therefore, made every effort on every given occasion to press for the complete prohibition of submarines and of submarine warfare, while France and Italy wished to maintain their submarine fleets.

Until Hitler announced the launching of his submarines in the spring of 1935, the fact of German naval armaments was to the British Admiralty only one of many problems. One of many, because during the one and a half decades following World War I, Britain found it increasingly difficult to keep the "Two-Power Standard" of her Navy, which in the 1930's had dropped below a "One-Power Standard." (The "Two-Power Standard" meant that Britain had a fleet of sufficient numbers to be capable of meeting the combined fleets of any two powers that might be brought against it).[10] Before the Washington Treaty of 1922, the British fleet, or the Royal Navy (which is known as the

[9] See Dr. T. Weber, "Az angol külpolitika irányvonalai" [Guidelines of British Foreign Policy], Külügyi Szemle, 1935, pp. 245—252. — F. Réczey, "Fegyverkezés a tengeren" [Rearmament on Sea], Külügyi Szemle, 1936, pp. 119—126. — Churchill, The Second World War, Vol. III: "The Grand Alliance", p. 98.
[10] Talbot-Booth, op. cit., p. 38.

Senior Service because it is the oldest one), had been the largest in the world. The basic idea of the Washington Treaty was to place the U. S. fleet on an entirely equal footing with the British Navy. It fixed the ratio with regard to *battleships* among the naval forces of the contracting powers up to the end of 1936. Accordingly, Britain and the United States could have 15 battleships each, Japan 9, France and Italy 5 each (meaning a ratio of 5 : 5 : 3 : 1.75 : 1.75). The London Naval Treaty of 1930 was designed to fill the gaps in the Washington Treaty. By maintaining the ratio of 5 : 5 : 3, the United States obtained parity with the British Empire also in respect to *light units* (as a consequence of which the British cruiser fleet fell below security standard). By the terms of the London Treaty the British fleet of 120 cruisers had to be reduced to 50, and only the 1936 British rearmament programme raised the lower limit to 70. Essentially this was only a tripartite agreement, because the two Latin nations, France and Italy, were unable to come to terms regarding smaller units and submarines.[11]

At the time the London Naval Treaty was concluded in 1930, the British Empire built and equipped only one cruiser, while France and Italy each completed three. This meant that the continental powers boasted a more up-to-date fleet, while the Royal Navy lagged behind.

Afterwards the situation only worsened, especially with respect to the submarines which were of such great strategic importance to Britain. As early as 1930—31, France commenced with the construction of another 14 submarines and Italy started to build 26 more. At the same time, Britain prepared to construct altogether 6 subs. Confronted with this large-scale submarine construction programme by the Mediterranean powers, England should at least have increased her efforts in her preparations for anti-submarine warfare. But the truth of the matter is that she cared less about it in those two years than she had before. "The Admiralty asked that a flotilla of 8 destroyers and a flotilla leader should be laid down in 1930, as in 1928 and 1929. The Labour Government under Mr. Ramsay MacDonald, however, appeared to think that this was quite unnecessary. They cut the destroyer-building programme for that year by half . . ." This did not fit into any fleet organization. (Later the remainder was joined to the Royal Canadian Navy.) In 1931, however, a whole flotilla was laid down.[12]

The Washington and London Treaties limited the total tonnage of the Royal Navy to 1,201,700 tons. This provision was to remain in force until the expiration dates of those treaties — December 31, 1936. Under the London Treaty, the United States and Japan were each allowed 52,700 tons for submarines. As has been mentioned before, France and Italy did not commit themselves in this respect. Thus France and Italy increased their strength in the sub-

[11] The Naval Treaties of Washington (1922) and London (1930) limited the tonnage of the different ship categories as well as their weapons. The great naval expert Admiral Sir Herbert Richmond, in an article written on the occasion of the Anglo-German Naval Agreement, questioned the rationale of limitation of the tonnage and the number of guns. He cited historical examples to prove that the naval battles had not been decided by the number of guns. He was strongly against the use and propagation of the "strategical jargon." See Sir Herbert Richmond, "The Battleship: Tonnage and Guns," *The Spectator*, June 19, 1935.

[12] K. Edwards, Lt. Comm. R. N., *Uneasy Oceans*, London, 1939, pp. 48—49.

marine category. The situation was quite different from the times when Britain had proposed a maximum of 250 tons for subs at the Disarmament Conference in 1932. In the late 1930's the five great powers had nearly 400 submarines.[13] (The French could argue that they had to protect not only France's north coast against possible German attack, but also the coasts of Southern France and North Africa against possible Italian attack.) In the middle of the 1930's, however, the British fleet was 60 per cent smaller and its personnel had 50,000 men less than in 1914. At the same time the U. S. Navy had increased by 130 per cent, the Japanese naval force by 75 and the Italian fleet by 96 per cent.

In the mid-1930's the British Navy was at the lowest point both in number of ships and in naval personnel. In 1914 the British Navy had 146,000 men; in 1935 95,000; in 1937 100,000; in 1938 120,000, and in 1939 133,000 men.[14]

After the Japanese occupation of Manchuria and after the party of Japanese militarists had come to power in 1931, Japan denounced the Washington and London Treaties in December 1934. This was still before the British fleet had sank to its low level. The action of the Japanese Government triggered an unrestricted race of naval armament, which found Britain in the most disadvantageous position at the worst possible moment. This was the case not only because of the very substantial reduction of her naval forces as a result of the terms of the Washington and London Treaties, but also because of the obsolete condition of her remaining vessels. (Twelve of her 15 battleships authorized under the Washington Treaty needed substantial overhauling.) It is true, however, that at the outbreak of World War II, Britain had managed to get out of this all-time low. This improvement was due to a large degree to the British naval strategy's awakening to the existing dangers and to the very important budgetary allocations which were made as a result of it.[15]

Between 1933 and 1935, while Britain was going her way downwards and had her potentialities muzzled by the Washington and London Treaties, Hitler continually circumvented also the Versailles provisions on the limitations of the German Navy. As is known, by the end of 1934, the German Army had trebled its numerical strength and in April of that year, General Ludwig Beck, Chief of the General Staff, was given to understand that by next spring Hitler would openly decree conscription and publicly repudiate the military clauses of the Versailles Treaty. It was ordered also that, "until then the utmost secrecy must be observed. Goebbels was admonished never to allow the words 'General Staff' to appear in the press, because Versailles forbade the very existence of this organization. The annual official rank list of the German Army ceased to be published after 1932 so that its swollen lists of officers would not give the

[13] IMT, Vol. 41, pp. 6—12: Doc. Raeder-13. Germany's largest submarine at that time was of 750 tons. After World War I about 315 German submarines had to be sunk. At the start of World War II Germany had 70 serviceable submarines... Regarding the different types of submarines in the period between the two World Wars, see details in Lévay, loc. cit., pp. 170—193: Dönitz, op. cit. (1958), pp. 33—35; Talbot-Booth, op. cit., p. 267. According to the latter the number of completed submarines in September 1939, at the outbreak of World War II, was as follows: Great Britain 57, France 78, Italy 104, Japan 60, United States 87.

[14] Talbot-Booth, op. cit., p. 38.

[15] Watt, loc. cit., p. 165.

game away to foreign intelligence. General Keitel, Chairman of the Working Committee of the Reich Defence Council, admonished his aides as early as May 22, 1933: 'No documents must be lost, since enemy propaganda will make use of it. Matters communicated orally cannot be proven; they can be denied'."[16]

The Navy was also warned to keep its mouth shut. On January 31, 1933, Admiral Raeder, Commander in Chief of the Navy, issued top secret directives to the Navy to support the German armament industry: "I attach particular importance to guaranteeing the continuous support of the industry concerned by the Navy, even after the present restrictions have been relaxed. If the purchasers are not made confident that something special is being offered them, the industry will not be able to stand up to the competitive battle and there-fore will not be able to supply the requirements of the German Navy in case of need."[17]

In March 1934 the German Naval Command Office wrote a top secret memorandum saying: "It is intended to include in the Establishment Organization 35 (AG-Aufstellungsgliederung) a certain number of auxiliary cruisers which are intended for use in operations on the high seas. In order to disguise the intentions and all the preparations, the ships will be referred to as 'transport ships' (0). It is requested that in future this designation only be used."[18]

In June 1934 Raeder had a long conversation with Hitler. On this occasion he noted down the Führer's instruction:

(1) It is forbidden to talk about displacement of 25 to 26 thousand tons, but only about repaired 10,000 tons. It is forbidden to talk about speeds of more than 26 knots.

(2) The Commander in Chief of the Navy expresses the view that the fleet must nevertheless be later developed against England, therefore from 1936 onwards the large ships must be equipped with 35-cm guns.

(3) The Führer insists on the necessity of keeping submarine construction secret also with regard to the Saar plebiscite.[19]

Admiral Raeder, Commander in Chief of the Navy, obtained a large measure of freedom for the development of the navy, which at that time was only limited in so far as the works of rearmament had to be kept secret because of the Versailles Treaty. Therefore, beside the public budget they retained also the former special budget, which was then substantially increased in view of the considerable working implements provided by the Reich for the purpose of rearmament. To put the said implements to use, a large authorization in keeping with the increased responsibilities of the chief of budgetary affairs was given to Captain Schüssler and in 1934 to Captain Foerster.[20] The German "Armament Plan (A.P.) for the 3d Armament Phase," as referred

---

[16] W. L. Shirer, *The Rise and Fall of the Third Reich*, London, 1961, pp. 281—282.

[17] CWT, Vol. X, p. 468: Doc. C.—29. Raeder's directive to the Navy to support the German armament industry, Berlin, January 31, 1933, Top Secret.

[18] CWT, Vol. X, p. 470: Doc. C.—166. Memorandum from Naval Command Office, March 12, 1934, Concerning auxiliary cruisers. Berlin. Top Secret.

[19] CWT, Vol. X, p. 472: Doc. C.—189.

[20] IMT, Vol. 34, p. 604.

to by the Naval Command directive of May 12, 1934, stated that "owing to the speed of military-political development since Germany quitted Geneva, and based on the progress of the army, the new A-plan will only be drawn up for a period of 2 years. The 3d A-plan lasts accordingly from April 1, 1934, to March 1936 . . . All theoretical and practical A preparations are to be drawn up with a primary view to readiness for a war without any alert period." The financial aspects of this new 2-year armament plan were also worked out. It was thought that the necessary funds were secured by the armed forces, including the navy.[21] On November 2, 1934, however, Raeder, in his conversation with Hitler, expressed the doubt whether the planned budget would be sufficient: (1) To his assertion that the total means that might be available to the *Wehrmacht* in 1935 would probably run to merely a fraction of the amount needed, which in turn might possibly hinder the navy in its plans, Hitler replied that he did not believe the funds would be reduced substantially. Raeder deemed it necessary to build up the navy rapidly until 1938, according to schedule. In case of need Hitler would ask Dr. Robert Ley to make 120 to 150 million available to the navy through his Labour Front with the justification that this money would again serve to promote labour. Afterwards the Führer explained also during his talks with Minister Göring and the Admiral, that he ascribed vital importance to the construction of the navy as planned, since it would be utterly impossible to make war should the navy not be able to secure the supplies of ore from Sweden. (2) When Raeder reminded him that in a critical political situation it would be desirable for six submarines to be assembled in the first quarter of 1935, Hitler declared that he would keep this in mind and tell Raeder if the situation required them to start the assembling process.[22]

After 1933 also I. G. Farben got instructions from the Nazi Government to raise its production of synthetic oil to 300,000 tons a year by 1937.

At the outbreak of World War II the numerical strength of the German Navy was not great. Let us refer to the following among the ships already built and under construction:

Three pocket battleships: the *Deutschland* had been completed by April 1, 1933; the *Admiral Scheer* by November 1934, and the *Admiral Graf Spee* by January 1936. These pocket battleships were officially said to be of 10,000 tons each, but during construction they were enlarged to 13,000 and 14,000 tons.

Two battle cruisers said to be of 26,000 tons each: the *Scharnhorst* had been completed by May 1938, the *Gneisenau* by September 1938. In reality they were of 31,300 tons each.

Two battleships alleged to be of 35,000 tons: the *Bismarck* was completed in February 1939, the *Tirpitz* in April 1939. In reality each of these ships was of 41,700 tons. This is quite remarkable because the London Naval Treaty had fixed 35,000 tons as the upper limit for British and U. S. battleships.

The tonnage limits set by the Anglo-German Naval Agreement ultimately made these discrepancies possible inasmuch as the tonnage units within the

[21] CWT, Vol. X, pp. 470—472. Naval Command Directive, May 12, 1934, Concerning the Armament Plan for the 3d Phase, Berlin, Top Secret.

[22] IMT, Vol. 34, pp. 775—776: Doc. C.—190.

various ship categories could be varied. Of course, whether the plus was taken from the tonnage unit of cruisers or lighter ships (the British used the latter method) was an open question. Eventually the Germans made use of the possibilities offered both by the Treaty of Versailles and by the 1935 Anglo German Naval Agreement as they saw it in the best of their own interest. It could have happened, as it did in fact, that Germany did not use in each ship category the possibilities given by the Anglo-German Naval Agreement, or if she did, she did it only when she found it to be best to her strategic advantage. With respect to battleships and submarines she passed over the permitted percentage entirely. At the time of the outbreak of World War II, Germany had 7 battleships in service. Some even believed that the British suspected foul play on the part of Germany but did not think this to be so decisive.

The first cruiser, the 5400-ton *Emden*, was finished in 1925; three 6000-ton cruisers, the *Königsberg*, the *Karlsruhe* and the *Köln*, were launched in 1929; a similar ship, the *Leipzig*, was completed in 1931, and the *Nürnberg* in 1935. Thus, before the conclusion of the Anglo-German Naval Agreement, Germany had constructed six cruisers. She added to this number another four in 1937—38 and 1939; these were 10,000-ton cruisers. (Properly speaking, these vessels corresponded to the 10,000-ton battleship class allowed by the Versailles Treaty. The contemporary press described also one of the cruisers of this category constructed after 1935, the *Prinz Eugen*, as a battleship which the wife of Hungary's Regent Admiral Horthy was asked to christen during the naval parade at Kiel in August 1938.)[23]

What in the 1930's Germany attained in the construction of warships, even despite the small number of the vessels, astonished the naval experts of ot her countries, especially the great powers of Western Europe, in the first place Great Britain. Even though they despised and condemned the methods of German naval rearmament, they had to admit that German planning and construction did a very good job in the field of shipbuilding. They valued especially highly the ingeniousness of the "pocket battleships." The sensation was that these pocket battleships gave Germany a fast and homogeneous — from the gunnery point of view — squadron capable of operating effectively at great distances from a base. It was also embarrassing to the other naval powers because those ships possessed a margin of speed exceeding those of existing battleships and had a greater firepower than cruisers. They ingeniously bridged the gap between the two ship categories, creating thereby a new and very serious danger to maritime trade. (What was in fact the use of escorting a convoy of merchant ships by cruisers and destroyers if they were open to attack from a pocket battleship which was faster and had better guns?) The pocket battleships and cruisers (with the exception of the *Emden*) could carry aircraft and, being equipped with catapults, could also launch aircraft from their decks. The strength and effectiveness of German battleships and of the

[23] Edwards, *op. cit.*, pp. 101—107, 170. — IMT, Vol. 41, pp. 84—85: Doc. Raeder—127; pp. 6—12: Doc. Raeder—13; pp. 1—3: Doc. Raeder—8. — IMT, Vol. 34, p. 188: Doc. C.—023. — DGFP Ser. C. Vol. IV, No. 165; App. 1, p. 344 — Shirer, *op. cit.*, pp. 488—489. — Observans, "Külpolitikai szemle" [Foreign Political Review], *Magyar Szemle*, Oct. 1938, p. 178.

entire German Navy lay in their being a novel and up-to-date armed force which was equipped according to the latest plans and with the most modern technical innovations. There was hardly a single outmoded ship in the German fleet, a situation which no other navy in the world could have claimed.

By the mid-1930's, Germany had recovered her great power status, but in spite of her over expanding overseas trade and growing naval forces she could not become a really notable maritime power as long as she lacked most essential naval bases on the seas and oceans. For this reason, Hitler started campaigning systematically for the return of the former German colonies practically from the first moment of his coming to power. He was prompted to do so also by the growing German need for raw materials. The usual way of naval development was for a country, if it had overseas colonies vulnerable to outside attack, to build up its fleet to protect those territories and ensure thereby unhampered communication between the metropolitan country and its colonies. Germany went the opposite way. First she wished to equip her land and naval forces in order to get back her former colonies. (It is certain, however, that Hitler wanted to build the navy within the scope of Germany's continental policy, and in 1933 he still believed, as he explained to Raeder during their first conversation, that he would never intend to go to war with Britain, Italy, and Japan.)[24]

It was already known at that time that a future naval war would be waged in three dimensions: on the sea, over the sea, and under the sea. Conscious of her superior strength, of course, Britain very much preferred "to come out into the open." Even the White Paper of March 1935 stressed therefore that the battleship was to remain an essential element of the British Navy and that Britain's whole naval strategy was based on it. British military experts debated this principle at that time. We shall discuss this issue later on. In order to redress this inferiority, Nazi Germany — in spite of the fact that she tried to construct her battleships as efficiently as possible in the knowledge that she would remain at all times a naval power only second to Great Britain — resorted to the methods of "unseen hands." She urged the development of a modern and fairly sizable fleet of submarines.[25] She, therefore, tried under the Anglo-German Naval Agreement of 1935 to ensure, that "Germany had the right to possess submarines of equal tonnage with that of all submarines of the Members of the British Commonwealth of Nations without exceeding the ratio 35 : 100 concerning the aggregate tonnage."[26] The German explanation was that the submarines "had been built purely for coastal defence service, with more than a hint that in view of the growth of the Soviet submarine flotillas in the Baltic it was a matter of obvious necessity for Germany to

[24] E. Raeder, *Mein Leben*, Vol. II, "Von 1935 bis Spandau 1955," Tübingen, 1957, p. 33.
[25] On questions of the pocket battleships and German naval tactics, *cf.* Edwards, *op. cit.*, pp 101, 107, — Sir Herbert Russell, K. B. E., *Sea Warfare Today*, London, 1940, pp. 15, 41. See also Note 13 above.
[26] Halmosy, *op. cit.*, p. 371. (That Britain accepted this provision may probably be explained by the fact that at the time the aggregate number of French and Italian submarines was exceedingly large. We shall deal with this question in detail when evaluating the Anglo-German Naval Agreement.)

66

respond to this menace."[27] In December 1938 the German submarine force consisted of 118 ships completed or still under construction, of which 26 were seaworthy at the outbreak of the war.[28]

From the experience of World War I the German naval experts knew very well that in case of another war, Britain's powerful naval force would blockade Germany again. Admiral Raeder, who, from 1933 onwards, had been the theoretical and practical executor of the strategy of German naval rearmament, was aware that in the given case, in spite of all his efforts, a British blockade would again counteract all efforts made by Germany. That is the reason why he was striving first of all to construct submarines and minelayers even in excess of the financial appropriations. The Naval High Command of Germany shared Reader's views. They were less confident that Germany's submarine strength alone would be able to paralyze British maritime trade or to re-create the situation of 1917—18. But they did believe that the ruthless deployment of minelayers and aerial bombers, added to submarine activities, might reduce England to poverty and economic insufficiency. The German naval officers almost without exception were also convinced that should war once again break out between Germany and Britain, Germany's naval strategy would be to launch immediately an attack on British seaborne trade in order to cut off the British Isles from their raw material resources, to break the maritime communications of the Empire, still before the metropolitan country could accommodate itself to the wartime requirements or to start organizing the protection of its naval operations. This was the basis of all German plans for sea warfare against Britain. In view of the wide disparity of naval strength between the two countries, it was about the only line of war policy open to Germany. It was fortunate that the British military command inferred by intuition and by other means what the Nazi German strategy and tactics were.[29]

[27] Russell, *op. cit.*, pp. 102—103. — The German submarines were practically of three types: (1) The small "coastal" type of 250 tons. Units of this type were as far afield as Spain, Portugal and the Western Mediterranean. (2) The "seagoing" type of over 500 tons. Its first unit was launched in February 1936. (3) The "ocean-going" type of about 750 tons. The use of the word "ocean-going" by Germany is noteworthy since her plea to be allowed to build submarines was that they were essential to the defence of her coasts in the North Sea and particularly in the Baltic. Edwards, *op., cit.*, p. 107.— During World War I German submarines of exactly the same tonnage (250) did much damage in the North Sea and in the English Channel. The small submarines built by Germany, alhough they were a valuable asset to her fighting fleet, had as their primary function the training of personnel for the new submarine service. *Ibid.*, p. 176.

[28] Watt, *loc. cit.*, p. 175. According to him Germany started World War II with 57 completed submarines. The aforecited data speak of 70 units, but this figure included also the submarines under construction. Actually, by virtue of the Anglo-German Naval Agreement, the Germans in 1938 had fewer submarines. To explain the difference, the German Naval Command in December 1938 announced that it would build a submarine fleet equal in tonnage to the British. This was officially made public on January 18, 1939. *Cf.* DGFP Ser. D, Vol. IV. pp. 293—294. The truth is that Germany had begun the construction of this tonnage much earlier. See Watt, *ibid*.

[29] Chatterton, *op. cit.*, p. 93. — Russell, *op. cit.*, p. 96.

The German naval strategy was of course determined by Germany's admittedly bad strategic position: practically opposite to her own coastal line run the long shores of her dreadful enemy — England. Germany herself had no naval base on the seas and battleships could not stay away from their base beyond a couple of weeks. The heavy armoured ships could not even operate beyond a few days. On the other side, Britain had many naval bases at her disposal. (Second in this respect was France.) This factor is an important point in judging the naval strength of any country, though it usually not included in the charts comparing naval figures. The German Naval Staff had always studied how it would be possible to overcome most effectively this drawback. They did not shrink — as was later completely clear to the British — from resorting to the illegal means of breaking treaties as well as agreements, just as they did at the start of the war when they often sprang "nasty surprises" on the world — e.g. torpedoing neutral ships, laying mines in British territorial waters, and employing other "shock tactics." The German naval warfare on the whole was later, in World War II, called "mosquito warfare." At the same time the Nazi High Command, including the Naval Staff, did not stop in their attempts to acquire naval bases of vital importance to Germany. There was very good reason to suspect that the Germans counted upon setting up supply bases at various points along the Spanish coast in return for the help which they had some time before forced upon General Franco. Hitler needed the iron ore of the Basque provinces and, even more, the bases located in Spain and in overseas territories controlled by Spain (Spanish Morocco, Rio de Oro, Canary Islands). They would have not only provided excellent stepping stones towards the regaining of the former German colonies in West Africa but, situated close to the trade routes to South America and South Africa, they would have also helped the German naval strategy of attack on seaborne trade. Speculations about naval bases also played a part in the German sympathies towards Italy as well as in the underground work conducted by Nazi agents in South America.[30]

German naval strategy directed its main line of offensive against the enemy's maritime trade not only in the event of war. Hitler wanted colonies, rich in natural resources such as oil, iron ore, and timber. Over and above his scheming in Europe, primarily in Eastern Europe, Hitler wanted his densely populated country to recover first of all the ex-German colonies — mostly with British approval, as we have seen from his conversation with the British appeaser Lord Lothian. Hitler intended to create a situation which under the threat of war would compel the Western European great powers to give back the colonies to Germany rather than to take the risk of war. When Hitler was aiming at his future enemies' maritime trade, he contemplated also cutting them off from the colonial territories he had in mind for himself. Hitler's Central European policy so much enraged the great colonial powers that on this pretext they refused to yield on the question of their own colonies. This was a natural result of the interaction and interdependence of political and economic interests. It is well known that the aim of Hitler's expansionism in Europe, in addition to acquiring new territories, was to lay hands on larger supplies of food and raw materials. However, it is seldom mentioned that

[30] Edwards, *op. cit.*, pp. 178—179. — Russell, *op. cit.*, pp. 67—68.

underlying this aim was the fear which also was based on the experience of World War I, i.e. that in the case of another war a new British blockade might disintegrate Germany. Objectives, such as "self-determination," "the right of minorities," "a menace to the security of the Reich" — were only excuses. Germany refused to admit the economic aspects of the question. For example she gained as a result of the Austrian *Anschluss* iron ore, magnesite, salt, lead, zinc, copper, coal and graphite, as well as the agricultural products of Austria and the vast resources of her forests. "Germany also obtained control of a great number of livestock. Livestock is not only important for food. It provides one of the most important sinews of war. It is not simply cattle that Germany wanted, but fat cattle, because there is hardly an explosive which can be made without animal fats. Lard yields approximately one-tenth of its own weight in glycerine. A thousand tons of lard will therefore produce a hundred tons of glycerine. From one part of glycerine, two parts of nitro-glycerine are obtainable. Since the propellent contains one-third of nitro-glycerine which the Germans used for firing their heavy guns, a thousand tons of lard provided for six hundred tons of gun ammunition to be manufactured."

Czechoslovakia was a much richer country than Austria, particularly with regard to minerals. By her rape of Czechoslovakia, Germany gained coal, radium, gold, silver, iron, graphite, lead and forests. Forests also were valuable to Germany not only because of the direct uses of timber, but because Germany produced from wood a substitute for the greatest of all the sinews of war — fuel oil. No amount of substitutes could, however, compensate Germany for her lack of mineral oil. Similarly, the agricultural produce of Austria and Czechoslovakia were insufficient to cover the needs of the German population in times of war. It was for this reason that Germany bribed and threatened Rumania into the conclusion of a trade pact designed to give Germany virtual control of the Rumanian oilfields and the products of her wide grain-lands. The Rumanian oilfields, however, could only just meet her peace-time requirements. In 1938 Germany's mineral oil requirements were about seven million tons, of which over four and a quarter million tons were imported. The total exporst of oil from Rumania in 1938 amounted to four and a half million tons.[31]

[31] Edwards, *op. cit.*, pp. 264, 267—268. Moreover, the main Rumanian oilfields were very steadily exhausted, as shown by the reduction in exports in spite of increased demand. In 1936 Rumania exported 6,884,000 tons of oil and in 1938 only 4,500,000. New oilfields of proved value were not found in Rumania at that time when also the mining laws restricted exploration. — At that time the militaristic nations, principally Germany but Italy as well, were facing the general problem of how to meet their economic needs, either by means of taxation, inflation or loans. In the mid-1930's the national debts of both countries were enormous and taxes were heavy. They should have raised their exports, but did not know how to achieve this. Germany had to import textiles, iron, metal, etc. She did her utmost to increase her exports, but to no avail. Regarding the rich literature of the question and the relevant surveys see Iván T. Berend and György Ránki, *Közép-Kelet-Európa gazdasági fejlődése a 19—20. században* [The Economic Development of Central Eastern Europe in the 19th and 20th Centuries], Budapest, 1969. *Cf.* pp. 290—312 especially with regard to the *"Neuer Plan"* and Germany's external trade policy in Central and Eastern Europe. — For a contemporary elaboration of the issue from the British point of view, see G. Crowther, "The Finance of Military Adventures," *The Spectator*, July 19, 1935.

Denmark was a valuable agricultural country with a very large supply of fat livestock. It was understandable, therefore, that Denmark should fear German invasion. Let us dwell for a little while on Germany's push northeastward and her endeavours to control the Baltic countries. That Germany wished to dominate the Baltic was obvious. On March 22, 1929, the occupation of Memel was a part of this process. Hitler went from Swinemunde to Memel in the pocket battleship *Deutschland* which was escorted by the two other "pocket battleships," *Admiral Graf Spee* and *Admiral Scheer;* in addition to the cruisers *Nürnberg* and *Köln;* two divisions of destroyers; three flotillas of torpedo-boats, and a flotilla of escort vessels. "Herr Hitler went by sea in order to avoid having to cross Polish territory, but the fact that he took with him a large fleet emphasized the view that the occupation of Memel, although a military operation, had as its chief objective the naval domination of the Baltic." Possession of the Baltic was indispensable for German trade on the North Sea. Although in the mid-1930's, Britain might have found it advantageous to have the North Sea and the Baltic controlled by Germany in order to keep the Russians in check, the occupation of Memel caused a complete turn in the British attitude. Facing German aggression, Britain found the Soviet Navy, already strong in submarines and minelayers, to be a good partner when needed in a blockade of Germany in the Baltic and North Seas. The military invasion and annihilation of Poland became a necessity for Germany as a countermove to Anglo-Soviet interests in the Baltic and North Sea areas, and also because under certain circumstances the Polish army could have become a threat to the German forces.[32]

We still have to refer to the German military strategists who believed that the anticipated "next war" should not be waged by Germany alone. The avowed ambitions of the Berlin—Rome—Tokyo "Axis" were as follows: Germany to dominate the Baltic and be in a position to dispute the control of the North Sea by any nation; Italy to dominate the Mediterranean, and Japan to have

[32] Edwards, *op. cit.* p. 264. Concerning the history of the first half of the 1930's let us note the following: According to Count Szembek, a former Polish Under-Secretary for Foreign Affairs, Göring offered Pilsudski command of the joint German-Polish forces in case he would agree to an attack on the Soviet Union. *Cf.* S. Mackiewicz, *Colonel Beck and His Policy*, London, 1944, pp. 25—26. — It is not without interest to note that in the summer of 1938, when the Polish Foreign Minister and Duff Cooper, First Lord of the Admiralty, met during the latter's tour of the Baltic, the British side expressed the view in the course of their examination of the Eastern European situation, that it attributed the greatest importance to Poland. As to the Anglo-Polish relations in foreign affairs, these were found to be closely dependent on Poland's Baltic policy, which did credit to Beck's "foresight" and was based upon common Polish, Estonian, Lettish, Finnish, and Scandinavian interests between the German and Russian powers. And here we have to know the relations of Britain towards the Scandinavian states, first of all Sweden, which is rich in iron ore. In order to understand the Anglo-Swedish relations we have to know how Britain, ahead of the German market, took an option on Sweden's iron ore for long years to come and how the situation was with regard to the close ties between the British Navy and the naval forces of the Scandinavian states. *Cf.* Observans, *loc. cit.*, p. 181.

the hegemony of the Western Pacific. Both Italy and Japan had large enough submarine fleets to live up to these expectations.[33]

The construction of the German Navy and the development of the concept regarding its utilization were calculated strategic steps which commenced at the time when the Nazis came to power and were part and parcel of all of Hitler's political moves.

When we compare the position and strategy of the British Navy with those of its German rivals, pursuing the Nazi aims, we come to the conclusion that we find ourselves faced with an object and its shadow image, or rather with the two halves of a sphere. The German Naval Staff was set on obstructing Britain's seaborne trade and the British Admiralty wanted to ward off this contingency. The Germans were building submarines and the British took pains to paralyze the operation of submarines, etc. Let us examine the difficulties with which the British naval chiefs were confronted, what organization was available to them, what authority and influence they could wield, and the kind of prestige they enjoyed among the leading public figures and government agencies.

The First Lord of the Admiralty (Sir Bolton Eyres-Monsell from 1931 to 1937), a government-appointed civilian, was always a full member of the Cabinet just like the Secretary of State for War or the Secretary of State for Air. The Cabinet decided the strategy of war on the basis of political and economic considerations. The three Chiefs of Staff sitting on the War Council decided as to the military practicability of the Cabinet's proposals. If combined action was necessary, each Chief of Staff drafted the general operational orders of his own service, and, each knowing his part in the enterprise, the three carried it out after coordination. An Admiral was not asked if he would cooperate with a General, as had been the case in Gallipoli. He was told what the objectives were and the part he was expected to play in the enterprise. In that case, the Admiral was relieved of the responsibility of making a major decision. It was made for him. The method of operation was left to his judgment, however, as well as the decision whether actions should commence at all when it came to the critical point. In short, his power of discretion as a high naval commander was left unfettered. The War Chiefs took it for granted that if he did not do what had been laid down in the operational instructions, he would have to have a very adequate explanation for his own decision. In the period from 1933 to 1938, the Chief of Naval Staff, Lord Chatfield, proved to be a leader of much greater stature and efficiency than his two colleagues, the Chief of Air Staff and the Chief of the Imperial General Staff. According to the famous historian of the British Navy, A. Marder, "Admiral of the Fleet Sir Ernle (afterward first Baron) Chatfield, the First Sea Lord and Chief of Naval Staff, was the finest officer the Royal Navy produced between the wars. He had character, charm (even if he always looked rather severe and lacked a sense of humour), administrative ability, professional knowledge ... His deputy chief of naval staff has written: 'He (Chatfield) could very quickly master the contents of a docket or disentangle a problem and make his decision. Unlike some of his contemporaries he never wasted time on unimportant matters

[33] Russell, *op. cit.*, pp. 101—102.

and so always found time to enjoy the sports and games . . . He was the best 'all-rounder of his day and age'. Chatfield completely dominated the Board of Admiralty, and it was he who conducted all the more important business arising from the crisis.' "[34] Both on the military and the social scale, at official meetings of leading circles, at friendly gatherings, as well as at festive dinners, Admirals took precedence over Air Marshals or Generals.

In the second half of the 1930's, leaders of the Board of Admiralty tried on their part to have the division of labour among the defence portfolios carried out in a well-considered manner or at least within strict limits. The defence of home waters was placed entirely under the administration of the Air Ministry aided by the Coastal Command of the Royal Air Force, an organization specially set up for this purpose. The Coastal Command of the Royal Air Force did not gain an independent status until 1936. It had always been the Cinderella of its own service throughout the preceding years. In 1937 its duties were enlarged by common consent to include the task of minelaying aircraft connected with the German blockade. Later the Area Combined Headquarters (ACHQs) were established adjacent to the naval bases of Plymouth, Chatham and Rosyth. In those headquarters all three services were represented but their main function was to exercise joint control over the Navy's and the Coastal Command's forces.

The best of the British naval officers were trained at the Imperial Defence College founded in 1926. The establishment of this College and the education it provided, meant the first step towards the extensive study of war and its prevention. A cardinal thesis of theoretical education was to attain a degree of strategic readiness that would preclude the possibility of Gallipoli repeating itself. The Royal Navy was painfully affected during the period of the disarmament talks. Neither this institution nor the Board of Admiralty could be expected to develop. The latter was called downright an "inflated" office. It even happened that a special commission inspecting the Admiralty building went from room to room questioning closely every one of the employees about their jobs. Towards the middle of the 1930's the situation changed completely. The Science and Research Department of the Admiralty was doing serious and fine work. Their findings were verified in every respect by the events of the initial years of the war. The German moves were of no surprise because they were new only to the extent as to the practical application of a principle which already had been known. The Science and Research Department of the Admiralty had been more interested in investigating the antidote than developing the method.[35]

The basic principle of British naval strategy, which had been stressed by every expert up to Churchill himself ever since World War I, and which we

[34] For a characterization of Sir Ernle Chatfield and Sir Bolton Eyres-Monsell, cf. A. Marder, "The Royal Navy and the Ethiopian Crisis of 1935—36," The American Historical Review, June 1970, p. 1336. — As to the Chatfield quotation, cf. Sir Ernle Chatfield, The Navy and Defence, London, 1942, p. 247. — Russell, op. cit., pp. 83—84. — Liddell Hart, op. cit. Vol. I, pp. 325—326. — It was in February 1939 that Chamberlain appointed Chatfield (then already Lord Chatfield First Baron) Minister for the Co-ordination of Defence.

[35] S. W. Roskill, The Navy at War, London, 1964. — Russell, op. cit., pp. 32—33, 91—92.

also have described above, though in a different context and not as succinctly, was expressed by Churchill in these words: "Amid the torrent of violent events one anxiety reigned supreme. Battles might be won or lost, enterprises might succeed or miscarry, territories might be gained or quitted, but dominating all our power to carry on the war, or even keep ourselves alive, lay our mastery of the ocean routes and the free approach and entry to our ports."[36] After the work was done by scientists and researchers, the problem, strictly speaking, was not merely how to parry the attacks on the British sea routes. This was considered a task for the tacticians as well as engineers and technicians. The problems were of a different nature.

In a decade and a half after World War I, there had been hardly any change in the composition of the British fleet. The categories had remained the same (or possibly have lost in importance). This can be simply explained by the fact that the British fleet had to meet all sorts of naval warfare and to be ready for service in any part of the world. Although the various categories remained, nevertheless, a great deal had changed in the blueprints of the different types of ships within each category and in their execution as a result of technological developments. Thus the interrelation of classification and function became broader. The changes served chiefly defensive purposes. The fighting value of a ship was increased by her capacity of resistance. British designers had to reckon with attacks over the sea, on the sea and under the sea alike. The old "combat-worthy" warships had to be modernized from time to time to remain capable of resisting attacks from above and from below. By the way, this modernization cost much more than the equipment of a new ship. The invention of new devices of attack always had preceded the developments of the defensive techniques by some time. It is also natural that the development of these weapons also had an effect upon the improvement of the means of their uses. As a consequence of all this, the brain trust of the Admiralty had to concentrate primarily upon the following problems:

1. How to secure the simultaneous protection of British interests in the Far East and in Europe.

2. How to organize defence so as to have also striking power, capable of attacking.

3. How to solve the question of submarine warfare.

4. How to solve the question of battleships.

The four problems are obviously interrelated. If the British Empire were to be attacked simultaneously in the Far East, in the Mediterranean and in the North Sea, then the question was if the Royal Navy should either protect the British Isles, the metropolitan country, and leave the other parts of the Empire to their fate, or defend the different British possessions and leave the heart of the Empire unprotected.[37] Beginning as early as 1935, the Baldwin Government, and after 1937 also the Chamberlain Cabinet, took great care, at least with regard to Europe, that the Royal Navy should not be unprepared for a

[36] Churchill, op. cit. Vol. III, p. 98.

[37] The Royal Navy's distribution was the following: Home Fleet (formerly Atlantic Fleet), Mediterranean Fleet, China Station, American Station, African Station, West Indies Station, East Indies Station, Royal Australian Navy, Royal Canadian Navy, Royal Indian Navy, New Zealand Division.

possible war with Germany, or even with both of the two fascist powers, Germany and Italy. ("It would be unjust to the Chamberlain administration and their service advisers to suggest that the Navy had not been adequately prepared for a war with Germany and Italy," wrote Churchill when describing the situation upon his taking over the Admiralty in 1939.)[38] At the same time it was impossible to compare the British Navy with the fleet of any European country. If we take for example Hitler's proposed ratio of 35 : 100 in the Anglo-German Naval Agreement, how is it possible to compare the fact that Germany had to protect her coast on the North Sea and the Baltic with the fact that the British Navy was deployed over seven seas? Thus the proportion of the defence of the European coasts became utterly disparate.

In the British view, rightly and reasonably, the merchant fleet plays just as important a part in the national defence as the Royal Navy. Moreover, it can be considered to be the heel of Achilles of the entire defensive system. Not a single airplane, tank, lorry and ship can be set in motion without the vital fuel supplies transported continuously by units of the merchant fleet. In the middle of the 1930's, Britain had about 2000 merchant ships less, than in 1914. What mattered for the defence of the country was not the displacement tonnage but the number of merchant vessels. About 1400 deep-drawing merchantmen and 1650 coasting vessels, to mention but the larger ones, had to be protected over a route of 85,000 nautical miles across the oceans. For example, for grain transports it was better to use three small ships than one big vessel. An average merchantman carried about 8000 tons of freight. Ships unloaded on a daily average in England about 110 thousand tons of commodities and 50 thousand tons of food. This task could not be taken over by the air fleet. The protection of the merchant ships, therefore, remained a pivotal point of Britain's naval strategy. At the same time, leaders of the Admiralty defined their defence policy usually in these terms: Britain had to be prepared to play a strategically defensive and tactically offensive role. Regarding the number one enemy in Europe, Germany, they took the view that the Germans would start and conduct the next war on the same principles followed in World War I, since it was difficult to imagine what else they could do. At the time of the preparation of the Great Naval Rearmament Programme, the Admiralty suspected that Germany was trying to cheat as far as the tonnage categories laid down in the 1935 Anglo-German Naval Agreement was concerned, and was building a great number of 250-ton submarines designed for action chiefly in the English Channel and other narrow sea passages. Churchill kept on warning that the Germans were steadily developing their submarine fleet with the intention to attack the British merchant fleet. Later, when World War II was already in process, he stated that it would have been wise for the Germans to stake all their efforts upon it.[39]

[38] Quoted by J. Macleod, *N. Chamberlain*, London, 1961. — In 1939 the composition of the Royal (British) Navy, including the Dominions, was as follows: 11 battleships built and 9 building; 3 battle-cruisers; 15 large cruisers; 43 light cruisers built and 19 building; 5 aircraft carriers built and 6 building; 179 destroyers built and 9 building; 57 submarines built and 13 building, plus about 120 smaller units built and 30 building. *Cf.* Talbot-Booth, *op. cit.*, p. 285.

[39] Churchill, *op. cit.* Vol. IV: "The Hinge of Fate," p. 107.

Beside Churchill, also Liddell Hart was incessantly occupied with the strategy of the British Navy and the questions of defence. In a booklet written in 1925 he had affirmed that the Navy might have unbroken strength on the high seas, but on a narrow lane of sea it was exposed to the dangers deriving from new weapons: "After studying its bearings on the seas around the British Isles I passed on to the Mediterranean, another long and narrow sea channel through which runs our artery with the East, and where our main naval force is now concentrated. Note that our ships, naval or mercantile, must traverse the length of this channel and, worse still, have to filter through a tiny hole of each end — the straits of Gibraltar and the Suez Canal — while midway there is a narrow 'waist' between Sicily and Tunis barely ninety miles across. After pointing out how the potential radii of submarine attack from the ports on the European and African coast intersected this long single line of British sea communications, the question was posed: Is it not obvious that if, in a future war, any Mediterranean power was numbered among Britain's enemies, her fleet would find it difficult enough to protect itself against submarines, let alone protect merchant convoys and troop transports? When the proven menace of submarine power is added to the potential effect of aircraft attack against shipping in the narrow seas, it is time the British people awoke to the fact that, in case of such a war, the Mediterranean would be impassable, and that this important artery would have to be abandoned. Thus as a strategical asset, the Suez Canal has lost a large part of its value in face of modern naval and air development — for in such a war we should be driven to close the Mediterranean route and divert our imperial communications round the Cape of Good Hope."[40]

As we have seen, from 1918 till 1936, the year of the Great Naval Rearmament Programme, Britain had had fewer submarines constructed than any other naval power, but this did not mean that the Admiralty so fatally underestimated the danger of the submarine warfare as it had in 1917—18. On the one hand, the Admiralty provided for the construction of a small number of submarines entirely adequate to certain functions; on the other hand, it was preparing for submarine warfare from a quite different point of view than the other sea powers. These powers were working hard to have an increasing number of subs constructed, while the British Admiralty was striving to neutralize those efforts in case of war and to find the most efficient means of destroying the enemy submarines. It was for this end that the Anti-Submarine School was established in Portland and it was due to the systematic and successful work being performed there (N. B. the submarine-detecting device known as Asdic) that the damage caused by the German submarines during World War II was decreased, although not as much as was desired.[41]

[40] Liddell Hart, op. cit., Vol I, pp. 327—328. — In his opinion the interrelations of the naval and air forces, in the long run, were not sufficiently appreciated in higher quarters until after the outbreak of World War II. His reasoning about the Mediterranean aspects of war also proved correct. After the German occupation of France, Britain had to annihilate a large part of the invaluable French fleet lest it should be captured by the Germans.

[41] Russell, op. cit., 78—79. — Asdic, the apparatus for the detection of submarines, was handled by excellent specialists. Consequently, A. J. P. Taylor wrote, "the

Finally came the question of the battleships. In the mid-1930's, especially during the war in Ethiopia, the debate concerning the use of the battleship in modern warfare became particularly heated in the British Parliament, in the press, and among naval and aviation experts. Should Britain make bombs or battleships? Liddell Hart wrote in *The Times:* "The real question is not whether a bomb can sink a battleship, but whether new methods of warfare can prevent battleships from carrying out their traditional functions and discount their utility."[42] His observations led him also to the conclusion that "to most admirals the respective value of battleships and aircraft was not basically a technological issue, but more in the nature of a spiritual issue. They cherished the battle-fleet with a religious fervour . . . a battleship had long been to an admiral what a cathedral is to a bishop." Liddell Hart's observations were refuted in the House of Lords by a recently retired admiral, who declared that "one thousand warplanes could be built for the cost of one capital ship and . . . it was pure lunacy to hesitate in the choice of policy."[43] To this we still can add that it took three years to build a battleship and seven years to train a seaman.[44]

Towards the close of 1935, a committee was appointed which, as the "Sub-Committee of the Committee of Imperial Defence on the Vulnerability of Capital Ships to Air Attack," investigated the question of battleships in connection with aerial attack. Sitting on this Sub-Committee were the Chief of Naval Staff, the Chief of Air Staff and specialists from the Admiralty and the Air Ministry. The report of its findings was issued on March 26, 1936, and it exercised a decisive influence upon the shipbuilding policy soon afterwards disclosed in the Great Naval Rearmament Programme. In simple and succinct terms the conclusions of the report were the following: "The advocates of the extreme air view would wish this country to build no capital ships (other Powers still continuing to build them). If their theories turn out well founded, we have wasted money; if ill founded, we would, in putting them to the test, have lost the Empire."[45] In the final paragraph under the heading of "Conclusions and Recommendations" the experts of "both sides" — the members from the Admiralty and the Air Ministry — stated that, on the assumption that capital ships were indispensable, the real question arose whether their design was such as to secure the maximum of immunity from air attack. The Admiralty's view was that there was no reason why the ships could not be designed to meet air attack just as in the past they had been designed to meet other dangers. The effect of this report was to assure the capital ships a new lease of their threatened lives. At that time and following the release of the report, new battleships of the Royal Navy were built one after another. Since they were recognized as large targets, they were armed with dozens of

---

Admiralty were confident that ASDIC, their device for submarine detection, would master the U-boats." A. J. P. Taylor, *English History 1914—1945*, London 1965, p. 563 But in 1939 still very few ships were equipped with radar and at that time not effective enough. *Cf.* Roskill, *op. cit.*, p. 27.

[42] Liddell Hart, *op. cit.*, Vol. I, p. 333.

[43] Russell, *op. cit.*, pp. 12, 38.

[44] Talbot-Booth, *op. cit.*, p. 38.

[45] Liddell Hart, *op. cit.*, Vol. I, p. 335.

14-inch and later 16-inch guns.[46] In spite of the optimism of that report, Liddell Hart upheld his opinion that attacks might be expected from three directions (from above, from below, and from the sea by pocket battleships). This could cause serious complications to the defences of the country. "But already the Cabinet had virtually committed itself to the building of a new battle-fleet, without any adequate re-examination of the question, whilst its attention was occupied with the Abyssinian crisis. It might be termed a decision by default."[47]

In the 1930's, therefore, failure was manifest not only in the conduct of foreign affairs but — in spite of the fact that the leading man of the Royal Navy was evidently master of his business — also in the execution of the British naval strategy. The British fleet, as a result of this, suffered great losses both in ships and in human lives during World War II.[48]

[46] Russell, *op. cit.*, pp. 38, 114—115. — Chatfield was of the opinion that "under certain circumstances attacks from the air will be a very serious menace to warships but it is at present pure conjecture as to what those circumstances will be, and what the degree of the vulnerability of the ships will be." *Cf.* his letter signed "Sailor," published by *The Times* on March 19, 1935. Quoted by Marder, *loc. cit.*, p. 1344.

[47] Liddell Hart, *op. cit.*, Vol. I, p. 331. It is worth to quote from his leading article published in *The Times* on February 10, 1936: "We have to take into account the fact that 20 years ago the submarine attack on our shipping routes nearly brought us to disaster despite the unassailable supremacy of our battle-fleet. If we are disposed to forget this, other powers do not. And it would be folly to shut our eyes to the fact that they are counting on aircraft and high speed surface craft to multiply greatly the past performances of the submarine for direct attack on sea traffic. We should remember also that before a new battle-fleet less susceptible to air attack can be built several years must elapse: during that time the means of attack may be improved proportionately. Moreover, a battle-fleet is dependent on bases. The bases that we might develop today out of reach may be within easy range or air attack 3 years hence . . ."

[48] *Cf.* Lévay, *loc. cit.*, p. 193. — See also Roskill, *op. cit.*, pp. 447—448.

"There is no policy that is more costly,
both to the taxpayer and to peace, than
a policy of missing the bus."

(From A. Eden's speech on July 11, 1935)

THE PREPARATION AND CONCLUSION
OF THE NAVAL AGREEMENT

Despite and amidst different statements by politicians on both sides, the preparation of the Anglo-German Naval Agreement was already in progress during April and May 1935. The preparations were not of an *ad hoc* nature but were part of the British defence policies which, with the aid of well-informed military and civilian Sub-Committees of the CID, had always sized up what had to be done in a given situation at a given moment.[1] The generally valid statement, made by the Defence Requirements Sub-Committee concerning the relationship between foreign policy and defence, can be accepted as pertinent for the period under review.

"We consider it to be a cardinal requirement of our national and imperial security that our foreign policy should be so conducted as to avoid the possible development of a situation in which we might be confronted simultaneously with the hostility, open or veiled, of Japan in the Far East, Germany on the West and any Power on the main line of communication between the two." (See Appendix VII, p. 203.)[2]

---

[1] The conclusions of these Sub-Committees were presented to the Cabinet by the Defence Policy and Requirements Sub-Committee through the CID. Probably depending on the subject, or on who opposed and who proposed the matter at issue, information was supplied, in addition to Cabinet members, also to other competent personages. In England a very important role is played by the Cabinet within the Government and this may explain the many divergences of domestic opinion regarding the Anglo-German Naval Agreement. This will be discussed in more detail in the next chapter.

[2] *Third Report of the Defence Requirements Sub-Committee* (D. P. R. 52, 21 Nov. 1935, not yet considered by the Cabinet). Memorandum by the Chief of the Imperial General Staff. P. R. O. Cab. 24/259. Secret. C. P. 12/36. Copy No. 52. —This seems to be confirmed from a different angle by the opinion of Geyr von Schweppenburg, the German Military Attaché in London, who wrote: "The British General Staff's authority was increased, where certain aspects of General British Policy were dictated by military strategy. For example the General Staff would see to it that Britain's policy should be conducted in such a way as to rule out any possibility of war with the U. S. or France or with Japan before the middle of 1935, as the

With regard to Japan, the Far Eastern peril, leaders of the Admiralty in the early 1930's had explained in their most secret memoranda repeatedly that the main weakness of Great Britain's strategic position in the Far East was the inadequacy of the defence of her bases and the lack of anti-submarine devices capable of hitting back at the steadily growing submarine forces of foreign states.[3] Competent and resolute personalities like Sir Ernle Chatfield and Sir Warren Fisher had stated unanimously that Great Britain would be able to protect her Far Eastern interests only if Singapore and Hongkong were developed into unconquerable places and if the first phase of Singapore's military defence programme would have been completed by 1936.[4] They knew precisely that Japan was continually rearming in the air, on land and on sea and that she had become a great power in all three arms as early as the middle of the 1930's. The modernization of the capital ships of the Japanese fleet was in process and was due to be completed in 1937. At that time, Japan was supposed to have nine powerful ships at her disposal. The naval air force of Japan at the same time was superior already to the British Fleet Air Arm and was expected to be almost double the size of the British by 1938. The Japanese position was very strong. Their warships could operate close to the main islands of the Japanese Empire, the centre of their force. (See Appendix VI, p. 199.)[5] It is easy to understand, therefore, that from early 1934 onwards

harbour construction at Singapore was not yet complete." Cf. Geyr von Schweppenburg, *The Critical Years*, London, 1952, p. 94.

[3] Cf. Notes on Navy Estimates for 1933. C. P. 25/33. Most secret. P. R. P. Adm. 116/3434. Annex II.

[4] The complete programme, Singapore's development into a British naval base, could not be envisaged until 1940. Sir Warren Fisher remarked that he would like to have it completed by 1938. According to Chatfield the base was serviceable practically a year before completion. P. R. O. Adm. 116/ 3434. — Also at the time of the Italo-Ethiopian war the question was raised as to what Japan would do if Britain declared war on Italy. In his memorandum of September 16, 1935 and in his letter to Hankey on September 25, Montgomery-Massingberd expressed his doubts: "It cannot be too strongly emphasized that it would be beyond our powers to secure our communications in the Far East, and still more to bring a war with Japan to a successful conclusion, if at the same time we were involved in a war in Europe." The British strategic position in such an eventuality would be desperate; Singapore could be defended but was "dangerously weak"; Hongkong could not withstand a "determined attack." — Looking back when the peak of the crisis had passed, Chatfield outlined how shaky the Far Eastern position would have become had war broken out with Italy: "If war were to be declared to-day against Japan — stated COS minutes, 174th meeting, May 13, 1936 — we should have only seven battleships available for operations in the Far East." Cf. Marder, *loc. cit.*, p. 1342. — On the same subject see also L. Ivanov, "The Breakdown of the London Naval Conversations and the Naval Policy of the Powers," Тихый Океан, 1/1935, pp 61—73.

[5] The General Strategic Situation in the Western Pacific vis-à-vis Japan. Part I, pp. 11/37, 12/41; Part II, p. 9/28. P. R. O. Adm. 116/3338. — Some facts from the history of the Japanese fleet: At the beginning of World War II the Japanese Navy, the third most powerful in the world, included some of the mightiest ships in naval history. Yet this great war machine was destroyed in barely four years. Nine out of ten battleships were sunk already in December 1941. We have to note that Japan possessed three super-battleships, the *Yamato*, the *Musashi* and the

the Committee of Imperial Defence and public personages in Britain kept their eyes fixed on any possible ominous indication of rapprochement or collaboration between Japan and Germany.[6]

Shinano, each with a displacement of 72,000 tons, while the British standard was around 35,000 tons. This achievement of Japan had required immense efforts and the amazing thing was that the building of those ships had been kept entirely secret. The Japanese Government denounced the Washington Treaty in December 1934 and decided at the same time to build super-battleships. (The construction of the *Yamato* was begun in 1936.) Just like Great Britain and the United States, Japan had not built warships for fifteen years and her older ships were not in excess of 35,000 tons. (There was a single 42,000-ton British battleship, the *Hood*, but she had been built as early as 1920, prior to the Washington Treaty.) The Japanese knew that if a competition of naval armaments should start they would be able to beat the enemy by superiority only in quality, not in quantity. They knew that the U. S. would not build battleships too large to pass through the Panama Canal. The Japanese battleships were designed exclusively for fighting and their execution expressed the real intentions of the Imperial Japanese Navy. (The three giant battleships were sunk within three months in World War II.)

Japan intended her submarines to play a vital role. This is why the Japanese representatives at the 1930 London Naval Conference had demanded 78,000 tons of submarine strength, while Britain and the U. S. had worked since 1922 for the abolition of submarines altogether. At last, after long and heated debates at the London Conference, it was agreed that each of the three powers might maintain 52,700 tons of submarines. The Naval General Staff in Tokyo did not give up, because it pinned great hopes on the submarines as part of Japan's "Invincible Armada." Japanese first-class subs were capable of cruising to California and back without refuelling. This feat can be paralleled only by today's achievements similar to those of the atomic-powered submarines of the American *Nautilus* type. Before World War II Britain and the U. S. were most afraid of the Japanese submarines. In 1941 Japan had 64 submarines ready for action and 126 more such boats were built during the war. At war's end, less than 50 Japanese submarines were left. The main cause of their failure was the lack of skilled commanders, so that they became entirely inoperable when the conduct of war had to be shifted from offensive to defensive. See Masanori Ito, *The End of the Imperial Japanese Navy*, New York, 1965, pp. 7—11, 16—19.

An article of a contemporary Hungarian magazine dealing with this question pertinently pointed out that Britain tried to hold up Japan's naval rearmament because she had to keep in mind that she would never be able to send her entire fleet to the Far East. See the article entitled "A flottakérdés" [The Naval Question], *Külügyi Szemle*, 1935, p. 72.

[6] We refer to another conclusion of the Defence Requirements Sub-Committee, dated February 28, 1934, which recommended to improve relations with Japan, to restore at least the old-time good relations and mutual respect, since there were certain signs of Japan's intention to broaden the relations with Germany. The success of such British attempts would create greater security and make it possible for Britain to stop or rectify the unwholesome trends of Japanese policy in this direction.

We can also refer to a letter from J. C. Smuts to Lord Lothian, who up to 1938 was one of the most influential and most effective appeasers. Smuts wrote in this letter that a Japanese-German combination must be prevented, for it might become disastrous and it could be avoided only if Britain stopped treating Germany as a pariah of Europe. Lothian Papers. G. D. 40. 17—445. December 14, 1934.

To assess properly Britain's European strategy we have to see the points of view of the British defence in the Far East. We can refer to a remark the Hungarian Minister in London made in a report in April 1935 — its interest lies in its being indicative of the diplomatic circles' judgment of the general opinion of the time — according to which "the British Government is most anxious to have a new accord replacing the Washington Treaty which will expire next year (1936). Aside from other factors, however, the situation has changed since 1922 only in so far as in the future it will be necessary to reckon with two more fleets which did not exist at that time, namely the German and the Russian. Although they were of no decisive importance, as far as the interests of the three principal sea powers were concerned, they still must be considered from the point of view of the general equilibrium. Thus England, by eliminating these difficulties now, would wish to prepare the ground for a future naval conference."[7] Whether or not this was the object to the preliminary negotiations for the Anglo-German Naval Agreement will be examined at a later part of this study. It is certain, however, that when Minister Széchenyi wrote those lines, the exchange of information in preparation of the Naval Agreement was in full swing already.

On April 12, 1935, Leopold Bürkner, an officer of the German Naval Command, noted down in a confidential memorandum that upon secret instructions from Admiral Reader, he had informed in private Captain G. Ch. Muirhead-Gould, the British Naval Attaché in Berlin, about the German Navy's construction programme but had given him no figures for submarines. When the British Attaché inquired after such figures, Bürkner remarked: "We haven't got that far." Bürkner was under the impression that he could have divulged the information about the submarine construction without arousing unfavourable reactions, since the Admiralty certainly was prepared to hear such news. He added that the Naval Attaché had said "he knew that we did not want to say anything about displacement, but he supposed that the cruisers were not of the 'Deutschland type'." Bürkner confirmed this and told the British Naval Attaché that the German representatives had been designated.[8] Equally from Bürkner's informative summary prepared for the German Foreign Office we know that on April 25, 1935, the Chief of the Naval Command, Admiral Raeder, had a conversation with the British Naval Attaché in Berlin, Captain Muirhead-Gould. The latter conveyed his Government's invitation (dated April 23) to Germany to attend preliminary naval conversations in London on May 1. Then he read to the Chief of the Naval Command the personal message from the First Sea Lord. The First Sea Lord wished to inform Admiral Raeder that the discussions would be of a general nature and it might well be that Germany and Great Britain would reach agreement on the subject of qualitative limitation of naval armaments. The message expressed the hope that Germany would be ready to put forward "a general outline of her minimum naval requirements up to 1942 in the form of a building programme, but this programme would not necessarily be considered binding." (Marginal note by

[7] Széchenyi's report from London, April 18, 1935. OL Küm. Pol. 1935—21/5—1393.

[8] Memorandum by an Officer of the Naval Command, Berlin, April 12, 1935. DGFP Ser. C. Vol. IV, No. 25, pp. 45—46.

the Germans: "The basis of the impending naval conversations will be different from what was first assumed by the German Naval Staff.") During his conference with Raeder, the British Naval Attaché made the following detailed observations:

1. Since the question was originally introduced in the conversations which the Führer and Chancellor had with Simon and Eden and was basically a political one, the British intention was to start the conversations with a short political introduction.

2. It was therefore thought that the delegations might be composed approximately as follows:

On the German side:

A political official,
an Admiral,
the German Naval Attaché in London (if Germany should think it desirable), and an additional German naval officer.

On the British side:

A political official from the Foreign Office,
an Admiral, and
an additional naval officer.

3. The discussions would take about two days and be spread over three or four meetings, of which the first should be political in character and the others should be reserved for the exchange of views between the experts.[9]

But the date of May 1 was not convenient to Hitler as the start of the naval discussions, because the German Government intended to make in the second week of May a statement on foreign policy in reply to the League of Nations Council resolution of April 17. The German Government would then propose a new date for the conversations.[10]

Yet the preparations were going on. On the day of the conversation with Raeder, April 25, the British Naval Attaché was informed by Bürkner about the facts of submarine construction in Germany. But Bürkner had received secret instruction to mention only twelve small boats of 250 tons being on the shipways and to refrain from revealing any other figures. He was instructed to give no information about the measures taken in Heligoland and *not* to start a conversation on this subject. The British Naval Attaché was astonished

[9] Record of a Conversation on April 25, 1935, between the Chief of the Naval Command, Adm. Dr. h. c. Raeder and the British Naval Attaché in Berlin, Capt. Muirhead-Gould. Secret. DGFP Ser. C. Vol. IV, No. 51, pp. 86—89.

[10] Following the Stresa conference the League of Nations Council was convened for April 15 to 17, 1935, at the request of the French Government, in order to examine the situation created by the announcement of the German rearmament programme. In its draft resolution the Council deplored the reintroduction of military conscription by which Germany had unilaterally repudiated the Versailles Treaty provisions regarding disarmament. The draft was submitted by France, Britain and Italy on April 16 and was adopted by all members of the Council except Denmark on the 17th. As to this and Hitler's response, *cf.* DGFP Ser, C. Vol. IV, No. 35, p. 65. Note by the State Secretary. Berlin, April 26, 1935, p. 86.

by the communication, as he had thought himself to have been fully informed about the immediate German naval construction plans earlier (certainly he had in mind his conversation with Bürkner on April 12).[11]

Next day, April 26, in another conversation between the British Attaché and Bürkner, the former said that the Admiralty did not seem to have been particularly "disturbed" by the news of German submarine construction. He said he did not know, however, how the news would be taken on the political side. Bürkner indicated that the German submarine construction was carried out in three phases, and Phase III had been started after April 7, 1935. He mentioned also that in Germany the furnishing of information about submarine construction was a political question. The military authorities had not the power to decide on it. The British Naval Attaché raised the question of the *Daily Telegraph* article of April 25, 1935, which had given an indication, based on technical press reports, that the German submarines were incomparably superior to the latest foreign types, especially in machinery, range of action, and armaments. Bürkner denied this. Mention was made also of MacDonald's article of April 25, which accused Germany of being responsible for the failure of international peace efforts. Nonetheless, the British Government, as was stated by MacDonald himself, had left the door open to Germany towards an equitable agreement in case of her joining the efforts of the states working for a system of European security. Bürkner described at considerable length that such articles would hardly contribute to good understanding between the two countries.[12]

Signs of good or bad relations between the two countries were registered also by the German Chargé d'Affaires in Great Britain, Prince Otto von Bismarck, who reported them to his Government at the end of April, after the announcement of the German submarine construction programme. Two influential papers, the *Observer* and the *Sunday Times*, tacked on to the announcement extremely hostile comments concerning Germany. These newspapers went as far as to threaten with the cancellation of the naval conversations. The original announcement on this subject was magnified into a first-rate political sensation, probably not without Foreign Office inspiration. Yet Bismarck saw a relaxation of the indignation of those who "designed to treat the rearmament question sensationally with a slant against Germany as a prelude to the foreign affairs debate of May 2."[13]

On April 29 Bürkner, who always acted upon instructions from above, mildly reproached the British Naval Attaché because the British press was making such a fuss about the submarine affair. Moreover, this must have been

[11] Conversation with the British Naval Attaché on April 25, Berlin, April 26, 1935. DGFP. Ser. C. Vol. IV, No. 52, pp. 89—90.

[12] Conversation with the British Naval Attaché on April 26. DGFP Ser. C. Vol. IV, No. 54, pp. 91—92. — Ramsay MacDonald's article, "Peace, Germany and Stresa," was published by all English daily papers, among them *The Times* of April 26. The Hungarian Minister in London, Széchenyi, referred to it in his report of May 7, 1935. OL Küm. Pol. 1935—2—158.

[13] The Chargé d'Affaires in Great Britain to the Foreign Ministry, London, April 29, 1935. DGFP Ser. C. Vol. IV, No. 55, pp. 93—94. In the House of Commons Sir John Simon on April 29 confirmed that the German Government had intimated that orders had been given for the construction of twelve 250-ton submarines.

known in Britain after the Führer had told Simon and Eden that all necessary measures were being taken for the defence of the Reich. Bürkner drew attention to the fact that the Versailles Treaty (and Part V) was no basis of negotiation for Germany. "The Naval Attaché replied that the Admiralty was aware of the German view. Part V of the Versailles Treaty affected only the preliminary naval negotiations in so far as those of its provisions which related to naval questions were to be replaced by other agreements."[14]

Admiral Raeder on April 30 also reproached the British Attaché because the series of confidential communications had obviously been misused for political ends by the British Government and the British press, although those releases were made at the request of the British Admiralty in order to clear the air for the naval conference. Admiral Raeder believed that "the Naval Attaché or the Admiralty could not prevent the Foreign Office, for whom this matter had apparently arisen at a politically convenient moment, from misusing confidential information."[15]

Meanwhile Captain Erwin Wassner, the German Naval Attaché in Great Britain, was watching the mood of the leaders of the Admiralty in the capital of England. On May 1 he informed the German Foreign Office that the mood of the Admiralty might still be described as calm and in favour of negotiating with the Germans. The Admiralty wished, as appeared from a statement made to a British journalist, "to find out, first of all, exactly what kind of increased navy the Germans have at the back of their minds," and also wanted to let them clearly know how far they could go without arousing British naval concern. According to Wassner's reliable reports, the Foreign Office was making every effort to prevent the naval negotiations with the Germans from taking place at all. The outlook prevailing against Germany of a broad section of the British public was reflected in most branches of the news media where it was energetically maintained and fostered. Press comments in general expressed the view that the appearance of a strong German Navy would disrupt the basis on which previous naval treaties had been built and "that new and undesirable naval activity would result, not only in the Baltic, but also among the other naval powers."[16]

Even Hoesch, the German Ambassador to London, in his telegram of May 3 to the Foreign Office in Berlin, gave account of his long conversation with Simon, who "explained with the utmost seriousness the extreme difficulties which he personally had had to overcome in order to carry through his own planned visit to Berlin in spite of our announcement of the introduction of universal military service. The notification of our submarine plans — he continued — of which nothing had been said in Berlin, had been taken here as a further instance of anticipating a position which should have been the subject of negotiation. Again he had to overcome great difficulties in insisting that the Anglo-German naval conversations should be held as planned. He was not

[14] Memorandum by an Officer of the Naval Command, April 30, 1935. DGFP Ser. C. Vol. IV, No. 58, pp. 97—99.

[15] Conversation between the Chief of the Naval Command and the British Naval Attaché on April 30, 1935. DGFP Ser. C. Vol. IV, No. 59, pp. 99—100.

[16] The Naval Attaché in Great Britain to the Naval Command and the Foreign Ministry, London, May 1, 1935. DGFP Ser. C. Vol. IV, No. 60, pp. 100—102.

sure whether the British Government would accept a third case of similar anticipation on the German side." The British Government had learned that the Führer was planning a political pronouncement for the middle of May. MacDonald's and Simon's own speeches of May 2 had been consciously designed in order to stimulate positive statements by the Germans about the security problems. As Hoesch pointed out, "the general impression gained from the conversation was that, although the British Government was much put out by the notification of our plans for submarine construction (which was very awkward for them at this particular time), they wanted to drop polemics as much as possible." The British had wished to give the Reich Government the incentive for making a pronouncement which in turn would enable Britain to pursue her mediatory policy, aiming at avoiding the encirclement of Germany.[17]

In a cipher letter of May 7 Hoesch told the German Foreign Office about his conversation with Sir Robert Craigie, head of the American Department of the Foreign Office in London. Craigie played a very important role on the British side in the preliminary naval conversations. He asked Hoesch if he knew who would lead the negotiations on the German side. The Ambassador said that Ribbentrop had been entrusted with the leadership of the German delegation, and while recognizing the great importance of the conversations, the Germans regarded them as negotiations of a technical character. Craigie agreed but added that Sir John Simon as well as he would take part in the naval conversations and keep a general eye on them. Sir Robert Craigie further asked Ambassador Hoesch to use his influence at home to prevent any further announcement from being made about German intentions in the naval sphere, not to excite British public opinion, and not to prejudice the chances of good results which might be forthcoming from the conversations. Relying on his personal impressions, Hoesch informed his superiors also of the misgivings of the British Admiralty, requesting the Germans not to delay the discussions. As Hoesch put it, "our delegation should hold itself ready for the naval conversations here immediately after the Führer's forthcoming pronouncement." He found it proper to send home another bit of information, which he had also obtained from the British Admiralty, namely that Sir John Simon had remarked "that further developments will entirely depend on the forthcoming speech by the Führer and that the British Government was anxiously awaiting it in the knowledge that nothing further can happen now until the Führer has stated his attitude to the situation anew." Marginal note: "The Führer is informed. M. May 11."[18]

In the meantime, during May, a number of strongly pro-German speeches were delivered in the House of Lords. We have to agree with the Italian historian Gaetano Salvemini that speeches in the House of Lords were unimportant when the Labour Party was in power, but they were of significance under Conservative Governments: "What the Tory Lords say today in the House of Lords usually becomes the line of action for the Tory Cabinet tomorrow."[19]

[17] The Ambassador in Great Britain to the Foreign Ministry, Telegram, London, May 3, 1935. DGFP Ser. C. Vol. IV, No. 66, pp. 118—120.
[18] The Ambassador in Great Britain to the Foreign Ministry, Cipher letter, London, May 7, 1935. DGFP Ser. C. Vol. IV, No. 74, pp. 132—133.
[19] Salvemini, op. cit., p. 220.

The speeches of the Tory Lords and of those Liberals who were more Tory than the Tories themselves showed clearly that an accord with Germany was in the making. Lord Mottistone stated on a number of occasions (e.g. on May 7 and 22) that during the many weeks he and a friend of his had spent in Germany they had found that there was not one single German from the top to the bottom who wished to antagonize Britain. But Germany had no navy. Could any intelligent person expect her to be satisfied with that position? He had had many interviews with Hitler, whom he found to be "absolutely truthful, sincere and unselfish." Lord Phillimore pointed out at the same time that Europe would have no peace unless the German people realized that Britain was their friend. And Lord Hutchinson demanded that the Government take the first opportunity to come to an agreement with Germany.[20]

This general mood was strengthened by Laval's trip to Moscow following the Franco-Soviet treaty. France's position became ever stronger also in consequence of the Franco-Italian alliance. Thus a number of even those Tory politicians who in March had still opposed the Anglo-German rapprochement, accepted Simon's and Baldwin's pro-German line in May. Among these politicians was also Neville Chamberlain, the future Prime Minister, who in early 1935 could not at all be accused of pro-German sympathies. Even Vansittart (an analysis of his attitude will be made in connection with the signing of the Naval Agreement), who took a different approach to this question, seemed sometimes as optimistic: "He is convinced," as appeared from his confidential talks he had with György Ottlik at the beginning of May, "that the German nation will understand sooner or later that Hitler's policy is bringing closer together the powers which are afraid of the German peril, and therefore will come to its senses. Then it will be possible to negotiate and to discuss a disarmament plan with success."[21]

Was this optimism justified by Hitler's much awaited speech of May 21? On May 16, Jan Masaryk, evaluating the changes in the British mood regarding Hitler and the expected effect of the speech, sent his Foreign Minister in Prague the following report:

"In spite of the pro-German manifestations in the House of Lords and in the Commons, Hitler's actions are rated way below the freezing point. At present there is in the Cabinet — as two members have averred to me — no one who would take sides with Hitler; even MacDonald has definitively gone over to the anti-Hitler camp. Public opinion has also understood that the increase in armaments — which requires enormous expenditures, and which will doubtless be reflected in an increase of direct taxation next year — is a consequence of Hitler's and Göring's policy, and the anger at Germany now seems to be general. I am afraid that Hitler's speech scheduled for next Tuesday will be far too pacificatory, and he will thereby again succeed in winning a few naive brains and consistently Francophobe individuals, but if I am not mistaken, the majority of the British population has comprehended that Hitler's

[20] Ibid.
[21] Széchenyi's cipher telegram from London, May 2, 1935. OL Küm. Pol. 1935—21/—954.
[22] J. Masaryk on the general political situation, London, May 16, 1935. AMZV P. Z. No. 124.

'pacifism' is not to be given much credit."[22] The British press was looking forward to Hitler's speech and several advance comments went so far as to predict that it would be a landmark of foreign policies in Europe.[23]

In a certain sense it certainly was a landmark. Far from disheartening the British ruling quarter, the speech rather influenced their mood and disposition, stimulated the claim for a special arrangement with Germany, an agreed derogation from the military provisions of the Treaty of Versailles, and thus the activation of the policy of appeasement. J. W. Wheeler-Bennett, the English historian of this period, is correct when, with reference to this speech, he quotes Hitler himself: "Even from the most impudent lie something will stick." Out of the maze of his mendacious promises made on May 21, Hitler obtained the one thing he wanted: the Anglo-German Naval Agreement. Hitler's policy of "divide and conquer" was working successfully.[24]

That speech is really worth studying, for it contains most of the tricks with which Hitler lulled the suspicions and raised the hopes of the gullible.[25]

But let us see what we can learn from an eye- and ear-witness to Hitler's speech, the American journalist W. L. Shirer, who at that time was correspondent in Germany for the *Chicago Tribune:* "On the evening of May 21 Hitler delivered another 'peace' speech to the Reichstag — perhaps the most eloquent and certainly one of the cleverest and most misleading of his Reichstag orations this writer, who sat through most of them, ever heard him make. Hitler was in a relaxed mood and exuded a spirit not only of confidence but — to the surprise of his listeners — of tolerance and conciliation."[26]

Apparently, this was a "peace" speech: "The blood shed on the European continent in the course of the last three hundred years bears no proportion to the national result of the events. In the end France has remained France, Germany Germany, Poland Poland, and Italy Italy . . . If these states had applied merely a fraction of their sacrifices to wiser purposes the success would certainly have been greater and more permanent," Hitler said among other things. Germany, he proclaimed, had not the slightest thought of conquering other peoples: "Our racial theory regards every war for the subjection and domination of an alien people as a proceeding which sooner or later changes and weakens the victor internally, and eventually brings about his defeat . . . As there is no longer any unoccupied space in Europe, every victory . . . can at best result in a quantitative increase in the number of the inhabitants of a country. But if the nations attach so much importance to that they can achieve it without tears in a simpler and more natural way—[by] a sound social policy, by increasing the readiness of a nation to have children. No ! National Socialist Germany wants peace because of its fundamental convictions . . . Germany needs peace and desires peace !"

At the end of his speech Hitler made thirteen proposals for maintaining the peace. He solemnly recognized and guaranteed France her frontiers as determined after the Saar plebiscite. He finally renounced all claims to Alsace-

---

[23] This is indicated also by the confidential report from V. Černý, the Czechoslovak Chargé d'Affaires in London, May 25, 1935. AMZV P. Z. No. 135.

[24] Wheeler-Bennett, *op. cit.*, p. 221.

[25] Bullock, *op. cit.*, p. 335.

[26] Shirer, *op. cit.*, p. 285.

Lorraine. He had concluded a non-aggression pact with Poland (already in 1934. — É. H. H.) and was adhering to it. He recognized Poland as the home of a great and nationally conscious people. Germany neither intended nor wished to interfere in the internal affairs of Austria, to annex Austria or to conclude an *Anschluss*. Though Germany was willing "at any time" to participate in a system of collective security, she had objected to the proposal for multilateral pacts, for this was the way of spreading war, not of localizing it. Moreover, the East of Europe, Hitler declared, was a special case, where the existence of a state, Bolshevik Russia, was a threat to the independence of Europe; a state with which a National Socialist Germany could never come to terms. Instead of the "unrealistic" proposal of multilateral treaties Hitler offered to sign non-aggression pacts with all of Germany's neighbours, except with Lithuania, whose continued possession of German Memelland was a wrong which the German people could never accept. He was prepared, on the other side, to agree to the British and French proposals for supplementing the Locarno Treaty. He was ready to agree to the abolition of heavy arms, to accept limitation of armaments, provided that it was to apply to all the powers. Hitler particularly stressed his willingness to limit German naval power to 35 per cent of the strength of the British Navy, since he had no intention of starting a new naval rivalry with Great Britain. That, he added, would still leave the Germans 15 per cent below the French in naval tonnage.[27]

There were few — inside Britain, especially among experts of defence — who paid attention to that part of the speech which, stressing respect for other articles of the Versailles Treaty, attempted to absolve Germany from her unilateral commitments (meaning, in short, freedom for Germany to rearm) on the grounds that other countries failed to observe their disarmament obligations and which announced also a peaceful territorial revision which might become necessary in the course of time. On the other hand, the Hungarian Minister to Berlin, a diplomat very receptive to any hope of a revision of the Treaty of Peace with Hungary, reacted at once to this pronouncement in these words: "... a responsible German statesman has now for the first time committed himself to the idea of a revision."[28]

Hitler's speech of May 21 incontestably mirrored the demands of the Western European democracies, and, surprisingly enough, he used a tone pleasing and convenient to them. This is interesting also because Hitler neither spoke any of their languages nor had he ever been in those countries. He was aware that the idealistic pacifists, the ill-at-ease liberals, the ordinary people desirous of peace, most gladly heard and wanted to hear these phrases. Members of the British Cabinet, chiefly Simon and Baldwin, responded to the speech very promptly and very positively. Simon's understanding and his activity in preparing the Anglo-German rapprochement were influenced by his personal ambition. This statesman of mediocre talents was after the premiership and

---

[27] M. Domarius, *Hitler, Reden und Proklamationen 1932—1945*, Munich, 1962. Vol. I, Book II: "1935—38," pp. 505—509. The speech is reviewed also by Shirer and Bullock. The full text in English is to be found in N. H. Baynes (ed.), *The Speeches of Adolf Hitler, 1922—39*, Vol. II, pp. 1218—1247.

[28] Hungary's Minister in Berlin, Masirevich, to Foreign Minister Kánya, Berlin, May 24, 1935. OL Küm. Pol. 1935—21—1766.

presumably wished to attain "results." In the same way as Ribbentrop, who hoped — and not without reason — that with the success of the naval negotiations his star would be rising meteorically. Baldwin in the House of Commons noted Hitler's utterances with great appreciation. On behalf of his Government he described the speech as a "strikingly elaborate" one which was worth considering with sympathy and without bias. At the same time, however, he instructed the British Ambassador in Berlin to ask for explanation regarding certain points in the speech.[29]

The Foreign Office was inquiring along other lines as well. The Czechoslovak Legation in London was asked by the British what the Czechoslovakian position was with regard to Hitler's proposals. The reply was as follows: "We adopt the position that bilateral pacts can by no means be regarded as adequate substitutes for the Eastern pact, especially if Lithuania is left out and Russia's security remains unsettled." Furthermore, Czechoslovakia would abide by the principles of the League of Nations and would be ready to negotiate a bilateral non-aggression treaty only if it was done within the framework of the League.[30]

After Baldwin's statement to the Commons, a part of the British press, as the Czechoslovak Chargé d'Affaires put it, was seized with "joyful enthusiasm." The lead was taken in this field by the most influential newspaper of the British Isles, *The Times*, which in Shirer's view welcomed Hitler's speech with almost hysterical joy: "No one who reads it with an impartial mind can doubt that the points of policy laid down by Herr Hitler may fairly constitute the basis of a complete settlement with Germany — a free, equal and strong Germany instead of the prostrate Germany upon whom peace was imposed sixteen years ago . . . It is to be hoped that the speech will be taken everywhere as a sincere and well-considered utterance meaning precisely what it says." According to Shirer, *The Times* was to play a dubious role in the disastrous British appeasement of Hitler. He knew better than anyone else that the London newspaper's Berlin correspondent, Norman Ebbutt, until he had been expelled on August 16, 1937, was fully informed about Hitler's doings and purposes. *The Times* editors must have read *all* of his dispatches, and so they knew what really was going on in Nazi Germany and how hollow Hitler's grandiose promises were.[31]

We have to agree with A. Bullock who stated that "the policy of appeasement is not to be understood unless it is realized that it represented the acceptance by the British Government, at least in part, of Hitler's view of what British policy should be."[32]

[29].Report by Dr. Čorný, the Czechoslovak Chargé d'Affaires in London, May 25, 1935. AMZV P. Z. No. 135.

[30] *Ibid.*

[31] Shirer had known all this from N. Ebbutt and it was later confirmed by several memoirists. On May 23, 1937, e. g. *The Times* editor, G. Dawson, wrote to his Geneva correspondent: "I do my utmost, night after night, to keep out of the paper anything that might hurt their [German] susceptibilities." Quoted by Shirer, *op. cit.*, p. 288. The problem has been discussed recently from a different angle by D. McLachlan, *In the Chair, Barrington-Ward of The Times 1927—1948* London, 1971.

[32] Bullock, *op. cit.*, p. 338.

That Hitler's oration of May 21 was full of mere tactical elements and emotional appeals and did not reveal his real intentions is proved by the secret Reich Defence Law of the same day, which put Dr. Hjalmar Schacht in charge of the war economy and the thorough reorganization of the armed forces. At the same time Chancellor Hitler became Supreme Commander of the Wehrmacht.[33]

Two days after Hitler's speech the Group for Naval Conferences in the War Ministry drew up a top-secret memorandum entitled "Directives for the Preliminary Discussions on the 1935 Naval Conference." Paragraph 1 laid down the principles which were not for discussion (that is, either the British would accept them, or there would be no further negotiations). Let us quote these principles "not for discussion":

"(a) Qualitative German equality of rights with regard to all types of vessels, fortifications, weapons, etc. and consequently the abolition of Part V of the Treaty of Versailles relating to the Navy, and of the provisions of Part III relating to Heligoland.

(b) The fixing of the German fleet at 35 per cent of the displacement of the British fleet.

(c) Germany's readiness for such *limitations of naval armament* as all naval Powers may ... undertake to carry out at the same time; on the other hand, non-acceptance of any provisions concerning a moratorium on construction or the like because this would impede the expansion of the German fleet while leaving the heavily armed Powers ... in possession of their naval establishments."

Paragraph 4 of the German memorandum is worth noting, which warned that "any attempts to take the requirements of the *Baltic Sea* area alone as the basis for our sea power will be *entirely unacceptable.* Such attempts would have to be *most sharply* rejected as being in conflict with the principle of equality of rights and as entirely ignoring the defence requirements of Germany's North Sea coast and the major trading centres situated here. Our maritime requirements in the North Sea must be set forth in so vigorous and convincing a manner that Britain will not be able to ignore our arguments, precisely because we shall be using the very arguments which she employs to justify her own demands (protection of supplies coming by sea, the vital importance of these supplies, and the fact that our position with regard to naval strategy is definitely unfavourable)". Paragraph 5 of the memorandum explained why it would be more favourable for Germany to demand an overall tonnage than one itemized by types (divided into categories). The former would give Germany complete freedom to allocate the tonnage among the various classes of ships. If, however, a settlement by categories should be agreed to, then efforts

---

[33] Shirer writes in some detail about the Reich Defence Law (*op. cit.*, p. 285): "The Reichswehr of Weimar days became the Wehrmacht. Hitler as Fuehrer and Chancellor was Supreme Commander of the Armed Forces (Wehrmacht) and Blomberg, the Minister of Defense, was designated as Minister of War with the additional title of Commander in Chief of the Armed Forces. The camouflage name of *'Truppenamt'* in the Army was dropped for the real thing and its head, General Beck, assumed the title of Chief of the General Staff." The changes produced by this law are described in DGFP Ser. C. Vol. IV, App. I, Charts A and B.

should be made to achieve the greatest possible latitude for tonnage distribution. The question of laying down in detail the *number* of vessels of individual types should not be discussed. Paragraph 9 stated that the size of the budgetary and financial questions were internal German affairs, discussion of which should be refused. Paragraph 10 said that should the British inquire as to the date by which the 35 per cent were to be realized, the reply should be: between 1942 and 1946, depending on financial and shipyard conditions and other factors which as yet cannot be foreseen. (Paragraph 10 was pasted over an earlier version which read: probably at the end of 1942 unless the political and military situation should demand speedier completion.) Paragraph 11 touched upon the delicate question of submarines. Since the war, Britain had consistently been striving for the limitation or outlawing of submarine warfare on commercial ships, as well as the abolition of submarines altogether. At the conversation the German reply should be: Germany would welcome a general humanization of war on commerce such as was attempted in the 1922 Washington draft and as was to some extent achieved in Part IV of the London Treaty.[34]

The day following the drafting of this memorandum the British Ambassador to Berlin, Sir Eric Phipps, sent a letter marked "urgent" to Foreign Minister Neurath. In this letter the Ambassador recalled a conversation he had had with Admiral Raeder two days before, when he had expressed the hope that the German Government would send their experts to London for the naval conversations as soon as possible. He explained to Neurath the British Government's recommendation not to lose time. He asked for information about the earliest possible date on which it would be convenient for the German Government's representatives to go to London. The Ambassador repeated this request to Foreign Minister Neurath in person. Sir Eric urged also Hans Dieckhoff, then head of Department II of the German Foreign Office, that talks should begin on June 1 at the latest. Bismarck had also telephoned from London to emphasize the importance which the British attached to an early start of the talks.

Minutes made by Hans Frohwein, a Senior Counsellor in Department II of the German Foreign Office, dated May 28, read: "Herr v. Ribbentrop has informed the British Ambassador that the naval delegation will schedule their arrival in London so that the conversations can begin on the morning of June 4." In a memorandum addressed to Neurath and also dated May 28, Ribbentrop recorded that Phipps had informed him by telephone that the British Government agreed with the proposal to start the conversations on June 4. Phipps had also consented that a press release on the date of the conversations ought to be issued simultaneously in London and Berlin on May 29.[35]

Craigie, head of the American Department of the London Foreign Office, an active promoter and participant of the naval negotiations, had discussed already on May 28 with the Counsellor of the German Embassy the proceedings

[34] Unsigned Memorandum, Berlin, May 23, 1935, Top secret, military. Directives for the Preliminary Discussions on the 1935 Naval Conference. DGFP Ser. C. Vol. IV, No 100, pp. 189—192.

[35] Regarding all this, *cf.* Ambassador E. Phipps to Neurath, Berlin, May 28, 1935. DGFP Ser. C. Vol. IV, No. 104, pp. 195—196.

of the naval conversations, the protocol and the official programme. The head of the German delegation, Joachim von Ribbentrop, on the day after his arrival on June 2, would open the proceedings with a talk at the Foreign Office with Foreign Secretary Sir John Simon and the First Lord of the Admiralty, Sir Bolton Eyres-Monsell. Agreement was reached also on who would attend the various meetings. Otto von Bismarck raised the question as to whether reports that Sir John and the First Lord would attend the opening session were correct. After a lengthy discussion, Craigie stated that if Ribbentrop wished to attend he would try to bring this about. He emphasized that the conversations were purely provisional and informal. He thought that the talks would be followed by discussions with the French, the Italians and probably also with the Russians, until eventually the full Naval Conference would be summoned, hopefully towards the end of the year. Craigie referred to his experience gained with other countries and emphasized that it would be desirable to conduct negotiations "entirely among experts." He would be taking part in all the conversations, since political questions could be expected to crop up any time. Finally Craigie earnestly begged that steps should be taken to prevent the press from magnifying too much the importance of the negotiations.[36]

Craigie phoned Hoesch already on May 30 and confirmed the date of the first conversation for June 3 and told him also that Foreign Secretary Simon would participate in the opening session.[37]

To the Germans, or probably to Ribbentrop who was leading the negotiations on the German side, it was very essential, for reasons of prestige, to get a high-ranking British politician, possibly the Foreign Secretary himself, to take part in the conversations. This, however, could not be justified by the participation of Ribbentrop. His rank at that time was only one of an Ambassador at Large in charge of this special mission. It was "justified" rather by his ambition to be able to announce Hitler's desire that Germany would not settle for less than 35 per cent right at the first session and in the presence of the British Foreign Secretary. Dr. Paul Schmidt, the German interpreter of the negotiations, wrote in his memoirs: "Ribbentrop was very like the dog listening to his master's voice on the label of an old gramophone record." Ribbentrop was so dependent on Hitler's will and disposition that if the Führer was dissatisfied with him, he would fall sick and go to bed like a hysterical woman.[38] How was it then possible that he was given this assignment which determined his future career when he had no position whatsoever within the German Foreign Office and previously had only acted as Hitler's disarmament commissioner?[39]

In order to understand Ribbentrop's career in spite of his lack of experience, we have to look into the relationship which existed between Hitler and his Foreign Office, Hitler's views of Anglo-German friendship, and Ribbentrop's personal ambitions.

[36] Report from Hoesch to the German Foreign Office, London, May 28, 1935, Airgram. DGFP Ser. C. Vol. IV, No. 114, pp. 221—223.

[37] *Ibid.*, note I. Reference to Hoesch's telegram No. 138.

[38] Dr. Paul Schmidt, *Statist auf diplomatischer Bühne, 1913—45*, Bonn, 1951, p. 312.

[39] As to the organization of the German Foreign Office, see details in DGFP Ser. C. Vol. IV, App. II.

Until 1934 the Foreign Office in Berlin had actually no reason to complain. There were a few minor incidents, however, no "imcompetents" interfered especially with the work of diplomats. As early as in 1933, Goebbels merged the Foreign Office Press Department and most of its staff with the new Ministry for Propaganda and thus monopolized the activities of cultural information formerly assigned to Wilhelmstrasse. But over and above this loss of minor importance, the Foreign Office's functions and personnel remained almost intact in the first eighteen months of the National Socialist administration. The situation changed when Joachim von Ribbentrop intruded into the sphere of foreign politics. As a rich businessman, having interests in the wine and champagne trade, he was more than casually acquainted with London and Paris. He had a number of influential friends in foreign business circles and also possessed a good command of languages. These evidences of cosmopolitanism must have impressed Hitler when he was entertained by the Ribbentrop couple for the first time in the spring of 1932 and listened to Ribbentrop's voluble political monologues. By 1932, the Ribbentrops had developed political ambitions and had so much ingratiated themselves with Hitler that many saw Ribbentrop as the coming man already in the first days of Hitler's chancellor-ship. His dishonesty and unscrupulous compliance with Hitler's wishes made him a useful servant of the Chancellor. At the same time, Ribbentrop made use of Hitler for advancing his own career. The wife of the Italian Ambassador Cerruti in Berlin, who at that time was stationed in Paris, said that only in Nazi Germany could a man with the superficialities of a Ribbentrop attain the high office of a Foreign Minister. For the Nazi foreign policy, which primarily was a threatening policy of strength, these qualities of Ribbentrop could and — as could be seen from his subsequent career — did bring him advantages. Ribbentrop incurred almost unanimous condemnation in the literature of political memoirs.[40]

According to Geyr von Schweppenburg, the German Military Attaché in London, Ribbentrop — nicknamed Herr Brickendrop — had a mind that was at once sluggish, obstinate, and confused. At first Hitler requested Foreign Minister Neurath to show Ribbentrop how to do things, but Neurath saw — and allegedly even told Hitler — that Ribbentrop was a hopeless case.[41]

But Hitler did not let himself be influenced by such trifles. Ribbentrop was for him a tool, but one that also could profit from this situation. Ribbentrop always had an ear for Hitler's maniacal pronouncements and schemes — including the idea of the Anglo-German alliance. That enabled him to refer to them at a propitious moment, thereby making their meetings pleasant occasions. Ribbentrop himself told a noble English lady that "you should see me and the Führer rolling on the floor together at Berchtesgaden and roaring with laughter after one of us has made a joke."[42]

[40] G. A. Craig, "The German Foreign Office," in G. A. Craig & F. Gilbert (ed.), *The Diplomats, 1919—39*, Vol. 2: The Thirties, pp. 419—420. — *Cf.* Maisky, *op. cit.*, pp. 549, 553—556.

[41] Schweppenburg, *op. cit.*, p. 92. — Maisky, *op. cit.*, p. 557.

[42] *H. Dalton's Diary 1937—40*, 18—23. April 8, 1937. London School of Economics Library. Manuscript.

Ribbentrop did not come up with original ideas which could realize Hitler's wishes and ideas. Foreign statesmen and journalists considered him a stupid man. Sir John Simon once said that Ribbentrop was the most stupid diplomat he had ever come across.[43]

And this was coupled, as was pertinently stated by the German interpreter, with a good deal of vanity and arrogance. Interpreter Schmidt also says that, although Ribbentrop could shape his thoughts and questions well, he (Schmidt) never had the feeling that a statesman was standing by his side during his long years of experience with Ribbentrop. In the course of negotiations, Ribbentrop never was able to find a new idea to refute the opponents' arguments.[44]

It is thus understandable that the old men of the German foreign service, from Neurath to Secretary of State Bülow and to the highly cultured Ambassador in London, Hoesch,[45] who were aware of Ribbentrop's poor abilities, could not consider him as a rival. "Bülow could not regard as a serious competitor a man who had had no formal training in diplomacy, who could not write a report in correct German, who did not listen carefully enough to the remarks of foreign statesmen to interpret them correctly, and who insisted upon seeing possibilities of alliance where none existed." Bülow thought that no formal protest against Ribbentrop's activities was necessary, since their patent foolishness could not long be hidden even from Hitler.[46]

But in fact, contrary to the calculations of career diplomats, Ribbentrop was rising in Hitler's esteem. Ribbentrop was clever to choose the field of foreign policy. The only other man who, within the National Socialist Party, had been widely considered as Hitler's expert in foreign affairs — Alfred Rosenberg — was already a spent force. During a visit to London in the summer of 1933, Rosenberg had discredited the Nazi system in front of influential British

---

[43] Schweppenburg, *op. cit.*, p. 92.

[44] Schmidt, *op. cit.*, p. 312.

[45] Schweppenburg wrote of Hoesch that he was a very efficient and talented man, an excellent diplomat and learned lawyer. The reports written from his dictation were exemplary. *Cf.* Schweppenburg, *op. cit.*, p. 98. — As regards Hoesch, we can read in H. Dalton's manuscript that his sudden death in 1936 was not from natural causes. Hoesch was succeeded by Ribbentrop as German Ambassador to London. A friend of Dalton's, an army captain, who knew Hoesch well, had talked to him two days before he died of a heart stroke. Hoesch had told him that he had recently sent a dispatch to Berlin stating that if the present policy of the German Government was to continue, there would be a major war in Europe; that in such a war Germany would once more, as in 1914, find England against her. And that such a war could only end in the defeat and complete annihilation of Germany. Hoesch also warned Berlin in his dispatch not to pay attention to the Londonderrys and Lothians, who in no way represented any important section of British opinion. "Von Hoesch continued that the reply to this dispatch was an intimation that he would be recalled from London and dismissed from the diplomatic service. Then a private messenger had arrived from Berlin and had told von Hoesch that, if he returned to Germany, his life would not be safe, and that it would be better that he should commit suicide first." *Cf. Dalton's Diary 1937—40*, 18—23. April 15, 1937.

[46] Craig, *loc. cit.*, pp. 423—424.

circles. Therefore, the only hurdle Ribbentrop still had to overcome was the opposition of the German career diplomats assigned to the Foreign Office and to the Embassies abroad. From 1934 a good number of German Ambassadors accredited to Western European states had tried, more or less openly, to convince Hitler that his current foreign policy might result in isolating Germany. This "pessimism" was not to Hitler's liking. Then Ribbentrop entered the scene. He began to emphasize with extreme audacity that the foreign service people took a wrong view of the international situation. Only he and Hitler were able to make realistic appraisals. Soon the occasion presented itself, in the so-called Barthou note of April 17, 1934, for Ribbentrop to demonstrate his "excellent" abilities before Hitler. Ribbentrop offered to negotiate in the Western European capitals for the adjournment of the session of the Bureau of the Disarmament Conference. "It was from the outset a hopeless undertaking. In their respective capitals, Sir John Simon and Mussolini listened politely to this extraordinary envoy who came armed with nothing but a proposal that they adjourn the meeting of an organization of which Germany was no longer a member." Ribbentrop's debut as negotiator was a failure, however, it seemed to be a success because really nothing eventful occurred in the Bureau of the Disarmament Conference. As a result, Hitler encouraged his eager friend to extend his activities.[47]

Ribbentrop established then an agency of his own, the so-called *Dienststelle* (or *Büro*) Ribbentrop, in a building that faced the Foreign Office across the Wilhelmstrasse. It was staffed with ex-journalists, disappointed businessmen, graduates from the *Hitlerjugend* and aspiring party members who had hitched their wagons to Ribbentrop's star. This Bureau was presumably intended to collect and analyze foreign intelligence, but it tried to absorb other Foreign Office functions as well. Before his trip to London, Ribbentrop had been appointed Special Commissioner for Disarmament Questions and had been given the right to see all diplomatic correspondence dealing with this subject. This privilege was now extended, on Hitler's express orders, to include all dispatches which were not specially marked "For the Foreign Minister" or "For the Secretary of State." Ribbentrop both used and misused this right. He "developed a habit of scanning the incoming correspondence, seizing upon telegrams which required action; he secured Hitler's assent to replies which he had himself drafted, before the Foreign Office had time to consider the cases."[48]

The "Ribbentrop Bureau" took the whole world for its own province. Ribbentrop himself — under Hitler's influence or just because the subject was close to Hitler's own heart — was particularly interested in Anglo-German relations. He disregarded what the professionals considered to be realities and persuaded Hitler that what the Führer wanted to believe was true, for example that the British Government was yearning for a comprehensive agreement with Germany. In November 1934, he made another journey to

---

[47] As to this and what follows, see Craig's study *loc. cit.*, p. 422 ff.

[48] Two works by E. Kordt (*Wahn und Wirklichkeit*, Stuttgart, 1947, and *Nicht aus den Akten*, Stuttgart, 1950) are quoted by Craig's aforecited study, *loc cit.*, pp 422—423. E. Kordt was a Secretary at the German Embassy in London and took part in the naval negotiations.

London and talked with such notables as Sir Austen Chamberlain (formerly Chancellor of the Exchequer and Foreign Secretary) and G. B. Shaw, and also with Lord Lothian. Chamberlain and Shaw were decidedly cool and sardonic. Lord Lothian admitted his sympathy with Germany's right to rearm and his belief in the natural affinity of the two countries. Ribbentrop returned to Berlin and told Hitler that all classes of English society — members of Parliament, journalists, businessmen, and ordinary citizens — desired close collaboration with Germany. Hitler was delighted to see his hopes confirmed, and remarked that Ribbentrop was the only man who told him the truth about foreign countries.[49]

Consequently, against the expectations of Bülow and other responsible leaders of the German Foreign Office, Ribbentrop strengthened his position further. Hitler's trust was expressed also in the fact that, after the emergence of the Stresa front, he entrusted Ribbentrop with the leadership of the Anglo-German naval negotiations which were extremely important to him and held out the promise of his growing prestige. For some time now, the idea had been maturing in Hitler's mind that the career diplomats were blind to realities and overcautions. Years later Hitler said: "In 1933—34 the reports of the Foreign Office were miserable. They always had the same quintessence: that we ought to do nothing."[50]

Ribbentrop was not only willing to carry out Hitler's conceptions and to suggest details for them, but — as is shown by the Anglo-German Naval Agreement — he was also able to produce results.[51]

---

[49] Kordt, *op. cit.* (1950), pp. 83—88. Quoted by Craig, *loc. cit.*, p. 423.

[50] H. Picker, *Hitlers Tischgespräche im Führerhauptquartier, 1941—42*, Bonn, 1951, p. 86. — Craig, *loc. cit.*, p. 425.

[51] The German Embassy in London and the German Foreign Office did not feel hurt by the fact that the naval conversations were being led by Ribbentrop. At that time officials in both places were certain of Ribbentrop's coming failure. Moreover, when Ribbentrop took over the London Embassy after Hoesch's death (Aug. 11, 1936) and Hitler encouraged him by saying: "Bring me the British alliance with Germany," Ribbentrop did more harm than good to the Anglo-German relations. He began his activity (Oct. 20, 1936) by declaring at a press conference that in Hitler's view the greatest peril to Europe was Communism, this malady of mankind. That the two peoples should work together to ward off that peril. The famous Margot Asquith, who once sat next to Ribbentrop during a reception, told him bluntly: "You are the very worst Ambassador that Germany has ever sent to this country." Ribbentrop was much taken aback, looked at her very solemnly and asked: "Do you really think so?" "Yes," she replied, "you have absolutely no sense of humour or else you would not have given the Nazi salute when you were presented to the King." *Cf. Dalton's Diary, 1937—40*, 18—23. April 8, 1937. The relationships between Ribbentrop and the right-wing Cliveden set in Britain would call for a special analysis, which we cannot undertake here. — Göring also knew that Ribbentrop was misinforming Hitler regarding the nature of the Anglo-German relations. *Ibid.*, September 5, 1938. Also according to Schweppenburg, the German Military Attaché in London, the influence of Ribbentrop on Anglo-German relations was "definitely unhealthy." Characteristic of Ribbentrop was also the fact that he asked Schweppenburg whether the British General Staff could be made to take a bribe. Like many other fellow diplomats, Schweppenburg also was always puzzled and he tried in vain to get an answer from Berlin to the

The majority of the sources offer evidence that Hitler had given definite instructions (for the last time he did so during a ninety-minute confidential conference held at his home in Munich on May 31, 1935) not to let the 35 per cent already fixed be reduced. The German delegation should rather return empty-handed than to give in.[52] There is, however, some indication also that Hitler would in fact have been ready "to make concessions," as the German Ambassador in Paris confided to his Hungarian colleague there, "when the Anglo-German naval discussions would indicate that Britain would in no way accept Germany's claim to the 35 per cent ratio between the two fleets."[53] But whether or not Hitler would have been ready to make concessions, Ribbentrop was determined to follow the instructions received at the Führer's home.

It was on one of those days that the Soviet Ambassador to Great Britain, I. Maisky, at the request of ex-General Spear, delivered a speech in the committee room of the House of Commons. Ambassador Maisky talked about armament issues, including the proportions of German rearmament. He made known the numerical strength of the German armed forces and paramilitary organizations and revealed figures relating to German naval construction, including references to the number of completed submarines of over 250 tons.[54] This, however, could not influence the course of events. A three-engined Junkers was already flying over the Elbe with the German delegation bound for the London naval negotiations. The German delegation was received on June 3 in the Locarno Hall of the Foreign Office by Sir John Simon, the Secretary of State for Foreign Affairs, in the presence of Sir Robert Craigie, then Assistant

---

question: What is the relationship between the Military Attachés and the Ribbentrop Bureau? The entire German Foreign Office was in the same quandary throughout 1935—36. Although Hitler personally was still fond of Neurath, he had lost all confidence in the German Foreign Office and in 1936, for example, the occupation of the Rhineland and the denunciation of the Locarno Treaty were effectuated rather through the Ribbentrop Bureau than through the services of the Foreign Office. Ribbentrop as Ambassador to London was not subordinated to the German Foreign Office. The cultivation of the Anglo-German relations became Hitler's and Ribbentrop's private affair. (In a different context, after the assassination of Dollfuss, the case was the same with the Vienna ambassadorship of Franz von Papen, who also was answerable to Hitler alone.)

The functions of the Foreign Office in respect to the diplomatic missions abroad were gradually taken over by the "*Auslandsorganisation*" (AO) of the National Socialist Party. As far as the German Foreign Office, the AO, and the Ribbentrop Bureau were concerned, this situation lasted until 1937.

[52] E. Raeder, *op. cit.*, Vol. I: "Bis zum Flottenabkommen mit England 1935," Tübingen, 1956, p. 301. This conversation was attended of course by Hitler, Raeder, Blomberg, Neurath, Lammers, Ribbentrop, and Schuster.

[53] Secret report from Paris by Khuen-Héderváry, the Hungarian Minister to France, June 4, 1935. OL Küm. Pol. 1935—2/25—1933.

[54] Confidential report by Széchenyi, Hungary's Minister to London, May 31, 1935. OL Küm. Pol. 1935—2/28—1912. According to this report: "It would happen at time that some outstanding foreign personage, at the request of one or another member of the House of Commons, gave invited members of Parliament information on some topical political question . . . A fairly good number of M. P. s were present."

Under-Secretary of State for Foreign Affairs, and Vice-Admiral Sir Charles Little, Deputy Chief of the Naval Staff, as well as a few British officials and officers. Simon then outlined briefly the purpose of the conversations but made no mention of numerical ratios.[55]

The first official conversation took place at the Foreign Office in the morning of June 4. The participants were, on the German side: Ambassador von Ribbentrop, Rear-Admiral Karl Georg Schuster, Lieutenant Commander Kiderlen, Captain Erwin Wassner, the Military Attaché in London, Counsellor Dr. Paul Schmidt as interpreter, and Secretary of Legation Erich Kordt; on the British side: Foreign Secretary Sir John Simon, Under-Secretary Craigie, Admiral Little, Captains Danckwerts and Scott, and another officer. The British press and public were eagerly looking forward to the negotiations. Representatives of Britain and Germany met at the negotiating table for the first time since the Great War. Let us pick a few interesting items from the many press comments. According to the *Manchester Guardian* (June 4) it was mere chance that the head of the British delegation to the conference was an expert in submarine questions. The *Daily Herald* (June 5) stated that the Admiralty wished to force the Germans to declare their final naval requirements, the total naval force which Germany considered indispensable for the protection of her coast and her commerce.

In the morning of June 4, Foreign Secretary Simon opened the meeting and welcomed the German delegation. He referred to the passage in Hitler's speech of May 21 in which the Reich Chancellor had stated, that he had no more intention to enter into competition with Britain in the naval field than Britain intended to compete with Germany in the field of land forces.

Ribbentrop made a lengthy declaration. He mentioned that he had maintained personal ties of friendship in Britain for twenty-five years, stating that the German Government and the German naval leaders were very pleased to see this important discussion taking place. In the interest of a successful outcome of the negotiations, he said by way of introduction:

"1. In his Reichstag speech on May 21, the German Reich Chancellor stated: 'The German Government, in consequence of the failure of the other States to fulfil their disarmament obligations, have thus on their part renounced those Articles which, as a result of their one-sidedness, had placed a burden on Germany contrary to the provisions of the Treaty; this has constituted a discrimination against Germany for an unlimited period of time.' By means of this pronouncement by the Chancellor . . . Germany has re-established her absolute equality of rights with regard to armaments.

"2. The necessity to safeguard the German Reich and its access to the sea, on the one hand, and the recognition of Great Britain's historic claim to supremacy at sea, on the other, have led the Chancellor of the German Reich to fix the requirements of German naval tonnage at 35 per cent of the total tonnage of Great Britain. The Chancellor has been able to accept this voluntary limitation of its maritime defences by a Sovereign State only because he has ruled out once and for all the possibility of Great Britain as an enemy of Germany's defensive planning. The Government of the German Reich is entitled to express

[55] Malanowski, *loc. cit.*, p. 411.

the hope that this generous decision of the Chancellor's will be fully appreciated as a great and historic German contribution towards the future shaping of relations between our two countries and to the pacification of Europe as a whole.

"3. Under these circumstances it is perhaps hardly necessary for the German Delegation to point out that it can only expect these negotiations to be successful and that it can only take part in these conversations, which carry such importance, if this ratio of Great Britain 100 to Germany 35 is accepted as an inviolable and firmly established relationship. In order, however, to avoid any possible misunderstanding on this point, the German Delegation would be very grateful to the British Delegation for confirmation that there is agreement on this basic principle. It is impossible to overestimate the value of the advantage to be gained by both our countries from such an enduring solution of the naval question. Hitler has further stated that Germany would regard this ratio, once it had been fixed, as final and enduring, and that the question of the possession of colonies would not make any difference to this settlement."

It was, however, not these considerations alone which induced the Reich Chancellor to perform this "generous act of self-restraint." With his deep insight into the future and in anticipation of the irresistible historical developments to come, the German Reich Chancellor came to certain conclusions, which had influenced his political thinking for many years, and which had become the corner-stone of his political philosophy, namely:

"I. That a repetition of the only conflict in history between the two great nations of a common race must under all circumstances be avoided. II. That a co-ordination of their vital interests and a certain common and realistic basic attitude on the part of the two Powers towards the major problems of Europe are, in the long run, the only things which can bring about a solution of these problems and, above all, a German-French settlement, which the German people desire and without which there can be no peace in Europe. Only in this way will it be possible at last to establish on firm foundations that solidarity of European nations which is so essential and on which the work of construction can be started. If we approach the problems of Europe in this spirit we shall find many points of mutual interest in the field of naval armaments as well."

It was approximately in these terms that Ribbentrop concluded his long oration. Sir John Simon in his reply reminded his negotiating partner that the object was to prepare the ground work for a future naval conference and an all-round naval agreement in which the great naval powers would have to participate. The aim was, therefore, first to pave the way for a multilateral agreement and, secondly, to determine what the relative strengths meant in terms of absolute tonnage. For the rest, it seemed to him that the German delegation's demand was something which properly belonged not to the beginning but to the end of the negotiations.

Ribbentrop replied in strong terms and repeated that only if a clear basis was created in advance, which made frank and friendly discussions possible, could the German delegation hope for any success from the naval discussions, and only then could they take part in them. The ratio of Great Britain 100 to Germany 35 represented not simply a demand by the German side but a final decision by the German Chancellor, which he had only reached after long and careful consideration and which stood absolutely firm. Therefore he asked once more for a clear answer to the German question.[56]

The German interpreter, Dr. Paul Schmidt, noted down in his memoirs that Simon's face had reflected the impact of Ribbentrop's shocking behaviour, "his bluntness of speech." As he had translated Ribbentrop's words, Simon's face flushed. His benignant eyes became dark with the clouds of anger. "It is not customary to stipulate such conditions at the very beginning; I for one cannot give any reply to this," he said and left the room with a cool nod of the head.[57] Then Craigie took the chair and said that from his very long experience of naval negotiations he knew of no previous case in which a foreign delegation had at the very beginning of the discussions put forward such rigidly defined conditions. It was not so much a question here of any fundamental difference of opinion, but rather of differing views about the methods to be followed.

Ribbentrop replied that he knew Hitler was not the sort of man to say one thing one day and do another thing the next day. He (Ribbentrop) was disappointed about the British refusal to accept the great historic proposals of the Reich Chancellor as the self-evident basis of honest discussions. Germany had restored her military sovereignty and had now come as an entirely free nation to take part in negotiations. As a result of the Versailles Treaty, Germany was in no position to build up her level of defences freely and undisturbed as other powers had been able to do. Before there could be any agreement, Germany would have to create the basis for participating in future international negotiations under the same conditions as other countries. If the German claim had come as a surprise to the British, he would propose that the British delegation submit the question to their Government and ask for instructions.

After that the negotiating parties agreed as to the character of the press coverage and information to be given out to the other naval powers simultaneously (Craigie) or after the conclusion of the negotiations (Ribbentrop) and of the communications to be made by common accord.

At the afternoon meeting of June 4, Craigie and Ribbentrop continued the tug-of-war about the issue of the German delegation's insistence on an immediate answer to the German claim for 35 per cent. If the Germans insisted, Craigie said, the British delegation might have to consult the other naval powers. Ribbentrop expressed his fear that such a procedure would only lead to complications and difficulties. Britain and Germany ought in fact to agree between themselves. Craigie asked whether the German claim for 35 per cent of the British naval strength was to be understood to mean that Germany would not demand any increase of the 35 per cent even if a third power increased the strength of its own fleet and if Britain did not. He gave as a theoretical example that of France, whose present level of tonnage was approximately 50 per cent of the British naval strength. Craigie asked whether in the case of an increase in the French fleet Germany would propose an increase of her 35 per cent,

[56] Unsigned Memorandum, 1935, London. Record of the meeting at 10 a. m. June 4. DGFP Ser. C. Vol. IV, No. 131, pp. 253—262. Allegedly the German Foreign Office had sent the very shrewd and highly cultured Baron Lesner (a former army officer) to London to spy upon Ribbentrop, while he was there negotiating the naval pact. See W. E. Dodd, *Ambassador Dodd's Diary*, London, 1941, p. 256.

[57] Schmidt, *op. cit.*, p. 312.

supposing that Britain for her part saw no cause to reply to the increase of French naval strength with an increase of her own. Ribbentrop pointed out that Germany wished to be guided in principle by British naval strength. At the present time French naval strength comprised about 50 per cent of the British, that is, 15 per cent more than Germany's. This did not mean, however, that Germany recognized French naval superiority in principle. Germany would find it absolutely incomprehensible if, in the light of the modest level of Germany's final naval strength, France felt justified in claiming an increase of her own proportionate strength. There would be nothing to justify such an attitude on the part of France. Measures undertaken by a third Government would not, however, lead to any increase in the claim for 35 per cent, although Germany must proceed from the assumption that Britain would maintain her naval strength in a definite proportion to that of other European naval powers.[58]

On June 5 the conversations took a different complexion. Craigie and Ribbentrop had talks in private during the afternoon. Craigie showed Ribbentrop the draft of a memorandum which the Admiralty wanted to submit to the British Government in order to secure its consent to the recognition of the precondition laid down by the German side. Ribbentrop and Rear-Admiral Schuster (whom he called in) studied this document and requested British appreciation for the earlier German concerns at a possible increase of French tonnage. They asked for the inclusion of this understanding in the memorandum. Craigie emphasized that the British Government would naturally not be able to exert any "pressure" on the French Government in order to dissuade them from taking an incomprehensible and unjustified step. This time and also later, at the seven-o'clock meeting at the Admiralty and at the resumed taks in the German Embassy, the question of global tonnage or distribution of tonnage among the various categories was discussed further. Germany with her small fleet must have the greatest possible freedom in the distribution of tonnage among the various categories. For the major naval powers this was not of such great significance as for the minor ones. Ambassador Ribbentrop pointed out that Germany was claiming complete equality of rights with the other nations with regard to submarines. Finally they agreed on the formulation and the details that should be included in the memorandum to be submitted to the British Government.[59]

This memorandum drawn up by the British Admiralty and the proposal submitted by the British delegation to its Government — which have been discovered only recently among the British Cabinet papers and which have been missing from all published Foreign Office documents — are very interesting inasmuch as these were essentially the factors which brought the British Government to accept immediately the German conditions put forward in a rather unusual form and through aggressive methods.

[58] Record of the meeting at 4 p. m. London, June 4. DGFP Ser. C. Vol. IV, No. 132, pp. 262—265.
[59] Unsigned Memorandum, London, June 5, 1935. Record of a Private Discussion between Mr. Craigie and Ambassador von Ribbentrop on the afternoon of June 5. — Unsigned Minute, London, June 5, 1935. Record of a Discussion at the Admiralty on June 5, 1935, at about 7 p. m. — Unsigned Memorandum, London, June 5, 1935. Discussion at the German Embassy during the evening of June 5, 1935. DGFP Ser. C. Vol. IV, No. 135—137, pp. 269—273.

The Admiralty memorandum began with stating that the German claim for 35 per cent must be considered in relation to the general strategical situation. The Chiefs of Staff described this situation in their Annual Review for 1935 in the following terms:

(a) "The ability of the One-Power Standard to satisfy our strategical needs is dependent upon a sufficient margin between the strength of the one Power on which the standard is calculated and the strength of the next strongest naval Power. The existing margin is only sufficient on the supposition that France will not be our enemy in Europe and that we are not without allies."

(b) "That we should be called upon to fight Germany and Japan simultaneously without allies is a state of affairs to the prevention of which our diplomacy would naturally be directed. With France as our ally the naval situation in Europe would wear a different complexion and the main British fleet would be available to defend our Empire in the East."

(c) "Although His Majesty's Government in the United Kingdom would never, we presume, confide the *entire* protection of this country and its vital sea communications to a foreign navy in the absence of our Main Fleet, yet if France were our ally, her naval forces could undertake part of this responsibility. A British capital ship cruiser and destroyer strength in home waters equal to that of Germany is probably the least that we could accept."

(d) "It would be important to have sufficient warning to enable us to bring forward our capital ships undergoing large repairs before we were called upon simultaneously to face Germany in European waters and to send our Main Fleet to the Far East. Subject to this proviso, and, except for the shortage of cruisers, we should, in the next three or four years, be able to provide naval security in an alliance with France against Germany, while at the same time defending ourselves against Japanese aggression."

The Admiralty memorandum then went on to state:

"3. At the present time Japan's total naval strength by tonnage is about 64 per cent of ours and Germany's is less than 11 per cent. In the vital matter of capital ships, the percentages are 57 per cent and 15 per cent, so that at the moment the margin is ample. If, when Germany has reached a strength of 35 per cent of our own, as is her announced intention, Japan's relative strength remains the same as at present, we should, *on a purely tonnage basis*, have a margin sufficient to fulfil the requirements set out in paragraph 2 *(c)*.

"4. Since our strategical requirements must take account of both Germany and Japan, it is evidently to our advantage that the naval forces of each or either of them should —

(a) Be limited.
(b) Be limited at as low a figure as it is possible to secure.

"5. The statements of Herr Hitler, as amplified by the German representatives in the current conversations, make it clear that there is no prospect whatever of Germany coming to agreement on any question, including the extremely important one of qualitative limitation, except on the 35 per cent basis.

"The German representatives have made it clear also that they are prepared to preserve this strength relative to British strength whatever France or any other country may do.

102

"6. We have also received the impression that the German Government genuinely consider that they have made a generous and self-sacrificing decision, and that if the opportunity to close with the offer is lost, it is improbable that they will stop short at the 35 per cent level in building up their fleet.

"7. Our information leads us to suppose that the German resources are amply sufficient to enable them to complete the whole of the tonnage necessary to bring them up to this level by the year 1943, and that they have made arrangements for manning the fleet as it is constructed

"8. The foregoing represents the ultimate position, stated in general terms. There are, however, other aspects of the matter which necessitate more detailed examination. As stated in the body of this report, the German representatives have declared that Germany intends to calculate her tonnage in principle by categories.

"9. In the first place the capital ship modernization programme that has been undertaken by Japan, has already made us relatively weak in modern or modernized ships. Until the middle of the year 1939 we shall, except for a short period, have only 11 ships available for service and, quite apart from the German battle-fleet, we shall have no margin in modernized ships over Japan alone.

"10. From this point of view it is important that every endeavour should be made to slow down the rate of increase of the German fleet.

"11. Germany at present possesses three ships of the *Deutschland* Class, a type of capital ship, which, although small, cannot be opposed ship for ship by existing cruisers. In addition, Germany is building two further ships which it is believed will be an improved and enlarged *Deutschland* Class of 20,000 tons or over.

"12. A 35 per cent ratio of the British tonnage in the capital ship category would permit Germany to lay down two further capital ships of the maximum size.

"13. Thus, when the programme under consideration is completed, we shall be faced with a German battle-fleet of seven ships, of which four may be of the most powerful type allowed. During this same period Japan may have completed four new capital ships (assuming they are content with the programme suggested unofficially by Admiral Yamamoto).

"14. Against this total of eight new large capital ships plus three *Deutschland* Class, the tentative British programme will only produce six ships. In these circumstances it may be essential for the Naval Staff to recommend a more rapid replacement of the British battle fleet, in order to ensure that in *new ships* the British Fleet does not fall behind the capital ship strength of Japan and Germany combined.

"15. This is a position which cannot be avoided by refusing to recognize the German decision and indeed such refusal is more likely to lead to an acceleration of the German programme with consequent disadvantage to ourselves. Amelioration of the position can only be brought about by persuading the Germans to increase their navy at a moderate rate. This they are unlikely to agree to do if we do not accord them the recognition for which they are asking."

Paragraphs 16 to 18 of the Admiralty memorandum dealt with specific questions of cruisers, destroyers, and submarines. In regard to submarines it stated that, "failing general agreement for the abolition of this type, Germany would ultimately acquire a right to build them. Although the German representatives have stated their intention to calculate their tonnage category by category in principle, yet they have made it clear that if other Powers are granted in a future Treaty or retain in fact the right to have parity with the British Empire in the Submarine category, Germany will expect a similar right, although she will not necessarily build up to this level."

In this case Germany would have some 50 to 60 submarines, a situation which must give rise to some misgiving, but — the memorandum said rather naively — "it is quite apparent from the attitude of the German representatives that it is a question of *'Gleichberechtigung'* which is really exercising their minds, and not the desire to acquire a large Submarine fleet. In the present mood of Germany, it seems probable that the surest way to persuade them to be moderate in their actual performance is to grant them every consideration in theory. In fact, they are more likely to build up to Submarine parity if we object to their theoretical right to do so, than if we agree that they have a moral justification.

Apart from this psychological aspect of the question, the only other way to ensure a reasonable limitation of German submarine building is to keep our own tonnage as low as possible."

In the knowledge of Hitler's strategy and tactics, there is no need to comment on all the foregoing. The conclusions appended to the memorandum categorically specify the course of action to be followed by the British Government:

"(a) On general strategical grounds, a 35 per cent ratio of our naval strength for Germany is acceptable.

"(b) The increase of the German Fleet makes it essential to preserve our Washington Treaty ratio *vis-à-vis* Japan.

"(c) A more rapid replacement of the British battle Fleet than is visualized in the tentative British programme may be necessary in order to ensure that in *new ships* the British Fleet does not fall behind the capital ship strength of Japan and Germany combined.

"(d) Our present contemplated rate of increase in cruiser strength is sufficient to balance the probable rate of German building in this category.

"(e) In other categories there are no particular comments.

"(f) *From the point of view of general limitation of naval armament it would be greatly to our advantage to recognize the decision of the German Government lest the demand should be increased.*"[60]

This memorandum of the Admiralty, together with a summary of Ribbentrop's introductory and closing speeches, was submitted to the Cabinet by Foreign Secretary Simon, who added also the report of the British delegation.

---

[60] German Proposal for a 35 per cent Naval Ratio, Naval Staff Memorandum. Anglo-German Naval Discussion. Annex III. P. R. P. Cab. 24/255, pp. 169—171. (My italics. —E. H. H.) — According to Prime Minister Baldwin the signing of the Anglo-German Naval Agreement was put through mainly at the insistence of First Lord of the Admiralty Sir Bolton Eyres-Monsell. *Cf.* Th. Jones, *A Diary with Letters, 1931—1950,* London, 1969, p. 186. Jones was a public figure close to Baldwin and had been Secretary of the Cabinet in the 1920's.

This report truly recorded the events of the first two days of the conference, the demands of the German delegation, and decidedly took the view that it was in the British interest to accept Hitler's offer "while it is still open." For, if it should be declined, Germany would build her fleet above the 35 per cent level. (This affirmation was supported by the Admiralty memorandum and not by any information inferred from Germany's war potential.) The British admitted at the same time that the German proposals had also some "elements of bluff," but in view of the proportions of German land rearmament, they alleged, it would be a mistake to believe that the Germans would leave their offer open for an indefinite time; so it would be a blunder not to stop Germany's naval development at this proposed limit.

If, on the other hand, the British Government should be willing to accept Hitler's offer, Britain would have to consider the repercussions on other European powers, since it had been tacitly agreed that no bilateral agreement should be concluded between the parties to the Washington Treaty. Yet the German offer was of such outstanding importance that it would be a mistake to decline it merely on the ground that other powers might be temporarily annoyed by the British action. Nevertheless, it would seem advisable and desirable to give those powers an opportunity to express their views on the Anglo-German Naval Agreement before a formal British answer was given to the Germans. Therefore an oral communication should be addressed to the United States, Japan, France and Italy, emphasizing that the Anglo-German naval conversations were of great importance to the cause of future naval limitation and constituted an assurance for the future security of all other countries. Still before that, however, the German delegation should be informed confidentally that the British wished to forward the above communication to the other powers. It was believed that the Germans would be satisfied and the discussions would proceed on a secure basis. In conclusion, the British delegation thought, for psychological and political reasons alike, that the answer should not be delayed, because it would be unfortunate if the Germans should return home for Whitsuntide without being able to report anything concrete. The German offer would gain in effectiveness with the speed of its acceptance, as was confidentially pointed out on the German side.[61]

This British proposal was drafted on June 5 and, together with a memorandum and the Admiralty's written opinion, was submitted to the Cabinet on June 7. Simon recorded in his memorandum that the Admiralty had intensively studied the German claim for 35 per cent at several meetings and that he (Simon) had been authorized to inform the German delegation of the British acceptance of the offer. The First Lord of the Admiralty and he went to see Ribbentrop and his delegation on June 6 and reached a confidential agreement with them. They explained that before giving a formal reply, the British Government must communicate with the other signatories of the Washington Treaty and inform them so as to enable them to offer observations. The essence of the British communication made to the other powers was that the Anglo-German Naval Agreement was definitive and it was not to be modified by any possible subsequent German colonial acquisitions or by the increase of the fleet of

[61] Anglo-German Naval Discussions, Report by the British Representatives Annex I. P. R. O. Cab. 24/255, pp. 167—169.

third powers, and that the tonnage limits allowed were fixed by ship categories and not globally. (See Appendix III, p. 177.)[62]

The conversation held on June 6 in the Board Room of the Admiralty, which was attended on the British side by Sir John Simon and Sir Bolton Eyres-Monsell as well as by Admiral Little and Commander (Captain) Danckwerts, proceeded in such a way that Ribbentrop asked for clarification whether the communication to the foreign Governments was to be interpreted as a tacit admission of the right of these powers to raise objections, or whether, on the contrary, it was a matter of *international courtesy*. "Simon for his part was in favour of as short a Whitsun break as possible and stated that he had the distinct impression that both sides of the table could congratulate themselves on having made a valuable contribution to a reasonable limitation of armaments, to the furthering of peace and to the establishment of good and friendly relations between the two countries."[63]

Ribbentrop then flew home with his success of "historic importance" and reported the result to Hitler on June 8. Foreign Secretary Simon was not so lucky. The British Government was reshuffled on June 7. The change was necessitated by the fact that MacDonald's illness prevented him from discharging his functions. For this and other reasons, he was unable to lead the national coalition before the approaching General Election. Within the National Cabinet composed of Conservatives, National Liberals, and National Labourites, the leadership passed from the hands of Labour Prime Minister MacDonald into the hands of Baldwin, the Conservative Party leader, who wielded the absolute majority both in the Coalition and in the House of Commons. The Government preserved its character of national coalition, but Conservative domination was evident. Fifteen out of 22 ministers were members of the Conservative Party. As the British newspaper magnate, Lord Beaverbrook, put it, "Hitler, by making Britain weak in the air, has made the Conservative party strong in the country."[64]

The most important of the personal changes was the dismissal of Foreign Secretary Sir John Simon. He was believed to be the least popular person within the Cabinet and his dismissal was not much deplored, neither in Parliament, nor in press circles, nor in the Foreign Office where he did not enjoy much sympathy either. He had lost the confidence of those with whom he had ever had dealings not only at home but also abroad. The charges raised against him were that he was prejudiced and had missed "favourable opportunities" rather than that he had committed concrete errors. It was the general opinion that in the British Cabinet Sir John represented the pro-German and wavering element. He was inapt to direct the course of events, although he was skilful

[62] Anglo-German Naval Discussions. Note by the Secretary of State for Foreign Affairs, P. R. O. Cab. 24/255, p. 167. — Sir John Simon to His Majesty's Representatives at Washington (No. 155), Paris (No. 140), Rome (No, 315) and Tokyo (No. 99). F. O. June 7, 1936. Ibid., p. 171.

[63] Unsigned Memorandum, London, June 6, 1935. Record of the Anglo-German Discussion held in the Board Room of the Admiralty. DGFP Ser. C. Vol. IV, No. 141, pp. 277—281.

[64] From Beaverbrook's letter of June 4, 1935. See A. J. P. Taylor, FBA, *Beaverbrook*. London, 1972. p. 354.

in manoeuvering when he found himself in unexpectedly serious predicaments. Simon stubbornly clung to his ministerial seat. It was his final gratification that he was appointed Home Secretary, and, on top of it, Deputy Leader of the House of Commons. MacDonald and Simon were succeeded by "genuine" Tories, Stanley Baldwin and Sir Samuel Hoare. A Hungarian news commentator wrote at that time: "The surprise — and on this score British public opinion shared the feelings of the French and the Italians — was that the predominantly Conservative Government inclined towards Germany more readily and more swiftly than its predecessor imbued with Labour and Liberal pacifism. After barely three weeks of negotiations, namely on June 18, they definitively concluded the agreement with the German naval delegation led by Ribbentrop."[65]

It is true that the Naval Agreement was ultimately concluded by Sir Samuel Hoare, the new Secretary of State for Foreign Affairs, but — as we are going to see — this was not an unambiguous act on his part, because he practically obtained it "ready-made," or inherited it, from Sir John Simon. We must again look into the power struggle. In fact, many — first of all Sir Warren Fisher and Sir Robert Vansittart — wanted to see the 38-year-old Eden take over the Foreign Office, but Prime Minister Baldwin found the successful and sympathetic politician too young for the position. Baldwin was held to be a man of good intentions, but one who showed little interest in the matters of defence, and who, as in domestic policies, applied also in foreign policy, towards the European dictators, the dangerous principle that most problems would be solved by themselves.[66] Of course, both he and Hoare, as well as Vansittart who stood behind them, were to a certain extent influenced in their decision by a very peculiar event of home politics in the summer of 1935, the so-called Peace Ballot, which was organized by the Labour and Liberal parties in cooperation with members of the League of Nations' association and which — as was seen from the result published on June 27 — showed that ten million and a half out of more than eleven million voters said "yes" to disarmament.

What made Sir Samuel Hoare look more suitable than Eden for the conduct of British foreign policy were his age and experience. Eden was a target of strong criticism from the Italians. There were many who set afloat the name of Churchill, whom some intended to become First Lord of the Admiralty. However, at about that time, the German Ambassador in London submitted a

---

[65] Ottlik, *loc. cit.* — To give a characterization of Simon we have used also the report by László Széchenyi, Hungarian Minister in London, dated June 12, 1935. OL Küm. Pol. 1935—2/1—2043. — From among the recent English memoirs, see the diary of a British Ambassador to France, who had earlier been Private Secretary and a close adviser to Anthony Eden. In the view of the author, Simon was "slippery and evasive, a moral coward." Cf. *The Diplomatic Diaries of Oliver Harvey, 1937—1940*, Ed. by John Harvey, London, p. 448.

[66] Liddell Hart, *op. cit.*, Vol. I. — Beaverbrook wrote of Baldwin pertinently: "For the biggest paradox about Mr. Baldwin is that he claims to be right when he does a thing, and claims also to be right, when he undoes it. The truth is that Mr. Baldwin is always right when he contradicts himself . . . In April 1935 his government made a solemn declaration along with the French and the Italians, against German rearmament in defiance of the Treaty of Versailles. But in June of that same year Mr. Baldwin made a naval treaty with Germany in defiance of the Treaty of Versailles." See Taylor, *Beaverbrook*, p. 374.

protest against one of Churchill's articles hurtful to Hitler. This incident and other reasons made it impossible to include Churchill in the Government.[67] When Sir Samuel took office, it was stressed that he had known the Soviet Union well as early as the time of his mission following the Great War (in 1921 he was League of Nations Assistant Commissioner in charge of the welfare of Russian refugees) and that "he had a strong antipathy towards the Bolsheviks" while on the other hand he was a great admirer of Masaryk and was on good personal terms with his son, the Czechoslovak Minister to Great Britain.[68]

Hoare, who was already 55 years of age at that time, had been a minister in 1922, and Secretary for India in 1931. Hoare's short and notorious tenure of the Foreign Office, in comparison to Simon's, revealed also differences of opinion as well as personal differences.[69] These differences of opinion, however, could of course not come up during the second phase of the naval negotiations, after Whitsuntide, when chiefly questions of detail were being discussed between experts of the two sides.

As we have already mentioned, Ribbentrop gave on June 8 Hitler a detailed account of the developments. The Naval Conference Group (SK = *Gruppe für Seekonferenzen*) of the German War Ministry was getting busy. It conveyed the questions of the London delegation and forwarded the decisions of the Ministry. In a secret memorandum of June 12, SK requested a decision on two points proposed by the London delegation:

"1. When announcing our claim for parity of submarine tonnage in principle... it seems best to limit ourselves for the near future to a smaller tonnage, in order not to give the British unnecessary cause for suspicion, particularly since on personnel grounds we cannot go substantially beyond our present programme (35 per cent). We should therefore tell the British that, on principle and on grounds of our equality of rights, we must claim parity of submarine tonnage outside the otherwise applicable framework of the 35 per cent, we would, however, limit ourselves during the period of our expansion to build only about 45 per cent of the British tonnage. According to present British strength, as laid down by treaty, this would amount to 23,680 tons, i.e. only 5,200 tons more than 35 per cent. From the military point of view this would be of no great advantage, but we would have established in principle our departure from the 35 per cent in the category of submarines, avoiding at the

[67] Concerning Churchill, see the report by Királdy-Lukács, Hungarian Chargé d'Affaires in London, November 19, 1945. OL Küm. Pol. 1935—2/1—3597.

[68] Report by Masirevich, Hungarian Minister to Berlin, June 15, 1935, Strictly confidential. OL Küm. Pol. 1935—2/1—2030.

[69] Hoare was born the son of a rich family of financiers and businessmen. He was short of stature, but an active, intellectually agile, determined politician, and also a sportsman. He had worked hard to acquire the necessary skill and experience. When he was appointed Secretary of State for Foreign Affairs, he was already a wearied and ailing old man, but he had retained his strong ambition to hold public functions. In his memoirs (Lord Templewood, *Nine Troubled Years*, London, 1951) he discloses interesting points about important details of the British policy of appeasement, about Baldwin, Eden, and Vansittart. On the other hand, Lord Simon's memoirs (*Retrospect*, London, 1952) are of very little practical use, tiresome, inaccurate, the poorest example of contemporary memoirs.

same time the chance of inviting an appreciable hardening of the British position on account of the trifling increase. SK, therefore, propose to settle for 45 per cent (but to leave it to the delegation's discretion whether to claim 50 per cent at first for tactical reasons, so as to be able to retreat to the lower figure . . .).

"2. SK take the view that it would be preferable to demand rounding-off the figures in each case when this seems best on the grounds of equity."

On the next day, Admiral Reader replied in a telegram to the naval delegation in London as follows:

"1. Discussion has resulted in a figure of 45 per cent. Will take effect on construction programme only after 1936.

"2. No general rule for rounding-off. Provide for agreement as cases arise."[70]

On the same day, June 13, Hoesch, the German Ambassador in London, had the first official conversation with the new British Foreign Secretary, Sir Samuel Hoare. (Hoare became head of the Foreign Office on June 7, 1935.) The talk was of a general nature and provided some insight into the foreign political problems of the British Government.[71] Hardly a word was said of the naval negotiations, a clear indication that Hoesch had been left out of that deal.

On June 13, Ribbentrop came back to London, and on the 17th he joined in the naval conversations at the Carlton Hotel.[72] On this occasion, Ribbentrop

---

[70] Memorandum by the Chief of the Group for Naval Conferences, Berlin, June 12, 1935, Secret. Raeder's telgram: 7790/E 559837, June 13, DGFP Ser. C. Vol. IV, No. 148, pp. 295—296.

[71] In a talk with Hoesch, Hoare referred to the difficulties which threatened in regard to relations between Japan and China as well as in regard to the Ethiopian question. He then turned to European problems, and expressed the view that a decision would have to be taken within the next twelve months as to whether a final settlement was possible or whether affairs in Europe would assume ever more threatening forms. Hoesch made reference to the German—British naval negotiations and stressed the complete harmony of views which had been achieved between Germany and Britain on the air question. In connection with the Eastern pact he explained that looming behind it was an anti-German alliance which the Soviet Union was trying to use more than ever for penetrating the heart of Europe. Hoare repeatedly stated that he could not believe that Russia constituted a threat to Germany and said he thought that Germany would do herself and the world a great service if she were to facilitate the settlement of the remaining questions and particularly the conclusion of the Western air pact, by adopting a positive attitude to the Eastern pact. The Ambassador in Great Britain to the Foreign Ministry, London, June 13, 1935. DGFP Ser. C. Vol. IV, No. 151, pp. 304—306.

[72] The conversation was also attended, on the German side, by Admiral Schuster, Dr. Kordt, and Dr. Schmidt; on the British side, by Craigie and Danckwerts. In the view of the interpreter, Dr. Schmidt, Ribbentrop was very distrustful. Before the talks Ribbentrop conferred with the members of the German delegation in his apartment in the Carlton Hotel. The officials huddled around him in the middle of the room, lest the British should listen to their secrets by means of microphones hidden in the walls. At times Schmidt could hardly refrain from laughing when the people were putting their heads together round Ribbentrop and kept whispering about battleships, cruisers, and tonnages. Cf. Schmidt, op. cit., p. 315.

objected to the British having inserted in the final text — at variance with an understanding arrived at earlier and again on that very morning — the sentence stating that the Anglo-German Naval Agreement should serve to facilitate an international agreement. Craigie explained that this had been done for the sake of the French; besides, it was in harmony with their earlier understanding. It should be evident that their accord was intended not to impede but to facilitate their relationships with other countries, or it might be a disservice to them. It was in the interest of both countries to show the agreement as an arrangement most advantageous to the French. Ribbentrop was reassured. He said that he would do everything in order to avoid giving the impression in other countries that this agreement involved anything particularly secret. Though he could not understand the reasons why the French should be upset by the outcome of the present negotiations. This first step was at last a possible contribution towards the limitation of armaments. This was supposed to be a generous gesture on Hitler's part, especially since it might be expected that a third power would increase its armaments. No one could know what to expect from the Russo-French military alliance and from Russia's entirely "obscure" attitude. Craigie did his best to soothe Ribbentrop's anxiety, saying that the state of agitation among the French was due to their Latin temperament. After settling a few details and removing some differences in the drafting, they agreed on the final text of the agreement.[73]

And there came at last the day of June 18, when the Anglo-German Naval Agreement was signed at the British Foreign Office. In his opening address Foreign Secretary Sir Samuel Hoare stressed that the agreement did not only serve the interests of the two countries, but was also an important factor in promoting the conclusion of a general agreement for the limitation of naval armaments. The British Government and public opinion regarded it as "an event of historic importance," but it would be of still greater importance if the two Governments regarded it also as a stepping stone on the road towards a general international treaty designed to avert that most serious of all evils — unlimited competition in the construction of naval armaments. Ribbentrop said that he associated himself in the name of his delegation fully and completely with those remarks. He believed that this agreement constituted the first practical step towards a limitation of armaments and the pacification of Europe in general after years of negotiations and conferences. Any naval rivalry was for ever rendered impossible. Thus began a new chapter in the history of their countries and the foundation was laid for a future friendship of the two great countries. Sir Bolton Eyres-Monsell, First Lord of the Admiralty, then said that the British delegation were handing the German delegation the note defining the agreement that had been reached, although it was an unusual procedure to sign a Naval Agreement until the details had been examined. The British delegation did so in full confidence that the German delegation would now bring forward their proposals regarding the strength and building programme of the German Navy. Ribbentrop in reply said the German delegation was of the opinion that, now that an agreement on the matter of principle had been

[73] Record of the Anglo-German Naval Discussion at 6 p. m. on Monday, June 17, 1935. (At the Carlton Hotel, London, June 17, 1935.) DGFP Ser. C. Vol. IV, No. 154, pp. 311—315.

110

concluded, there should be no obstacle in the way of open and frank discussions on the details.

The text of the Naval Agreement, as included in an exchange of notes read as follows:

"1. During the last few days the representatives of the German Government and His Majesty's Government in the United Kingdom have been engaged in conversations, the primary purpose of which has been to prepare the way for the holding of a general conference on the subject of the limitation of naval armaments. I have now much pleasure in notifying Your Excellency of the formal acceptance by His Majesty's Government in the United Kingdom of the proposal of the German Government discussed at those conversations that the future strength of the German navy in relation to the aggregate naval strength of the Members of the British Commonwealth of Nations should be in the proportion of 35 : 100. His Majesty's Government in the United Kingdom regard this proposal as a contribution of the greatest importance to the cause of future naval limitation. They further believe that the agreement, which they regard as a permanent and definite agreement as from today between the two Governments, will facilitate the conclusion of a general agreement on the subject of naval limitation between all the naval Powers of the world.

"2. His Majesty's Government in the United Kingdom also agree with the explanations which were furnished by the German representatives in the course of the recent discussions in London as to the method of application of this principle. These explanations may be summarized as follows:

"*(a)* The ratio 35 : 100 is to be a permanent relationship, i.e. the total tonnage of the German fleet shall never exceed a percentage of 35 of the aggregate tonnage of the naval forces, as defined by treaty, of the Members of the British Commonwealth of Nations or, if there should in future be no treaty limitations of this tonnage, a percentage of 35 of the aggregate of the actual tonnages of the Members of the British Commonwealth of Nations.

"*(b)* If any future general treaty of naval limitation should not adopt the method of limitation by agreed ratios between the fleets of different Powers, the German Government will not insist on the incorporation of the ratio mentioned in the preceding sub-paragraph in such future general treaty, provided tha the method therein adopted for the future limitation of naval armaments is such as to give Germany full guarantees that this ratio can be maintained.

"*(c)* Germany will adhere to the ratio 35 : 100 in all circumstances, e.g. the ratio will not be affected by the construction of other Powers. If the general equilibrium of naval armaments, as normally maintained in the past, should be violently upset by any abnormal and exceptional construction by other Powers, the German Government reserve the right to invite His Majesty's Government in the United Kingdom to examine the new situation thus created.

"*(d)* The German Government favour, in the matter of limitation of naval armaments, that system which divides naval vessels into categories, fixing the maximum tonnage and/or armament for vessels in each category, and allocate the tonnage to be allowed to each Power by categories of vessels. Consequently, in principle, and subject to *(f)* below, the German Government are prepared to apply the 35 per cent ratio to the tonnage of each category of vessel to be maintained and to make any variation of this ratio in a particular category or categories dependent on the arrangements to this end that may be arrived at in a future general treaty on naval limitation, such arrangements being based on the principle that any increase in one category would be compensated for by a corresponding reduction in others. If no general treaty on naval limitation should be concluded, or if the future general treaty should not contain provisions creating limitation by categories, the manner and degree in which the German Government will have the right to vary the 35 per cent ratio in one or more categories will be a matter for settlement by agreement between the German Government and His Majesty's Government in the United Kingdom, in the light of the naval situation then existing.

"(e) If, and for so long as, other important naval Powers retain a single category for cruisers and destroyers, Germany shall enjoy the right to have [a] single category for these two classes of vessels, although she would prefer to see these classes in two categories.

"(f) In the matter of submarines, however, Germany, while not exceeding the ratio of 35 : 100 in respect of total tonnage, shall have the right to possess a submarine tonnage equal to the total submarine tonnage possessed by the Members of the British Commonwealth of Nations. The German Government, however, undertake that, except in the circumstances indicated in the immediately following sentence, Germany's submarine tonnage shall not exceed 45 per cent of the total of that possessed by the Members of the British Commonwealth of Nations. The German Government reserve the right, in the event of a situation arising which in their opinion makes it necessary for Germany to avail herself of her right to a percentage of submarine tonnage exceeding the 45 per cent above mentioned, to give notice to this effect to His Majesty's Government in the United Kingdom and agree that the matter shall be the subject of friendly discussion before the German Government exercise that right.

"(g) Since it is highly improbable that the calculation of the 35 per cent ratio should give for each category of vessels tonnage figures exactly divisible by the maximum individual tonnage permitted for ships in that category, it may be necessary that adjustments should be made in order that Germany shall not be debarred from utilizing her tonnage to the full. It has consequently been agreed what [sic] the German Government and His Majesty's Government in the United Kingdom will settle by common accord that [sic] adjustments are necessary for this purpose and it is understood that this procedure shall not result in any substantial or permanent departure from the ratio 35 : 100 in respect of total strengths.

"3. With reference to sub-paragraph (e) of the explanations set out above, I have the honour to inform you that His Majesty's Government in the United Kingdom have taken note of the reservation and recognise the right therein set out, on the understanding that the 35 : 100 ratio will be maintained in default of agreement to the contrary between the two Governments."[74]

---

[74] The Agreement (Anglo-German Naval Conversations, London, 1935, June 18) is published — on the basis of DGNF Ser. C. Vol. IV, No. 156, pp. 319—326 and a British White Paper, Cmd. 4953 — in *Documents on International Affairs 1935*, Vol. I, pp. 142—145. The signature was attended, on the British side, by Secretary of State for Foreign Affairs Sir Samuel Hoare, First Lord of the Admi-

After the first session of the British National Government. R. MacDonald leads
the Members. Behind him L. H. Thomas, Baldwin and Lord Reading, Snowden,
Sir Herbert Samuel, N. Chamberlain, Sir Samuel Hoare, Sir Philip Cunliffe-Lister,
Lord Sankey

Britain's two Ambassadors to Berlin, Sir Eric Phipps and his successor,
Sir Nevile Henderson

Nazi leaders celebrating the proclamation of conscription, 17th March, 1935

Sir Robert Vansittart, Permanent Under-Secretary of State, Foreign Office, 1930—1938

Sir Winston Churchill

M. M. Litvinov, the Soviet
Foreign Minister

Hitler's talk with A. Eden and Foreign Secretary Sir John Simon, 25th March, 1935

Ribbentrop at London Airport in June, 1935

Described like this, it all seems to be a fair bargain free of ulterior motives. (See also Appendix IV, p. 185.) If, however, one tries to look behind the appearance, one can see that before the final agreement the British had to make an important adjustment in order to remove the differences between the Foreign Office and the Admiralty. Moreover, some details even permit to arrive at certain conclusions regarding the undecidedness of various personalities. We have in mind here, first of all, the Permanent Under Secretary of State for Foreign Affairs, Vansittart. At the time of the Stresa conference Vansittart, speaking for his superiors, Foreign Secretary Simon and Prime Minister MacDonald, said: "You can't make two empty sacks stand upright." After the change of Government his relation to Hoare, the new Foreign Secretary, was different. Vansittart and the brain trust in the Treasury, Sir Warren Fisher, would have liked Eden as head of the Foreign Office, as we have already pointed out. Nevertheless, both could work better with Hoare than with Simon. Sir Robert and Sir Warren clearly saw Hitler's aggressive designs and, therefore, they combined their energies in the fight for British rearmament and for stalling for time. "Vansittart's fertile mind and unequalled knowledge of European politics," Hoare said, "were invaluable to me, whilst my more conventional methods may have been useful to him."[75] According to certain information it was Vansittart who at the last moment made an attempt to obstruct the conclusion of the Naval Agreement. The Foreign Office view, influenced by Vansittart, could also be seen from what Sir Eric Phipps, the British Ambassador to Germany, told the Hungarian Minister in Berlin, Masirevich, in the middle of June. He stated that "England has accepted as a basis of negotiation the 35 per cent ratio demanded by Germany, although this is a very high basis in view of the great difference between British and German maritime interests."[76]

In his memoirs written shortly before his death, Ribbentrop referred to Vansittart's attitude at the time of the signing of the Naval Agreement. He believed that Vansittart was responsible for a last-minute "hitch". When the Foreign Office tried to make ratification dependent on the agreement of other Versailles Treaty powers, Sir Robert Craigie took Ribbentrop aside and asked him not to call on Vansittart. But he did anyhow. Ribbentrop recorded: "I ... called on the Permanent Under-Secretary at the Foreign Office, Sir Robert Vansittart, but could not discover his real opinion ... He seemed

---

ralty Sir Bolton Eyres-Monsell, Assistant Under-Secretary of State R. L. Craigie of the Foreign Office, Vice-Admiral C. J. C. Little, Deputy Chief of the Naval Staff, Captain W. H Danckwerts of the Admiralty, Mr. R. C. Cox of the Foreign Office, and A. W. Clarke on behalf of the CID; on the German side: by Ambassador Extraordinary and Plenipotentiary Joachim von Ribbentrop, Rear-Admiral K. C Schuster, Captain E. Wassner, Lieutenant Commander H. Kiderlen, Secretary Dr. E. Kordt, and the interpreter, Dr. Paul Schmidt.

[75] Colvin, *op. cit.*, pp. 47, 64.

[76] Strictly confidential report by Masirevich, Berlin, January 15, 1935. OL Küm. Pol. 1935—2/5—2028. Thomas Jones, a trusted man of Baldwin, in 1936 recommended to the Prime Minister the removal of Phipps as an obstacle to better relations with Germany. Sir Eric Phipps was explicitly warning the British Government that the question in Germany was no longer "whether she shall expand but where and when." *Cf.* Colvin, *op. cit.*, pp. 47, 54.

to be extraordinarily nervous and I had the impression that he did not like the course which events had taken ... I wondered whether the reason was that he was such a pronounced Francophile... He was undoubtedly the great opponent of all German aspirations and throughout the world 'Vansittartism' has become the symbol of hatred for the Germans."[77]

Distressed at the policy of *The Times*, edited by Geoffrey Dawson and influenced by Lord Lothian, Vansittart wrote to a friend in May 1935 that, "only *The Times* and the weaker-minded members of the House of Lords could fail to be impressed by Germany's avowed military intentions."[78] Yet the same Vansittart at last gave his consent to the Naval Agreement. It is true, he was confronted with an unexpected situation. He later confided to Jan Masaryk, the Czechoslovak Minister in London: "The Germans came with a precise and elaborate plan. Actually they had the ships already on the shipyards so there was no question of any kind of agreement. Craigie, who on the part of the Foreign Office talked with Ribbentrop, when entering Vansittart's office said: We must decide at once, or else they will go home, although the experts are in favour of an agreement. Vansittart replied: thereupon I gave immediately my consent and with regard to the Foreign Office, I have assumed responsibility for a matter of far-reaching consequence. Because of this agreement, there will be 400,000 more tons of German shipping on the North Sea ... We seem to have arrived at a point where he who takes the initiative will succeed even if he is wrong about it."[79]

In the same month, however, Vansittart resolutely opposed the conclusion of another agreement — an air pact — with Germany.[80] He dissuaded Prime Minister Baldwin from meeting Hitler, either on board a ship in the North Sea or at Chequers, where the German Chancellor would have been pleased to fly. And it was he who at times, and still with success, prevailed upon the British Cabinet not to enter into pro-German negotiations contrary to the Versailles system. Sir Robert Vansittart pondered over his remarks and on November 7 wrote to Lord Wigram, the King's Secretary, a letter summarizing his views:

"I do not think it would be profitable to undertake any serious attempt to [make] an agreement with Germany until our own national re-equipment is well under way. It is clear that some agreements are always matters of bargain, [however], you can drive a much better bargain when you are strong than when you are weak. Secondly, it would be essential that any such exploration should be undertaken *à trois* and not *à deux*; in other words, that we should have to act with the French. If we did not do so, the French would be all the time going behind our backs at Berlin, and we correspondingly should be compelled to go behind theirs. The results would be that Germany would play one Power off against the other and raise her terms accordingly. In fact the terms might be too high to be payable.

[77] Published, on the basis of the Ribbentrop memoirs, by Colvin, *op. cit.*, pp. 64—65.

[78] *Ibid.*, p. 47.

[79] Masaryk to Beneš, London, July 12, 1935. AMZV Beneš Papers.

[80] Vansittart to Foreign Secretary Hoare, July 30, 1935, Vansittart Papers. Quoted by Colvin, *op. cit.*, p. 48.

"This question of terms brings one right up against the central difficulty. Any arrangement with Germany will have to be paid for, and handsomely paid for. Otherwise it will not even work temporarily, let alone hold permanently, and nothing that will not fulfil the latter requisite is really greatly worth while. Now I am convinced that modern Germany is highly expansive and will become highly explosive if it is sought to cramp her everywhere. But the inevitable expansion can only take place either in Europe ot Africa. Therefore, if we are to undertake eventually and seriously any negotiation, we must be prepared to pay in one of these two quarters. If the expansion were to be in Europe, it would be at other people's expense. If it is to be in Africa, it will be at our expense.

"I do not think there can be any question that it will have to take the latter form. Any attempt at giving Germany a free hand to annex other people's property in central or eastern Europe is both absolutely immoral and completely contrary to all the principles of the League which form the backbone of the policy of this country. Any British Government that attempted to do such a deal would almost certainly be brought down in ignominy — and deservedly. It would have been of no use to run the risk that we have recently been running to stand up for the League if we ourselves were going to destroy it later.

"Any suggestion that a British Government contemplated leaving, let alone inviting, Germany to satisfy her land hunger at Russia's expense would quite infallibly split this country from top to bottom, and split it just as deeply and disastrously as France is now split, though on rather different lines. This is an undoubted fact, whatever we may think of it, and I hope it will always be in the minds of our political folk.

"We therefore come down to the basic fact that if any lasting agreement is to be made with Germany, some expansion will have to be allowed for, and that expansion can only take place by restoring to her some of, not all of, her former colonies. This conclusion will do doubt raise considerable objection on the Right in this country, but it will have to be faced in the long run."[81]

The King, who was not in favour of "appeasement at any price," and whom Vansittart could turn to with confidence, died in January 1936. After his death the Cabinet's policy turned from collective security to appeasement. There was no mention any more of an Eastern pact. Heads of states and Ambassadors followed behind the royal bier from a Europe that would soon be no more. It is beyond doubt that — as we shall see — other thinking British politicians also were against the naval negotiations, yet Vansittart found himself in a position where he had to give his consent on behalf of the Foreign Office, unlike the Admiralty which had from the outset urged agreement. Admiral Chatfield, Chief of the Naval Staff, was in favour of the agreement for reasons similar to those for which Vansittart opposed it. But let us look at a few illustrating facts.

In 1938 the British Ambassador to Germany, Sir Nevile Henderson, reported about his conversation with Marshal Göring. On that occasion Göring had stated regretfully how little the 1935 Naval Agreement was appreciated in Britain. Having received this report of Ambassador Henderson, the British

---

[81] A letter from Sir Robert on November 7 to Lord Wigram, the King's Secretary. *Cf.* Colvin, *op. cit.*, pp. 50—51.

Admiralty requested the Foreign Office to let the Germans know that, on the contrary, "the Admiralty attached and still attaches the greatest importance to the Agreement," and called attention to a newspaper article which reflected a sensible appraisal and said among other things: "In British naval circles, at least, this agreement is held to be one of the greatest and most beneficial diplomatic achievements of the post-war era." (A competent official of the Foreign Office, who unintentionally expressed the still existing difference of opinions, added this marginal note: "Slight exaggeration !")[82]

Admiral Chatfield during his term as First Sea Lord dominated the CID. "His line was that we must cut our coat according to our cloth; that we cannot fight Germany, Italy and Japan at the same time; that therefore we must try and detach at least one member from this group; that probably Italy is the easiest to detach. [This was written in 1938.] Thus it seems that this Admiral is responsible for Chamberlain's foreign policy."[83]

In 1935—36, however, the attitude of Chatfield and the Admiralty had indicated that military circles in Britain were seeing Germany as the potential enemy.[84] According to well-informed Hungarian diplomats, the Anglo-German Naval Agreement "was opposed by the Foreign Office, and its conclusion was due solely to the firm stand of the British Admiralty, which viewed the agreement as an excellent deal for Britain."[85]

Besides, the British press did not conceal during the naval negotiations that the Admiralty had the firm intention not to miss the opportunity to prevent for ever the development of an Anglo-German naval competition and that the agreement between Britain and Germany would have as one of its important results the elimination of the possibility for the two countries to build their fleets in secret. Germany agreed in principle to the provision in Article 10 of the London Treaty which made it a mutual obligation of the interested powers to exchange information about naval construction.[86]

This view, which prevailed in Admiralty circles, was naive and tactically erroneous and also failed to recognize the real nature of Hitler's intentions and of his political machinations, requires no comment.

[82] W. Strang to Captain W. H. Danckwerts, May 16, 1938. P. R. O. Adm. 116/3378. The quoted article was written by H. Bywater and published by the *Daily Telegraph* on December 6, 1937.

[83] *Dalton's Diary*, 1937—40, December 8, 1938.

[84] Confidential report by Masirevich, the Hungarian Minister in London, July 23, 1936. OL Küm. Pol. 1936—2/7—2616.

[85] Report by Bóbrik, Counsellor of the Hungarian Legation in Berlin, July 6, 1935. OL Küm. Pol. 1935—21/5—2246. Bóbrik obtained his information from G. Köpke, head of Department II in the German Foreign Office.

[86] *Daily Telegraph*, June 4, 1935.

"Nothing will deter me. There is no international law, there is no treaty to deter me from grasping the opportunity that presents itself at any time."

(Hitler's words, quoted by H. Rauschning: *Gespräche mit Hitler*.)

THE EFFECT OF THE NAVAL AGREEMENT

During the rather important and specific discussions which followed the signature of the Naval Agreement, the British continually referred to the effects and to the repercussions the agreement had at home and abroad. Apparent deference to various manifestations in Parliament, in the press and to public opinion in general, is a traditional political practice of British Governments. Such was the case especially with regard to the political bargain which was questioned in advance by certain prestige groups and even official circles concerning its rightness and usefulness. Also serious foreign political consequences had to be faced, or at least it was expected that the agreement was to be attacked or criticized abroad.

How then was the Anglo-German Naval Agreement received in Britain and outside of the British Isles by other sea powers? How did the British Government try to overcome the objections and opposing opinions?

Part of the British press was rather surprised by the agreement, because — as was pointed out in a press survey issued by MTI (the Hungarian Telegraphic Agency) — the British Foreign Office insisted to the very last "that it is only a matter of preliminary conversations which will not lead to any agreement. The motives of Britain: (1) She has been disgusted that France and her allies are bringing the Soviet Union into the heart of Central Europe. (2) She is alarmed by Italy's obstinacy in Ethiopia which poses a serious menace to the British position in the Sudan."[1]

The general astonishment was soon followed by affirmative statements in the press. The moderately Conservative, Liberal, and left-wing British press gladly welcomed the Anglo-German Naval Agreement because it saw its value in the fact that Germany was limiting her naval strength relative to that of Britain without receiving any compensation, and that Berlin desisted once and for all from competing with the British naval forces.

The Labour Party's *Daily Herald* also found the agreement valuable. In the view of the columnist, the importance was not so much the accord in

[1] MTI (Hungarian Telegraphic Agency), June 19, 1935. OL K. 428. 565.

117

itself than Germany's unilateral and voluntary statement that she would keep her naval strength within certain limits.

The newspapers pointed out that Germany had been able to violate the military clauses of the Versailles Treaty without any major consequences and nothing would have prevented her from starting also a race in naval armaments. Thus political realism suggested that the elimination of this danger should be regarded as a positive factor.

According to *The Times*, the agreement was more specific and covered a wider area than had been thought at the outset. The next intention of the British Government was to continue now without delay the good work which started with the Anglo-German Naval Agreement and to invite France, Italy and Soviet Russia to talk over the adjustment of the new agreement to a general treaty on limitation of naval armaments. If France insisted on increasing her naval strength, then the British and German Governments certainly would have to raise their respective tonnage. Needless to say that Britain had not the slightest intention to cut off her existing obligations when she concluded the Naval Agreement. Locarno stood as valid as ever. Britain did not want any new agreement to become a detriment of old friendships. On the contrary, she was intent on persuading the other countries to enter into a general treaty on the reduction of naval forces.

The Times remarked among other things that in terms of submarines, Britain was rather weak as compared to France (only 51 against 96) and, therefore, Germany, with only one-third of Britain's tonnage, would be relatively at a much greater disadvantage with regard to France than Berlin might have assumed.

The *Daily Mail* wrote that the agreement, diplomatically interpreted, meant that Britain had resigned herself to the situation created by the violation of the military provisions of the Treaty of Versailles. Britain had obviously come to the conclusion that under the given circumstances it would be better to save what she could.

The *Morning Post* expressed the summary opinion that the agreement was satisfactory from the naval point of view, but alarming from the diplomatic point of view. On March 18, Britain had most energetically protested in Berlin against the repudiation of treaty obligations and three months later she openly helped Germany to violate the naval provisions of the Versailles Treaty. In such conditions France's attitude was quite natural.

According to the *Daily Telegraph*, the revival of Germany's naval power restored the old strategical importance of the North Sea and Britain's naval policies must be radically changed to suit the new situation. It was probable that the Scapa Flow naval base would reopen soon.

The same paper wrote also that the agreement allowed Germany a submarine fleet of 19,635 tons in addition to the twelve small submarines under construction, so that Germany would be stronger under the sea than she had been in August 1914, when she had possessed all in all twenty-six submarines. (See also Appendix, V, p. 189.)[2]

---

[2] *Ibid.* — A commentary upon the Naval Agreement published by the Conservative weekly *The Spectator* is of really documentary value. Here we quote it in full: "For what happened was that an opportunity was offered and was forthwith

So much for the press. In Parliament, in the House of Commons, and the night before in the BBC, First Lord of the Admiralty Sir Bolton Eyres-Monsell explained and evaluated the naval negotiations and the agreement. The essence of what he had to say was that, in the view of the Admiralty, Britain would have shouldered a serious responsibility if she had declined the German offer. After considering the foreseeable practical consequences, the British Government had accepted the proposal, not only in the interest of the future development of good relations between Britain and Germany, but also in order to create thereby an instrument facilitating the conclusion of a general treaty on naval disarmament. The Anglo—German Agreement would make it possible to avert for all time the threat of naval rivalry between the two countries.

The agreement might become of great importance also from the point of view of the interests of the other states and furnish a point of departure for further negotiations. The agreement, Sir Bolton said, can be an essential contribution to world peace.

The British Government considered only the actual situation when it entered into the agreement. It was aware that naval construction in Germany was already outside the limits set by the Treaty of Versailles. The critics had made even the point that Britain had no right to separate the issue of naval disarmament from the questions of land and air disarmament. The British Government could not accept this view, because it was of the opinion that the existing naval treaties must be replaced by a new one.

Britain wanted to proceed in this direction, in complete accord with the signatories of the Washington and London Naval Treaties. This did not mean, however, that, if a future general treaty of naval limitation should be reached, it would in any way hinder the British Government's efforts aimed at land and air disarmament. Quite to the contrary, in all three categories of armaments the British Government attached the greatest importance to the prevention of an armament race. But the British Government could not adopt the view

---

grasped. If it had not been it would in all likelihood never have been secured. We have had examples enough of what the disregard of German offers of armament limitation costs. Invariably the next offer forthcoming is at a higher level. Herr Hitler in his speech of May 21st openly declared his willingness to be satisfied with a navy not stronger than 35 per cent of the British. It was the French, after all, who rejected the German proposals of April 1934, which provided for a Reichswehr of 200,000 men. As a result the German army today is well over 500,000. With that and other examples before their eyes British ministers would have been guilty of criminal negligence if they had not taken Herr Hitler at his word and tested his sincerity. They have done so and the result is eminently satisfactory." *The Spectator*, June 21, 1935. p. 1049. — Three weeks later the same paper already lectured the British Government: "What is important about the German naval figures just disclosed is not the fact that Germany is proposing to equip herself with 25,000-ton battle cruisers — all that is well within the four corners of the recent naval agreement — but that vessels of this magnitude could be laid down in complete secrecy. There is, of course, a drastic censorship which has completely robbed the papers of any initiative for enterprise in news-getting, and there is no reason to believe that anything but preliminary steps in the construction of the vessels have been taken. But the incident demonstrates conclusively the need for effective international supervision of any disarmament agreement that may be concluded." *The Spectator*, July 12, 1935, p. 42.

that naval disarmament should be postponed until some progress had been made in the negotiations for land and air disarmament.[3]

Sir Bolton Eyres-Monsell took up also the question of submarines. In connection with the agreement, he said, Germany had declared that she would never again start unrestricted submarine warfare and was willing to accept forthwith the former (London) naval treaty's provisions regarding limitation of submarine warfare, if all sea powers acceded to those rules.

The debate following the statement of the First Lord of the Admiralty to the House of Commons singled out a few "delicate" issues. A question was put by M.P. Hall as to whether the British Government wished to call a conference of the signatories of the naval treaties in force, and whether it thought the Anglo-German Naval Agreement was not contrary to the clauses of the Treaty of Versailles.

Sir Bolton Eyres-Monsell replied that, with regard to the first question, discussions were under way with the other powers. As far as the second question was concerned, it raised a legal point, which must be addressed to the competent minister.

M. P. Hall asked the Prime Minister whether the House would be given an opportunity to consider all consequences of the agreement. Prime Minister Baldwin replied that bilateral negotiations were of a very delicate nature and if the honourable members should wish to debate all details, the Government could never conclude bilateral international agreements.

Lansbury, the leader of the Opposition, stated that members did not intend to cause difficulties to the Government, but extremely important questions were coming up and these ought to be put before the House of Commons. Prime Minister Baldwin said in reply that this might become possible when Parliament would discuss the budget of the First Lord of the Admiralty.

When the debate was resumed, Labour M. P. Cocks raised a few questions. He expressed concern about the fact that the German naval force might reach 35 per cent of the British and thus become supreme in the Baltic. He wondered whether the British Government had asked the governments of the Soviet Union, Sweden, Latvia, Estonia, Poland, Lithuania, and other Baltic States for their opinions regarding the Anglo-German Naval Agreement. The reply of Foreign Secretary Sir Samuel Hoare was a clear "no." He added that the Soviet Government had been officially informed about the contents of the Naval Agreement.

The interpellator continued questioning whether the British Government intended to guarantee the frontiers of those states which were left to the tender mercies of Germany as a result of this agreement by accepting the proposed Eastern pact. Sir Samuel Hoare again answered in the negative, rejecting at the same time the assumption that those small states were at the mercy of Germany. He asserted that the agreement was favourable not only to Britain and Germany but to all sea powers.

Another member of Parliament, Mr. Thorne, asked whether the Foreign Secretary was aware of the fact that the agreement constituted a breach of

[3] Statement by the Rt. Hon. Sir Bolton Eyres-Monsell, First Lord of the Admiralty, June 21, 1935. (In the House of Commons, *Hansard*, June 21, 1935, coll. 709—11.) *Documents on International Affairs 1935*, Vol. I, pp. 145—146.

the Versailles Treaty and the Stresa agreements and whether Anthony Eden, the Minister for League of Nations Affairs, would make a statement after returning home. (Eden had left on June 20 for Paris and Rome to "explain" the Naval Agreement.) Hoare said that a statement would probably be made, but he could not accept the interpellator's conclusions as correct.

M. P. Harris asked whether the full text of the agreement would be deposited with the League of Nations and submitted to the Disarmament Conference. The Foreign Secretary requested the member to make a special interpellation on this matter.[4]

In the House of Lords the debate over the Naval Agreement was opened on June 26. The first speaker was Lord Lloyd Dolobrand, a Conservative peer. In his view the Anglo-German Naval Agreement had dramatically changed the naval and military situation. He characterized as dangerous the system of percentage ratios or ratios by categories, which paid no attention to Great Britain's overseas commitments. He reminded the House of Lords that the country had to build ships not only for the North Sea but also for the Far Eastern and Indian stations and the Mediterranean. If Britain wished to have more destroyers in the Far East or in the Mediterranean, the force facing Britain in the North Sea would automatically and disproportionately grow. This was the reason why the ratio system was so dangerous. Great Britain was building warships in order to keep her fleet strong in the Far East, an essential action because of Japan's growing expansionism. As Britain is increasing her Far Eastern naval forces, so will also Germany's fleet grow. It was extremely peculiar also that such an agreement was signed three months after the British Government had presented to the German Government a note of protest concerning the introduction of general military service. It would be highly regrettable if the British Government would take any step which could make France likely to believe that Britain had changed her course of policy or that the solidarity and intimacy evolved in Stresa were in danger. One might suppose, the noble Lord explained, that the creation of the new German Navy was inevitable as the natural aspiration of a great nation which, although without overseas possessions, was already building up a rapidly expanding

---

[4] MTI, London, June 24, 1935. OL K. 428.565. — Labour M. P. Cocks, quoted in the text, also in the months following the conclusion of the Naval Agreement was strongly critical of the increasingly pro-German policy of the Government. On August 1, 1935, he stated in the House of Commons that he was "intensely alarmed by what he had seen of recent tendencies in British foreign policy to go rather on the side of Germany in the various discussions." He objected to the British Government's refusal to do anything whatever to prevent the export to Germany of aeroplanes, munitions of war and materials for munitions of war. A tremendous change "had been taking place in the Press almost universally during the last two or three months." He was informed that "very strong pressure" had been brought to bear upon newspapers by the British Foreign Office, "not to say anything very much about the real things that were taking place in Germany and to publish articles rather sympathetic to the Nazi regime, or at any rate, which were not hostile, but very conciliatory and sympathetic in character." The Labour M. P. continued that there had even been articles by well-known Labour correspondents which gave Hitler to understand that some Labour bodies in Britain were sympathetic to his policy or to his ideals. Cf. Salvemini, op. cit., p. 222.

121

maritime trade. It was comprehensible that Germany would want a larger fleet than the one authorized by the Versailles Peace Treaty. Not her claim, but her methods, were to be condemned. The German submarines had been in existence before the Naval Agreement was concluded. The Germans opened the negotiations with a *fait accompli*, thereby making this method clearly known to the whole world.[5]

Lord Lloyd's speech was followed by a long debate. Lord Lothian congratulated the Government on the conclusion of the Anglo-German Naval Agreement. His only objection was that the basis for the tonnage ratio was the fleet of the whole British Empire and not just of Great Britain alone.

Admiral Lord Beatty declared that on the whole he was glad to see the Anglo-German Naval Agreement. He thought Britain had to thank Germany for the offer of the 35 per cent ratio. Had Germany offered 50 per cent, he said Britain would not have been able to do anything about it. He was of the opinion that the German attitude eliminated definitively and entirely any possibility of naval competition between the two nations.[6]

Lord Beatty then referred to the objections made in respect of submarine parity between Britain and Germany and declared that the London Naval Treaty had envisaged parity with other powers. A few of the powers which had not signed the London Treaty had even surpassed that level. The submarine fleet of France amounted to 180 per cent of the British submarine force. Consequently, he went on to say, there was no danger of Britain having made a mistake with regard to Germany. The British Government should be satisfied that Hitler had declared the German Government's readiness to scrap the entire submarine fleet. It was a pity that a few other countries had failed to follow this British policy.

The leader of the Labour Opposition, Lord Ponsonby, stated that his party was not against the agreement as such, but was opposed to the methods which were used to bring it about. In his view Britain should have discussed it also with France.

The debate was closed by Lord Londonderry's statement, which was in fact a clever excuse for the Naval Agreement. He claimed that the British

[5] Quoted by Edwards, *op. cit.*, pp. 172, 175.

[6] Lord Beatty's position was in many respects debatable. Hitler would have settled for less than 35 per cent if the British had driven him to the wall, since his declaration of his willingness to eliminate submarines completely was not taken seriously by any sensible statesman. Hitler repeatedly told people in confidential circles in the summer of 1933, as well as earlier and later, that Britain was a "wash-out" and he thought it would be inevitable to finish with her. An "initiated" man of Hitler's, P. Hanfstängel, called attention to the fact that a studied perusal of *Mein Kampf* might demonstrate that anything contained therein relating to England was of mere tactical value; Hitler knew well why he wrote what. *Cf.* Rauschning, *op. cit.* — Incidentally, Admiral Beatty's words are quoted literally, obviously in excuse of the German position by E. Raeder in his memoirs (Vol. II, p. 24): "*Ich bin der Meinung, dass wir den Deutschen Dank schuldig sind. Sie kamen zu uns mit ausgestreckten Händen und erklärten, dass sie mit dem Stärkeverhältnis von 35 : 100 einverstanden seien. Wenn sie andere Vorschläge gemacht hätten, hätten wir sie auch nicht hindern können. Dass wir nur wenigstens von einem Lande der Welt kein Wettrüsten zu befürchten haben, ist wahrlich eine Sache, für die man dankbar sein muss.*"

Government was still adhering to the Franco-British declaration of February 3, 1935, which was reaffirmed in Stresa, and which stipulated that neither Germany nor any other power could unilaterally modify the Peace Treaties. But the British people were a practical people who liked to face the facts. Since Germany was already increasing her naval strength beyond the limits imposed by the Peace Treaty, it was better for Great Britain not to engage in a competition but to circumscribe the effects of Germany's decision by concluding an agreement with her. The essence of the German proposal was the limitation of the size of their fleet to 35 per cent of the British naval strength. What could have been done against such an offer? The issue of limitation of air armaments had been broached in 1933 and the figures discussed at that time had long since been surpassed. If Britain would have disregarded the proposal for limitation of naval rivalry, she might have missed also the opportunity to eliminate a competition of the fleets which had poisoned the atmosphere already a quarter century before. Lord Londonderry emphasized that (1) Germany had made her offer to Britain and to no one else; (2) the agreement did not affect the freedom of other countries to continue their naval construction, and (3) if Britain had insisted on consulting with other countries before concluding the agreement, she would have definitively missed the opportunity to conclude the agreement alltogether. This in turn would have had incalculable effects on the position of both Great Britain and the other naval powers, and even with regard to the peace of the world.

Lord Londonderry proceeded to explain that the agreement did not affect the situation with regard to the other sea powers. If other powers also succeeded in reaching agreement with Germany concerning their land and air forces, and if such an agreement should not oblige Britain to keep to any particular strength, then those powers would do an important service to Britain and the whole world. It would never occur to Britain to request other nations not to do what the British Government had done by concluding the Anglo-German Naval Agreement, provided that such accords promoted the general reduction of armed forces.

The French Government had been informed of the outline of the proposed agreement on June 7, at the same time as the other signatories of the Washington Treaty. The British Government had received the reply from Paris just before the conclusion of the agreement, however, the criticism contained in the French note was not of such a nature as to restrain London from signing the agreement which allegedly served the peace of the world. If the French Government had been able to obtain a complete picture of the situation, it certainly would understand that the British step had been taken in the interests of France as well. The Lord also mentioned that at present France's naval force was 50 per cent of the British, that meant that she would still have a superiority of 43 per cent over Germany's naval strength. This situation was considerably better than the situation prior to World War I, when the French fleet was 30 per cent below the strength of the German fleet. No argument could be offered which could prove that if Britain had refrained from concluding the Naval Agreement, the position of the French or Italian fleet would be stronger. Lord Londonderry gave also a detailed answer to the submarine question. Essentially he argued that the British submarine fleet was equal in strength with the fleets of most of the European states and also with the Japanese fleet, while some states had even larger submarine forces. Germany, therefore, had every reason to claim the right to parity in this respect as well. She even had offered spontaneously that for the time being she would remain satisfied with 45 per cent of Britain's submarine strength. Germany had the right to parity in this field all the more as the submarine was different from other types of warships. Submarines cannot be counted in the same manner as other warships. Parity in this category was not the same as parity in the category of, for example, cruisers. The anxiety nevertheless was understandable because England's security had been seriously threatened by submarine attacks in World War I. The country had gained, however, at great cost and through bitter losses, sufficient experience which will protect Britain against future submarine attacks. Furthermore, Germany had freely accepted Part IV of the London Naval Treaty, which meant that in a future war Germany would not engage in unrestricted submarine warfare. (This argument had been put forward also by the First Lord of the Admiralty.)[7]

During those days the debate was continuing still in the House of Commons. We are selecting from the many speeches and interpellations some which are of special interest.

M. P. Mander asked the Foreign Secretary whether the Anglo-German Naval Agreement provided for the reciprocal supervision of naval forces and whether it laid down that the naval forces of the two countries were part of the League of Nations system of collective security. Sir Samuel Hoare gave a negative answer to the first part of the question. He added that the British Government hoped that Germany would co-operate within the League as one of its members, and if this should be the case, then the position of the German naval forces in any combined security system would be like that of any of the other members of the League of Nations.

Mander continued his interpellation by asking whether the Government realized now that the way in which it had reached the agreement was wrong. Sir Samuel said he could not agree with this remark.

M. P. Mason put the question whether the point was raised regarding control of naval armaments in connection with Germany. Sir Samuel Hoare requested the member to prepare a special interpellation on this issue.[8]

During June and July a great part of British society was almost incessantly preoccupied with the agreement. The significance of the accord was discussed in private gatherings and in public meetings alike.

First Lord of the Admiralty Sir Bolton Eyres-Monsell and Winston Churchill attended late in June a dinner in a London club and spoke of the need to strengthen the British fleet. Churchill proposed the floatation of a national defence loan with a view to reconstructing the British Navy. He said that the naval parade held at Spithead in the King's presence had displayed warships which had been destined for replacement for a quarter of a century. The brave

---

[7] Lord Londonderry, like so many other British politicians, at that time still accepted the German proposals and promises as full guarantees. See his speech in the House of Lords. (*Hansard*. June 26, 1935, coll. 903—11.) *Documents . . . ,* pp. 148—153.

[8] MTI, London, June 27, 1935. OL K. 428.565.

British seamen should not be assigned to serve on ships which might become their coffin in case they encountered up-to-date vessels.

Sir Bolton Eyres-Monsell explained in his speech that ill-informed people had often fallen in the past for the fanatical propaganda which claimed that peace and budgetary savings can be the result of unilateral disarmament. He was pleased to note that in this respect a great change in the public mind seemed to have occurred. The First Lord of the Admiralty then stated with satisfaction that in the course of the past four years, despite financial difficulties, the Government had allocated large sums for the expenditures for the Royal Navy. The expenditures in 1934 had been 20 per cent higher than at the time when the Government took office. The greatest achievement since the war's end was that in the four years ending with December 31, 1935, the construction of fifteen new cruisers had been authorized. Then Sir Bolton Eyres-Monsell warned against overestimating air armaments.

Coming to the question of submarines, he stated that in the course of the last war the submarines had been regarded as a deadly peril, which indeed they were. On account of the technological development, however, the Admiralty today does not take the submarines as seriously as before.

In conclusion he declared that, although in Great Britain the strongest possible air fleet was considered desirable, in the interest of imperial security the British Empire rather needed a strong navy. One should never forget that the defence of the British Empire was almost completely dependent on the Royal Navy.

Prime Minister Baldwin declared in a public speech that the Anglo-German Naval Agreement did not mean that Britain was departing from the policy of co-operation with France and Italy, as confirmed in Stresa. He said among other things that they saw in the Naval Agreement a practical means of bringing about a general disarmament pact and that they felt this agreement was the first step taken towards disarmament since the war. He deplored that two members of the House of Commons had insisted that it was impossible to believe that the Germans would keep their promise. His opinion was that in the absence of mutual trust there was nothing else to do than return to the "jungle law" and give up any hope for progress. In concluding the agreement, Germany and Britain were inspired by the same spirit and by the same honest intentions.

Chancellor of the Exchequer Neville Chamberlain also dealt with the Anglo-German Naval Agreement at a meeting of the Conservative Party. In his speech he said among other things that this agreement not only meant the limitation of competition between the German and British fleets, but showed the enormous growth of "good will" in Europe. He regarded as the next task of Britain the strengthening of this good will during the forthcoming negotiations of the European nations about the various angles of the disarmament issue.[9]

As to the official explanations for the conclusion of the Naval Agreement and the press comments it had provoked, as well as the true reasons underlying the whole affair — which were not elucidated with total frankness either by

[9] MTI, London, June 30, 1935. *Ibid.*

Cabinet members or by the British press — we would like to present here two items.

First, Foreign Secretary Hoare's statement to the Commons on the foreign political situation, including the Naval Agreement, and the ensuing and very interesting debate. Secondly, the confidential explanation which Sir Samuel Hoare sent on July 19 to the British Ambassador in Paris with the instruction that he might show it privately to some responsible personage in the French Foreign Ministry.

In the foreign policy debate in the House of Commons on July 11, Sir Samuel Hoare spoke about the *air pact* (it was a matter of urgency for the five powers concerned to reach agreement on limitation of air armaments), the *Eastern pact* (there were danger signs of war in Central and Eastern Europe, thus it was considered important to conclude a Danubian non-aggression pact as soon as possible), the question of *Austria's independence* (the British Government had always regarded the status of Austria as a key question of Europe from both the strategic and the economic point of view; any change in Austria's independent status would shake the peace of Europe to its very foundations; it was for this reason in the first place that Britain would welcome the earliest possible conclusion of a Danubian pact of non-aggression and non-intervention), *collective security* (for which the most appropriate forum would be the League of Nations; as long as the League was working towards this end, Britain would always be ready to partake of the general responsibilities), and *French friendship* (Britain and France were primarily responsible for the settlement of 1919; Britain would, now as before, go hand in hand with her "old and intimate collaborator," since it was not the British way to sacrifice old friendships for the sake of new friendships). Speaking of the Naval Agreement, Hoare said that the maritime powers had always treated naval disarmament separately from land and air disarmament. The agreement provided for important restrictions and ruled out an Anglo-German competition which had been the cause of so much bitterness and friction before the war. If the British Government was unable to prevent Germany from rearming and evading the Versailles provisions which had been imposed upon her against her will, then it was a wiser course of action to take Hitler at his word and bind him to observe an agreement which he was willing to accept, an agreement which furthermore set relatively low ceilings to his maritime force. It was hoped, Hoare said, that if Germany was shown trust and was regarded as a great power enjoying equal rights both by treaty and on moral grounds, then an unfortunate naval competition might be avoided. If, on the other hand, the French proved to be right in their assumption that Germany had not been sincere in the conclusion of the agreement and will violate it, then Great Britain would have every right to apply sanctions against the treaty-breaker. Sir Samuel also pointed out that it became now apparent that the French Government in the spring of 1934 had made a great mistake by sending the notorious Barthou note which declined Hitler's offer to set at 300,000 men the maximum strength of the German land army. Now that the peacetime strength of the army of the German Reich had reached, or inevitably was going to reach, 550,000 men, thus exceeding in numbers the French armed forces, it was clear that the French had "missed the bus." In fact there is no policy more disastrous than that of missed opportunities. In conclusion Sir Samuel Hoare brought forth the argument — which had been used also by Lord Londonderry — that with this agreement Britain was protecting France's interests too. Before the war the German fleet was superior to the French Navy. Now, on the basis of the ratio of 35 : 100 between the German and British fleets, France, whose navy had a ratio of 52 : 100 in relation to the British, still could maintain a naval superiority of about 13 per cent over Germany.[10]

In the view of many observers a much stronger impression was achieved by the statement made by Eden to the Commons. His elocution was equal to the actual content of his message.[11] He also came to the rescue of the British Government's position: "Let me make it clear that His Majesty's Government do not admit that the conclusion of that Agreement is contrary to the principle of co-operation which was embodied in the London communiqué of 3rd February and in the Stresa Resolution, to which the Government remain firmly attached ... The purpose of this step has been to circumscribe by agreement with Germany the ultimate consequences of the unilateral decision to which Germany had already begun to give effect." The British Government had intended to prepare with this Naval Agreement an all-comprehensive land, air, and naval treaty which had been proposed as an objective in the London Protocol and by the Stresa conference alike. "That criticism that His Majesty's Government must not make treaties or agreements, two by two, applies equally to the Franco-Russian Treaty."[12] Eden also defended the British position by stressing the absurd belief that, "so far as naval armaments are concerned, Germany is prepared from now onwards to exchange, on a reciprocal basis with other Naval Powers, particulars in regard to dates of laying down and characteristics of future warships. This result would never have been achieved without the prior conclusion of the Anglo-German Agreement ... There is no policy which is more costly, both to the taxpayer and to peace, than a policy of missing the bus. The very fact that Germany is shown to have rearmed so much already is the strongest possible argument for accepting her offer to limit the future course of her naval armaments ... Would it not have been a tragedy for this country and the world had the history of land armaments

[10] In outlining Hoare's speech we have made use also of the report by Széchenyi from London, July 13, 1935 (OL Küm. Pol. 1935—2—2342), the MTI news bulletin (OL K. 428.566) and the evaluative summary by György Ottlik, *loc. cit.*, — Taking a view of the speech from the German side, Foreign Minister Neurath wrote that "the chilly attitude which Sir Samuel Hoare adopted to Germany and her demands could cause no surprise, since this corresponds to the familiar British policy of balance and since a renewed and marked inclination toward France after the conclusion of the Anglo-German Naval Agreement was generally expected not only by us." Circular of the Foreign Minister, Berlin, July 15, 1935. DGFP Ser. C. Vol. IV, No. 207, pp. 446—449.

[11] As for this, see the opinion of J. Masaryk, the Czechoslovak Minister in London. He stated that Hoare's speech — which was bad to hear but excellent to read — could taken as useful from the point of view of Czechoslovak policy. *Cf.* his letter to Beneš, London, July 12, 1935. AMZV Beneš Papers.

[12] Eden then skilfully argued to defend the Naval Agreement. But in his memoirs he condemns it with an interposed remark. This gives us reason to compare memoirs with contemporary pronouncements of their authors. *Cf. The Eden Memoirs*, p. 186.

been repeated on the sea?" Eden challenged the critics whether they would have wished the British Government to reject the German offer.[13]

In the July 11 debate the House of Commons heard a more interesting and more colourful speech than those of Hoare and Eden. It was Churchill who then contested the significance and advantages of the Naval Agreement. His logical arguments met with no response at that time, but later he was vindicated by the events. He said in clear terms that the advantages which the Naval Agreement conferred upon Britain were very doubtful: "Of course it is quite wrong to pretend that the apparition of Germany as a formidable naval Power, equipped with submarines and all the other apparatus of war, is the result of the Naval Agreement. That would have happened anyhow ... It has for some time been evident that Germany intends to embark upon a gigantic process of rearming by land, sea and air, which will make her the most formidable military Power in the whole world. I am not blaming upon this Agreement these events and the misfortunes which will follow from them, but when the Prime Minister says, as he did the other day, that he hoped this would be a great measure of disarmament, let me tell him that I am afraid it will not. I hazard the prediction that it inaugurates the arrival of Germany as a great naval Power."

Churchill made the following example to the situation: "Let us suppose that some distinguished and powerful person who has played a great part in life dies, and his posts, offices, appointments and possessions are distributed and then he suddenly comes back from the dead. A great deal of inconvenience would be caused. That is what has happened in the resuscitation of German naval power. The equilibrium — such equilibrium as we have been able to establish — in naval matters is entirely ruptured and deranged, and we shall find in every country, in the present temper of the world, that great constructions, replacing old ships or increasing the total tonnage, will be begun without the slightest delay. And let me say that if the first German programme, which has already been announced, and which is really last year's programme, the programme of 1934, is followed by similar programmes in the next few years, the German 35 per cent limit will have been laid down, if not completed, by 1938 or 1939. And in the same period, if we are not to endanger our naval security, it will be necessary for us to rebuild and lay down in new construction practically half the tonnage of our existing Fleet."

"I have never felt that there was very much in this offer," said Churchill another time, "which the Germans made to co-operate with us in abolishing the submarine ... it was a very safe offer for them to make — for any country to make — when the condition attached to it was that all other countries should agree at the same time, and when it was perfectly well known that there was not the slightest chance of other countries agreeing ... I should have thought that the French, the Italian, and the Japanese views would all be absolutely adverse to it ... Another statement which was made on the subject of submarines was that the Germans were willing to subscribe to the terms of the international agreement which many of the Powers have signed restricting the use of the submarine in such a way as to strip submarine warfare against

[13] Eden's reply to criticisms hurled at the Government during the House of Commons debate on July 11, 1935. Cf. A. Eden, *Foreign Affairs*, London, 1939, pp. 66—70.

commerce of inhumanity ... Lord Beatty said the other day that the battle fleet was now practically secure against submarines if properly protected by its flotillas, etc ... Submarines are not needed, then, for attack upon the battle fleet. If they are not needed for that purpose, and the Germans are not going to use them in the only way in which they can be effectively used, against commerce, it seems to me strange that they should dwell with so much reiteration on the importance of having not merely 35 per cent, but 45 per cent, and in the long run in some circumstances up to 100 per cent, of our tonnage in this category. If neither of the spheres of activity for submarines is to be used by them, it seems strange that they should attach so much importance to the possession of this weapon, which they have begun to construct in considerable numbers in flat defiance of the Peace Treaty. If we are to assume, as we must for the purposes of this discussion, the ugly hypothesis of a war in which Britain and Germany would be on opposite sides and the British blockade would be enforced on the coast of Germany as it was in the late war, who in his senses would believe that the Germans, possessed of a great fleet of submarines and watching their women and children being starved by the British blockade, would abstain from the fullest use of that arm? Such a view seems to be the acme of gullibility."

Churchill then asked what would have happened if Britain had refused the German suggestion: "The proper course would have been to say that this Agreement involves a breach of the Treaty, and that we have joined with other Powers in condemning breaches of the Treaty ... if that had been done the position would have not been worsened. The position is very bad. Do not let us underrate it. The German Fleet is to be 35 per cent of the British Fleet. We have seen the first year's programme of its construction. It is already far on the way; even the battleships are laid down. I do not know how the Admiralty came to be without information that even battleships, contrary to the Treaty, were being laid down before the end of 1934 ... We always believed before the war that battleships could never be laid down without our knowledge. The Germans were entitled to build 10,000-ton ships according to the Treaty, but they, by a concealment which the Admiralty were utterly unable to penetrate, converted these into 26,000-ton ships." (Churchill was much in the right, since even these figures were exceeded.) "It is time that if we take mere tonnage the First Lord is able to show a satisfactory arrangement for France in the percentage of superiority which she would possess, but what is to be the position of the French Navy if the Germans in the next four years build by four programmes a fleet of 35 per cent of the British Fleet? The entire navy of France, except the latest vessels, will require to be reconstructed. The new German Navy, although somewhat behind the French in the matter of percentages, would undoubtedly be overwhelmingly superior from the point of view of matériel ... I must say that I regret that we have condoned this flagrant breach of the Treaty. It would have been far better ... to have carried these matters forward to the League of Nations and endeavoured to use this further breach of the Treaty by Germany as a means of gathering forces for a policy of collective security among all the nations of the world.

"I do not believe for a moment that this isolated action by Great Britain will be found to work for the cause of peace ... Every day the German Fleet approaches a tonnage which gives it absolute command of the Baltic, and very soon one of the deterrents of a European war will gradually fade away. So far as the position in the Mediterranean is concerned, it seems to me that we are in for very great difficulties. Certainly a large addition of new ship-building must come when the French have to modernize their Fleet to meet German construction, and the Italians follow suit, and we shall have pressure upon us to rebuild from that point of view, or else our position in the Mediterranean will be affected. But worst of all is the effect upon our position at the other end of the world, in China and in the Far East . . . The First Lord said, 'Face the facts.' The British Fleet, when this programme is completed, will be largely anchored to the North Sea. That means to say the whole position in the Far East has been very gravely altered, to the detriment of the United States and of Great Britain and to the detriment of China . . . When this German Fleet is built we shall not be able to keep any appreciable position of the British Fleet so far from home . . . I do not say that they are reactions from the Naval Agreement, but from the fact that Germany is breaking treaties and re-establishing her naval power." Churchill finally drew the attention of the House to the enormous development of German armaments by land, sea and air, "converting the whole mighty nation and empire of Germany into an arsenal virtually on the threshold of mobilization. Britain ought to take the necessary measures in good time, to endeavour to secure a common front as far as possible against infractions of treaties. The facts are that Britain has to rebuild the Fleet with great rapidity, not a day should be lost in getting on."[14]

Churchill tried to mobilize against a great peril, and the Foreign Secretary at the same time endeavoured to mitigate the effect of a mistake, as we have already mentioned above, by his memorandum of July 17 sent to the British Ambassador in Paris (See Appendix V, p. 190). This writing contained elaborate answers to political and juridical criticism of the conclusion of the Anglo-German Naval Agreement:

"I. Criticism: —

(a) That His Majesty's Government have committed a breach of the Treaty of Versailles;

(b) That His Majesty's Government have condoned a breach by Germany of the Treaty of Versailles.

"(a) Where, as in the Treaty of Versailles, a treaty is concluded between one State on the one hand and a number of States on the other, the position is that the one party, Germany, contracts a series of similar obligations towards each of the other parties to the treaty severally. Each of the other parties, if it should wish to do so, has a legal right (apart from any specific undertakings to the contrary) by a separate agreement with Germany to waive its rights in any particular under the treaty. If it does so, it affects only its own rights and the provisions of the treaty remain in full legal force as regards the other parties thereto.

"(b) The German Government have declared that they no longer consider themselves bound by Part V of the Treaty of Versailles . . . The principal other

[14] Churchill's speeches in the House of Commons: Consequences in Foreign Policy, July 11, 1935; The Anglo-German Naval Agreement, July 22, 1935. In *Speeches by W. S. Churchill: Arms and the Covenant*, London, 1938, pp. 254—263.

130

parties to that treaty, His Majesty's Government included, taking the view that legally there was nothing to justify the German claim that conditions had come into existence rendering Part V no longer binding, protested against this decision, declared that it was a breach of the treaty and that nothing had happened to prevent the application of the usual principle that Germany could only obtain her release from Part V by agreement with all the other parties thereto. The other parties placed all this on record, but the German Government proceeded to act in accordance with their decision, and it was clear that the other parties were not going to take any action to enforce their view of the legal position upon Germany. The present bilateral Agreement with Germany is based upon the admitted *de facto* situation and constitutes an attempt to limit the consequences thereof. It contains no admission that the *de facto* situation was a legal one, though to the extent that the new Agreement is fulfilled it removes for the future the right of His Majesty's Government to protest against that situation further as regards naval armaments.

"II. Criticism: —

That His Majesty's Government have not acted in accordance with the London Communiqué of February 3 and under the Stresa Resolution.

"Throughout the discussions which led up to the drafting of these two documents no reference was ever made to the particular position of naval disarmament.... in the absence of any contrary statement by the other parties, His Majesty's Government are entitled to agree ... that naval armaments are in a separate category from land and air armaments, having been regulated by international treaties since 1922 ... This Anglo-German Agreement is in effect a contribution towards the General Settlement and not prejudicial to it ... Were it not for the Agreement, there is reason to believe that the first naval objective of Germany would have been not 35 per cent of the British fleet, but parity with France. Such a claim, if made, would have rendered yet more difficult the conclusion of that 'General Settlement' to which the London Communiqué referred. In this connexion it is perhaps worth while contrasting the attitude adopted by the French Government towards their own bilateral agreement with the Soviet Government and our bilateral agreement with Germany. When His Majesty's Government conclude a bilateral agreement with Germany, as their contribution towards those 'agreements regarding armaments generally' recommended in the London Declaration, it is a cause of criticism. But when the French Government conclude a mutual guarantee treaty with the Soviet Government as their contribution towards the 'conclusion of pacts freely negotiated between all the interested parties in Eastern Europe,' it is regarded as a matter for congratulation. It is to be observed also that when the French Government decided, not merely to negotiate but to bring their Russian Treaty into force in advance not only of the General Settlement, but of the so-called Eastern Pact to be concluded between all the parties concerned, they did so without requesting or awaiting the consent of His Majesty's Government.

"III. The criticism that we (Britain) gave the French Government no chance to influence our view and that the summary of the Agreement handed to them on June 7 was inadequate.

"The German representatives intimated that this was an offer which was made to this country, and to this country only ... We had good reason to believe that in making his offer, Herr Hitler had overruled the German Ministry of Marine, which, if we had hesitated to accept it, would have been favourably placed for securing an amendment of the German proposal in the sense desired by the German navy.

"We gave the French Government ten days in which to express an opinion, leaving them in no doubt that this was a matter on which our own minds were already made up. The real answer to this charge is that the acceptance of this German offer was a matter of vital interest to this country, that on the juridical side it did not constitute a breach of the Treaty of Versailles by this country; that it did not directly concern the naval construction of France nor prejudice the chances of an ultimate general settlement; and that no British Government could have taken the risk of losing the agreement simply on the ground that it might conflict with a French interpretation of the Declaration of the 3rd February. The French Government are also disposed to complain that the Aide-mémoire which was communicated to them on the 7th June was not an adequate summary of the Agreement which afterwards contained the clause about parity in submarines and the clauses about Germany's right to draw attention to any abnormal and exceptional construction by other Powers. The reason for this is that these clauses were only inserted at the last moment as the result of representations by the German representatives on their return from Berlin after Whitsuntide."

From among the many answers intended to reassure the French Government, we still refer only to the arguments contained in paragraph VI, which dealt with the criticism that "His Majesty's Government have withheld from the French Government information with regard to the German building programmes." In reply to this the British pointed out that such information had been given, at British insistence, by the Germans themselves on June 9, to the effect that "the German construction programme may be divided into two parts. The first is their 1934—35 programme, most of which has already been laid down. It consists of 2 capital ships of 26,000 tons each, 2 cruisers of 10,000 tons each, 16 destroyers, 20 submarines of 250 tons, 6 submarines of 500 tons, 2 submarines of 750 tons. Of the above, the two capital ships, the two 8-inch-gun cruisers, the sixteen destroyers and twelve of the submarines had already been laid down before the conclusion of the Anglo-German Naval Agreement. This fact had been conveyed to the British Naval Attaché at Berlin before the naval conversations commenced. The second part of what is known as the German building programme relates to the construction to be undertaken by Germany up to the year 1942. This part of the programme was communicated to Britain on a reciprocal basis. This part of the German programme, like the British and other programmes of all other nations, must for the time being of course remain confidential, for premature publication of advance programmes could only serve to increase the difficulty of arriving at an ultimate international agreement on this subject. The British Government informed the French Government that Britain is ready and anxious to communicate to them all the information communicated confidentially to her, if they will undertake to communicate to the British Government, for transmission to the German Government, the particulars of the French building programme up to the end of 1942. The British Government have not so far received from the French Government a reply to this suggestion. It will be seen from the above that one important result of the Anglo-German Agreement is that, in the matter of naval armaments, Germany is now prepared to depart from the policy of secrecy which, in connexion with armaments generally, has done so much to cause uneasiness throughout the world. Furthermore, so far as naval armaments are concerned, Germany is prepared from now on to exchange on a reciprocal basis with the other naval Powers particulars in regard to the date of laying down and characteristics of future warships, even in advance of the conclusion of a general naval treaty. This satisfactory result could never have been achieved without the prior conclusion of the Anglo-German Agreement."

Paragraph VIII dealt with the criticism that in concluding this agreement with Germany His Majesty's Government had acted purely from interested motives in contradiction to the spirit of the League of Nations:

"...The step which has been taken was an essential preliminary to the general limitation of naval armaments, and had it not been taken by His Majesty's Government, all foreign Powers must have suffered from the race in naval armaments which would have been resulted. As it is, other foreign Powers whose naval construction is not directly effected by the agreement know the limits of naval expansion and can regulate their programmes accordingly. One of the primary purposes of the League of Nations is to limit and, if possible, reduce world armaments and the League cannot suffer if, as a result of this agreement, which we regard as a useful contribution to a general settlement between all the naval Powers, the threatened race in naval armaments can be prevented."[15] (For subsequent comments on the Agreement by British diplomats, see also Appendix VIII. p. 229.)

In describing the reception in Germany of the Naval Agreement we begin with the statement which Ribbentrop made to the press before leaving London on June 23. Ambassador Ribbentrop characterized the agreement as the "beginning of a practical peace policy," as an event which settled the vital naval problems between Germany and Britain once and for all. After years of negotiations and talks, and ministers rushing from one capital to another, he said, "this is the first real achievement, the first step towards a limitation of armaments." All problems could not be resolved at once, as was envisaged by the system of collective security, one had to move on step by step, as was being done by Germany, whose policy was accompanied by acts, not theories. The Naval Agreement was of great importance, Ribbentrop said, because it meant that the ice had been broken in the rigid political situation in Europe: an atmosphere of appeasement might and should follow, and the culture of the old world would be preserved if Britain, France and Germany, and the other European nations, stood together. They (the Germans) believed in a strong Europe and in a strong British Empire, and they wished to forget the old griev-

---

[15] Answers to Criticisms directed from the Political and Juridical Point of View against the Conclusion of the Anglo-German Naval Agreement, Foreign Office, July 17, 1935. P. R. O. Adm. 116/3377.

ances. One had to believe in the renascence of the West, as Hitler had said, who had found in this the principal object of his life.[16]

As far as the German press is concerned, the *Völkischer Beobachter* (June 19) wrote that the London conversations had secured a very important advantage not only to the two interested states but also to all of Europe. The agreement was proof that German National Socialism acknowledged the consequences resulting from many centuries of European history and from the geographical situation of the particular states. National Socialism was aware that the British Empire needed a powerful fleet to secure communications between the countries of the Empire, in the same way as Germany was unable to protect her security unless she possessed a strong land army. The *Deutsche Allgemeine Zeitung* emphasized the rightness of the method of bilateral negotiations which Germany had been the first to use in disarmament matters. The *Berliner Tageblatt* wrote that the result was due, on the one side, to the wise restraint of the British Government and, on the other side, to the Reich Chancellor's clear-cut and definite objectives. According to information gathered by Masirevich, the Hungarian Minister to Germany, "the Berlin newspapers were given strict instructions to refrain from any rejoicing over the Naval Agreement, from commenting upon a loosening of Anglo-French friendship and from all kinds of such manifestations."[17]

Masirevich pointed out, however, also that no one should believe that following the Naval Agreement Great Britain would give up friendship with France; in another context this was formulated in a confidential Hungarian memorandum stating that the Germans regarded the Anglo-German Naval Agreement "as very important, but they do not overestimate it, that is, they do not think that it is probable that, by means of this and future negotiations, they would be able to get Britain to let France down. The essential thing is that the Versailles Treaty has been broken through".[18]

The Naval Agreement's importance to the Germans was summed up in a secret and unsigned memorandum prepared for the SK Group of the German War Ministry. The memorandum contained among other things the following: "The agreement arose from the Führer's decision to fix the relative strengths of the German and British Navies at 35 to 100. It was unswervingly maintained in face of initial British opposition, and the Germans' claims were put through in their entirety ... The Agreement is entirely satisfactory for the Navy. Any substantially larger figure than that permitted by the Agreement could hardly be reached in the next decade. It will give us the opportunity of creating a modern fleet which is appropriately constituted and in accordance with

[16] Statement by Herr von Ribbentrop, German Ambassador-at-Large. In an interview with Reuter in London, June 23, 1935. *Manchester Guardian*, June 24, 1935. — *Documents* . . . , pp. 146—148.

[17] Strictly confidential report by Masirevich, the Hungarian Minister in Berlin, June 25, 1935. OL Küm. Pol. 1935—2/19—2105. (It is said that in this case sanctions should have been applied already against the *Lokalanzeiger* and the *Essener Nationalzeitung*.)

[18] Information obtained by the head of Department VI/2 of the Ministry of Defence during his visit to Berlin from 23 to 27 June 1935, Conversations with the chief of the German record office about the military-political situation. OL Küm. Pol. 1935—21—2289.

our maritime needs. By means of the Agreement Britain has formally accepted the expansion *(Aufbau)* of the German Navy on the lines laid down by the Führer . . . The success of the Agreement lies principally in the political sphere. In this respect its consequences should not be underrated. As a result of the Agreement the most powerful of our former enemies and of the signatories of the Versailles Treaty has formally invalidated an important part of this Treaty and formally recognized Germany's equality of rights. The danger of Germany being isolated, which definitely threatened in March and April of this year, has been eliminated. A political understanding with Great Britain has been initiated by the naval settlement. The front recently formed against us by the Stresa Powers has been considerably weakened by the Agreement."[19]

It cannot be doubted that the Naval Agreement, apparently so advantageous to the British, profited in fact the Germans both politically and militarily. Admiral Raeder confirmed this in his confessions at Nuremberg and later in his memoirs, and even admitted that Germany had violated also the treaty-breaking agreement by exceeding the limits authorized by it.[20]

A couple of remarks in the memoirs of two contemporary observers — Ernst Weizsäcker, the German Minister to Switzerland at the time, and the ill-famed Otto Abetz, who was German Ambassador in Paris at the time of the German occupation of France — are worth mentioning. Weizsäcker noted that the Naval Agreement was better than an Anglo-German war, but it had the shortcoming that it failed to formulate guarantees reminding Hitler to refrain from any further arbitrary action. And Abetz called attention to the fact that the agreement had created a precedent enabling the Germans later to claim territorial revisions and refer to their rights as *Volksdeutsche*.[21]

Having been informed by phone about the signing of the agreement, Hitler declared, as he did so many times, that this was the happiest day of his life.[22] (For Hitler's interest in the British Navy, see also Appendix X, p. 239.)

Hitler really attached importance to the agreement and indeed there are a good number of indirect and very confidential pieces of information indicating this.[23] He kept repeating the significance of the agreement in his talks with

[19] Unsigned Memorandum, Berlin, August 28, 1935, Secret. DGFP Ser. C. Vol. IV, No. 275, pp. 587—588.
[20] IMT, Vol. 41, pp. 3—5: Doc. Raeder—12. — P. Gilbert, *Nürnbergi napló* [Nuremberg Diary], Budapest, 1967, p. 486. — Raeder, *op. cit.*, Vol, I, pp. 303, 304.
[21] Ernst von Weizsäcker, *Memoirs*, London, 1951, p. 100. — O. Abetz, *Das offene Problem*, Cologne, 1951, p. 43.
[22] Ribbentrop: *Erinnerungen*, P. 64. — The Anglo-German Naval Agreement is treated from the German viewpoint by R. Ingrim, *Hitlers glücklichster Tag, London, am 18. Juni 1935*, Stuttgart, 1962. — A dissertation of this subject is expected to be prepared, presumably containing material from the Bonn Archives: N. Wiggershaus, *England und die deutsche Aufrüstung 1933—35*, [Bonn].
[23] See, e. g., Királdy-Lukács' cipher telegram from London, October 4, 1935, reporting on his talks with the head of the Southern Department of the Foreign Office. The British official inquired after information other than published press reports about Hungarian Prime Minister Gömbös' journey to Germany. In reply to this report Foreign Minister Kánya in a cipher telegram wrote that, from his conversation with the Reich Chancellor, Gömbös had gained the impression that "Hitler attached extremely great importance to the conclusion of the Anglo-German

various statesmen. For example, still in the autumn of 1936 when talking to Lloyd George at Berchtesgaden, he explained in a manner characteristic of him what he had wanted and expected of the agreement. "He [Hitler] had been ready to recognize the vital interests of the British Empire. The Anglo-German Treaty was a proof of his eagerness to respect British vital interests. He thought that England should equally recognize in her turn what the vital interests of Germany required; particularly in regard to Germany's position on the Continent . . . In this connection the Chancellor enlarged upon the danger of Bolshevism." Lloyd George interposed: "Would Germany be prepared to agree to an air pact between the three powers?" Hitler replied: "Yes, provided the three powers (France, Germany and Great Britain) were able to reach a a common defensive position *(Abwehrstellung)*, but not otherwise. He had made attempts to conclude some agreement of this kind and as a first step they had concluded the Naval Treaty with Great Britain which secured Great Britain's supremacy on the High Seas and the security of Germany in the Baltic."[24]

Interesting information is available also on the views of responsible British military experts as to the reasons why Hitler had concluded the agreement. On February 14, 1936, Duff Cooper entertained as his guests Liddell Hart, Winston Churchill, Marshal of the R.A.F. Sir Hugh Trenchard, and Colonel (later Major-General) J. F. C. Fuller. In the discussion of defence problems the question of the value of the battle-fleet came up. Liddell Hart was of the opinion that the Germans were not worrying about Britain's battle-fleet — hence their indifference to the Naval Agreement — because they were so confident of the direct attack upon commerce, now with multiplied means.[25]

And what were the British diplomats' views on why Germany had entered into the Naval Agreement? Instructions drafted in the Foreign Office, based on consultation with the Admiralty, were sent in July 1938 to Sir Nevile Henderson, the British Ambassador in Berlin. The following confidential points of view were recommended for consideration should Marshal Göring again bring up the issue of the 1935 Naval Agreement (here we quote only the passages relating to the subject under review):

"2. The continued existence of the Anglo-German Naval Agreement of 1935 is naturally of great importance to us (Britain) from the point of view of our future naval policy and construction . . .

"3. On the other hand, it must not be assumed that the German Government obtained no advantage by subscribing to it and that they are still entitled to a further *quid pro quo* from us. At the time of the conclusion of the Agree-

Naval Agreement and spoke of the very optimistic terms about the possibility of friendly co-operation between England and Germany." OL Küm. Pol. 1935—21/7—3024.

[24] Dodd, *op. cit.*, pp. 252—253, 256. — Hitler's discussion with Lloyd George, September 4, 1936. — Gilbert, *op. cit.*, (1966), p. 198.

[25] Liddell Hart, *op. cit.*, Vol. I, pp. 302—303. — Churchill and Cooper both stressed the danger from Germany. In their opinion, there was nothing to stop the Germans, unless their country would be dismembered after the war. Liddell Hart remarked bitterly that there was no hope of any balanced solution based on facts and not on fancies, until the discussion of a problem could be properly organized. These important issues were not decided ultimately until a year later, in the autumn of 1937. *Op. cit.*, Vol. I, pp. 306—307.

ment the German Government were well aware that 35 per cent of our navy was probably the most that they could hope to achieve for a considerable period of years. This was their chief concern. The Agreement as far as they were concerned was valuable because it was a means of obtaining from His Majesty's Government (alone of the ex-Allied Powers) a formal acceptance of the German thesis that the naval provisions of the Treaty of Versailles had ceased to exist and because it enabled them to forestall the juridical objections of other signatories of the Treaty and to build with the approval of His Majesty's Government as much as they were likely to be able to build within the next few years. They did not concern themselves about the ultimate future because they no doubt reckoned, if the necessity should ever arise, on being able to free themselves from the Agreement by finding some plausible excuse.

"4. Field Marshal Göring's threat that in certain circumstances Germany might, presumably after denouncing the Anglo-German Naval Agreement of 1935, proceed to build up to 100 per cent of the British fleet is clearly bluff. In view of the great existing disparity in the size of the two navies this threat could only be excusable if British construction were to remain stationary over a considerable period of years whilst German tonnage was being built up to it. This would not occur. Although Germany is doubtless capable of realizing the 35 per cent figure by 1942 if she so desires, or even appreciably earlier, it seems unlikely (considering her difficulties in connection with raw material, foreign exchange and the necessity of giving priority to her vast rearmament on land and in the air and considering our own big programme) that she would appreciably exceed that figure during the course of the next few years . . .

"5. From the political aspect, the German Navy has we think been to Germany mainly an instrument for putting political pressure on this country. Before the war, Germany would have been willing to cease, or greatly moderate, her naval competition with this country, but only in return for a promise of our neutrality in any European conflict. Hitler has attempted the same thing by different methods, but he has seen one side of the picture, as all German politicians have only seen one side of the picture. It is clear from his writings that he was enormously impressed with the part played by the pre-war naval rivalry in creating bad relations between the two countries. From this he argued that the removal of this rivalry was all that was necessary to obtain good relations. By making us a free gift of an absence of naval competition he hoped that relations between the two countries would be so improved that we should not in fact find it necessary to interfere with Germany's continental policy. He overlooked, as all German politicians have overlooked for many years past, that this country is bound to react, not only against danger from any purely naval rival, but also against the dominance of Europe by any aggressive military Power, particularly if in a position to threaten the Low Countries and the Channel ports. British complaisance can never be purchased by trading one of these factors against the other and any country that attempts it is bound to create for itself disappointment and disillusion as Germany is doing." (See Appendices XII, XIII, pp. 243, 247.)[26]

The strongest reaction to the Naval Agreement, of course, came from France and Italy. In the view of French Premier Laval the agreement was a violation

[26] P. R. O. Adm. 116/3378—8678.

of the Franco-British accord of February 3, 1935 and Mussolini was convinced that it ended the Stresa front.

The conclusion of the Anglo-German Naval Agreement — especially the fact that the parties to the agreement had confronted the other signatories of the Versailles Treaty with an accomplished fact — caused resentment in Paris and to some extent in Rome as well, particularly because the British Government had already received the note by which the Paris and Rome Governments had protested against the Anglo-German negotiations and the agreement which was likely to result from them. Both Governments had pointed out that the discussion with Germany concerning the questions of naval, air and land disarmament was to be considered an indivisible whole and furthermore that the signatories of the Versailles Treaty could not alter the treaty provisions except by common agreement. Finally they stated that the London declaration of February 3 and the subsequent Stresa resolution had put the three Western powers under an obligation to negotiate all major European questions relating to Germany by common agreement and jointly. This latter standpoint — the maxim of the indivisibility of peace — was especially stressed in the note from Paris and in the comments of the French press following the publication of the agreement.[27]

But let us take a closer look at the grievances of the two countries. The nervousness of the French press had been manifest already at the time of the naval conversations. According to *Le Jour* (June 6) the British Admiralty, when trying to reduce not only the German but also the French naval forces, in reality wished to kill two birds with one stone. England worked for the total elimination of submarines and expected that the Germans would in all probability stop building up their submarine fleet if France followed suit. England was thus preparing another Trafalgar against the French fleet. The *Echo de Paris* (June 12) noted that Britain's security was not in every respect satisfied by arrangements which related only to the sea and air forces while disregarding the land forces. The semi-official *Petit Parisien* (June 13) wrote in brief that the German claims turned the Versailles Treaty naval provisions upside down. The *Excelsior* (June 13) objected that the British note had confronted the French Government with the "alternative" of simply agreeing to decisions taken without consulting it.

The French newspapers in general did not recognize that Germany needed as large a naval force as France. France was the second largest colonial power in the world and because of the scattering of her naval force, she would in fact become inferior to Germany. The moderate Republican paper *Homme Libre* (June 14) explained that Germany was able to concentrate her fleet consisting almost exclusively of new ships in the North Sea and the Baltic, while France had to distribute her naval force between the English Channel and the Mediterranean Sea. The Royalist *Action Française* (June 14) also considered the possibility of France falling behind and stated that in three to four years, Germany would have as many ships in the North Sea as France had in the Atlantic and the Mediterranean taken together. The *Paris-Soir* (June 14), sizing up the situation in a realistic manner, issued this warning: France should not forget that while Britain was a competent arbitrator in naval and air

[27] Ottlik, *loc. cit.*

138

questions, yet she was far too indifferent in regard to land armaments. If Germany was going by England in the field of naval construction, she must seek agreement with France on the issues of land armament. *L'Oeuvre* (June 15) complained about the great successes of the clever diplomacy of Germany, designed to disrupt the unity of the Anglo-French front. According to *L'Ordre* (June 15) Britain had in the past most resolutely insisted on general disarmament and now she was the first to make an agreement on rearmament. The *Journal* (June 17) thought the agreement was acceptable to France and Italy on the condition that in fixing the ratio between the fleets the special requirements of the particular states were taken into account. The requirements of Germany were different from those of Italy and France. The paper regarded as an achievement that Italy intended to co-ordinate her view with France's standpoint. In *Le Matin* (June 18) Admiral Docteur set forth that if France was in danger of her fleet falling far behind the naval forces of other nations, both in numbers and in quality, then she would have to double the number of her submarines and military aircraft. The next issue of the same paper wrote that England was pleasantly surprised by Germany's compliance. London had expected to be faced with excessive demands from the German side and hastened to sign the agreement because it feared that later Berlin would present higher claims. It was a sure thing, the paper stated, that the Naval Agreement would not facilitate the conduct of Laval's policy.

Indeed, Laval was in no easy position. This appeared from the French note which Ambassador Corbin on June 18 presented to the British Foreign Office in reply to the British memorandum explaining the Naval Agreement. This reply turned out to be sharper than expected. The French Government took the view that Britain was not entitled to allow Germany a naval ratio contrary to the provisions of the Peace Treaty. Therefore the French Government retained its freedom of action and did not consider itself bound by the pre-established ratio. The note recalled the five-power declaration of December 11, 1932, which had promised Germany equality of rights only within the framework of collective security.

In the *Echo de Paris*, on the very day of the signing of the agreement, the famous French journalist Pertinax analyzed the situation, pointing out that if it should come to Anglo-French naval conversations, they would have to take place in Paris, not in London. England could no longer exercise the functions of arbitrator as she had done in London without regard to the interests of France. England professed the inviolability of treaties when her colonial gains were at stake, but was ready to violate the treaties when her naval superiority had to be secured. And France should not let herself be dragged into the Ethiopian conflict, but should rely on the Geneva principles which England had just disregarded by signing the Naval Agreement. The same thought was explained in a different form by *L'Intransigeant* (June 19) which found in the Anglo-German Agreement a reason for France to approve of Italy's "work of civilization" in Ethiopia and to warn Britain that France would stand by her Latin sister.[28]

[28] Salvemini wrote that *L'Intransigeant* was "a paper intransigently loyal to Mussolini." *Op. cit.*, p. 223.

A few days later (June 22) the same paper published a statement by a French naval expert of high rank, whose name was not revealed, and who said among other things: "Whatever may happen, our Navy must not be surpassed by the German fleet. At this time around 146,000 tons of warships are under construction, but if need be, France can further intensify her work of construction, since she possesses seventeen shipyards." There were also voices in the press which tried to calm the general discontent. A news commentator wrote in the *Petit Parisien* (June 19) that Berlin would be disappointed in its calculations because the Franco-British relations would not relax. The Naval Agreement was open to objection from the juridical point of view, since it disregarded both the Treaty of Versailles and the Anglo-French declaration issued in London on February 3. Furthermore, Paris and Rome had been asked for their opinion at a rather late time and when the French objections hardly could do anything to influence the final settlement. Nevertheless, it would be useless to keep on complaining about an agreement which could not be prevented anyhow. Every nation was free to decide on how it wished to secure its future. Judging the thing from the purely naval standpoint, no serious harm had come to Italian and French interests.

While the majority of the French press went far in venting its anger and attacking Britain, a Hungarian news analyst wrote at the time, the French official quarters chose to point out that they thought the British were victims of their own good faith regarding Germany; and thus they objected not so much to the accord as to the fact that Britain had been so readily taken off her feet by the German representatives, although there was no guarantee that the agreement would be observed by the Germans. On the contrary, the fact that shortly after the conclusion of the agreement the Government of the German Reich announced for the current year the start of a naval construction programme covering half of the fleet authorized by the agreement, served as proof for the French that the Germans had no intention to observe its provisions. This "new" programme indicated also that part of the new construction "allowed" by Britain had been in progress already at the time when the German delegation arrived in London.[29]

In any case Britain took pains to destroy as quickly as possible the unfavourable effect which the London Agreement had produced in Paris. After the French note relating to the Anglo-German Naval Agreement had arrived in London, it was decided that Anthony Eden, the Minister for League of Nations Affairs, should go to Paris with the purpose of soothing the mood and explaining the Naval Agreement. It was also planned that Eden's visit to Paris should be followed by the visit to London of French naval experts. Certain consequences of the Naval Agreement, however, could not be averted. Laval had learned the news of the signature of the Agreement from the press and made an immediate protest with the British Ambassador in Paris. Presently, on June 19, the Franco-Italian treaty was signed which had been negotiated and prepared in the preceding months, and which defined the joint actions to be taken should Germany march on Austria.[30]

[29] Ottlik, *loc. cit.*
[30] Salvemini quotes Laval's reactions on the basis of the latter's memorandum of October 2, 1945: "A Franco-Italian military convention which had been

This treaty, in its turn, prompted the British to anti-French manifestations. In the British view this act seemed apt to assist in the realization of Italy's designs regarding Ethiopia. The British Government rejected the French Ambassador's request for information about the German naval construction programme. Such were the antecedents to Eden's trip to Paris, where he was given a rather cool reception. According to the *Paris-Soir* (June 19) Laval would think twice before deciding to align himself with Britain on the Ethiopian question. A columnist of *L'Intransigeant* (June 19) declared: "Eden will not persuade us to oppose Italy's aspirations in East Africa for the sake of enjoying Britain's inconstant favour." The British Government had given Eden detailed instructions on how to inform the French Government about the circumstances of the conclusion of the Anglo-German Naval Agreement. Eden wanted to take this opportunity for an exchange of views regarding the two Governments' guidelines in naval matters, for the purpose of promoting the conclusion of the Eastern pact and the Western air pact, and upholding the principle that separate accords might be concluded, which in his view could in no way mean any departure from the measures envisaged so far in London and Stresa, especially with regard to the Eastern and Danubian pacts.

Eden faced a difficult task. It seemed that, in spite of all his excellent personal qualities and the personal sympathies he enjoyed, he would be unable to carry out fully this rather delicate task imposed on him. Eden described this mission as follows: "... it was not so much the terms of the Agreement that aroused opinion in France and among France's allies. The way it was done was a classical example of the truth of Lord Salisbury's dictum that the methods by which a policy is executed in diplomacy are commonly as important as the policy itself. In these negotiations, London once again made the mistake of acting in isolation. Paris and Rome were inevitably offended and indignant when it was known that the Agreement had been signed without any consultation with them.

"... Laval's reproaches were sharp. The Agreement, he said, had caused great difficulties for the French Government. ... the recent French note was not generally regarded as sufficiently strong. Not only was the Agreement an

---

drawn up during the preceding months was immediately (June 19) signed by General Gamelin, Commander in Chief of the French forces, and General Badoglio, Chief of the General Staff in Italy. In the event of a German move against Austria, a French army would be sent to Italy, to join with Italian and Yugoslav forces in a march on Vienna and effect a junction with the Czech forces. At the same time an Italian army should be sent to France to operate between Belfort and the Swiss border, side by side with French units. The air forces of the two countries would join against southern Germany. The Italian Military Intelligence Service (SIM) suspended its activities in France and made arrangements to work hand in glove with the French Counter Espionage Office (2me Bureau) against Germany." Cf. M. G. Gamelin, *Servir*, Vol. II, Paris, 1946, pp. 163—169, 171; Laval's testimony at the Pétain trial on August 6, 1945, in the *Chicago Sun*. See also the testimony and memorandum of Roatta, Chief of SIM, and the testimony of Baistrocchi, Under-Secretary for War, in *Il Processo Roatta*, pp. 30—31, 81, 93, 200; quoted by Salvemini, *op. cit.*, p. 223. — It would be worth looking closer into the double-dealing of Italian intelligence (in Franco-Italian and German-Italian relations) at that time.

infringement of the Treaty of Versailles, but it was also contrary to the undertaking contained in our communiqué of February 3rd, that the various parts of the security and armaments problems were to be treated as an indivisible whole. Moreover, at Stresa we had, Laval thought he was right in saying, told the French that we would not accept a German claim of 35 per cent of the British fleet. The united front of Stresa was clearly broken in pieces. He asked me why other powers should not now deal separately with Germany. France might have, she had not done so and would not do so. It was German policy to deal separately with each subject and with each party. He wished to make peace with Germany, but on the condition that Germany would make peace with everybody else. These were fine arguments, but it was doubtful whether Laval, in view of the dubious bargain I suspected he had made with Mussolini over Abyssinia, was the man to put them.

"I replied that it had been the British intention to conduct only preliminary conversations with the German naval experts. The German representative had, however, refused to continue them, unless a definite answer were given as regards the 35 per cent. This offer was one which no government of the United Kingdom could possibly have refused, especially in the light of the experience of the past year and the increase in German claims in respect of land and air armaments. An increase in German claims for naval armaments, I continued, would be more serious than, for example, an increase in German claims for air armaments. It was bad enough to have to double the air force; it would be still worse to have to double the fleet in these days of budgetary difficulties. I understood that Germany might be trying to drive a wedge between our two countries, but she would not succeed. If we had refused the German offer to meet French criticism, the outcry in Britain might have driven such a wedge. I assured Laval that we would not have accepted the German offer if we had not been convinced that to do so was in the interest of both our countries.

"The discussion went on for two sessions. At the end of the first evening, June 21st, I telegraphed in a personal message to London: 'The Anglo-German Naval Agreement is regarded here as having struck a blow at the communiqué of February 3rd. Nothing that we can say will modify that judgement. None the less Monsieur Laval is himself not unduly disposed to cry over spilt milk. He is, however, determined to preserve what is left in the can of February 3rd.'

"Laval eventually admitted reasonably that it was more the form and method of which he had to complain. At intervals during two days we discussed the armaments and security problems of our two countries, including the possibility of an air pact. Laval was firm that we could not proceed by bits and pieces any further and I was sure that we must not give Anglo-French confidence another sharp jolt . . .

"This discussion was followed by one equally as long and as difficult on the question of further arms agreements with Germany . . . The contrast was between the British pragmatic approach and the French more legalistic one . . . The French were on the firmest ground when they argued that the piecemeal approach which now attracted us was not consistent with our joint policy declared on February 3rd. Why had His Majesty's Government changed their minds so soon? Laval asked me. He also reproached us with being too much impressed by Germany. Great Britain had shown weakness after weakness, he complained, and the result would be that Germany would have superiority

142

everywhere ... He had a genuine grievance and could hardly be blamed for exploiting it."

Eden saw clearly that France could not be talked into concluding the air pact. He also saw that Laval's position was very difficult. As a press correspondent pertinently remarked: "Eden failed to prevail upon Laval in the naval question, but gave him satisfactory information about further collaboration."[31]

Well-informed circles saw the main difficulty of the discussions in Laval's firm insistence that the question of different armaments should constitute an indivisible whole. Laval opposed the plan of the air pact because he was against its being negotiated immediately and independently of the other questions. Laval even mentioned that France was averse to the use of this method also because the prospects for a general limitation of armaments were very poor. The Paris correspondent of *The Times* reported that Eden had informed Laval that Britain would not regard a moderate increase of the French fleet as a reason to increase her own fleet, which might indirectly induce Germany to take similar steps. Eden gave France guarantees on several points. He expressed his complete understanding of the interdependence of the various spheres of disarmament as well as the interrelation between the disarmament problem and the different diplomatic methods of restoring security. Britain not only was ready but most earnestly wished to set about seeking the solution, if possible simultaneously, to these questions at an early date. Eden finally declared that Britain had not the slightest intention to start separate negotiations with Germany for an air agreement or to desert France in her future negotiations with Germany on the subject of land armaments.

After concluding his talks with Anthony Eden, the British Minister for League of Nations Affairs, Prime Minister Laval made the following statement: "We have discussed with M. Eden the various questions relating to the Naval Agreement between Britain and Germany. In addition we have talked over the problems arising out of the present international situation. We have further examined the formulas of the joint Anglo-French communiqué of February 3rd regarding co-operation between our two countries. We have found it necessary to seek practical means of solving the practical questions which we had discussed at London in February and which are of concern not only to both our countries but to a third European power as well. M. Eden has reported our conversations to his Government. After his return home from Rome I shall have another conversation with him. We have been in agreement with M. Eden that France and Britain will abide by their jointly undertaken commitments, and the two powers will do their utmost to build up peace in Europe by means of collective security ..."[32]

The French Minister of the Navy, F. Piétri, made references in a speech on June 27, over and above the problems indicated by Laval, to the objections to the Anglo-German Naval Agreement prevailing in French naval circles. In his view the agreement had upset the equilibrium of European fleets and

[31] As to the Laval—Eden conversations, *cf. The Eden Memoirs*, pp. 230—231. — The press correspondent is quoted by MTI, June 21, 1935. OL K. 428. 565.

[32] MTI, June 22, 1935. *Ibid.* — Pierre Laval was Prime Minister and Foreign Minister from June 1935 till January 22, 1936.

it was his task to study the new situation and draw the conclusions. With regard to battleships, France would have to speed up construction and to assign to this category a larger portion of the total tonnage. He emphasized that her geographical position, the vastness of her Empire with its dispersed possessions as well as the glorious traditions of her history reminded France to consider it as her duty to maintain her naval strength.[33]

By the end of June, however, the storm raised by offended French self-esteem had gradually come to a lull. On July 1, Béranger, the chairman of the Foreign Affairs Committee of the Senate, wrote a sensational article in the *Agence économique et financière*, hinting that the view of French foreign policy had changed somewhat with regard to the new British diplomatic methods. Some section of the French press might possibly show more understanding of Britain as far as the Anglo-German Naval Agreement was concerned, the author wrote and proceeded: "The astonishment expressed in this country in the wake of the London accord refers not so much to the British change of policy as rather to our undue inclination to gloat over misunderstandings. Neither the Stresa declaration nor the London communiqué forbade Britain to enter into a preliminary naval agreement with Germany, as also France had the right to come to terms with the Soviet Union, and as also Italy is free to act in Africa by herself. The three powers at Stresa undertook only to ask for one another's opinion before taking any action, and not to refrain from taking it. Britain asked for our opinion in a detailed note on June 7. We did not reply until June 17, and our reply was nothing else but procrastination. Thereupon Britain thought she had to grasp the opportunity for a limitation of the German naval force. Where is here any kind of betrayal, any change of front and objectionable attitude? . . . It may be that for many years we also have exasperated Britain with our fixed idea that all questions must be lumped together — without, however, having helped a single question closer to a solution. No wonder that the British, seeing the failure of our methods, chose to resort to different ones."[34]

A number of contemporary English historians take a summarily unfavourable view of the British Government's treatment of France at the time of the naval negotiations. One of them remarks only that it hurt the French feelings to see the Anglo-German Naval Agreement being signed on the 120th anniversary of the battle of Waterloo. Another writer, Wheeler-Bennett, uses stronger words: "The decision of the British Government to save what they could for themselves from the débâcle of the military clauses of the Treaty of Versailles is understandable, but that they should have done so without first consulting the French Government was not only unethical but stupid. Moreover, it was clear either that the British historical sense was at fault or that there was a definite intention to humiliate France, since the date selected for signing the agreement was the hundred and twentieth anniversary of the defeat of France at the hands of the British and Prussians at Waterloo. What appeared to the French to be an underhand transaction on the part of Perfidious Albion was long remembered and unforgiven . . . It was to bear fruit a year later in a

[33] From M. Piétri's speech on June 27, 1935. Quoted in *Documents* . . . , pp. 152—154.
[34] MTI, July 1, 1935. OL K. 428.566.

further and deeper misunderstanding between the two countries, and Adolf Hitler himself could not have devised a better and more effective instrument to create ill-feeling between Great Britain and France."[35]

Compared with the varying repercussions on the French side, the Italian reception of the Naval Agreement can be described as certainly calmer and steadier. According to the Palazzo Chigi, Italy was only indirectly affected by the Naval Agreement. If France decided to draw certain conclusions from it, the Italian Navy then would be built up proportionately as well.[36]

The Rome correspondent of *The Times* observed that the Italians did not adopt such a rigid attitude towards the Anglo-German "extra dance" as the French did. If, however, after having her naval requirements satisfied, Britain should obtain also a Western air pact and then, sitting back comfortably, keep aloof and refuse to take sufficient interest in the Danubian and Eastern pacts, the Italians would join with the French.[37]

The Italian press paid little attention to the Naval Agreement. The only exception was *Il Popolo di Roma*, which, in its usual weekly foreign political summary (June 23), dealt also with this event. First it stated that Germany had closed the naval discussions with a result beyond her expectations. The newspaper saw the greatest advantage to Germany in her submarine parity and in the absence of a limitation in time of armaments. The columnist found it strange that Britain should have failed not only to consult the other powers in advance, but also to make the agreement dependent on their consent.

Coming to the Italian considerations, the newspaper stated that the Anglo-German Naval Agreement was ultimately favourable to Italy from the technical standpoint, because it withdrew part of the French and British fleets from the Mediterranean, and so Italy might in a short time become supreme on the "Mare Nostro." It added that the solution was favourable also to the other interested powers, because they had no choice between a rearmed and a disarmed Germany. The question rather was whether Germany would reorganize her navy without restrictions or within certain limits.

It became more or less widely known that Mussolini endeavoured to make use of the Naval Agreement for bringing his Abyssinian designs towards realization. A refined diplomatic form of blackmail was manifest, for example, in the conversation which, one of the days following the conclusion of the Naval Agreement, Mussolini had with Sir Eric Drummond, the British Ambassador to Rome.

The London correspondent of the Paris paper *Information* published portions of the conversation between Mussolini and Sir Eric Drummond. The Duce declared, wrote the correspondent, that Italy would not hesitate to quit Geneva if the League of Nations were to pass a resolution hurtful to Italian interests in the Ethiopian question. Mussolini stressed repeatedly that the only way of settling the Italo-Abyssinian conflict was by granting Italy a protectorate over Abyssinia like the French protectorate over Morocco or the

---

[35] *Cf.* L. C. B. Seaman, *Post-Victorian Britain 1902—51*, London, 1966, p. 265. — Wheeler—Bennett, *op. cit.*, p. 248.

[36] Cipher telegram by Villani, Hungary's Minister in Rome, June 21, 1935. OL Küm, Pol. 1933—2/27—2054.

[37] MTI, June 26, 1935. OL K. 428.566.

British protectorate over Egypt. In this case Italy would do no greater harm to Ethiopia than the Anglo-German Naval Agreement of London did to the Treaty of Versailles. Sir Eric Drummond reminded Mussolini that Italy's attitude might result in the disruption of the Stresa front. Mussolini retorted, according to the newspaper, that the Stresa front was much more threatened by the Anglo-German Agreement signed in London.

Sir Eric Drummond, who was an enthusiast of the League of Nations, excitedly reported to his Government this conversation with the Duce. It was allegedly under the impact of this report and in the interest of appeasement that the British Government decided to send Eden to Rome.[38]

Eden's journey to Rome was commented upon by many and in many ways. The French were watching jealously whether the relaxation of Anglo-Italian tensions would be to their detriment. The French papers wrote with satisfaction that during Eden's visit to Rome Mussolini spent four hours in talks with French Ambassador Chambrun.[39] The explanation offered was that even if Italy held to her own position, she would not on occasion depart from France's policy. Although Eden went to Rome because of the criticism of the Anglo-German Naval Agreement, it had been decided already earlier at a Cabinet meeting in June that Eden should go there and present Mussolini with a compromise plan for the solution of the Ethiopian crisis. The essence of the offer was that Great Britain would compensate Ethiopia with part of British Somaliland, including the port of Zeila, in order to provide Ethiopia with an access to the sea. Ethiopia in return would cede part of the Ogaden Province to Italy and also would make some economic concessions which were to be defined later.[40]

[38] MTI, June 21, 1935, *ibid.*

[39] Right after Eden's arrival in the evening in Rome, Ambassador Chambrun, who had just come back from Paris, called on Suvich and presented Laval's message. Laval had instructed Chambrun to inform Mussolini that he would be faithfully adhering to the policy laid down in the Rome agreements. Neither England nor any other country would be able to disturb Italo-French friendship. Suvich asked whether Geneva would be able to disturb it, and the Ambassador replied: "Laval trusts that the Ethiopian question will be settled without causing any trouble at Geneva . . . Laval hopes also that the Italian demands will be accepted without any recourse to arms." In conclusion, the Ambassador affirmed that on the Ethiopian question France was for Italy. Quoted from Mario Toscano, "Eden at Rome on the Eve of the Italo-Ethiopian Conflict," *Nuova Antologia*, Jan. 1960.
— *Cf.* Kirkpatrick, *op. cit.*, p. 300.

[40] In the view of the Hungarian Minister in Paris Khuen-Héderváry, this proposal would be gravely prejudicial to the economic interests of French Somaliland on the Red Sea. Strictly confidential report by Khuen—Héderváry, July 4, 1935. OL Küm. Pol. 1935—2/19—2230. — According to the Hungarian Minister in Rome, Villani, who usually obtained his information from Suvich, the British proposal contained the following points: (1) Ethiopia should cede the Ogaden to the Italians; the entire area of this territory is desert country which can be put to no use. (2) The boundaries should be fixed in accordance with the Italian demands. (3) The two Italian colonies, Eritrea and Somalia, might be connected by rail across Ethiopian territory. (4) Italy should gain economic concessions. In compensation the Negus should receive from Britain a coastal strip of British Somaliland with the seaport of Zeila (in the immediate vicinity of Djibouti). In case this port would

Eden arrived in Rome on June 23 and talked with Mussolini on two occasions. The unfounded rumor circulated which claimed that the discussion had been violent, that Mussolini had offended his British visitor, and they had aroused a mutual antipathy that was to leave its marks on the future relations between the two states. The well-informed Sir Ivone Kirkpatrick (a former high-ranking officer at the British Embassy in Rome and later at the British Mission accredited to the Holy See) denies all this, though he admits that surely neither of the two was a man of flatteries, and that no contemporary dictator was glad to see the "British self-assurance" and stubbornnes with which Eden represented the intentions of his Government.

The first conversation took place at the Palazzo Venezia on June 24 and dealt formally with questions of disarmament and several problems aired mainly in the British press: the Naval Agreement, the Western air pact, the Danubian pact, and others. This part of the conversation, or rather the result thereof, was confidentially made known by Suvich to the Hungarian Minister to Italy, F. Villani, who summed it up in these terms:

"1. The Anglo-German Naval Agreement: Italy objects to the method of procedure; the substantive part of the solution is of only indirect interest to her. If France expands her naval programme, Italy will do the same. In so far as the French will be ready to discuss the naval problem in London, the Italians also will send their representatives.

"2. The negotiations for an air pact will be attended by Italy, too. In addition to the five-power treaty France wishes to conclude bilateral agreements as well.

"3. The Eastern pact was touched upon only in broad generalities. Nothing new.

"4. Mussolini pressed for the Danubian pact. Eden declared that Britain was in favour of its conclusion and . . . he may possibly have said that, although Britain will also in the future secure her freedom of action, she will do nothing (against Germany) that might be harmful to Austria.

"According to Suvich it is doubtful whether they will return to the plan by which the three great powers (France, Italy and Germany) would guarantee the independence of Austria by treaty, if the conclusion of the pact encounters too many difficulties. This, of course, will depend on the position to be adopted by the Reich.

"5. The Mediterranean pact, which is now called the 'South-Eastern pact', did not even come up in the course of the conversation."[41]

The most essential part of the Mussolini—Eden conversations was on the British offer concerning Ethiopia. The plan was made known in advance neither to the Italian nor to the French Government. When Eden put forward the British scheme, Mussolini declared at once that it was unacceptable to him for three reasons. First: Ethiopia would thereby be made into a sea power and might increase her influence. Second: Britain would appear to be Ethiopia's

---

be enlarged, it might compete with the French by attracting the entire traffic going to and from Ethiopia. This in turn would be both economically and politically profitable to Britain. Strictly confidential report by Villani from Rome, June 2, 1935. OL Küm. Pol. 1935—2/27—2200.

[41] From Villani's report of July 2, 1935. OL Küm. Pol. 1935—2/27—2199.

protector. Third: Italy could not agree to territorial changes through the mediation of a third power. Moreover, Italy could not in the least be satisfied with the area in question. She had already spent a thousand million lire and made serious attempts to solve the Abyssinian question. The only way of peaceful solution might be for Italy to be given all those territories inhabited by non-Ethiopian races. The military solution would wipe Abyssinia off the map. Eden was very disappointed[42] and explained that the difficulty would arise from the fact that Abyssinia was a member of the League of Nations. Suvich, who was present, interposed that France was also a member of the League, yet she took a different view of the Abyssinian problem. In Eden's opinion, based on information obtained from Laval, the promise that France would let Italy have a free hand applied only to economic matters. Mussolini contested this. Eden did not wish to retreat from the hopeless dispute. He used all his eloquence and referred to the good relations between their two countries, to Mussolini's interests; for it was not worth the trouble to engage in an adventure whose outcome might be dubious. The Duce, on the other hand, argued that he had already spent untold sums on behalf of Eritrea and, therefore, could not afford to withdraw his troops without firing a shot. He had to produce something in return for the great efforts made. The two statesmen agreed on a single thing: they decided to meet again on the next day.

The main topic of the conversation on June 25 in the afternoon was again Ethiopia, but no progress was made. Eden had by necessity come to understand that the proposals he had brought with him, could not be used as the basis of negotiation.

"Eden's visit to Rome, far from resolving the deadlock, only crystallized it. On his return to London, it was impossible to avoid statements in Parliament, and the publicity given to them and to the circumstances of his abortive mission altered public opinion, which in turn stiffened the attitude of the Government. Mussolini was not insensitive to this development and launched an anti-British campaign in the press. Relations between Italy and Britain deteriorated and the prospect of a negotiated settlement began to fade."[43]

All this hardly seemed to have anything to do with the Anglo-German Naval Agreement. Indirectly, however, through French mediation, the agreement made itself felt also in the Italian relations and gave Mussolini his trump card to play in the execution of his Abyssinian designs.

Another European power that was directly hit by the Anglo-German deal was the Soviet Union. If not taken entirely by surprise, Moscow felt, quite understandably, rather uneasy with regard to the Anglo-German arrangement. The Soviet Ambassador to London, I. Maisky, an excellent diplomat, got a clear insight into the calculations of British foreign policy and saw, behind the British policy of imperial defence, the anti-Soviet Conservative

[42] Allegedly, when Eden put forward the proposals, Mussolini continually interrupted him and in reply to a question as to what he demanded eventually, he made a broad movement of the hand indicating the whole of Ethiopia. In the same afternoon he declared that he was definitely determined to carry out the Ethiopian enterprise. See Villani's strictly confidential report of July 2, 1935. OL Küm. Pol. 1935—2/27—2200.

[43] Cf. Kirkpatrick, op. cit., pp. 300—303.

forces seeking reconciliation with Hitler at any price. Nonetheless, the possession of a better knowledge of Hitler's policy-making process prompted the Soviet leaders, as had been the case during the Stalin—Eden conversation in the spring of 1935, to inform the British of their own experiences. In June 1935 Hugh Dalton noted in his diary a conversation with Maisky: "Speak with Maisky. He is worried by Labour attitude in Parliament on rearmament. He says 'by all means talk with Hitler . . . But talk to him with a rifle in your hand, otherwise pay no regard of your wishes. We know him with Japan.' "[44]

According to the U. S. Ambassador in Moscow, W. C. Bullitt, the Soviet Government was intensely disturbed by the naval pact. He wrote in a report to the Department of State in Washington: "Litvinov has expressed himself to me three times on this subject in language more violent than any he has used with regard to any event since I have been here. He now refers to the British as 'the blacklegs' and fears that the effect of the Anglo-German naval agreement will be disastrous not only in Europe but also in the Far East.

"It is, as the Department knows, the theory of Litvinov and the French that Hitler may be restrained only by a 'chain' of states armed to oppose Germany. Litvinov is convinced that England has now broken this 'chain' and that the defection of Italy and other states is likely to follow.

"The most serious concern of the Soviet Government, however, is with regard to the effect on Japan of the Anglo-German naval agreement. The Russians point out that the construction of the new German fleet will make it necessary for England to retain the greater part of her naval forces in the North Sea, that she will have to diminish her forces in the Mediterranean, and that it will be absolutely impossible for her to send a fleet to Singapore.

"From this they draw three conclusions: (1) That the Japanese henceforth will have a completely free hand in the Far East as the United States will not oppose Japanese advance either in China or against the Soviet Union unless assured of British support; (2) That the Anglo-German agreement is definitely against the interests of England unless the British Cabinet proposes to cultivate much closer and friendlier relations with Hitler's Government than have hitherto existed, that therefore a strengthening of the ties between London and Berlin and a weakening of the ties between London and Paris is to be expected; (3) That Great Britain could not have tied her hands so completely in the Far East unless she had arrived at a private and secret agreement with Japan. It is, therefore, believed that the British have made a secret agreement with the Japanese with regard to the limits of the Japanese aggression in China and the protection of British interests in the Far East: In other words, a revival, in the form of a secret understanding, of the Anglo-Japanese Alliance.

"In this connection, Mr. Wheeler-Bennett, who for many years has been connected with the British Secret Service and has just visited several European capitals, said to me recently that he and all the British diplomatists he has seen since the conclusion of the Anglo-German agreement, believe that henceforth Singapore will be totally useless."[45]

[44] *Dalton's Diary*, June 1935.
[45] Report by W. C. Bullitt, U. S. Ambassador in Moscow, June 28, 1935. FRUSDP 1935, Vol. I (Washington, 1953), pp. 168—169.

It was clear also from Bullitt's report, and it was common knowledge by then, that the Soviet Union was at least as much occupied with the Far Eastern power relations as with the relations of forces in Europe. And it is assumed that after the conclusion of the Naval Agreement Litvinov was not especially touched when the British Ambassador in Moscow, Lord Chilston, called on him and presented a message from His Majesty's Government stating that London would be willing to discuss also with the Soviet Government the question of naval armaments. The afore-mentioned Wheeler-Bennett not only described but also influenced the events of those times. He saw things correctly: "A process of disillusionment had begun in Russia with the conclusion of Anglo-German Naval Agreement in the previous June. It began to be believed in Moscow that the protestation of Britain against a possible aggression by Germany could be stilled if such were to be to her advantage, and that a tacit condoning of German depredation in Europe might always be possible if Britain did not consider herself directly threatened, and if such depredation could be effected by peaceful means."[46]

The U. S. Ambassador in Paris reported to the Secretary of State in Washington the opinion of J. Paul-Boncour, who "stressed his belief that the results of German construction to 35 per cent would inevitably cause the Soviet Government to embark upon a vast programme."[47] What else could Moscow have done?

At first the Baltic States welcomed the Naval Agreement, but their mood changed shortly, as diplomats reported from Riga: "The Latvian Government became panicky," and "Britain abandoned Latvia". The question was the main item on the agenda of the Conference of the Ministers Plenipotentiary of Latvia on June 28. The Riga and Tallinn newspapers were alarmed at what Germany would do with her 400,000 tons. A Latvian journalist proposed that the Baltic States must strengthen their naval and coast defences. He quoted also Scandinavian papers stating that the balance of power had completely

---

[46] Wheeler-Bennett, *op. cit.*, p. 279. — Regarding the repercussions of the Naval Agreement, *cf.* also P. N. Miloukov, *La politique extérieure des Soviets*, 2nd ed., Paris, 1936, pp. 504—505. — M. Beloff, *op. cit.*, pp. 133—134. — The literature of the history of the Naval Agreement has been enriched by a number Soviet historians; *cf.* the articles by Л. Б. Поздеева in Вопросы истории 4/1952, and in the volume entitled Из истории агрессивной внешней политики германского империализма [From the History of the Aggressive Foreign Policy of German Imperialism], Moscow, 1959; Л. Иванов: "Англо-германское морское соглашение и проблема воздушного пакта" [The Anglo-German Naval Agreement and the Problem of the Air Pact], Мировое хозяйство и мировая политика, 8/1935, pp. 25—39; И. Ерухимович: "Англо-германское соглашение и угроза новой войны" [The Anglo-German Naval Agreement and the Threat of a New War], Мской сборник, Leningrad, 8) 1935, pp. 9—22; В. Корнев: Творцы англо—германского морского соглашения" [The Authors of the Anglo-German Naval Agreement], Новый мир, 7/1935, pp 169—185; В. Повлов: "Расплата за недальновидную политику: К истории англо—германского морского соглашения 1935 года" [Payment for a Short-sighted Policy: On the History of the Anglo-German Naval Agreement of 1935], Международная жизнь, 11/1963, pp. 96—103.

[47] The Ambassador in France (Straus) to the Secretary of State, Paris, June 19, 1935. FRUSDP 1935, Vol. I, p. 166.

changed in the Baltic and the North Sea. A high-ranking official of the Latvian Foreign Ministry, Mr. Munters, expressed in private his complete agreement with the author of *The Times* article "Sea power in the Baltic" published on July 6, 1935. The writer set forth that both Poland and Sweden would have to embark upon a naval building programme.[48]

Japan's part in the preparation of the Anglo-German Naval Agreement is not entirely clear. According to Turkish and Japanese sources it was Japan who had advised Germany not to retreat from the 35 per cent.[49] This was confirmed in a general way by U. S. Secretary of State Cordell Hull on the basis of confidential information from Britain and he made it also known to his Ambassador in Tokyo, J. C. Grew.[50] (The communication read: "Germany is being pressed by Japan to ask for restoration of naval strength.") The fact of the matter is that both Japan and the United States noted with approval the conduct and the result of the Anglo-German naval negotiations. Secretary of State Hull on June 11 had dispatched the following Aide-mémoire to the London Foreign Office: "While the American Government desires to co-operate fully with Great Britain in seeking a solution of all phases of the naval question, it feels that inasmuch as American interest in the size of the fleets of the Continental Powers is necessarily less immediate than that of Great Britain, the differential between the British and German fleets is primarily one for British decision."[51] On June 12 President Roosevelt conferred with members of his Government. Afterwards they released a statement to the effect that the United States was not opposed to any settlement acceptable to Britain. The U. S. policy regarding the fleet issue at that time was essentially determined by two considerations, parity with Britain and superiority over Japan.[52]

An analyst of Roosevelt's foreign policy takes the view that the Naval Agreement met with general approval in the United States, however, the arguments he adduces in support are far from being held uniformly. It is true that the *Cincinnati Enquirer*, the *Des Moines Register* and the *Albuquerque*

[48] See the reports by F. Cole, the American Chargé d'Affaires in Riga, July 11 and 18, 1935. FRUSDP 1935, Vol. I, pp. 298—299, 304—305. It could be no accident that the start of World War II was signalled by a cannonade opened from Hitler's battleship *Schleswig—Holstein* on a Baltic peninsula, the Polish Westerplatte (a section of the Danzig harbour). — Regarding the Baltic questions, see also Note 32 in the chapter on the "Position and Strategy of the German and British Fleets."

[49] Personal communication from D. C. Watt, Professor of the London School of Economics, a specialist on naval questions. See also the advice given to the German delegation by Avata Oka, the Japanese Naval Attaché in London. Quoted by H. A. Jacobsen, *Nationalsozialistische Aussenpolitik 1933—1938*, Frankfurt, 1968, p. 415.

[50] The Secretary of State (C. Hull) to the Ambassador in Japan (J. C. Grew), March 1935. FRUSDP 1935, Vol. I, pp. 26—46. The U. S. Ambassador in Tokyo wrote in his memoirs (*Ten Years in Japan*, New York, 1944) that Japan regarded the Soviet Union as her enemy No. 1. Tokyo was afraid of Bolshevism and deemed it necessary to drive this peril out of Asia.

[51] Hull to Bingham (U. S. Ambassador in London) on June 11, 1935. FRUSDP 1935, Vol. I, p. 5.

[52] Report by Balázsy, Counsellor of the Hungarian Legation in Washington, August 12, 1935. OL Küm. Pol. 1935—2/25—2672.

Journal were praising the pact, while the influential *New York Times* (June 20), the *Washington News* (June 20), and *The Chicago Daily News* (June 19), on the other hand, were highly critical of British appeasement which amounted to "a breach of international law."[53]

W. E. Dodd, the U. S. Ambassador to Berlin, in his confidential personal letters, expressed his grave concern — which was really worthy of attention but went unheeded — just after the signing of the Anglo-German Naval Agreement. In a letter to Secretary of State Cordell Hull he wrote that the naval pact was to his mind the first step taken by the Germans to encircle Russia and get absolute control of the Baltic. And in a letter to his friend the appeaser Lord Lothian, he wrote from Berlin on June 19, the day following the conclusion of the Naval Agreement: ". . . Just now it seems to me that navy building and aircraft activity only indicate how hopeless the prospect is . . . Especially since both our countries permit great capitalists to go on making arms of all kinds and making enormous profits with governmental approval . . . It looks as if our children would once more be engaged in such a struggle as Lloyd George describes so dramatically in his Volume 3."[54] (The work in question is Lloyd George's six-volume *War Memoirs*.)

[53] Ch. C. Tansill, *Back Door to War: The Roosevelt Foreign Policy 1933—41*, Chicago, 1952, p. 302.

[54] See Dodd's letter to Hull, July 15, 1935. Quoted by Tansill, *op. cit.*, p. 303, and Dodd's letter to Lord Lothian, Berlin, June 19, 1935. Personal and confidential. Edinburg. Scottish Record Office. Lothian Papers. G. D. 40.17—319.

SUMMARY AND OUTLOOK

The Naval Agreement was followed immediately by a process of reorganization and combining of all forces which felt the urge to take action and which, for one reason or another, pressed for an increase of Britain's defensive forces. A very accurate and elaborate document to this effect is the report, unpublished until now, which was submitted on November 21, 1935, by Sir Warren Fisher and Sir Robert Vansittart, together with other leading figures of the defensive forces (among them Sir Ernle Chatfield, Sir Edward Ellington, Sir Archibald Montgomery-Massingberd, and Sir Maurice Hankey, secretary of the Committee of Imperial Defence), and whose concluding, recapitulative sentence reads as follows: "Our Report is based on a reasonable estimate of what is required to meet our responsibilities in respect of the security of the Empire, and does not provide a margin for every conceivable danger, such as an unexpectedly rapid increase in the naval strength of Japan or the air strength of Germany: a sudden attack in time of normal diplomatic relations such as was deemed possible before the war."[1] By 1937, the year Chamberlain became

[1] This document was an accurate situation report on Great Britain's international relations. It adapted the imperial defence requirements to the new conditions. It reckoned with German naval reorganization, foresaw that Italy might be a potential enemy on the sea route to the Far East, and that continual and heavy air attacks would come. It called for new standards in respect of the fleet on two points:

"(a) To enable us to place a Fleet in the Far East fully adequate to act on the defensive and to serve as a strong deterrent against any threat to our interests in that part of the globe. (b) To maintain in all circumstances in Home Waters a force able to meet the requirements of a war with Germany at the same time." The memorandum stated at the same time that the survey was looking three years ahead. In this immediate period Britain could not afford to be opposed by a hostile Italy. It envisaged £417.5 million for a five-year period, including £239 million for the first three years. Interestingly, the general part of the document commented that it was advisable to prepare the population for increased defence requirements, to convince the people of the necessity of such measures and at the same time to ensure that education laid as strong an emphasis on the problems

153

Prime Minister, the prevailing political power relationships had made it clear that, although the Baldwin ministry did not induce determined action — it not only had taken the road of active appeasement but also had become the breeding ground of the political attitude of appeasement — it nevertheless saw the need to raise the defensive forces to the highest possible level, and tried to get a clearer picture of the number one potential enemy in Europe: Germany.[2] This understanding was promoted by a well trained staff of correspondents, intelligence agents and diplomatists working under the ambitious young Foreign Secretary, Eden, a staff which continually issued danger signals even though certain quarters steadily endeavoured to confuse them.[3]

---

of defence as on propaganda for peace and the idea of the League of Nations. Programmes of the Defence Services. P. R. O. Cab. 24/259.

The rearmament programme had become known to diplomatic circles as early as October 1935, even though precise figures did not leak out. The Hungarian Chargé d'Affaires also had been informed that the defence portfolios "have fully succeeded in winning the Government over to their view . . . The entire war industry is already working with full capacity. The largest Vickers plant, which had stood still since the war, has resumed production. To all indications Britain has begun rearming on such a large scale which a short time ago looked entirely hopeless even to the most eager imperialists." Report by Királdy-Lukács from London, October 5, 1935. OL Küm. Pol. 1935—2/5—3081.

[2] Anthony Eden, who had been appointed Foreign Secretary in December 1935, had some part to play in this. He was a diplomat of smart looks, but of not so smart brains in the view of some, one who had made a "meteoric rise." His appointment was "a victory for 'The Left,' for 'the pro-Leaguers.' " Cf. Chips, *The Diaries of Sir Henry Channon*, ed. by R. R. James, London, 1967, p. 65. — In January 1936 Eden circulated to his fellow Cabinet members a very confidential memorandum together with a collection of the report for 1933—35 by the British Ambassador in Berlin. He said in that paper that "Hitler's foreign policy may be summed up as the destruction of the peace settlement and re-establishment of Germany as the dominant Power in Europe. The means by which this policy is to be effected are twofold: *(a)* Internally through the militarization of the whole nation in all its aspects, *(b)* externally by economic and territorial expansion so as to absorb as far as possible all those of German race who are at present citizens of neighboring States, to acquire new markets for German industry and new fields for German emigration, and to obtain control of some of the sources of those raw materials at present lacking to Germany. The forms and direction of this expansion is the one still doubtful factor in Germany's plans for the future." Eden drew two conclusions from the situation thus presented: "*(a)* That it is vital to hasten and complete our own rearmament. In view of what is so openly proceeding in Germany, we must be ready for all eventualities. *(b)* Whilst pursuing our rearmament it will be well to consider whether it is still possible to come to some *modus vivendi* with Hitler's Germany which would be both honourable and safe for this country and which would at the same time lessen the increasing burden in Europe caused by the growth of Germany's strength and ambitions . . . I do not conceal from my colleagues that in the present temper of the German Government and people, this solution of our problem will not be easily realized." The German Danger. Very confidential. P. R.O. Cab. 24/259.

[3] A good example of this was the case of the Berlin correspondent of *The Times*, N. Ebbutt. The attitude of Sir Robert Craigie, who played an important role in the negotiation of the Anglo-German Naval Agreement, still remains to some extent to be elucidated. In November 1936 Craigie received the copy of a memoran-

154

Improvement of the forces of defence and more reasonable assessment and judgement of the aims of Hitlerite Germany, however, did not alter the essence of the principles and methods of British policy. The Anglo-German Naval Agreement was an important landmark in the evolution of European policies, including Anglo-German relations, and, by encouraging Hitler and the British appeasers, it determined the political developments of both countries for years to come.

The results of the study of the Anglo-German Naval Agreement indicate also that we cannot know the whole truth, either with regard to Great Britain or to any other great power, if we judge events exclusively from the European viewpoint.

We still have to tell the rest of the story. Churchill, who reorganized the British fleet in 1911 and who took over the helm of his nation on the verge of an ultimate catastrophe, had said in 1901: "The only weapon with which we can expect to cope with great nations is the Navy."[4]

But the Naval Agreement of 1935, which should have safeguarded the position of the British fleet and set limits to the building of German submarines, which were recognized as a dangerous military instrument as early as World War I, provided just on this point unlimited opportunity to the Germans who, on top of the bargain, violated the agreement precisely on this point. In May 1938 Hitler told senior officers of the German Navy that Britain was to be counted as a potential enemy and in the autumn of 1938 these officers began to draw up the tactical plan of annihilating the British merchant fleet. This purpose was served by what was called "Plan Z" to be carried out within six years. (Admiral Doenitz who succeeded Raeder, relying on the experiences of World War I, was convinced that in the naval warfare to be carried on against Britain, the submarines would play a key role.)[5]

---

dum, which said that a diplomatist in London "had been shown by a friend in the German diplomatic service a circular to the German Embassies abroad explaining the circumstances in which the Anglo-German Naval Treaty had been concluded. The circular was dated about 10 days after the conclusion of the Treaty in the summer of 1935 and it emphasized that one of the motives directing the German Government's attitude was that Germany was not, at the time of the signature of the Treaty, in a position to build more than one-third of the British Fleet. The circular continued that as soon as the German yards were able to build a larger fleet, the whole situation would be reviewed." In a confidential private letter to the Admiralty, Craigie refuted this quite reasonably, while remarking at the same time that "it seems to me most improbable that even had the German Government intended from the first to play us false . . . what has probably happened is that some relatively harmless passage in the circular, if circular there was, has been twisted into the present story. The German Government will be as little desirous of entering into a naval race with Britain after they have reached their 35 per cent strength as they are at the present time." This was Craigie's personal estimate and his opinion was shared by the First Lord of the Admiralty, as is seen from a memorandum forwarded to Craigie by another official. P. R. O. Adm. 116/3378.

[4] Sir Peter Gretton, *W. Churchill and the Royal Navy*, London, 1966, p. 338.

[5] The German U-boats were widely known to be practically not submarines but submersible ships. The problem with them was that they ran faster on the surface

And this view was not changed in the slightest by the fact that in autumn 1938 the Anglo-German communiqué, issued at the time of the Munich Pact (September 30, 1938), included the following two sentences: "We regard the agreement signed last night and the Anglo-German Naval Agreement as symbolic of the desire of our two peoples never to go to war with one another again. We are resolved that the method of consultation shall be the method adopted to deal with any other questions that may concern our two countries, and we are determined to continue our efforts to remove possible sources of difference and thus to contribute to assure the peace of Europe. (Signed:) A. Hitler, N. Chamberlain."[6]

In December 1938 Herbert von Dirksen, the German Ambassador in London, on instructions from his Government sent Foreign Secretary Halifax a confidential note stating that the time had come to exploit the possibility offered by the 1935 Naval Agreement and its ratification in 1937, namely to create a parity of tonnage between German and British submarines. (See Appendix XIV, p. 251.)[7]

When on March 31, 1939, Britain — at the same time as France — gave a unilateral guarantee to Poland, Hitler wanted to denounce the Naval Agreement immediately, but he changed his mind for the time being and only declared that if Britain no longer felt bound by the agreement, Germany would not oppose its termination. In April, however, a great deal happened: an Anglo-Polish declaration of mutual assistance was issued on the 6th; Italy invaded Albania on the 7th and annexed the country on the 12th; on the 13th the British and French Governments gave assurances to Rumania and Greece, etc. Ultimately Hitler made the Anglo-Polish declaration a pretext for denouncing on April 27 the Naval Agreement and the Polish–German Non-Aggression Declaration dating back to 1934. Addressing the Reichstag on April 28, 1939, he recounted that the Germans had felt respect and admiration for Britain, but Britain had cheated them and pursued a policy of encirclement towards Germany, therefore, the basis of the Naval Agreement had been removed.[8]

Today we know that Hitler gave the *Wehrmacht* an order on April 3 to prepare a war of agression on Poland ("Case White"). Admiral Raeder had the naval policies of the plan worked out: the entrance to the Baltic was to be guarded by submarines with two pocket battleships, and two battleships

---

than in the depths of the sea, so that they were less effective than expected. By the time this problem was solved World War II had been ended. In the course of 1942—43 Anglo-American technicians solved the question of precisely locating submarines. This put an end to the submarine danger. In World War II sixty-six per cent of the German submarine fleet were sunk with their crews and officers. Such losses have seldom occurred in naval history.

[6] Quoted by Halmosy, *op. cit.*, pp. 437—438. — We know from one of Chamberlain's biographers that, still prior to Munich, Hitler repeatedly talked to Chamberlain about the Naval Agreement and this might have given Chamberlain the idea of including this passage in the text of the Anglo-German communiqué. *Cf.* J. Macleod, *op. cit.*, pp. 236—255.

[7] Dirksen to Halifax December 1, 1938. P. R. O. Adm. 116.3369.

[8] Shirer, *op. cit.*, p. 471.

with the rest of the submarines were to stand in readiness for the battle of the Atlantic.[9]

At that time such a short-sighted and all-out advocate of Anglo-German co-operation as Sir Nevile Henderson, the British Ambassador to Germany, already had to admit that it was impossible to make any further concessions. In 1937 he still reported to his superior in the Foreign Office: "I regard the Anglo-German Naval Agreement as the foundation and test stone of any present and future understanding with Germany . . . I am very disinclined to believe in the reality of Germany's aggressive intentions against Great Britain unless and until she goes back on the Naval Agreement." (See Appendix XI, p. 241.)[10] Hitler made no scruples at brushing aside the "foundation and test stone" of co-operation.

It is also a part of the story of the Naval Agreement that after eighteen months of negotiation an Anglo-Soviet Naval Agreement was signed on July 18, 1937. The instruments of ratification were exchanged in London on November 4, and the agreement came into force the same day. The antecedents and the essence of this agreement are the following:

As it is well known, the great powers concluded a treaty for the limitation of naval armaments in Washington in 1922, followed by another in London in 1930. They attempted to prolong those treaties upon expiration in 1936. (It is believed by some, as we know, that it was in preparation for this step that the Anglo-German Agreement was made.) This, however, came to nothing because of Japanese opposition. Japan had demanded that her naval strength should be on a par with the U. S. Navy and the British Navy. The two great powers did not accept this demand. In 1936, therefore, Great Britain, France and the United States concluded an agreement for a qualitative limitation of warships. After the conclusion of this three-power arrangement Britain invited the Soviet Union to enter into a similar agreement with her. The related conversations, in which the Soviet Union was represented by Ambassador Maisky and Naval Attaché Antsipo-Chikunsky, started in London on May 20. The Soviet Union accepted the British proposal with two reservations: (a) that Britain should conclude a similar agreement with Germany, too; (b) that the agreement should not impose restrictions on the building of the Soviet Far Eastern fleet, with regard to Japan.

Stipulating the above conditions and an exchange of information, the two powers signed the agreement on July 30. According to confidential reports a secret clause was also agreed upon between the British and the Soviet Government: the Soviet Union allegedly undertook to set certain limits to its fleet-building programme, in order to avoid the danger of Germany denouncing the 1935 Anglo-German Naval Agreement under the pretext of Soviet naval superiority. It is further alleged that the Soviet Union undertook not to bring its Far Eastern fleet to European waters under any circumstances whatsoever. According to diplomatic sources in Moscow, the Soviet Union launched a big programme of naval construction and "England is alarmed at the supposition that the Soviet Union may expand its fleet to

[9] *Ibid.*, p. 488.
[10] N. Henderson's personal note to the Foreign Secretary, Berlin, July 1, 1937. P. R. O. Adm. 116/3378.

157

such an extent as it did its land and air forces; the arrangement has been proposed in order to prevent it from doing that uncontrolled". (See also Appendix IX, p. 233.)[11]

The Anglo-Soviet Naval Agreement was of course brought into connection with the Montreux Convention of the Straits, signed on July 20, 1936. The Convention of Montreux restored the sovereignty of Turkey over the Straits, giving her the key to the Dardanelles and the Bosporus. The convention gave the right of passage through the Straits to all merchant vessels, as well as to warships of the Black Sea powers in times of peace and war alike, but the right of passage of the warships of non-Black Sea powers was strictly limited also in peaceful times. Under the Montreux Convention the Soviet Union might have actually relied on Turkey for its defence in the Black Sea, and consequently concentrate its forces in the Baltic. It is supposed by some that there was a connection between the secret clause of the Anglo-Soviet Naval Agreement and the British concessions made at Montreux.[12]

This was the prelude to the signing on July 18, 1937, of the Anglo-Soviet Naval Agreement, followed half an hour later by the signing of another Anglo-German treaty. The agreements thus seemed to secure the future from many sides. Slowly but most surely, moves and countermoves became indicative of irreconcilable future conflicts of interests. A historian of the British diplomacy of appeasement wrote: "If Hitler's promises were those of a rational statesman, in the Stresemann tradition, then the agreement was clearly a triumph. Nor is there evidence that Baldwin, Neville Chamberlain, Anthony Eden, or Lord Halifax doubted Hitler's trustworthiness when the agreement was signed. They all believed that it would prove effective. They all chose to ignore the growing signs of danger and deception."[13] Unfortunately, this choice created

[11] Excerpt from the report by Jungerth-Arnóthy from Moscow, May 29, 1936. OL Küm. Pol. 1937−2/28−1928. — See also the strictly confidential report by Masirevich from London, August 6, 1936. OL Küm. Pol. 1937−2/28−27566. — On the other hand, the British argued that the German naval construction programme did not endanger the European equilibrium. Cf. Anglo-German Naval Conversation at the Foreign Office, February 13, 1937. P. R. O. Adm. 116/3378. — As to the development of the Soviet Navy in the 1930's, cf. С. Е. Захаров: История военно-морского искусства [A History of Naval Strategy], Moscow, 1970, pp. 168−170.

[12] Regarding Montreux we still have to note that the British delegation, under German pressure, found something to object to in the Soviet proposals submitted at Montreux (the right of Soviet warships to innocent passage through the Straits in times of peace and war alike, the closing of the Straits to all other warships). But when Maisky had told the Foreign Office in London that Litvinov would leave the conference, the British retracted. Of course, they did so not only for this reason By means of the Anglo-Egyptian treaty of alliance, whose preparation was advancing as scheduled, Great Britain obtained full military control of the Suez Canal, dominated over the Western gate of the Mediterranean from her Gibraltar stronghold, kept a strong naval base on Malta in the Mediterranean, and was gradually developing Alexandria and Cyprus into similar bases. In other words, Britain was in a position, as was formulated by Masirevich, "to bottle up in the Mediterranean any possibly hostile Russian fleet coming from the Black Sea." Report by Masirevich, July 29, 1936. OL Küm. Pol. 1936−2−2755.

[13] Gilbert, op. cit., (1966), p. 150.

158

a situation far too dangerous for the whole of Europe. That is why the sympathies of the historians go to such less famous past diplomats who, however, were of a more realistic vision and mind as for example, the Czechoslovak Minister in Paris, Stefan Osuský, who, filled with anxieties, wrote in December 1935 as follows:

"Germany is preparing to solve big questions. There is every indication that she will raise the question of partitioning, not the colonies, but the raw material resources. She will try to enforce such claims also against Russia in an effort to use it for extending there her sphere of political and economic control. The years ahead of us, I cannot deny, will be much more difficult than we could surmise. The German problem exists, it is here, and Germany is seeking to solve it."[14]

[14] S. Osuský to Dr. M. Hodža, Paris December 19, 1935. AMZV P. Z. No. 35.

APPENDICES

APPENDIX I*

The issue of Imperial Defence before the Cabinet

IMPERIAL DEFENCE.

For some years when the Votes of the Defence Services have been debated in the House of Commons, the suggestion has been made that their consideration should be preceded by a Debate on Imperial Defence as a whole. The Government have always been sympathetic to this proposal, but owing to the limitations of the parliamentary time-table, they have not found it possible hitherto to adopt it. In the present year the case for some such procedure is stronger than it was in past years, for the reason that the course of events has rendered unavoidable an increase in the total Defence Estimates, and it is hoped to be able to provide an opportunity for the discussion of Imperial Defence. The following notes are circulated, not to supersede the White Papers accompanying the Estimates of the Defence Departments, but in order to indicate generally the policy of the Government in Imperial Defence, and the reasons for the increase.

I.

2. The establishment of peace on a permanent footing has long been the principal aim of British foreign policy. The first and strongest line of defence of the people's territories, cities, overseas trade and communications of the British Empire is provided by the maintenance of peace. If war can be banished from the world, these vast and world-wide interests will remain free from the dangers of external attack, and the great work of civilisation and trade will proceed unhampered by the fears that have hindered their progress from the earliest recorded times until to-day. That is why *every* British Government is bound to use its utmost endeavours to maintain peace.

3. In recent years the chief methods by which His Majesty's Government in the United Kingdom have pursued the establishment of peace on a permanent footing have been as follows: —

* Transcripts of Crown-copyright records in the Public Record Office appear by permission of the Controller of H. M. Stationery Office.

(1) *By unswerving support of the League of Nations*, which His Majesty's Government in the United Kingdom regard as essential machinery for promoting the preservation of peace by the facilitating and regularising of the means of international co-operation.

(2) *By the promotion, in co-operation with other nations, of international instruments designed to produce collective security and a sense of security among the nations.* — Among the more important may be mentioned: —

(*a*) The Briand—Kellogg Pact of 1928 for the renunciation by every signatory of war as an instrument of policy.

(*b*) The Quadruple Pacific Treaty and the Nine-Power Treaty regarding the Far East, both designed to promote peace in that area and in the Pacific.

(*c*) The Locarno Treaties, designed, by a system of mutual guarantee, to maintain the peace in those countries of Western Europe, to the situation of which this country has never been and can never be indifferent.

The latest development in this direction is the Anglo-French proposal of the 3rd February for regional and mutual arrangements to deter aerial aggression and thereby provide immunity from sudden attacks from the air.

(*d*) Various proposals for increasing security in Eastern Europe and the Danube Basin, with special reference to the maintenance of the independence and integrity of Austria. These involve no military commitments, direct or indirect, by this country.

(3) *By efforts to promote international understanding in general, and in particular to bring back into the comity of nations the ex-enemy countries.* — Successive Governments in the United Kingdom have taken a leading part in such measures as the suspension of the Penalties provisions of the Treaty of Versailles; the election of ex-enemies to membership of the League of Nations, including, in the case of Germany, permanent membership of the Council; the evacuation of the Rhineland five years in advance of the date fixed by the Treaties; the gradual rationalisation and virtual settlement of reparations at the Lausanne Conference of 1932; the Saar plebiscite; the action in connection with the Disarmament Conference referred to below in (4).

(4) *The reduction and limitation of international armaments in order to promote the work of pacification and steadily to reduce the means of making war.* — The best known instances of disarmament are the Washington Treaty of 1922 and the London Naval Treaty of 1930, both of which are to form the subject of an International Conference during the present year. After six years of preparation the Disarmament Conference, promoted by the League of Nations, opened at Geneva on the 2nd February, 1932, and ever since the present Government have sought unremittingly to obtain a successful result. In pursuit of this object they have been foremost among the nations in taking the initiative as, for example, to mention only a few instances, their declaration in connection with Germany's claim to equality of rights, of the 17th November, 1932 (Cmd. 4189); the British draft Convention of the 16th March, 1933 (Cmd. 4279), and their proposals of January 1934 (Cmd. 4498).

4. Hitherto, in spite of innumerable setbacks, public opinion in this country has tended to assume that the international machinery for the maintenance of peace can be absolutely relied on, and that we can gradually dispense with the older methods on which we have hitherto depended for our security in the last resort. The force of world events, however, has shown that these assumptions

are premature, and that sustained efforts will be required over a long period of time before this stage is reached. Nations vary in their temperaments, needs and state of civilisation. Some are resentful at past misfortunes, or harbour the desire to recover their losses, or seek new fields of expansion, owing to increase in population or other causes, and it must not be forgotten, in this last connection, that the United Kingdom and the rest of the British Empire are, perhaps, more fortunately placed than anyone else. All are suffering, in varying degrees, from the economic pressure of the times, which is itself due to human folly in the past. Events in various parts of the world have shown that nations are still prepared to use or threaten force under the impulse of what they conceive to be a national necessity, and that once action has been taken the existing international machinery for the maintenance of peace cannot be counted upon to provide an adequate protection.

5. The National Government intends to pursue without intermission the national policy of peace by every practicable means and to take advantage of every opportunity, and to make opportunities, to make peace more secure. But it can no longer close its eyes to the fact that a second line of defence is still required in order to secure the Empire's survival, so that it may continue to play its full part in maintaining the peace of the world.

II.

6. During the years that all parties in this Country have been seeking to carry out the policy outlined above, there has been a steady decline in the effective strength of our armaments by sea and land. In the air we virtually disarmed ourselves in 1919, and, subsequently, from time to time postponed attainment of the minimum air strength regarded as necessary to our security in the face of air developments on the Continent. It is not that British Governments have neglected to keep themselves informed of the position. Every year the state of our armaments has been anxiously considered, and if risks have been run they have been accepted deliberately in pursuit of the splendid aim of permanent peace. Again and again, rather than run any risk of jeopardising some promising movement in this direction by increasing expenditure on armaments, Governments have postponed the adoption of measures that were required when considered from the point of view of national defence alone. In this way we have taken risks for peace, but, as intimated by the Secretary of State for Foreign Affairs in the debate on the address on the 28th November, 1934, "disarming ourselves in advance, by ourselves, by way of an example — has not increased our negotiating power in the Disarmament discussions at Geneva."

7. Parliament and people, however, have been warned again and again by Ministers and other public men that serious deficiencies were accumulating in all the Defence Services; that our armaments could not be maintained at their present level, and that unilateral disarmament could not be pursued indefinitely.

165

III.

8. Last midsummer the position was as follows: —

(1) The Disarmament Conference through still in existence, had virtually come to a standstill, and there was no reasonable prospect that any measure of international disarmament was likely to result without prolonged negotiations, the issue of which could not be foreseen. It was clear that these negotiations would be hampered by very serious difficulties that had arisen in recent years both in Europe and elsewhere, and by the fact that Japan and Germany had both given notice of their withdrawal from the League of Nations; while Germany, in addition, had left the Disarmament Conference.

(2) A mass of evidence had made clear Germany's intention to re-arm on a large scale, and not least in the air, despite the provisions of Part V of the Treaty of Versailles. All the larger Powers, except the United Kingdom, had adopted measures of re-armament and were in different stages of putting them into execution.

(3) Detailed examination prolonged over many months had been made into the serious deficiencies that had accumulated in our defence forces and defences. It had been established that unless a programme was put in hand to recondition them and bring them up-to-date, the country and the Empire would no longer possess an adequate standard of defence. And if, unhappily, in spite of all our efforts to keep the peace an aggression should take place directed against ourselves, we should be incapable of keeping open our sea communications, or of feeding our people or of defending our Capital and our principal cities and their population against the menace of air attack. Much less should we be in a position to fulfil our obligations under the Covenant of the League of Nations or the Locarno Treaties, or to take effective part in any system of collective security.

9. In the above circumstances, His Majesty's Government feel that they would be failing in their responsibilities if, while continuing to the full, efforts for peace by limitation of armaments, they delay the initiation of steps to put our own armaments on a footing to safeguard us against potential dangers. A co-ordinated programme has been drawn up for re-conditioning our defence forces and defences. In the case of the Navy (whose strength in certain respects is at present limited by Treaty) and Army, these programmes involve for the most part a process of making good technical deficiencies, providing up-to-date equipment and adequate personnel and reserves of war material, without which our forces would be helpless either to defend our most vital interests against an aggressor or to co-operate in any system of collective security by sea, land or air.

10. In the case of the Royal Air Force alone were any appreciable increases of units deemed immediately necessary, and for this reason they were announced in Parliament on the 19th July, 1934, and debated by the House of Commons on the 30th July, and by the House of Lords on the 14th November. Increases will also be necessary in the anti-aircraft defences provided by the Army.

166

11. On the 28th November, 1934, His Majesty's Government drew public attention to the re-armament which Germany has undertaken, and announced a speeding up of the increases in the Air Force already announced. The action of His Majesty's Government did not, of course, imply condonation of a breach of the Treaty of Versailles. It merely noted and made public, as a first step, what was known to be proceeding. This re-armament, if continued at its present rate, unabated and uncontrolled, will aggravate the existing anxieties of the neighbours of Germany, and may consequently produce a situation where peace will be in peril.

12. His Majesty's Government have noted and welcomed the declarations of the leaders of Germany that they desire peace. They cannot, however, fail to recognise that not only the forces but the spirit which these leaders are organising among the population, and especially the youth of the country, lend colour to, and substantiate, the general feeling of insecurity which they have already and incontestably generated. Anxiety in turn reflects itself in the armaments of other countries.

IV.

13. If peace should be broken, the Navy becomes the first line of defence for the maintenance of our essential sea communications. Our special problems of defence arise *firstly*, from the dependence of this country for its existence on seaborne supplies of food and raw materials, and *secondly*, from the unique conditions of the British Empire, its world-wide distribution, and the fact that all parts of it are, to a greater or less extent, dependent on communications by sea for their well-being, or in some instances for their very existence; furthermore, in the last resort, it is on the transport of adequate forces and their supplies by sea that the different parts of the Empire rely to resist aggression and to ensure the security of their interests and the integrity of their territory.

Thus it is that the security by sea passage to this country, as well as to and from all parts of the Empire, forms the basis and foundation of our system of Imperial defence, without which all other measures can be of but little avail.

14. So long as the Navy is strong enough to perform this task, and the other defence services are equipped to co-operate in the defence of ports and of the narrow seas, our food supplies will be safeguarded; the Members of the British Commonwealth of Nations will be able to render each other mutual support to the extent that each may decide, and the trade of the different parts of the Empire, both with one another and with the rest of the world, will be maintained. Failure to make sufficient provision for the Navy and the other Defence Services will, in the event of war, reduce supplies to the point of starvation, render impossible mutual support within the Empire, lead to a cessation of trade, and inflict incalculable suffering on the community.

15. Developments in the power and range of air forces have increased the vulnerability of this country in certain circumstances, but this is an added burden of defence, and when it has been faced and shouldered, the protection of the sea communications of these Islands as well as of the rest of the Empire remains. While also the growing power of air forces has increased the efficiency

and range of shore defences, our merchant ships on the vast ocean spaces are still open to naval attack. The principles of naval defence remain therefore unaltered.

16. The Main Fleet is the basis upon which our naval strategy rests, but the cover it can provide is rarely complete, and it may always be expected that detached enemy units may evade the Main Fleet and carry out sporadic attacks on territories and trade. To deal with these attacks, considerable numbers of cruisers are required over and above those forming part of the Main Fleet.

17. In the Main Fleet the capital ship remains the essential element upon which the whole structure of our naval strategy depends. The age of our battleships, however, together with this and other factors, renders it necessary to commence their replacement at an early date. The advent of air attack in its present form was unforeseen when our battleships were designed; but the anti-aircraft armament of the present ships is being increased to enable them to perform their primary function.

18. The strength of the Navy, as already mentioned, is at present fixed by the Washington and London Naval Treaties which are due for reconsideration this year. Divergencies in national points of view have developed since the negotiation of those treaties, as evidenced by the recent notice by Japan to terminate the Washington Treaty, and by the programmes effected and contemplated by some of the European Powers. Much will therefore depend on the next naval conference and on the ability of all concerned to translate into action the undoubted desire for a satisfactory international settlement.

19. It is the hope of His Majesty's Government to secure an arrangement that will avoid competition naval armaments whilst leaving us free to maintain a fleet at the minimum strength necessary for our absolute requirements. This involves a calculation of the number of ships of each type which together make up the fleet, and it is essential that the minimum numbers so calculated should be maintained. It is equally essential that our fleet should be kept up to date in all respects, including a sufficient and highly trained personnel, adequate provision of aircraft (which are becoming more and more important to the Navy), the most modern weapons, repair facilities, and the necessary reserves of fuel, ammunition and stores of all kinds at convenient bases. Without these facilities, or if at the outbreak of war our ships are less well equipped than those of the enemy, our fleets may be unable to fulfil their tasks and our ships may suffer destruction.

V.

20. The bases and fuelling stations of the Fleet and the harbours where merchant ships are loading and unloading require defences against sea-borne and air attack on scales that vary with their geographical position and the other circumstances of each port. Without these defences, the docks, repair facilities, fuel, stores, as well as merchant ships in port, would be liable to destruction by an enemy, and the action of the Fleet might be paralysed.

21. At the present time the defences of our ports are inadequate and out of date. Under modern conditions the defence of ports involves concerted action

between the three Services, but the heaviest expenditure falls on War Office votes.

22. The Army estimates, besides providing for the improvement and installation of coast defences on a considered scale of priority, make provision for the large expansion of the anti-aircraft defences which are a necessary corollary to the increase in our air forces. In addition, the mobile forces require to be brought up to the standard of a modern army by the provision of modern equipment, mechanisation, transport and reserves of war material of all kinds which have fallen below modern standards. If these essentials are not provided, our Army may one day be called on to go into action with inferior equipment and a totally inadequate reserve of ammunition, and to submit to heavy loss, suffering and possible disaster which might have been avoided by reasonable foresight and expenditure.

VI.

23. The Royal Air Force has, as its principal role, to provide (with the co-operation of ground defences) for the protection of the United Kingdom and particularly London against air attack. It also provides Air Forces for general defence purposes in the Middle East, India and the Far East, as well as for co-operation in Coast Defence (a subject which is being closely studied by the three Defence Services in co-operation at the present time); and, in addition, furnishes specially trained and equipped squadrons for co-operation with the Army and a proportion of the Fleet Air Arm personnel for work with the Navy. The Air Squadrons at home provide, in addition, a reserve of air squadrons for employment in any part of the world in an emergency.

24. Technical development in the air is taking place very rapidly in respect, for example, of such matters as speed, height, endurance, carrying capacity and potentialities for destruction. The range of territory on the continent of Europe from which air attacks could be launched against this country is constantly extending and will continue to extend; and if, in war, an enemy were in possession of the countries bordering the Channel, the area of Great Britain liable to his attacks would be still further increased. The weight of the attack would be much greater, owing to the quicker "turn round" of the bombers and their increased bomb load at shorter ranges. The increase in speed, range and height accentuates the difficulty of obtaining warning in time to bring defensive aircraft into action in favourable conditions to repel attacks. For these reasons the importance of the integrity of certain territories on the other side of the Channel and North Sea, which for centuries has been, and still remains, a vital interest to this country from a Naval point of view, looms larger than ever when air defence is also taken into consideration.

25. If adequate forces for air defence were not provided, the only deterrent to a sufficiently armed aggressor would be a moral one, and no effective means of defence or counter-attack would be available to us. In view of the time required to provide the necessary defensive forces, and the obscurities of the international situation, no Government mindful of its responsibilities could neglect to provide such defence as it deemed necessary to secure the safety of the country.

169

26. As was stated in the House of Commons on the 30th July, 1934, His Majesty's Government intend to develop, simultaneously with the active air defence of this country, a system of passive air defence for the protection of the civilian population. Corresponding action has already been taken by most of the countries on the continent of Europe, and, by common consent of all those who have studied the subject, this is an essential complement to defensive measures in order to reduce, so far as possible, the inevitable losses and suffering that must result from air attack.

27. It would as yet be premature to forecast what may be the ultimate effect on our armaments of the Anglo-French proposals of the 3rd February. But it is desired to emphasis that the measures now proposed are elastic. They will not only be subject to frequent review in the light of prevailing conditions, but may from time to time be adjusted in either direction if circumstances should, in the opinion of His Majesty's Government, warrant any change.

28. His Majesty's Government are convinced, and they believe that all thinking and unprejudiced fellow countrymen having the cause of peace at heart will agree, that the influence of the United Kingdom as a stabilising force in the councils of the world could only be weakened by the knowledge that the United Kingdom was no longer in a position to defend herself, to fulfil her responsibilities towards the rest of the Empire, to honour her agreements, or to perform her part as a member of the League of Nations. It is to avoid these conditions that the defensive programmes of the Defence Departments, which have been concerted in common, and an instalment of which will appear in their estimates for 1935—36, have been designed.

PRO. Cab. 24/253

February 14, 1935.

APPENDIX II

Sir John Simon and Mr. Anthony Eden meet Hitler in Berlin. (Excerpt).

THIRD MEETING.

March 26, 1935, at 10.30 a. m.

NAVAL ARMAMENTS.

SIR JOHN SIMON said that he regarded that morning's proceedings as a continuation of those of yesterday; and therefore had no general remarks, to make at the moment. He proposed to take up the next subject on the programme, namely, armaments. He wished to make a statement about the naval side of this matter.

The German Government would be aware that representatives of His Majesty's Government had recently been engaged in bilateral conversations with representatives of a number of other Governments in view of the fact that in 1935 the continuation or modification of existing naval treaties comes under consideration. He would like to inform the Chancellor what had been happening. Separate conversations had taken place in London with representatives of the United States of America and Japan, and somewhat less elaborate conversations with representatives of France and Italy. The object in each case was to prepare the ground for the naval discussions of 1935.

The first thing he had to say was that His Majesty's Government hoped that the German Government would take part in any general conference of naval Powers that might be held in the near future. With this in view, it would be useful if informal exchanges of views could now take place on the naval question between representatives of His Majesty's Government and the German Government. London would probably be the best place for these. The conversations with the United States. France and Italy took place in London, and were conducted on their part by Ambassadors helped by technical assistants. His Majesty's Government would like in these discussions to learn from the German representatives the view of the German Government as to the requirements which Germany would wish to be discussed at a naval conference.

It would be understood, of course, that this proposal was made without prejudice to the validity of existing treaty provisions, and was made with all reserve on this point and without prejudice to any agreement regarding armaments generally which might be reached as part of the general settlement oreshadowed in the London communiqué.

There was one other communication he would like to make on this subject. He wished to inform the German Government that the method that His Majesty's Government thought most likely to give results was not to raise or seek to formulate proposals in the form of ratios, but to consider whether it was possible to reach agreement about programmes for the next period of years. During the preliminary discussions in London it had been suggested that this period might run to 1942. No country was able in a very limited number of years to construct at an unlimited rate, whatever its ultimate programme might be. This applied to Great Britain as well as to other Powers. He therefore hoped that, in the preliminary Anglo-German discussions in London on naval issues preparatory to a general naval conference, this method would be thought practicable by the German Government. At the present stage, however, it was necessary to do no more than make the enquiry as to a preliminary meeting. The method His Majesty's Government hoped would be adopted would not pre-judge or lay down figures for the distant future by the method of ratios.

HERR HITLER asked what would be the date of the Naval Conference. He said that this proposal came as a great surprise, and was completely new. Hitherto naval conferences had tried to fix ratios. The Washington Treaty had laid down ratios up to which the parties were free to build or not as they wished. So far as the new proposal was concerned, he thought it necessary to say that a number of States were fully equipped with fleets sufficient for their needs under previous conferences. Under building programmes, building would be limited, or there might be no building at all. It might, for example, be arranged that there should be no fresh construction for a period of five years. In that event Germany would not be able to build anything for five years, and Germany's sovereign rights, which she could not in any event give up, would merely exist on paper.

SIR JOHN SIMON said that the date for the naval conference had not yet been fixed and was a matter for negotiation.

He wished at once to explain that the Chancellor was mistaken in supposing that he had proposed or indicated a method that was entirely novel. There were two quite distinct points. The first was the proposal that there should be a preliminary meeting between British and German representatives to see whether an exchange of views on naval subjects would be useful in preparation for the naval conference. He would be glad at some convenient time to receive a reply to this proposal. This proposal was, of course, made subject to reserves and without prejudice to the provisions of existing treaties.

The second point was merely a piece of information, and not a proposal. His Majesty's Government were trying to do with Germany what they had already done with the other naval Powers. He wished therefore to inform the German Government that the method that His Majesty's Government had found most useful to consider was whether it would be possible to propound programmes. It was better that he should tell the Chancellor this than that he should not tell him. There was no occasion for surprise. The Chancellor may not have understood that the method did not mean that each State should have the same programme. What was intended was that States should discuss what their respective programmes should be. It was not suggested that X should be the same for all. Each country would discuss with every other whether their requirements over a period of years could be stated in programmes rather than in ratios. This, surely, was not a very revolutionary proposal.

BARON von NEURATH said there might have been a misunderstanding.

HERR HITLER said that the first proposal was accepted.

He added that even the proposed building programme would have some relation to each other, and that in the end the effect would be similar to that of ratios. It was obvious that, if Russia reconstructed her fleet, this must have repercussions on the German programme. In the same way, if France built giant ships of high speed, this must have its effect upon the German programme. There was bound to be interaction. It would probably not be possible to discover the best method until the conference met.

On a point of principle, he wished to say that Germany did not want to pursue an unlimited naval armaments race as had been the case before the War. Germany did not think it politically necessary, and had not the necessary financial resources for such a race. On the other hand, Germany must take account of certain vital necessities in the matter of her own protection, and could not make those necessities dependent upon a conference the date of which had not been fixed and the results of which were not certain. While he was prepared to give every assurance to His Majesty's Government that there would be no naval armaments race between Germany and Great Britain, Germany could not subordinate the requirements of her own security to a conference the date and result of which were unknown. If Russia and France increased their fleets, Germany must be in a position to do what she thought necessary to safeguard her own security. No responsible Government could do otherwise.

He wished also to make the reservation that, at least from the theoretical point of view, a possible new agreement reached at the conference would not necessarily replace the Treaty of Versailles.

SIR JOHN SIMON said, as regards this last observation, that the results of the naval conference were of course a matter for the future, but His Majesty's Government earnestly desired that an agreement should be reached which would take the place of existing provisions. All that he was concerned to make plain was that, in inviting the German Government to send representatives to London for a preliminary discussion on naval matters in preparation for the naval conference, it was clearly understood that this invitation was not an abandonment of existing treaty provisions, but was given and accepted with all reserve on this point, because it was for the future negotiation to reach a new agreement.

Sir John Simon continued that Herr Hitler had been good enough to say that Germany was not contemplating an unlimited armaments race in the naval sphere. The British Ministers were, of course, very glad to hear that. He thought, since they were speaking with such complete frankness and in order to inform one another, that he ought to point out that a figure which he believed had been mentioned to the British Ambassador of 35 per cent. of the British fleet would appear to the British Government—apart from any other question—to be so large as to make general agreement almost impossible.

173

The result would therefore be, if that figure were insisted upon, to promote the unlimited armaments race which the Chancellor said the German Government wished to avoid.

Such a figure would inevitably increase the demands of France, for the French figure was, roughly speaking, 50 per cent. of the British figure. If it really was contemplated that the German Government intended to build up to so large a figure as that indicated, that meant new tonnage, and therefore the most efficient ships. It was quite obvious that this must result in putting up the size of the French and therefore also of the Italian navy. This would have serious results on the British figures.

The consequence would be that the unlimited armaments race which Germany wished to co-operate in avoiding would, in fact, be stimulated and hastened.

Sir John Simon made this observation because he did not want the German Government to be under any misapprehension as to the view which the British Government would take on any such figure. But he understood that the Chancellor agreed that the preliminary meeting should take place in London, and that the best way in which the needs and intentions of the different Powers could be formulated would be a matter for consideration at that meeting.

He only made the statement which he had just made because he thought it would be of no advantage to any one if there was any misunderstanding as to the grave impression which would be made on the British Government by the mention of the figure in question.

HERR HITLER said that there had been a mistake. The present ratio of the French fleet, he understood, was 35 per cent. of the British fleet, though under the Washington Agreement it had been 50 per cent.

SIR JOHN SIMON said that the French fleet was at present in tonnage 50 per cent. of the British fleet or rather over. The Washington Treaty was not the only treaty which had to be considered. The Washington and London treaties must be taken together. In fact, if these two treaties were taken together, it would be found that French tonnage was 667,000, as against 1,200,000 tons of the Britis fleet.

Those were the present figures.

BARON von NEURATH then went out of the room to check these figures. He returned after a few minutes and admitted that the British figures were right.

HERR HITLER said that his claim to 35 per cent. of the British fleet implied unequivocal recognition of British naval superiority. He emphasised that he did not make this claim for a limited period of 2, 5 or 6 years. Any assurance which he gave with regard to it would be for ever.

On the other hand he did not see any heavenly or earthly authority who could force Germany to recognise the superiority of the French or Italian fleets.

Germany's requirements for the protection of her trade were just as great as those of France or Italy for the protection of their trade.

In those circumstances it was hard for him to see how a figure of 35 per cent. of the British fleet claimed by Germany could give any right to France to increase her percentage demand.

He claimed 35 per cent. of the British fleet for Germany, but not 35 per cent. for all the different categories of ships.

He based his claim on the need for the protection of the long coastline in the Baltic in particular, and further on the protection of German communications with East Prussia, which, for Germany, had almost become an overseas colony.

As regards the objection that the 35 per cent. would be new tonnage, Herr Hitler said that he could not possibly build up the 35 per cent. within three or five years. It would take much longer than that, and that would give other countries an opportunity to modernise their fleets.

Further, his 35 per cent. would be burdened with the ships built under the Versailles conditions. The cruisers so built were too slow and inadequately armed.

SIR JOHN SIMON took note of the agreement in principle for a meeting in London under the conditions indicated.

HERR HITLER wished at this point to make an observation of principle. The meetings of the 25th March and of that morning were the first which he had had in this highly official manner with the representatives of the British Governement.

He thought that they were not in that room concerned with the problems of to-morrow or of the day after.

But it was necessary to define the German conceptions and wishes as clearly as possible, so that on the basis of those clear definitions co-operation over a long period might be possible with all countries.

He would therefore think it wrong to advance demands now in order to increase them after two or three years; and he would think it just as wrong to remain silent on demands which Germany would put forward after two or three years.

For that reason he had very frankly and fully explained the conceptions held by the German Government as to the conditions to which Germany's return to the League of Nations must be subordinated and as to the possibilities of concluding a naval agreement.

He had put forward Germany's demands in respect of that naval agreement frankly; he was guided not by the circumstances of the moment, but was taking account of a more distant future.

It would be an impossible situation if Germany returned to the League to put forward new demands so far unknown to the world after two or three years. That might imply, if those demands were rejected, a fresh German withdrawal from Geneva.

Thus there would be continuous disturbances and uneasiness.

It was because he had put forward certain demands at that moment that he had thought it best to indicate those demands frankly. He well understood that their fulfilment could for the moment only be a fulfilment of principle; and that their practial realisation, *e.g.*, as regards the navy, would have to take place in the course of time.

PRO. Cab. 24/254

APPENDIX III

Sir John Simon's note on the Anglo-German naval discussions, with a
report by the British representatives (Annex I.) and
a Naval Staff memorandum (Annex III.)

ANGLO-GERMAN NAVAL DISCUSSIONS.

Note by the Secretary of State for Foreign Affairs.

HERR von RIBBENTROP and the other members of the German Naval
Delegation, whom we invited to come here after the visit to Herr Hitler for
the purposes of preliminary consultation, have been in London this week.
At the opening of the Conference the German representatives invited His
Majesty's Government to recognise the decision announced by the German
Chancellor laying down for the future a relationship between the German
fleet and the British fleet in the proportion of 35—100. The meaning of this
proposal was investigated in subsequent meetings and has been the subject of
very careful examination by the Admiralty. As a result the British representatives reported to the Ministerial Naval Committee in the terms annexed
(N.C.M. (35) 50) and the Committee authorised me to intimate to the German
representatives the acceptance of the proposal. The First Lord and I accordingly
saw Herr von Ribbentrop and his colleagues yesterday afternoon and agreement was confidentially reached. We explained that before giving our formal
reply, His Majesty's Government must communicate with the other parties
to the Washington Treaty and give them the opportunity of offering any observations. What we are communicating is our decision to accept the arrangement which will be a perpetual one and which Germany expressly states will
not be varied even though Germany should hereafter acquire colonies or if
the construction of third Powers should be altered.

I annex a copy of the telegram which has been sent to the other capitals.

J. S.

Foreign Office, June 7, 1935.

Naval Conference, 1935.

ANGLO-GERMAN NAVAL DISCUSSIONS.

Report by the British Representatives.

1. IN the course of the meetings held yesterday and to-day, the German naval representatives made it clear that, before proceeding with further naval discussions, they would like to know whether His Majesty's Government would be prepared "to give a clear and formal recognition of the decision taken by the German Government laying down a relationship between the British and German fleets in the proportion of 100 per cent. to 35 per cent." The German representatives explained that the German Government would regard this ratio, if accepted by His Majesty's Government, as "final and permanent," and that the subsequent possession of colonies would not modify it.

2. In the course of the discussions the German representatives gave the following important clarifications of their proposal:—

(*a*) Once agreement had been reached between Great Britain and Germany on a ratio of 35 per cent., the German Government would adhere to this limitation independently of the construction of third Powers. As an example it was stated that if, for instance, France should decide to increase the proportionate strength of the French navy to the British navy, and His Majesty's Government were to decide not to respond to this by increasing British construction, Germany would likewise adhere to a level of 35 per cent. of the British fleet.

(*b*) At the same time, the German representatives stated that they assumed that, in the event of France deciding to make any considerable increase in her naval strength, the British Government would do their best to deter her from taking this course.

(*c*) The German Government would not insist on the incorporation of this ratio in any future international treaty, provided that the alternative method eventually adopted for the future limitation of naval armaments gave Germany full guarantees that this relationship between the British and German fleets would be maintained.

(*d*) The German Government believe in the system of limitation by categories, and they are prepared in principle to calculate the 35 per cent. ratio on the tonnage in the separate categories, any variation from this ratio in a particular category being dependent upon the arrangements to this end that may be arrived at in a future general treaty of naval limitation. Should no international treaty be concluded, or should the question of limitation by categories not be dealt with in a future international treaty, the question of the calculation of the 35 per cent. ratio in the categories would be a matter for discussion between the German and British Governments.

3. The text of the German declaration on this point, of which the relevant passages will be found in paragraph 2, sub-sections (2) and (3), is attached as Annex I.

4. The German representatives fully recognised that, owing to the present domestic situation here, the answer of His Majesty's Government might be slightly delayed. They pointed out, however, that there had been a certain disappointment in Germany that His Majesty's Government had not felt able to accept more promptly what the German Government regarded as an offer of the highest historical importance, under which a sovereign State voluntarily agreed in advance to accept a permanent naval inferiority of 65 per cent. as compared with the British Fleet, and for this reason it was important that the answer should be delayed as little as possible. It would be particularly appreciated if the answer could be returned before Whitsuntide. An extract from the British record, giving the text of Herr von Ribbentrop's observations on this point at today's meeting, is attached as Annex II.

(The foregoing paragraphs have been submitted to the German representatives, who agree that they correctly represent the view of the German Government.)

5. The British representatives fully explained to the German representatives the difficulties in the way of the course they suggested, pointing out in particular that, even were His Majesty's Government prepared to accept such a relationship in so far as the British Navy was concerned, there remained the question of the repercussions on the other naval Powers, with whom there was a tacit understanding that, in advance of any international conference, there should be no bilateral agreements during the present conversations. The fact that the whole essence of the British proposal was to do away with the element of ratio and to substitute voluntary declarations of programme was also stressed. Despite these arguments, the German representatives declared that it was essential for them to learn at the outset whether His Majesty's Government were or were not in a position to proceed on this basis.

6. The British representatives have since had time to consider this proposal carefully, and they are definitely of the opinion that, in our own interest, we should accept this offer of Herr Hitler's while it is still open. They are confident that, if we now refuse to accept the offer for the purposes of these discussions, Herr Hitler will withdraw the offer and Germany will seek to build up to a higher level than 35 per cent. A Naval Staff memorandum dealing with the strategical aspects of the question is attached as Annex III.

7. It is true there may be a certain element of bluff in these proceedings, but it is felt at the same time that, in view of Herr Hitler's action in regard to land armaments, it would be a mistake to believe that such an offer on the part of Germany will remain indefinitely open in the absence of a British acceptance of it. Having regard to past history and to Germany's known capacity to become at will a serious naval rival of this country, it is felt that we may have cause to regret it if we fail to take this chance of arresting German naval development at the level stated.

8. Even, however, if His Majesty's Government, for their part, were prepared to accept this offer, they have to consider the repercussions on other European Powers and also whether such acceptance would not be a breach of the tacit understanding which has governed our discussions with those Powers, namely, that there should be no bilateral agreements between any of the Washington Naval Powers in advance of any general naval conference.

9. This German offer is of such outstanding importance that it would be a

mistake to withhold acceptance merely on the ground that other Powers might feel some temporary annoyance at our action. It is, however, both desirable and necessary that we should give the Governments of those Powers with whom we have had previous naval conversations an opportunity to express their view on the point before we give a formal answer to the Germans. It is therefore proposed that we should as soon as possible address an oral communication to the United States, Japanese, French and Italian Governments in the following general sense:

10. After informing them of the nature of the German offer, we should state that we consider that it is a contribution of great importance to the cause of future naval limitation and also furnishes an important assurance for the future security of this and other countries. We should emphasise points (a) and (c) mentioned in paragraph 2 above and say that we intend accordingly to recognise this decision of the German Government as the basis of our future discussions between the British and German naval representatives in London. Before, however, giving our formal reply to the German representatives we should be glad to learn whether the Governments concerned desire to furnish any observations, and in view of the urgency of the matter we trust that we may receive their observations in the course of the next few days.

11. It is believed that if the German representatives could be informed confidentially, either on Thursday or Friday, that it was our intention to make the above communication to the other interested Powers they would be content and the discussions could proceed on a satisfactory basis. There is, in fact, every reason to believe that, once this difficulty is out of the way, there is a good prospect of the British and German representatives finding themselves in agreement on all other points.

12. It may be thought that His Majesty's Government are being asked to take too hurried a decision and that the matter should wait over until after Whitsuntide. The German representatives quite anticipate that such course may be necessary, but at the same time they would regret the necessity because of the misunderstanding which it would create. In the view of the British representatives it would be unfortunate both from a political and psychological standpoint if the German representatives returned to Germany for Whitsuntide under the impression that His Majesty's Government are still hesitating as to whether or not the German proposal can be accepted. It is obvious, of course, that the effect of an acceptance of the German offer will decrease in proportion to the length of time that His Majesty's Government take to consider it, and this is particularly the case in view of the confident expectation of the German Government that the acceptance of His Majesty's Government would have been forthcoming very shortly after the offer was made publicly in Herr Hitler's speech of the 21st May.

June 5, 1935.

GERMAN PROPOSAL FOR A 35 PER CENT. NAVAL RATIO.
Naval Staff Memorandum

The significance of the construction by Germany of a fleet of 35 per cent. of our own must be considered in relation to the general strategical situation that has to be faced.

2. This was recently described by the Chiefs of Staff in their Annual Review for 1935, in the following terms:—

(a) "The ability of the One-Power Standard to satisfy our strategical needs is dependent upon a sufficient margin between the strength of the one Power on which the standard is calculated and the strength of the next strongest naval Power. The existing margin is only sufficient on the supposition that France will not be our enemy in Europe and that we are not without allies."

(b) "That we should be called upon to fight Germany and Japan simultaneously without allies is a state of affairs to the prevention of which our diplomacy would naturally be directed. With France as our ally the naval situation in Europe would wear a different complexion and the main British fleet would be available to defend our Empire in the East."

(c) "Although His Majesty's Government in the United Kingdom would never, we presume, confide the entire protection of this country and its vital sea communications to a foreign navy in the absence of our Main Fleet, yet if France were our ally, her naval forces could undertake part of this responsibility. A British capital ship cruiser and destroyer strength in home waters equal to that of Germany is probably the least that we could accept."

(d) "It would be important to have sufficient warning to enable us to bring forward our capital ships undergoing large repairs before we were called upon simultaneously to face Germany in European waters and send our Main Fleet to the Far East. Subject to this proviso, and, except for the shortage of cruisers, we should, in the next three or four years, be able to provide naval security in an alliance with France against Germany, while at the same time defending ourselves against Japanese aggression."

3. At the present time Japan's total naval strength by tonnage is about 64 per cent. of ours, and Germany's is less than 11 per cent. In the vital matter of capital ships, the percentages are 57 per cent. and 15 per cent., so that at the moment the margin is ample. If, when Germany has reached a strength of 35 per cent. of our own, as is her announced intention, Japan's relative strength remains the same as at present, we should, *on a purely tonnage basis,* have a margin sufficient to fulfil the requirements set out in paragraph 2 (c).

4. Since our strategical requirements must take account of both Germany and Japan, it is evidently to our advantage that the naval forces of each or either of them should —

(a) Be limited.

(b) Be limited at as low a figure as it is possible to secure.

5. The statements of Herr Hitler, as amplified by the German representatives in the current conversations, make it clear that there is no prospect whatever of Germany coming to agreement on any question, including the extremely important one of qualitative limitation, except on the 35 per cent. basis.

The German representatives have made it clear also that they are prepared to preserve this strength relative to British strength whatever France or any other country may do.

6. We have also received the impression that the German Government genuinely consider that they have made a generous and self-sacrificing decision, and that if the opportunity to close with the offer is lost, it is improbable that they will stop short at the 35 per cent. level in building up their fleet.

7. Our information leads us to suppose that the German resources are amply sufficient to enable them to complete the whole of the tonnage necessary to bring them up to this level by the year 1943, and that they have made arrangements for manning the fleet as it is constructed.

8. The foregoing represents the ultimate position, stated in general terms. There are, however, other aspects of the matter which necessitate more detailed examination. As stated in the body of this report, the German representatives have declared that Germany intends to calculate her tonnage in principle by categories.

9. In this first place the capital ship modernisation programme that has been undertaken by Japan has already made us relatively weak in modern or modernised ships. Until the middle of the year 1939 we shall, except for a short period, have only 11 ships available for service and, quite apart from the German battle-fleet, we shall have no margin in modernised ships over Japan alone.

10. From this point of view it is important that every endeavour should be made to slow down the rate of increase of the German fleet.

11. Germany at present possesses three ships of the *Deutschland* Class, a type of capital ship, which, although small, cannot be opposed ship for ship by existing cruisers. In addition, Germany is building two further ships which it is believed will be improved and enlarged *Deutschland* Class of 20,000 tons.

12. A 35 per cent. ratio of the British tonnage in the capital ship category would permit Germany to lay down two further capital ships of the maximum size.

13. Thus, when the programme under consideration is completed, we shall be faced with a German battle fleet of seven ships, of which four may be of the most powerful type allowed. During this same period Japan may have completed four new capital ships (assuming they are content with the programme suggested unofficially by Admiral Yamamoto).

14. Against this total of eight new large capital ships plus three *Deutschland* Class, the tentative British programme will only produce six ships. In these circumstances it may be essential for the Naval Staff to recommend

a more rapid replacement of the British battle fleet, in order to ensure that in *new ships* the British Fleet does not fall behind the capital ship strength of Japan and Germany combined.

15. This is a position which cannot be avoided by refusing to recognise the German decision and indeed such a refusal is more likely to lead to an acceleration of the German programme with consequent disadvantage to ourselves. Amelioration of the position can only be brought about by persuading the Germans to increase their navy at a moderate rate. This they are unlikely to agree to do if we do not accord them the recognition for which they are asking.

16. With regard to other categories of ships, on a basis of 50 cruisers the situation would be unsatisfactory. When, however, we have 70 cruisers, and supposing the German ratio to be calculated with respect to our under-age tonnage only, the position can be accepted. Our present contemplated rate of increase is sufficient to balance the probable rate of German building.

17. In regard to destroyers, if the German calculation is based on our under-age destroyer tonnage, the situation would be satisfactory.

18. In regard to Submarines, it was inevitable that, failing general agreement for the abolition of this type, Germany would ultimately acquire a right to build them. Although the German representatives have stated their intention to calculate their tonnage category by category in principle, yet they have made it clear that if other Powers are granted in a future Treaty or retain in fact the right to have parity with the British Empire in the Submarine category, Germany will expect a similar right, although she will not necessarily build up to this level.

Should Germany exercise her power to build up to parity with ourselves in submarines, she could produce a formidable force of some 50 to 60 submarines (allowing for the fact that her first 12 are to be 250 tons each). This is a situation which must arouse some misgiving, but it is quite apparent from the attitude of the German representatives that it is a question of "Gleichberechtigung" which is really exercising their minds, and not the desire to acquire a large Submarine fleet. In the present mood of Germany, it seems probable that the surest way to persuade them to be moderate in their actual performance is to grant them every consideration in theory. In fact, they are more likely to build up to Submarine parity if we object to their theoretical right to do so, than if we agree that they have a moral justification.

Apart from this psychological aspect of the question, the only other way to ensure a reasonable limitation of German submarine building is to keep our own tonnage as low as possible.

It is in any event satisfactory to know the limit beyond which the Germans do not intend to proceed. Under these circumstances, it is considered that the situation is acceptable.

19. The German decision to preserve a 35 per cent. ration *vis-à-vis* the British Fleet limits the German Navy to 70 per cent. of that of France, assuming that France maintains her present ratio of naval strength with us, which is about 50 per cent. In the opinion of the Naval Staff, France will be wise to accept the proposal, and in informing the French Government, as also in any subsequent naval discussions, it must be our aim to endeavour to persuade

them to avoid any consequential increase of the French Fleet, as such an increase might call for similar action on our part in the event of the political situation changing.

20. *Conclusions.*

(*a*) On general strategical grounds, a 35 per cent. ratio of our naval strength for Germany is acceptable.

(*b*) The increase of the German Fleet makes it essential to preserve our Washington Treaty ratio *vis-à-vis* Japan.

(*c*) A more rapid replacement of the British battle Fleet than is visualised in the tentative British programme, may be necessary in order to ensure that in *new ships* the British Fleet does not fall behind the capital ship strength of Japan and Germany combined.

(*d*) Our present contemplated rate of increase in cruiser strength is sufficient to balance the probable rate of German building in this category.

(*e*) In other categories there are no particular comments.

(*f*) From the point of view of general limitation of naval armament it would be greatly to our advantage to recognise the decision of the German Government lest the demand should be increased.

PRO. Cab. 24/255

APPENDIX IV

The Cabinet's Satisfaction with the Anglo-German Naval Agreement

Conclusions of a Meeting of the Cabinet held at 10, Downing Street, S.W.1, on Wednesday, 19th June, 1935, at 11.0 a.m.

PRESENT:

The Right Hon. Stanley Baldwin, M.P., Prime Minister. (In the Chair).

The Right Hon.
J. Ramsay MacDonald, M. P.,
Lord President of the Council.

The Right Hon.
The Viscount Hailsham,
Lord Chancellor.

The Right Hon.
Sir Samuel Hoare, Bt., G.C.S.I.,
G.B.E., C.M.G., M.P., Secretary
of State for Foreign Affairs.

The Right Hon.
The Viscount Halifax, K.G.,
G.C.S.I., G.C.I.E., Secretary of
State for War.

The Right Hon.
Sir Philip Cunliffe-Lister, G.B.E.,
M.C., M.P., Secretary of State
for Air.

The Right Hon.
Malcolm MacDonald, M.P.,
Secretary of State for the Colonies.

The Right Hon.
Sir Bolton Eyres Monsell, G.B.E.,
M.P., First Lord of the Admiralty.

The Right Hon.
Lord Eustace Percy,
Minister without Portfolio.

The Right Hon.
Oliver Stanley, M.C., M.P.,
President of the Board of Education.

The Right Hon.
Ernest Brown, M.C., M.P.,
Minister of Labour.

The Right Hon.
Neville Chamberlain, M.P.,
Chancellor of the Exchequer.

The Right Hon.
Sir John Simon, G.C.S.I.,
K.C.V.O., O.B.E., K.C., M.P.,
Secretary of State for Home
Affairs.

The Most Hon.
The Marquess of Londonderry,
K.G., M.V.O., Lord Privy Seal.

The Right Hon.
J.H. Thomas, M.P.,
Secretary of State for Dominion
Affairs.

The Most Hon.
  The Marquess of Zetland, G.C.S.I.,
  G.C.I.E., Secretary of State for
  India.

The Right Hon.
  Walter Runciman, M.P.,
  President of the Board of Trade.

The Right Hon.
  Anthony Eden, M.C., M.P.,
  Minister for League of Nations
  Affairs.

The Right Hon.
  Walter Elliot, M.C., M.P.,
  Minister of Agriculture and
  Fisheries.

The Right Hon.
  Sir Kingsley Wood, M.P.,
  Minister of Health.

The Right Hon.
  W. Ormsby-Gore, M.P., First
  Commissioner of Works.

Colonel Sir M.P.A. Hankey, G. C.B., G.C.M.G., G.C.V.O., ... Secretary.

2. The Secretary of State for Foreign Affairs made a statement to the Cabinet on the subject of the exchange of Notes between His Majesty's Government in the United Kingdom and the German Government regarding the limitation of naval armaments (Cmd. 4930). He pointed out that the Agreement was based on the proceedings of the late Cabinet and of the Committee of Ministers to whom the question had been referred by the Cabinet at the Meeting mentioned in the margin. He and the First Lord of the Admiralty had thought it important to conclude an Agreement which would enable us to control German programmes of naval armaments, instead of the probable alternative of an Anglo-German competition in naval armaments. In recent years many opportunities of achieving disarmament had been lost through delay in seizing the favourable moment. It had been clear to the two Ministers that a better Agreement could not be obtained from Germany and that it was essential to seize the present opportunity and secure the German signature to an Agreement. Everything possible had been done to obtain the good will of France and Italy. Nevertheless, the French had started a Press campaign on the subject, and the French Government had sent a Note which could be described as one of criticism rather than of outraged surprise. The attitude of other Powers had been not unsatisfactory. He proposed that the Minister for League of Nations Affairs should proceed on Friday next to Paris to meet N. Laval and to explain all the circumstances.

The First Lord of the Admiralty gave the Cabinet a statement from the Naval point of view, in which he said that the Naval Staff were satisfied and had been anxious to bring about an agreement, more especially as they rather suspected that if there had been any delay the German Naval Staff would have tried to whittle away what was proposed. He gave particulars to show that the Agreement was advantageous to the French Navy no less than to our own. As the existing Naval Agreements would come to an end in 1936 it was very valuable to be able to record this Agreement with Germany, and it ought to help towards further Agreements. The arrangements as to submarines were the most likely to be criticised, but it had to be remembered that the London Naval Treaty gave equality in submarines and that the submarine was not the

186

defensive reply to attacks by submarines: in addition, the Admiralty were rather less apprehensive of submarines today than they had been during the War.

In reply to questions the Cabinet were informed by the Foreign Secretary and the First Lord that the actual programmes of construction were still being discussed with the German Delegation. Questions such as the rate at which the Germans intended to build up to the 35 per cent, and of over-age and under-age tonnage, and other technical matters, would be dealt with in these discussions. The German Delegation had given the British Delegation to understand that they would spring no surprises during these discussions. If, after Germany had built up a Fleet on the 35 per cent. basis, we were to enter into an agreement with other Powers reducing our own tonnage, the Germans would, under this Agreement, have to make a corresponding reduction. If, later on, we were to agree with other countries to abolish Capital Ships or Submarines, Germany would have to do the same. It was quite clear, both from the White Paper and the record of the discussions, that if Germany should acquire colonies this Agreement would none the less remain unaltered, and it was laid down that "the ratio of 35—100 is to be a permanent relationship".

In connection with the question of the ratio attention was drawn to the following passages in Sir Samuel Hoare's Note to Herr von Ribbentrop:—

Paragraph 2 (c);
"Germany will adhere to the ratio 35 : 100 in all circumstances, e.g., the ratio will not be affected by the construction of other Powers. If the general equilibrium of naval armaments, as normally maintained in the past, should be violently upset by any abnormal and exceptional construction by other Powers, the German Government reserve the right to invite His Majesty's Government in the United Kingdom to examine the new situation thus created. . . . ."

Paragraph 3;
"With reference to sub-paragraph (c) of the explanations set out above, I have the honour to inform you that His Majesty's Government in the United Kingdom have taken note of the reservation and recognise the right therein set out, on the understanding that the 35 : 100 ratio will be maintained in default of agreement to the contrary between the two Governments."

The above, it was pointed out, rendered the ratio a fairly tight one.

The attention of the Cabinet was also drawn to the following passage in the leading article of "The Times" of even date:—

"If France insists on increasing her naval strength, then the British and German Governments will clearly have to consider increases also."

This point, it was suggested, was bound to be raised by M. Laval in his conversation with the Minister for League of Nations Affairs. (*See Conclusion (c) below.*)

The Cabinet agreed —

(a) That the Agreement set forth in the exchange of Notes of June 18, 1935, between His Majesty's Government in the United Kingdom and the German Government regarding the limitation of Naval armaments (Cmd. 4930) was an advantageous one:

187

(b) To take note that the Minister for League of Nations Affairs would visit Paris on Friday, June 21st, for the purpose of explaining to M. Laval the advantages of the Naval Agreement and the circumstances in which it had been necessary to enter into it without delay. He would make it quite clear that there was no question of Germany having driven a wedge between the United Kingdom and France, or anything of the kind, but that it had been essential not to miss this fleeting opportunity for a favourable agreement:

(c) In case French Ministers were to raise the point mentioned in the extract from the leading article of "The Times" mentioned above, the Minister for League of Nations Affairs was authorised to reply to the effect that supposing the French Government considered it necessary from the point of view of French national defence to make an increase to their Navy. His Majesty's Government in the United Kingdom would examine the effect of that increase on their own naval strength and might or might not decide to make some increase themselves: but that under the new Agreement Germany was not entitled to make any increase except in the event of an increase to the British Navy. The utmost that Germany could do would be to invoke paragraph 2 (c) of Sir Samuel Hoare's Note, which is quoted above: that is to say, to invite His Majesty's Government in the United Kingdom to examine the new situation thus created.

PRO. Cab. 23/82

APPENDIX V

An unsatisfied letter on the bargain (The Spectator, June 28th, 1935) and Sir S. Hoare's memorandum on answers to criticism of the Agreement

German Submarine Strength.
(To the Editor of the Spectator.)

Sir, — on April 23rd 1917, I had the melancholy duty of explaining at length to the War Cabinet the grave results of the German submarine blockade, which had at that date made such progress that in the then preceding 22 days we had lost 600,000 tons of shipping. A gloomy discussion of two and a half hours followed, and it was for the first time realized that the nation was in sight of defeat. That defeat was narrowly averted because we had an ally in the richest nation in the world, whose supplies were made available by a specially protected Atlantic Concentration of Shipping. There is no guarantee, of course, that such a scheme would be again practicable.

The submarine blockade nearly succeeded although Germany entered the war in 1914 with only some 30 submarines available for duty.

The new Anglo-German Naval Pact concedes to Germany a submarine strength 45% as strong as that of the British Empire, which means roundly that she can build 20,000 tons of submarines. This tonnage whether expressed in U-Boats great or small, will give Germany a very much greater submarine strength than she possessed in 1914. I will not enlarge upon the further concession that, in certain undefined circumstances, Germany may claim up to 100% of the British submarine strength, nor will I develop any argument upon the plain case stated. I will only add that, as one who lived with the terrible facts that unfolded themselves in 1917, I would not like to be responsible for signing the Anglo-German Naval Convention of 1935.

Your obedient servant

Royal Societies Club

Leo Chiozza Money.

CONFIDENTIAL.

[A 6441/22/45]

Sir Samuel Hoare to Sir G. Clerk (Paris).

(No. 1356.)

Sir,

Foreign Office, July 19, 1935.

I TRANSMIT to you herewith copies of a memorandum containing answers to the criticisms directed from the juridical and political point of view against the conclusion of the Anglo-German Naval Agreement.

2. My impression is that the agitation in France against this agreement has now considerably diminished, and I certainly wish to do nothing to revive it.

3. On the other hand, the answers to certain of these criticisms have a bearing on matters now under discussion or about to be discussed, notably the air pact and air limitation, future negotiations leading up to the naval conference and the limitation of land armaments.

4. In these circumstances it seems to me to be very desirable that the French Government—and indeed informed French opinion—should be aware of the view taken here of the criticisms directed against the agreement. I should therefore welcome any steps which you could take to secure this: and I should even have no objection were it possible for you or a member of His Majesty's Embassy to show a copy of the enclosed memorandum privately and confidentially to someone in authority at the Ministry for Foreign Affairs. The memorandum would in no sense be a communication to the French; and the purpose of showing it to them would simply be to let them know in a friendly way how we feel on the points dealt with.

5. For your own information I may say that His Majesty's Government would regard with some anxiety any attempt by the French Government to hold up further progress in naval limitation as a means of pressure on His Majesty's Government in connexion with the limitation of land armaments or, indeed, a French decision to embark on such an increase in fleet as would render a general naval agreement impossible. There is at the moment a prospect of making real progress towards a general limitation of naval armaments if France will co-operate, but if the present opportunity is missed as a result of non-co-operation by France, the impression created on British public opinion is bound to be adverse.

I am, &c.
SAMUEL HOARE.

Enclosure.
Answers to Criticisms directed from the Political and Juridical Point of View against the Conclusion of the Anglo-German Naval Agreement.

I.

Criticism:—

    (i) *That His Majesty's Government have committed a breach of the Treaty of Versailles;*

    (ii) *That His Majesty's Government have condoned a breach by Germany of the Treaty of Versailles.*

(i) Where, as in the Treaty of Versailles, a treaty is concluded between one State on the one hand and a number of States on the other, the position is that the one party, Germany, contracts a series of similar obligations towards each of the other parties to the treaty severally. Each of the other parties, if it should wish to do so, has a legal right (apart from any specific undertakings to the contrary), by a separate agreement with Germany to waive its rights in any particular under the treaty. If it does so, it affects only its own rights and the provisions of the treaty remain in full legal force as regards the other parties thereto. Therefore, though Germany has to obtain the assent of all the other parties in one way or another before she is released from any particular obligation under the Treaty of Versailles, there is no reason as a matter of law why this cannot be done piecemeal by separate agreements with the other parties individually, and, if this course is followed, any of the other parties who concludes such an agreement commits no breach of the treaty but is merely doing what it is entitled to do. The recent agreement with Germany has the effect of a waiver, so far as the United Kingdom is concerned, of any obligations incumbent on Germany under Part V of the Treaty of Versailles in the matter of naval armament, provided that German armaments are kept within the limits of the new agreement. The rights of France and other parties to the Treaty of Versailles to claim that the Versailles limits must be observed are legally unaffected; and His Majesty's Government have committed on breach of the treaty.

(ii) The German Government have declared that they no longer consider themselves bound by Part V of the Treaty of Versailles. The latest pronouncement to this effect was contained in Herr Hitler's speech of the 21st May last, the relevant extract from which will be found in Annex A. The principal other parties to that treaty, His Majesty's Government included, taking the view that legally there was nothing to justify the German claim that conditions had come into existence rendering Part V no longer binding, protested against this decision, declared that it was a breach of the treaty and that nothing had happened to prevent the application of the usual principle that Germany could only obtain her release from Part V by agreement with all the other parties thereto. The other parties placed all this on record, but the German Government proceeded to act in accordance with their decision, and it was clear that the other parties were not going to take any action to enforce their view of the legal position upon Germany. The present bilateral Agreement with Germany is based upon the admitted *de facto* situation and constitutes an attempt to limit the consequences thereof. It contains no admission that the *de facto* situation was a legal one, though to the extent that the new Agreement is fulfilled it removes for the future the right of His Majesty's Government to protest against that situation further as regards naval armaments. The countries who complain of this "condonation" in fact still contemplate and desire agreements with Germany under which Germany will have the right to armaments in excess of those of Part V. From this point of view what would be the difference between such agreements and the action taken by His Majesty's Government, except that these agreements are intended to have more parties thereto? But this does not alter the fact that, if His Majesty's Government's action in arriving at an agreement involved condonation, then these other agreements would involve it also. The procedure of acting together or separately is irrelevant to the "condonation" point.

II.

Criticism:—

That His Majesty's Government have not acted in accordance with the London Communiqué of February 3 and under the Stresa Resolution.

The relevant passages from these two documents are quoted in Annexes C and D. Throughout the discussions which led up to the drafting of these two documents no reference was ever made to the particular position of naval disarmament. In the absence of any such reference it is impossible to say that any of the parties concerned adopted any definite line in the matter. But in the absence of any contrary statement by the other parties, His Majesty's Government are entitled to argue that they have always maintained that naval armaments are in a separate category from land and air armaments, having been regulated by international treaties since 1922, and that therefore when subscribing to the London and Stresa Declarations they assumed that the limitation of naval armaments would be negotiated separately from the other elements constituting the proposed General Settlement. The possibility that these separate negotiations might result in the conclusion of a direct Anglo-German Agreement was, it is true, not contemplated before the Anglo-German naval talks took place, but in so far as we can argue that this Anglo-German Agreement is in effect a contribution towards the General Settlement and not prejudicial to it, the French Government have no reason to object to it on that score. This argument involves the practical appreciation of existing circumstances rather than the legal interpretation of texts. Viewed in this light it is reasonable to maintain that the Anglo-German Agreement is an essential prelude to the conclusion of a general naval settlement, since Germany had (1) already definitely decided to increase the size of her fleet; (2) was already giving practical effect to that decision; and (3) was not prepared to enter upon any negotiations for an international settlement until the basis of her future naval relationship to this country had been finally established.

If there is to be any future general limitation of naval armaments, it can only be on the basis of one or both of the following systems:—

192

Qualitative limitation, *i.e.*, limitation of the sizes of ships in each category and the armament which they may carry; and

Quantitative limitation, i.e., on the basis of an exchange of declarations of programme (a settlement on the basis of agreed ratios being now definitely out of the question).

The placing of a limit on the expansion of the German navy cannot be held to prejudice the chances of an ultimate general agreement on the basis of either of these systems of limitation. Were it not for the Agreement, there is reason to believe that the first naval objective of Germany would have been not 35 per cent. of the British fleet, but parity with France. Such a claim, if made, would have rendered yet more difficult the conclusion of that "general settlement" to which the London Communiqué referred.

In this connexion it is perhaps worth while contrasting the attitude adopted by the French Government towards their own bilateral agreement with the Soviet Government, and our bilateral agreement with Germany. When His Majesty's Government conclude a bilateral agreement with Germany, as their contribution towards those "agreements regarding armaments generally" recommended in the London Declaration, it is a cause of criticism. But when the French Government conclude a mutual guarantee treaty with the Soviet Government, as their contribution towards the "conclusion of pacts freely negotiated between all the interested parties in Eastern Europe", it is regarded as a matter for congratulation. It is to be observed, also, that when the French Government decided, not merely to negotiate but to bring their Russian Treaty into force in advance not only of the General Settlement, but of the so-called Eastern Pact to be concluded between all the parties concerned, they did so without requesting or awaiting the consent of His Majesty's Government.

III.

The criticism that we gave the French Government no chance to influence our view and that the summary of the Agreement handed to them on June 7 was inadequate.

The German representatives intimated that this was an offer which was made to this country and to this country only, and that, as it was made independently of the construction of third Powers, they saw serious objection to the prior consultation with such Powers before His Majesty's Government gave their answer. Furthermore, we had good reason to believe that, in making his offer, Herr Hitler had overruled the German Ministry of Marine, which, if we had hesitated to accept it, would have been favourably placed for securing an amendment of the German proposal in the sense desired by the German navy.

We gave the French Government ten days in which to express an opinion leaving them in no doubt that this was a matter on which our own minds were already made up. In doing so we ran the risk of letting the Germans proceed to Germany and return—as they did—with an offer less satisfactory from our point of view than the original offer. The real answer to this charge is that the acceptance of this German offer was a matter of vital interest to this country:

that on the juridical side it did not constitute a breach of the Treaty of Versailles by this country; that it did not directly concern the naval construction of France nor prejudice the chances of an ultimate general settlement; and that no British Government could have taken the risk of losing the agreement simply on the ground that it might conflict with a French interpretation of the Declaration of the 3rd February.

The French Government are also disposed to complain that the aide-mémoire which was communicated to them on the 7th June was not an adequate summary of the Agreement which afterwards contained the clause about parity in submarines (paragraph 2 (*f*)) and the clauses about Germany's right to draw attention to any abnormal and exceptional construction by other Powers (paragraphs 2 (*c*) and 3). The reason for this is that these clauses were only inserted at the last moment as the result of representations by the German representatives on their return from Berlin after Whitsuntide. In actual fact, neither point has the significance which the French Government at first appeared disposed to attach to it. The aide-mémoire of the 7th June contained an exact representation of the position as it stood at that date. These points have since been explained to the French Ambassador.

IV.

Criticism :—
    (a) *That, by concluding the Naval Agreement with Germany, we have deprived France of a trump card in connexion with the negotiations on land and air.*
    (b) *That by endangering France's communications with North Africa we have made it impossible for France to take account of her North African troops in any discussion of military parity with Germany.*

(1) We cannot admit that the Naval Agreement has taken a trump out of the French hand for securing land limitation. It has for some time been more than questionable—if indeed there is any doubt at all on the subject—whether Germany is prepared to pay anything for the recognition of her right to rearm in defiance of Part V of the Treaty of Versailles. In his speech of the 21st May Herr Hitler definitely stated that he had taken that right to himself; and his contention was that it was not taken in defiance of Part V, as the ex-Allied Powers themselves had broken that part of the treaty and therefore destroyed it. Further, Germany has already announced the strength of her peace-time army, viz., thirty-six divisions, the rough equivalent of 550,000 men. Lastly, it is pertinent to recall that, though the ex-Allied Powers were "solid" in their disapproval of all three kinds of German rearmament through the year 1934, this in no way prevented Germany from rapid expansion in all three spheres.

(2) It is further necessary to contest the French contention that the Naval Agreement has endangered the French communications with North Africa; and that that would consequently be a reason in itself why France could not now agree to count in the North African troops in any calculation of parity with Germany. As a matter of fact, what the Naval Agreement has done is, without restricting the French freedom of action, to limit the expansion of the German fleet, and to enable France to maintain a permanent naval superiority over Germany which must be at least 43 per cent. if France preserves her present level of naval strength *vis-à-vis* the British Commonwealth.

V.

The criticism that His Majesty's Government have not acted in accordance with the spirit of Anglo-French co-operation.

Acceptance of the principle of co-operation does not mean that one party gives any special rights of control over its actions to the other party, but that both parties recognise that the actions of each shall in every case be the subject of consultation between them and shall be directed towards the common objective which both have in view. If such co-operation is to be wholehearted and fruitful, it must not be used for the purpose of preventing one of the parties from taking action which it considers essential to its own vital interests. In the present case the French Government have ignored our naval interests, which to us are vital, and have shown a wish to refuse us the latitude necessary to secure them. Such an attitude on their part is, in our view, entirely contrary to the whole spirit of that co-operation to which we are both pledged, and gives us strong ground for complaint. In a word, Anglo-French co-operation must on both sides be supple and dynamic; it must be constructive and not obstructive.

VI.

The criticism that His Majesty's Government have withheld from the French Government information with regard to the German building programmes.

The German construction programme may be divided into two parts. The first is their 1934—35 programme, most of which has already been laid down. This was published in Berlin on the 9th July (largely at our instigation). It consists of—

2 capital ships of 26,000 tons each, with 11-inch guns.
2 cruisers of 10,000 tons each, with 8-inch guns.
16 destroyers of 1,625 tons each, with 5-inch guns.
20 submarines of 250 tons.
6 submarines of 500 tons.
2 submarines of 750 tons.

Of the above, the two capital ships, the two 8-inch-gun cruisers, sixteen destroyers and twelve of the submarines had already been laid down before the conclusion of the Anglo-German Naval Agreement. This fact had been conveyed to our naval attaché at Berlin before the naval conversations commenced. The information as regards the size of the ships and their guns was communicated to our representatives during the conversations, and, at our suggestion, it was communicated direct to the French, Italian, United States and Japanese Governments in advance of publication.

The second part of what is known as the German building programme relates to the construction to be undertaken by Germany up to the year 1942 (the year originally suggested by this country as that up to which building programmes should be exchanged in any future agreement). This part of the programme was communicated to us on two conditions: (1) that we should communicate our own programme to Germany on a reciprocal basis; and (2) that we should only communicate this programme to other foreign Powers on a reciprocal basis, i.e., in return for the building programmes of those Powers up to and including 1942. This part of the German programme, like our own and other programmes of all other nations, must for the time being of course remain confidential, for premature publication of advance programmes could only serve to increase the difficulty of arriving at an ultimate international agreement on this subject.

We have informed the French Government that we are ready and anxious to communicate to them all the information communicated confidentially to us if they will undertake, within a reasonably short time, to communicate to us, for transmission to the German Government (or else to communicate direct to the German Government), the particulars of the French building programme up to the end of 1942. We have not so far received from the French Government a reply to this suggestion.

It will be seen from the above that one important result of the Anglo-German Agreement is that, in the matter of naval armaments, Germany is now prepared to depart from the policy of secrecy which, in connexion with armaments generally, has done so much to cause uneasiness throughout the world. Furthermore, so far as naval armaments are concerned, Germany is prepared from now on to exchange on a reciprocal basis with the other naval Powers particulars in regard to the date of laying down and characteristics of future warships, even in advance of the conclusion of a general naval treaty. It may confidently be asserted that this satisfactory result could never have been achieved without the prior conclusion of the Anglo-German Agreement.

VII.

The suggestion that His Majesty's Government would raise strong objection if other Powers were to conclude similar arrangements with Germany (e.g., in regard to land and air armaments) as that which we have just concluded in regard to naval armaments.

The answer is that, far from objecting, we should regard the conclusion of such separate agreements as a great step in the direction of peace and appeasement, provided that our own liberty of action remained unimpaired (just as the liberty of action of other foreign Powers remains unimpaired under the Anglo-German Agreement), and provided that the purpose of the agreement was to facilitate that "general settlement" referred to in the London communiqué of the 3rd February.

VIII.

The criticism that, in concluding this agreement with Germany, His Majesty's Government have acted purely from interested motives in contradiction to the spirit of the League of Nations.

This criticism is to some extent answered in the reply to point VII, but it can be added that the step which has been taken was an essential preliminary to the general limitation of naval armaments and, had it not been taken by His Majesty's Government, all foreign Powers must have suffered from the

196

race in naval armaments which would have resulted. As it is, other foreign Powers whose naval construction is not directly affected by the agreement know the limits of German naval expansion and can regulate their programmes accordingly. If France remains at her present level (approximately 50 per cent. of the tonnage of our navy), she will still retain a permanent superiority in tonnage over Germany of 43 per cent. (as compared with an inferiority of about 30 per cent. before the war).

One of the primary purposes of the League of Nations is to limit and, if possible, reduce world armaments, and the League cannot suffer if, as a result of this agreement, which we regard as a useful contribution to a general settlement between all the naval Powers, the threatened race in naval armaments can be prevented.

Foreign Office, July 17, 1935.

PRO. Adm. 116/3377

APPENDIX VI

Admiralty notes on the general strategic situation in the Western Pacific
vis-à-vis Japan on the August, 1935,
(Excerpts)

MOST SECRET.

THE GENERAL STRATEGIC SITUATION IN THE WESTERN PACIFIC VIS-À-VIS JAPAN.

34. As the result of the above unsatisfactory state of affairs I telegraphed (China telegram timed 1539 of 23rd February, 1935) and reported in China No. 313/01526 of 27th February, 1935, that I recommended that an additional Fighter Bomber squadron and additional overseas land reconnaissance machines be sent out in 1935, bringing *the total peace equipment up to 51 machines, exclusive of reserves.* Although it was reported that the hangars for the above reinforcements would not be complete before about September, 1936, I was informed by the Air Officer Commanding, Far East, that temporary accommodation would be available by the end of 1935.

35. The question of strengthening the R.A.F. forces at Singapore is now (August, 1935) under consideration by the authorities at home, as also is the question of establishing R.A.F. landing grounds at Kuantan (Federated Malay States), Kuching (Sarawak) and Bintulu (Sarawak). These should enable land aircraft from Singapore to carry out valuable distant reconnaissance over the seaward approaches to Singapore from the south China Seas.

An Expeditionary Force and M.N.B. Defence Organisation.

36. I have asked Their Lordships (China No. 255/01514 of 1st March, 1934) whether it is Their intention to send out *an expeditionary force and/or a M.N.B. defence organisation* when considering Phase III of a Far Eastern war. In order to carry out the advance, the seizure and defence of one or more advanced bases I consider such a force is required. At the present time there are no stores available on the China Station for any form of M.N.B. organisation.

The Japanese Military Situation.

37. The modernisation of the capital ships of the Japanese Fleet is being pressed forward and is due to be completed in 1937, by which time they will have nine powerful ships at their disposal.

38. The Japanese Navy attains its maximum efficiency and readiness in October each year. At this time the 4th Fleet, which is composed of ships

normally in reserve, is mobilised and fully manned. This Fleet, together with the 1st, 2nd and 3rd Fleets, has by then undergone its annual period of intensive individual ship, squadron and fleet training, which culminates in September in the Grand Manoeuvres.

If, on completion of these manoeuvres, the relegation of the 4th Fleet ships back into reserve was secretly postponed, then *from October onwards the whole Navy would be at the peak of its powers and ready to act at a moment's notice.*

It is of interest that this time corresponds with *the end of the typhoon season in the China Seas.*

39. Since 1932 the re-equipment of the Japanese army with modern weapons has been carried out and now is considered to have been largely completed except parts of the field artillery. Japan is therefore in possession of an up to date army of such a size that she could easily afford to launch expeditions to attack Hong Kong and Singapore and simultaneously to seize advanced bases on the China coast, in Borneo or in Siam.

40. Combined operations receive their fair share of attention annually in Japan and are regularly practised. Ujina, the main army depot, is conveniently situated within a few miles of the major Naval Base at Kure, and as they lie within the Inland Sea, expeditions can be organised in complete secrecy.

41. In recent years those in power in Japan have been successfully educating the people towards air-mindedness. Japan is now a great Power in the air as well as on the land and the sea, though it is thought that she lags behind other Powers in technical development and knowledge. There is no separate air force, the Navy and Army each having their own services. There has been an alarming increase in both Services in the last few years. The Japanese Naval Air Force is already larger than our Fleet Air Arm and in 1938, if the present rates of development are maintained, it will be almost double the size of ours.

42. With the above information (corrected for the Year of Grace in which this Memorandum is read) it may be of interest to examine the following example of the skeleton framework of a *possible* Japanese strategic plan for attacking Singapore.

It is obvious that the possibility of such a plan being carried out cannot be lightly dismissed.

Our naval forces *might* with good fortune achieve a successful night attack on one of the Japanese expeditionary forces, but the chances are that our naval forces would be brutally swept out of the path by overwhelmingly strong Japanese escorting forces.

SUMMARY.

28. These notes are intended to give some clue to the strategical possibilities of the Sea of Japan in a great war in the Far East.

The strength of the Japanese position is very great. They would be operating close to the main Islands of the Japanese Empire, that is to say, *close to the centre of their force, and if they can deny access to* the Sea of Japan to their enemy surface vessels and protect themselves against submarines and control the air, then they should be able, as already explained, to run supplies across from the great Korean ports which they are devoloping on the east coast of Korea.

200

29. Their situation will undoubtedly be vastly improved if and when they take the Maritime Province from Russia, and particularly if they can force the Russians back to the westward of Lake Baikal, with a buffer state between them and the Russians.

30. In Section II the possibilities of Japan getting supplies across from the Yangtse or further north on the China Coast are discussed.

Aerial Operations and Commercial Flying.

31. In recent years the Japanese have paid great attention to the devolopment of their air services and are taking special steps to make the whole Japanese nation air-minded.

In regard to naval operations to the northward of Tokio, it is of interest to note that for their 1935 Naval Grand Manoeuvres the Japanese mobilized their naval bases at Maizuru and Ominato as well as that at Yokosuka. At the opening of the final phase the Combined Fleet was at Hakodate.

PRO. Adm. 116/3338

APPENDIX VII

The CID's "reasonable estimate" of what is required to meet the responsibilities in respect of the security of the Empire (Excerpts)

Printed for the Committee of Imperial Defence. February 1936.

MOST SECRET.

Copy No. 44

D.P.R. (D.R.) 9

COMMITTEE OF IMPERIAL DEFENCE.
Sub-Committee on Defence Policy and Requirements.

PROGRAMMES OF THE DEFENCE SERVICES.
REPORT.

I.—INTRODUCTION.

IN October 1935 the Cabinet were informed (C.P. 187 (35)) that the (Official) Defence Requirements Committee had been instructed to re-examine the question of Defence Requirements with special reference to the programme of the Navy, Army and Air Force and to make recommendations for the future. The terms of reference of the Committee, for this purpose, were communicated at the same time to the Cabinet, who approved the procedure which had been adopted (Cabinet 45 (35)).

2. The Report of the (Official) Defence Requirements Committee was presented to the Prime Minister on the 21st November, 1935, and was referred to the Committee on Defence Policy and Requirements, the membership of which was, by direction of the Prime Minister, slightly varied for the specific consideration of this Report; the consequent constitution of our Committee is given in Annex A.

3. We have had nine meetings, and now submit to the Cabinet our observations and recommendations on the Report before us, a copy of which, with its Schedules, is attached hereto.

II.—THE INTERNATIONAL SITUATION.

4. We appreciate that in the Section dealing with the International Situation the Defence Requirements Committee desired to analyse the various factors which tend to disturb the peace and so to lead up to the measures which they recommend the Government to adopt to remedy a situation which is admittedly fraught with grave danger to this country. We have read this important Section of their Report in this light, and we agree that it represents a generally accurate picture of the state of international affairs. The wording and the emphasis is, of course, that of the Defence Requirements Committee, and, whilst we accept the general reasoning, it should not be assumed that it necessarily represents in detail our own views.

5. We can, however, fully associate ourselves with the deduction reached in paragraph 22 of the Report of the Defence Requirements Committee as to

the four possible policies on which this country's international relationships may be based, *i.e.:*—

   (i) Adherence to the system of collective security provided for in the Covenant of the League of Nations;

   (ii) A more limited system of collective security on the Locarno model;

   (iii) The pre-war system of alliances and *ententes;* or

   (iv) Isolation.

The leadership of a strong Britain is now clearly essential to the success of the Covenant system; if the Covenant were to fail, co-operation and aid may be expected from other nations only to the extent that Britain is recognised as being strong and ready; an isolationist policy would undoubtedly require the greatest strength of all. We are in full agreement with the views thus expressed by the Defence Requirements Committee and with their deduction (paragraph 23 of their Report):—

> "The lesson we draw from recent events is the paramount necessity whatever our policy in future, for making ourselves sufficiently strong to enable us to take our full share in maintaining the peace of the world and so to preserve ourselves, in the hope that a time may ultimately come when mutual reductions of armaments by consent may become possible without upsetting the equilibrium. That time, however, is not yet."

III.—DEFENCE REQUIREMENTS (GENERAL).

6. Continuing from their review of the international situation, the Defence Requirements Committee proceed to outline their views on Defence Requirements as a whole, recording the new factors of a recrudescence of German naval strength; the possibility of a hostile Italy on our main line of communications to the Far East; and the possibility of heavy and continuous air attack from Germany. In connection with our communications to the Far East the Defence Requirements Committee remark that our defence requirements are so serious that it would not be possible within the three-year period with which this Report mainly deals, to make provision for the case of a hostile Italy; we feel that the view that it is not urgently necessary nor feasible to make provision for a permanently hostile Italy should be endorsed.

7. But even excluding Italy, the new considerations in the situation of to-day have led the Committee to make recommendations for revised standards of security in the case of all three Services. It will be convenient if we record our views on these new standards individually in the following Sections dealing with each Service concerned.

IV.—NAVY PROGRAMME AND REQUIREMENTS.

8. Since 1932 the standard of naval strength has for practical purposes been based on the following formula:—

> "We should be able to send to the Far East a Fleet sufficient to provide 'cover' against the Japanese Fleet; we should have sufficient additional forces behind this shield for the protection of our territory and mercantile marine against Japanese attack; at the same time we should be able to

retain in European waters a force sufficient to act as a deterrent and to prevent the strongest European Naval Power from obtaining control of our vital Home terminal areas while we can make the necessary redispositions." (N.C.M. (35) 12.)

The coming increase in German naval power combined with continuing anxiety for the safety of our possessions in the Far East have properly led the Defence Requirements Committee to a careful reconsideration of our naval needs, and they recommend a *new* standard of naval strength defined as follows:—

(i) To enable us to place a Fleet in the Far East fully adequate to act on the defensive and to serve as a strong deterrent against any threat to our interests in that part of the globe.

(ii) To maintain in all circumstances in Home Waters a force able to meet the requirements of a war with Germany at the same time.

Included in (i) and (ii) would be the forces necessary in all parts of the world, behind the cover of the main fleets, to protect our territories and merchant ships against sporadic attacks.

During the next three years, however, there are difficulties from the point of view of provision both of material and personnel, which render it difficult to take any considerable steps towards the attainment of the proposed new standard. Moreover, what would be involved by the adoption of the new standard has not yet been worked out in detail, and we consider that approval for this standard should be reserved until the practical effects can be more precisely estimated.

9. In the same connection we have had some discussion on the Cruiser replacement programme, which at present involves the building of five ships a year between 1936 and 1939. A new naval standard of security will no doubt involve a higher strength in cruisers, as well as in other types of ships. In these circumstances we agreed to ask the Admiralty—

(i) to work out the naval programme required to give effect to the new standard of naval security as soon as the necessary data are available; and

(ii) to make suggestions as to any items in the new programme that can be put in hand before the expiration of the next three years;

and to withhold, until that information was received a recommendation for approval for the new standard of naval strength referred to.

10. Items of naval requirements based on past standards are put forward by the Defence Requirements Committee as follows:—

Capital Ships.

A replacement programme of seven ships in the period 1937—39 inclusive (2 . 3 : 2). This will provide equality in new ships with Germany and Japan in 1942 on the important assumption that Japan does not start building at a greater rate than has been assumed by the Admiralty.

Aircraft Carriers.

Four new Carriers (some of a smaller type) within the period 1936—42.

Cruisers.

The proposal is for a replacement programme of five ships a year, but since our ultimate provision of cruisers is dependent on a number of factors, including the acceptance or otherwise of a "new standard" of naval defence, we consider that this programme should be adopted, for the present, provisionally and subject to later review.

Destroyer Leaders and Destroyers.

A further flotilla of destroyer leaders in 1936—37, and subsequently a flotilla of destroyers in alternate years up to 1942.

Submarines, Sloops and Small craft.

To continue at the present rate of about three submarines and five or six sloops a year.

Deficiencies.

The provision of reserves of ammunition, anti-submarine equipment, stores, &c., together with the modernisation of Capital Ships. Complete modernisation is proposed for three of our Capital Ships and partial for four more. The *Nelson, Rodney* and *Hood* will not require modernisation. The question of the modernisation of the remaining five ships must depend on future developments, one of the most important of which will be the extent to which other Powers retain their older Capital Ships.

Personnel.

An expansion in strength by some 35,600 spread over 1936—42.

Fleet Air Arm.

An increase from 1900 aircraft (embarked in carrier and catapult ships) in 1935 to 357 in 1939, and 504 in 1942. The corresponding anticipated figures for the United States of America and Japan, in 1938, are 670 and 374 respectively.

Expediting Naval Construction.

Emphasis has been laid on the desirability of expediting construction by laying down ships earlier in the year than has hitherto been usual. Several months' acceleration could thereby be gained yearly.

11. With all the above proposals, which lie within the existing approved standard of naval strength, we are in agreement and recommend them for approval by the Cabinet, with the reservation that the cruiser programme should be adopted only provisionally and subject to later review.

The provision of a new standard of naval defence, decision on which is postponed for the present, would necessitate an increase in all classes of ships and also of personnel.

The Relationship between Foreign Policy and Defence.

16. We consider it to be a cardinal requirement of our national and imperial security that our foreign policy should be so conducted as to avoid the possible development of a situation in which we might be confronted simultaneously with the hostility, open or veiled, of Japan in the Far East, Germany in the West, and any Power on the main line of communication between the two. So far as Japan is concerned, in our previous Report we emphasized strongly the importance of an ultimate policy of accommodation and neighbourliness with that country. Recent events accentuate the desirability of that policy, difficult though it may be to carry out.

17. The establishment of friendly relations with Germany on a durable basis, while equally desirable strategically, presents difficulties which are even greater than in the case of Japan. This object might founder on Germany's restless desire for expansion, either to the East or South-East in Europe, or by the acquisition of colonies, or both. If either of these ambitions were to be conceded or condoned by a Government in this country, widespread opposition and division of public opinion may be anticipated. The former case would, indeed, be wholly incompatible with our membership of the League, or with the existence of the League. Nevertheless, we see every advantage in keeping our relations with Germany on as friendly a basis as possible. Herr Hitler has in several occasions affirmed his desire for friendly relations, and by concluding the recent Naval Agreement he has given to it some practical expression. In view of the urgent need of peace and the grave dangers to which this country, its Capital and the whole Empire, would be exposed in the event of a breach of the peace in Western Europe, to say nothing of the danger of its extension to the Far East, we consider that we should respond as favourably as circumstances permit—though circumstances are likely to impose a concrete limit—to Herr Hitler's attitude, and do everything we can, in conjunction with France, to promote and maintain friendly relations with Germany. It is possible, especially if M. Laval remains in power, that France may attempt to force the pace in this respect. The subject is at least one to be borne constantly in mind, though it bristles with practical difficulties, both internal and external.

18. So far as Italy is concerned it would be premature to forecast what is likely to develop from present events; how long Italian resentment will endure after an exhausting war; in what kind of condition the country will emerge; whether the Italians, who are complete opportunists and will take without scruple the course that suits them best at the moment, will wish to return to the League and the Franco-British group or to gravitate towards Germany; or whether the Germans, who are more formidable realists, will go out of their way to bring within their orbit a nation, probably in an exhausted condition and one of whose doubtful reliability they have bitter experience. These matters are beyond calculation, but, from the point of view of Imperial Defence, we would urge that, before Italy can again become a formidable factor, our long-range policy should be so aligned that we can never get into a position where we would not have a certainty of French military support in the event of war with Japan and Italy at the same time, and *a fortiori* if we were involved simultaneously with Germany and Japan. This, however, is, of course, subject

to the reservations on the weakness of France, as explained in paragraph 7, and of the unreliability that always flows from division and can only be corrected by an increase in our own strength.

The Need for increasing our Defensive Armaments.

19. From the above observations one fact stands out pre-eminently. Whatever means we adopt to forward our main policy of preserving peace, there is no alternative to our raising our armaments to a far more effective standard than they will attain when existing approved programmes are completed. Our defence forces must not only be strong enough but must be ready to meet an emergency such as the one that arose so suddenly this summer, for graver ones may come and come shortly.

20. These are urgent necessities, whether viewed from the standpoint of the past, the present or the future. Had we been reasonably strong at sea in 1931—33 our influence with Japan would have been much greater than it was, and we might have averted that defiance of the League of Nations which has provided so unfortunate an example to Germany and Italy. Had we been reasonably strong, Germany might well have hesitated before re-arming in breach of the Treaty of Versailles. If we had been less weak to-day it is almost certain that Italy would never have dared to set herself against the public opinion of the world and would have responded to the Paris peace offers; and, even if Italy had remained obdurate, France (feeling more assurance about England and therefore less dependent on Italian support) would have been willing from the first to play her proper part in defending the Covenant of the League instead of being split from top to bottom on the question of sanctions, and breaking out into anti-British manifestations.

21. Looking to the future, a strong Britain is no less essential to the peace of the world. If the policy of collective security contained in the Covenant survives the present test, it is certain that it can only succeed under the leadership of a re-equipped Britain. As the Japanese, German and Italian incidents show, the United Kingdom alone among the more powerful States Members of the League is so placed as to be able to give whole-hearted *expression* to the moral ideals underlying the Covenant: expression (be it noted), but owing to our weakness, not effect. We can secure the plaudits of the smaller nations who are at a safe distance from the centres of disturbance, but we cannot be sure of obtaining the active material and moral support of the larger nations which, acting together, alone can provide that overwhelming deterrent to war that lies in the background of the Covenant, because they know, and have long known, that we lack the power to support our words effectively by deeds. With a strong Britain the League would be a far more effective instrument for the maintenance of peace, and as a deterrent to war. If we fail, moreover, to provide this strength, we cannot exclude—particularly if we embark on further forward policies—the possibility of a European combination against us.

22. As we see it, there are four possible policies on which to base our international relationships:—
(i) Adherence to the system of collective security provided for in the Covenant of the League of Nations;
(ii) A more limited system of collective security on the Locarno model;

(iii) The pre-war system of alliances and *ententes*; or

(iv) Isolation.

We have already shown that the leadership of a strong Britain is essential to the success of the Covenant system. If the Covenant fails and we are driven back on some other and more limited system of collective security or alliance, our co-operation will only be desired to such extent as we are recognised to be both strong and ready. Like Germany we shall attract satellite nations in proportion to our strength, and so increase our influence for peace. Either of the first three systems, therefore, demands strong defence forces on our part and needless to say an isolationist policy, if anyone still had leanings that way, would require the greatest strength of all.

23. Hence, the lesson we draw from recent events is the paramount necessity, whatever our policy in the future, for making ourselves sufficiently strong to enable us to take our full share in maintaining the peace of the world and so to preserve ourselves, in the hope that a time may ultimately come when mutual reductions of armaments by consent may become possible without upsetting the equilibrium. That time, however, is not yet.

III. — Defence Requirements (General).

24. From the previous section of this Report it will be seen that important new factors have been introduced into Imperial Defence. Formerly, if a war of the first magnitude was brewing, it was usually possible to foresee it and to take the necessary precautions. But if a war is brought into sight owing to the operation of collective security, the crisis is apt to arise with very little warning, as illustrated by the Manchurian and Abyssinian episodes, and as may in the future happen in the case of, *e.g.*, Austria. It is almost impossible to forecast the nations with which we might be brought into conflict owing to a breach of the Covenant and still more impossible to forecast those on whose material support we could count. If the Covenant breaker were Germany, that support would be even less reliable than in the present case. And if we were to become embroiled in war on behalf of, or as a consequence of the action of, the League of Nations, it might be that one or other of our vital world-wide interests became exposed, as at the present time. It is also difficult to calculate what the composition of our naval, military and air forces should be, as no reasonable warning of the conditions under which we might have to operate can be given.

25. Consequently there arise three completely new considerations in the situation:—

(*a*) As the result of the principle of collective security we must be more instantly ready for war than before.

(*b*) There is from now onwards the possibility of a hostile Italy on our main line of communications.

(*c*) As the one big Naval Power of the League we may have to exhaust ourselves to the detriment of the balance of security against Japan and Germany, who are outside it.

to these must be added a fourth new consideration affecting the Navy exclusively:—

(*d*) As a result of the resumption by Germany of the right to build up a new Navy free of the restrictions of the Treaty of Versailles, the Navy of that country (though fortunately now limited by agreement to 35 per cent. of our own strength) has to be taken into account.

And although there has been a *partial* recognition of the implications of air attack, we are more than justified in regarding the following as a fifth new consideration:—

(*e*) In view of the enormously increased output capacity of Germany, there is the possibility of attack so continuous and concentrated and on such a scale that a few weeks of such an experience might so undermine the morale of any civilian population as to make it difficult for the Government to continue the war.

26. The remedy of the deficiencies of the three Defence Services as contemplated in this Report will meet the first of these new considerations by rendering more possible rapid mobilisation and concentration wherever our forces are required.

27. As indicated above in paragraph 18, the significance of the second consideration is impossible to appraise as yet, as it depends upon future developments subsequent to Italy's Abyssinian adventure. For the present her eventual political orientation remains a matter of conjecture. Much will depend on the degree of her exhaustion after the present venture, for on this, of course, will depend the degree of the rancour of an opportunist State. Much will also depend on how far France recovers from her present outbreak of angry irresolution. We shall have to make the best of her, and in the last resort France needs our support so much for her own security *vis-à-vis* Germany that, provided we are strong, she may recover her perspective. We must recognise, however, that Anglo-French co-operation against aggression by Italy has been shown to be dubious, and we must not under-estimate Italian capacity for mischief if we were in conflict with Germany, and Italy joined in on the German side.

28. Our defence requirements are so serious that it would be materially impossible, within the period with which this Report deals, to make additional provision for the case of a hostile Italy. We take the view, therefore that, for the moment at any rate, it is neither urgently necessary nor feasible to make provision for the contingency of a permanently hostile Italy, especially if, as suggested above in paragraph 18, an appropriate policy can be pursued in the international field in order to counter this.

29. It will in any event be necessary to watch the situation carefully and to make a close study of the Mediterranean strategical problem. But for the above reasons we have limited ourselves for the present to the same hypotheses as in our first Report (D.R.C. 14, also C.P. 64 (34)), namely, the provision of an adequate deterrent to Germany and Japan, and a protection to the United Kingdom and the rest of the Empire in the event of war with these countries.

30. Even when the problem is limited to these hypotheses, however, new factors have arisen, particularly so far as the Navy is concerned. Since 1932 the standard of naval strength has, for practical purposes, been based on the following formula:—

"We should be able to send to the Far East a Fleet sufficient to provide 'cover' against the Japanese Fleet: we should have sufficient additional forces behind this shield for the protection of our territory and mercantile

210

marine against Japanese attack: at the same time we should be able to retain in European waters a force sufficient to act as deterrent and to prevent the strongest European Naval Power from obtaining control of our vital Home terminal areas while we can make the necessary redispositions." (N.C.M. (35) 12.)

So long as Germany was bound by the Treaty of Versailles it may have been safe to assume a situation in which the "necessary redispositions" could be made to meet an emergency arising out of difficulties with Germany while still maintaining a strong defensive in the Far East. This is now more difficult as a result of the resumption by Germany of the right to build up a new Navy free of the restrictions of the Treaty of Versailles, and the Navy of that country has to be taken into very definite account. By 1942 Germany, it is calculated, will have afloat 5 new capital ships in addition to 3 Deutschlands (the "Pocket Battleships"), and Japan will probably have completed 2 new capital ships. Even by the 31st March, 1939, Germany will have 3 Deutschlands and 2 new 26,000-ton battle cruisers; if there was a serious emergency in the Far East we should have no margin of security in the event of a threatening situation in the West, even assuming superior fighting efficiency.

31. We cannot over-emphasise the difficulties of conducting naval warfare against highly efficient enemies in two theatres so widely separated. The present troubles with Italy, which have necessitated the concentration in the Mediterranean of naval forces from all over the world, including the Far East, afford some slight indication. But it would be suicidal folly to blind our eyes to the possibility of a simultaneous or practically simultaneous threat on both fronts; and if we do not possess forces sufficient to provide a deterrent this double emergency is the more likely to occur. If there is danger from Japan at all, it reaches its maximum from the point of view both probability and extent when we are preoccupied in Europe. Unless we can provide a sufficient defence for that emergency, Australia, New Zealand, India, Burma, the rich Colonies East of Suez and a vast trade will be at their mercy, and the Eastern half of the British Empire might well be doomed.

32. In the circumstances we recommend the new formula set forth in paragraph 34, which states more effectively than the one quoted in paragraph 30 that our standard of naval strength should cover both the two contingencies mentioned. Further, we consider that, as soon as is materially possible, our naval strength to carry out the formula ought to be calculated on a wider margin of safety; for hitherto our margin has been illusory, and we are now confronted with the prospect of an increase in the naval strength of our potential enemies, while in any event nations contemplating an aggression will naturally select the moment when they are at their maximum numerical strength and we, perhaps, at our average.

33. Unfortunately, for reasons which are given later in Section IV, it is not possible to bring the Navy even to the present standard by the 31st March, 1939, or for some years thereafter, partly owing to the Naval Treaties, and partly to the difficulty of increasing the personnel and material to a sufficient extent within three years. Even in later years the situation will depend on the results of any international naval arrangement that may be entered into in substitution of the existing Treaties; but, subject to this, we think that every effort should be made to achieve the requisite standard.

34. The standards of security which we believe to be necessary may be summarised briefly as follows:—

In the case of the Navy.

We should aim at a *new* standard of naval strength defined as follows:—
> (i) To enable us to place a Fleet in the Far East fully adequate to act on the defensive and to serve as a strong deterrent against any threat to our interests in that part of the globe.
> (ii) To maintain in all circumstances in Home Waters a force able to meet the requirements of a war with Germany at the same time.

Included in (i) and (ii) would be the forces necessary in all parts of the world, behind the cover of the main fleets, to protect our territories and merchant ships against sporadic attacks.

In the case of the Army.

> (i) To maintain garrisons overseas on the present general basis for purposes of Imperial Defence.
> (ii) To provide for the military share in Home Defence, which includes anti-aircraft defence, Coast Defence and internal security.
> (iii) To enable us to provide reinforcements and/or a Field Force from Home in time of emergency or war, with adequate equipment and reserves.

Under (i) and (ii) the most important requirements are a substantial improvement in coast defences at Naval bases at Home and Abroad, and the completion of the Army's share in the Air Defence of Great Britain.

Under (iii) the most important requirement is to organise a Field Force which can be sent abroad at short notice for the protection of our vital interests, and to enable us to honour our international obligations, particularly under the Treaty of Locarno, which would involve effective co-operation with other signatories on the Continent of Europe. This includes the occupation for ourselves and the denial to the enemy of advanced air bases in the Low Countries.

In the case of the Air Force.

We regard as a *minimum* the strength already decided for the Royal Air Force at Home, viz., 123 squadrons (1,512 first-line aircraft) to be completed by April 1937. This figure was based on the assumption that by that date the number of German first-line aircraft will amount to some 1,500. In the absence of any agreement for the limitation of air forces there is, however, no guarantee that she will not build up to an even higher figure of first-line strength. It is therefore vital that the position should be kept under the closest continuous review.

In addition we propose:—
> (i) Provision of war reserves, without which the Air Force could only fight for a very short time.
> (ii) Strengthening of the air forces overseas and, in particular, those required to meet the possibility of war with Japan in the Far East.

(iii) Additions to the Fleet Air Arm to correspond to the naval programme.
(iv) Additions to the Army Co-operation Squadrons (mainly auxiliary squadrons) to provide the requirements of the four contingents of the Field Force.

For all three Services.

An effective scheme for the expansion of industry in time of war and the provision of reserves of war material sufficient to maintain them from the outset of war until industry is able to supply their needs from current output.

35. The financial aspects of these proposals are discussed in Section IX. For the moment it is sufficient to state that they would result in an increased annual expenditure over the £124 millions (original Estimates) voted for the three Defence Services in 1935 of the order of £49,650,000 in 1936, £86,750,000 in 1937, £102,400,000 in 1938, £88,450,000 in 1939, and £90,050,000 in 1940. In other words, an increased expenditure, compared to the 1935 rate, of about £239,000,000 in the next three years and a further £178,500,000 in the following two years. In addition, there is a proposed increase in the Home Office vote of £1,847,000 a year for each of the next three years, for Air Raids Precautions equipment; and a recommendation that increased provision should be made for Secret Service work up to £500,000 per annum.

All estimates contained in this Report are given with the utmost reserve and are liable to substantial alteration in the light of experience.

36. The summary given in paragraph 34 above is only intended to convey some idea of the general scheme for Imperial Defence as a whole before describing the requirements of each of the Defence Services to enable the plan to be implemented. The Sections which follow, namely, IV (Navy), V (Army), VI (Air Force), VII (War Production) and VIII (Miscellaneous), contain fuller particulars. Schedules I, II, III, IV and V, which were prepared by the Departments concerned for the use of our Committee, contain a good deal of further detail.

IV.—Navy Programme and Requirements.
(For details, see Schedule I.)

(*a*) PROGRAMME.
Basis of the Construction Programme.

37. In paragraph 34 above we recommended that the standard of naval strength should be increased so as to render it adequate to protect our interests simultaneously against Japan in the Far East and Germany in Europe. It must take a certain time to work out this standard, as it is dependent largely on the probable programmes of other Powers, as to which more information may be available after the coming Naval Conference. It is accordingly not possible for us to make concrete proposals in connection with such a standard at the moment. Still less is it possible to increase the Navy to the new standard within the period of three years with which this Report is primarily concerned for the reasons given below.

213

The Difficulties of Rapid Expansion.

38. The limiting factors in a rapid expansion of the Fleet are twofold, namely, those of (i) material, and (ii) personnel.

39. The material difficulties are due, firstly, to the large amount of leeway to be caught up, which is strikingly illustrated later in the case of capital ships and, secondly, to the diminution in our national industrial resources for armament work resulting from the relatively small naval orders in recent years combined with the almost complete disappearance of foreign orders. In these circumstances the Admiralty, within the next three years, cannot do much more in naval construction than commence the replacement of over-age and out-of-date ships in order to bring the Navy abreast of the existing approved standard quoted in paragraph 30.

40. Apart from this, it would not be possible to raise and train the naval personnel required to man additional new ships. Even to comply with the requirements of the existing approved standard, a large addition to the personnel of the Fleet is required (as described below in paragraph 58), and further increases could not be made, in the opinion of the Admiralty, without serious loss of efficiency.

41. If it were decided to make a large increase in the size of the Navy within the next few years, it would be necessary to resort, so far as both material and personnel are concerned, to extraordinary measures, such as those adopted in the case of the Royal Air Force expansion. Anxious though they are to reach the new standard as early as possible, the Admiralty wish to avoid methods which, in their opinion, would prejudice the efficiency of the Service.

42. There is, however, one step that can usefully be taken to expedite naval construction generally, namely, to lay down ships earlier in the year. In recent years, for reasons of economy, the practice has grown up of laying down ships in the last quarter of the financial year. We strongly recommend that during the next few years ships should be laid down as early as possible in the financial year.

Immediate Policy.

43. In the above circumstances it is clear that during the next three years we cannot make much progress towards the new standard of naval strength proposed in paragraph 34. For the time being we must concentrate on the requirements of the existing standard, doing all we can at the same time to prepare for a fresh programme designed to bring the Navy up to the new standard if it is approved by the Government.

44. Although the situation as to any international agreement on the size of Fleets is not yet clear, we recommend that the Government should at once adopt the new standard in principle and instruct the Admiralty—

    (i) to work out the naval programme required to give effect to it as soon as the necessary data are available; and

    (ii) to make suggestions as to any items in the new programme that can be put in hand before the expiration of the next three years. These will probably be limited by material considerations to the smaller classes of warship.

214

45. *In the meanwhile, we wish to make it clear that the naval construction set forth in this Report and summarised below is limited to the existing approved standard of naval strength as set forth in paragraph 30.*

Capital Ships.

46. The programme of capital ship construction proposed by the Admiralty, in which we concur, involves laying down 7 ships in the period 1937—39 inclusive (2—3—2). This replacement programme will provide equality in new ships with Germany and Japan, *on the important assumption* that Japan does not start building at a greater rate than has been assumed by the Admiralty.

47. The high rate of replacement for the years 1937—39 has been forced on the Admiralty by the London Naval Treaty, which precluded the building of new capital ships in the last five years and thus rendered impossible a steady replacement of out-of-date vessels. After the completion of the ships laid down in 1937—39 (approximately by 1942) the more immediate necessities of capital ships will have been met, and, after one more year with two ships, it may be possible to revert to a normal rate of replacement, provided that no new factors arise. For example, after 1940 it would only be necessary to lay down one capital ship a year for normal replacement purposes, but this would have to be exceeded if Japan or Germany should lay down more ships than the Admiralty at present anticipate. Further, if the quantitative restrictions of the Naval Treaties on capital ship construction are not renewed in any form, it is possible that Japan, apart from new construction, may retain old ships that would have been scrapped under the provisions of the Naval Treaties and thus increase her total of capital ships. In that event, it will be necessary for the Admiralty to go further than is at present contemplated in the modernisation of our older capital ships in order to maintain the balance, and to provide some reasonable margin as is necessary for the new standard we now propose, if it is adopted by the Government. For these reasons the situation must, in any case, be carefully watched in case, after 1940, a larger capital ship programme than one capital ship a year may be requisite.

Aircraft Carriers.

48. In aircraft carriers, the Admiralty propose to lay down 4 carriers (some of a smaller type) within the period 1936—42.

Cruisers.

49. The ultimate number of cruisers to be aimed at must depend, to some extent, upon construction in Japan and Germany, but we are of the opinion that *for the time being* it is sufficient to adopt the Admiralty's cruiser replacement programme, which involves the building of 5 ships a year between 1936 and 1939. In the unlikely event of Treaty restrictions comparable with those at present in force still existing, the future programme could be reduced to 1 replacement cruiser per annum for a few years. Otherwise, however, and in any event if the new standard of naval strength is adopted, it will probably be necessary to continue at a higher rate and also to retain more over-age vessels.

Destroyer Leaders and Destroyers.

50. For some years now a steady replacement programme of destroyers has been proceeding at the rate of one flotilla a year. In view of the large numbers of destroyer leaders in several foreign navies, we learn with great satisfaction of the recent Cabinet decision to increase this year's approved building programme by 7 flotilla leaders of a special type. The Admiralty contemplate laying down a further flotilla of these vessels in the financial year 1936—37. After this programme only one more new flotilla will remain to complete the present approved total of 12 under-age flotillas. The Admiralty proposals consequently only visualise the laying down of a flotilla in alternate years up to 1942 which will complete our strength unless an increase of our total destroyer strength is decided upon. An increased programme of the vessels will be required if the Government decide to adopt the higher standard of naval strength recommended in paragraph 34.

Submarines, Sloops and Small Craft.

51. As regards other construction, for instance, submarines, sloops, other small craft and auxiliaries, to maintain our present strength it will be necessary to continue at the rate which has been carried out in the past, that is to say, for submarines about 3, and for sloops about 5 or 6 a year.

Cost.

52. It will be seen from Schedule I, Appendix 6, that the construction programme involves an expenditure of approximately £ $19^1/_4$ million in 1936, rising to a peak of £$36^1/_2$ million in 1939. If quantitative international restrictions similar to those at present in force under the Naval Treaties are renewed, the cost of new construction will drop considerably in subsequent years. With no such restrictions, it must be assumed that the cost may be increased and continue high, more especially if the standard of naval strength is adopted. The above figures do not, of course, represent a net addition. In a normal replacement year calculated on the present strength of the Fleet and the life of the various classes of ships, the new construction Vote would amount to some £$16^1/_2$ million. The figure has only been below this in recent years (£11 million in 1935) because capital ship replacement has been deferred.

53. The additional cost now proposed over that which was put forward in our previous Report (D.R.C. 14, also C.P. 64 (34)) is due firstly to the more rapid rate of replacement rendered necessary by more recent estimates of German and Japanese programmes, and secondly to the issue of the preliminary Naval Conversations over the last year which leave no doubt that owing to the attitude of the United States of America we are unlikely to secure international agreement to reduce the present maximum size of capital ships and cruisers.

54. If the above building proposals are adopted, on the 31st March, 1939, the figures for naval strength for the United Kingdom, Germany and Japan will be as follows:—

Completed Ships.

Class of Ship	British Commonwealth	Japan	Germany
Capital Ships ...	3 modern 3 modernised 9 non-modernised 15 Total	2 modern 6 modernised 9 Total	2 new 3 *Deutschlands* 5 Total (excluding 4 very old ships)
Aircraft carriers ...	6([1])	5([2])	1
8-inch Cruisers ...	15	12([4])	3
Large 6-inch Cruisers	12([3])	6	0([6])
Small 6-inch Cruisers	28([5])	18	6([6])
Destroyers ...	144([7])	93([8])	38
Submarines ...	45	39([9])	38

NOTES—It is assumed that British Commonweath and Japan adhare to London Naval Treaty provisions; this affects 6-inch cruiser, destroyer and submarine totals.

[1] Assumes *Argus* scrapped.

[2] Assumes *Hosho* scrapped.

[3] Assumes 4 *Hawkins* class retained rearmed with 6-inch guns.

[4] Excludes 7 old cruisers classed as special service and coast defence vessels.

[5] Assumes 8 6-inch cruisers scrapped to comply with London Naval Treaty.

[6] It is probable that about two more new cruisers (size unknown) may be completed.

[7] Includes 16 "V" large type.

[8] Includes 23 large type and excludes 20 torpedo boats 500—600 tons each.

[9] Assumes about 17 submarines not yet over-age are scrapped prematurely to comply with London Naval Treaty.

(b) DEFICIENCIES.

55. We concur in the Admiralty proposals for making good deficiencies, and the necessary provision has, as far as practicable, been inserted in the programme years 1936, 1937 and 1938. There remains, however, unavoidably a certain residue which it would not be possible to make good in these years; and of a total of approximately £29 million required some £ $4^3/_4$ million is left to be met subsequent to 1939. The deficiencies dealt with include the modernisation of capital ships, anti-submarine equipment, reserves of ammunition, stores, &c., and, in consequence of the fact that on this occasion we are reporting upon the *total requirements*, as against those only needed merely to make good the worst deficiencies, the Admiralty Estimates necessarily exceed those contained in our last Report. This is particularly the case with the modernisation of capital ships. Subsequent to the estimate put forward in Paper No. D.R.C. 14 (C.P. 64 (34)) information received as to the extent of modernisation

217

of these ships by other Powers has shown that considerable extra work was necessary on our own ships if they were to be comparable with those of the Powers concerned.

56. Complete modernisation is proposed for three of our capital ships, and partial for 4 more. The *Nelson*, *Rodney* and *Hood* will not require modernisation. If quantitative restrictions on the lines of the international agreements are continued after 1936, the Admiralty do not suggest modernising the remaining 5 capital ships. On the other hand, as we have already mentioned, if no such restrictions continue and other Powers retain their older ships when they have completed their new construction, it may be necessary to take in hand our remaining capital ships for modernisation in order to maintain the requisite superiority. Details of the deficiency proposals are contained in Appendix 2 to Schedule I, and the estimates there do not include the modernisation of the 5 ships referred to above.

57. We draw attention in particular to the new Item 17 of Appendix 2 to Schedule I for the immediate construction of a further Boys' Training Establishment. This is of the utmost importance if the future naval personnel requirements are to be met.

Personnel.

58. The figures for personnel are given in Appendix 3 to Schedule 1 and they provide, in general, for an expansion of strength by some 35,600 spread over the years 1936—42. The Admiralty are reluctant, for reasons of efficiency, to shorten the period within which this personnel should be provided and, as already mentioned, this affects the rate at which ship replacement can be usefully undertaken. The desirability of shortening the period of training, however, will be kept in view. These increases, in conjunction with those already made in 1934 and 1935, result in an annual charge of £820,000 in 1936, rising ultimately to an annual total direct charge of over £6$^1/_2$ million.

Fleet Air Arm.

59. The cost of aircraft for new construction has been included in the Naval Construction Programme, and the Admiralty's proposals contained in Appendix 4 to Schedule I cover the provision of aircraft for the new carriers and for re-armament or completion of existing flights; and also for the maintenance of the Fleet Air Arm during the period of expansion. The proposals are spread over the years 1936—42, mainly for the purpose of keepisng in step with new construction, and the total required in these years amounts to £28 million. Maintenance of the whole Fleet Air Arm by that time will have trebled itself as compared with 1936 and will amount in 1942 to £3 million per annum.

60. The first-line Fleet Air Arm strength allowed for in our proposals will amount to 504 aircraft by 1942. The need for the increase in the strength of the Fleet Air Arm from the present figure of 190 is clear when the present relative strengths of the principal Naval Powers is considered.

The above numbers do not include aircraft in operational shore-based units capable of carrying out sea reconnaissance and other duties in co-operation with naval forces. Differences of air organisation as between United Kingdom, U.S.A. and Japan respectively preclude exact statistical comparisons in respect of this category of units. But it is observed that U.S.A. have 170 and Japan has 182 first-line aircraft of this nature. It is to be noted that the latter country has great advantage in the North China Sea, where she could make use not only of ship-borne aircraft, but also shore-based aircraft working from islands in her possession. We possess a certain number of units which are so located that they are able to co-operate with the Naval forces in various areas, but it

Aircraft Embarked in Carrier
and Catapult Ships.

	1935	1939 (anticipated)
United Kingdom	190	357
U.S.A.	403	670*
Japan	258	374*

is clear that we are at present definitely inferior in numbers of aircraft in coastal units, both to the U.S.A. and to Japan. Our position in this respect will, however, be improved by the present Air Force Expansion Scheme and by the proposals in this Report. Moreover, the Admiralty propose to discuss with the Air Ministry means whereby our position in this respect may be further improved, particularly in respect of mobility (see paragraph 81 below).

61. These increases in the strength of the Fleet Air Arm and its ever growing naval importance will necessarily require more shore accommodation for maintenance and training, and the Admiralty, in Schedule I, paragraph 10 (d), have drawn attention to their opinion that a Fleet Air Arm base ashore is a vital requirement for the efficiency of the Fleet Air Arm, and they have tentatively mentioned a figure of £5 million for that purpose. This is not, however, included in the summary of the Naval estimates of cost, and is a matter for discussion between the Admiralty and Air Ministry, whose own Estimates, it may be observed, include considerable (£2 million) provision for additional shore accommodation for the Fleet Air Arm.

Possible New Mediterranean Base.

62. The Admiralty (paragraph 10 (e) and Appendix 5 to Schedule I) draw attention to the question of a possible base in Cyprus to supplement our base facilies in the Mediterranean. A very tentative estimate of the cost of the establishment of a complete base has been made, amounting to approximately £122$^{1}/_{2}$ million. The proposal raises many big questions and the cost has not been included in the summary of estimates attached to this Report.

63. As already mentioned in paragraph 29, we are of opinion that the Mediterranean situation is one which needs watching, and one factor in this is the question of such a base in Cyprus. It might be that some partial work, such as the building of a breakwater and the provision of a dock with certain repair facilities only, would be the correct solution of the problem.

General.

64. In the foregoing summary of the Admiralty estimates for making good
deficiencies and providing for new construction, it is important to emphasise
that nothing has been included for the inevitable expansion at the Admiralty
and at ports in the matter of staff to cope with the large volume of extra work
that will be involved.

V.—Army Programme and Requirements.
(For details see Schedule II.)

The Field Force.

65. The role which we propose for the Army in paragraph 34 requires the
following provision, viz., a Regular Field Force Contingent of 4 Divisions, a
Mobile Division (see next paragraph), 2 Air Defence Brigades and Army
Cooperation Squadrons of the Royal Air Force, together with the necessary
Complement of G.H.Q. Corps and L. of C. troops, the whole provided with all
its essential needs as regards modern armament and material. This Force
would form the first contingent of the Field Force, and would number about
155,000 men.

66. Under these proposals the present Cavalry Division will be reorganised
as a mobile division, consisting of 6 mechanised Cavalry Regiments and a
Tank brigade, together with appropriate supporting arms and services. Provision is also made for 3 new Army Tank Battalions, which, with the one now
existing, will provide one per Infantry Division of the 1st (Regular) Contingent of the Field Force. These are considered essential for the support of Infantry under modern conditions of warfare. In addition, the four Infantry
Divisions would be mechanised in regard to their transport, in accordance
with programmes already initiated.

67. We regard rapidity of mobilisation as essential, and we therefore propose
that arrangements should be speeded up so as to enable the Cavalry (Mobile)
Division and Air Defence Brigades to be disembarked on the Continent in a
week, and the remainder of the 1st Contingent a week later. This involves an
ultimate increase of the annual recurrent expenditure from £ 1,100,000 to
£ 1,500,000 as regards personnel (*vide* Schedule II, paragraph 6), and, in addition, further expenditure, may prove necessary in acquiring more rapidly
other essential requirements for the force. It is becoming more and more obvious that if our assistance to Continental allies is to be effective, it must be
available within a fortnight of the outbreak of war.

XI.—Summary of Conclusions and Recommendations.

140. Our conclusions and recommendations may be summed up as follows:
(1) The system of collective security provided by the Covenant of the League
of Nations, which has been adopted by successive Governments with strong

popular support as the basis of our foreign policy, has been shown by recent events to complicate the calculation of defence requirements. The Manchurian episode of 1931-33, and more especially the Italo-Abyssinian affair, show that this system is liable:—

    (a) to involve this country, as the only great sea-power in the League, in unforeseen commitments at very short notice;

    (b) to embitter our relations, almost without warning, with countries like Japan, Italy and France, with whom we had deliberately cultivated close relations in order to exclude them from the range of possible enemies; and

    (c) to produce unexpected reactions on our own security for which we were totally unprepared (*e.g.*, in the Far East in 1931—33; in the Mediterranean in 1935). (Paragraphs 10 to 15.)

(2) From the point of view of national and imperial security it should be a cardinal principle to avoid a situation in which we might be confronted simultaneously with the hostility, open or veiled, of Japan in the Far East, Germany in the West, and any Power on the line of communications between the two (Paragraph 16.)

(3) Recent events accentuate the importance of a policy of accommodation and friendliness with Japan as recommended in our first Report. (Paragraph 16.) Similarly as regards Germany it is very desirable that we should respond as favourably as circumstances permit—though circumstances are likely to impose a concrete limit—to Herr Hitler's desire to be on good terms with this country and that we should do everything we can, in conjunction with France, to promote and maintain friendly relations with Germany. (Paragraph 17.)

(4) Before Italy can so far recover from her present embarassments as to become a permanent factor in calculating our defence requirements, our long-range policy should be so aligned as to ensure that we shall never be in a position of hostility to Japan and Italy at the same time, to say nothing of Germany, without the certainty of French military support. (Paragraph 18.)

(5) The outstanding feature of recent world events is that a strong Britain is essential to the peace of the world. The policy of collective security contained in the Covenant can only succeed under the leadership of a strong and re-equipped Britain. With that backing the League would be a far more effective instrument for the maintenance of peace and as a deterrent to war than it is to-day. To the League system of collective security the alternatives are a more limited system of collective security in the Locarno model; the pre-war system of alliances and *ententes;* or isolation. For any of these systems to prove effective our armaments must be raised to a far more effective standard than has hitherto been aimed at. (Paragraphs 19 to 23.)

(6) The following new considerations affecting the calculation of our Defence Requirements have arisen:—

    (a) As the result of the principle of collective security our forces must be more ready than before;

    (b) There is now the possibility of a hostile Italy on our main line of imperial communications;

    (c) As the one big Naval Power of the League of Nations, we may have to exhaust ourselves to the detriment of the balance of security against Japan and Germany, who are outside it;

(d) As a result of the assumption by Germany of the right to build up a new navy free of the restrictions of the Treaty of Versailles, the Navy of that country (though fortunately now limited to 35 per cent. of our own strength) has to be taken into account;

(e) In view of the enormously increased capacity of output by Germany. there is the possibility of attack from the air so continuous and concentrated, and on such a scale, that a few weeks of that experience might so undermine the morale of any civilian population as to make it difficult for the Government to continue the war. (Paragraph 25.)

(7) With reference to (6) (b) above, the eventual position *vis-à-vis* Italy is as yet too obscure to appraise in terms of defence requirements. The situation will have to be watched carefully and a close study of the strategical problem in the Mediterranean will have to be made. In any event, it would be materially impossible, within the three-year period with which this Report is primarily concerned, to make additional provision for a hostile Italy. For these reasons we have limited ourselves to the same hypotheses as in our first Report (D.R.C. 14, also C.P. 64 (34)), namely, the provision of an adequate deterrent to Germany and Japan, and a protection to the United Kingdom and the Empire in these two contingencies. (Paragraphs 27—29.)

(8) The standards of security at which we should aim are as follows:—

Navy.

A new standard of naval strength defined as follows:—
(i) to enable us to place a Fleet in the Far East fully adequate to act on the defensive and to serve as a strong deterrent against any threat to our interests in that part of the globe;
(ii) to maintain in all circumstances in Home Waters a force able to meet the requirements of a war with Germany at the same time.

Included in (i) and (ii) should be the forces necessary in all parts of the world, behind the cover of the main fleets, to protect our territories and merchant ships against sporadic attack.

Army.

(i) To maintain garrisons overseas on the present general basis for purposes of Imperial Defence;
(ii) to provide for the military share in Home Defence, which includes anti-aircraft defence, Coast Defence and internal security;
(iii) to enable us to provide reinforcements and/or a Field Force from Home in time of emergency or war, with adequate equipment and reserves.

Under (i) and (ii) the most important requirements are a substantial improvement in coast defences at Naval bases at Home and Abroad, and the completion of the Army's share in the Air Defence of Great Britain.

Under (iii) the most important requirement is to organise a Field Force which can be sent abroad at short notice for the protection of our vital interests, and to enable us to honour our international obligations, particularly under

222

the Treaty of Locarno, which would involve effective co-operation with other signatories on the Continent of Europe. This includes the occupation for ourselves and the denial to the enemy of an advanced air base in the Low Countries.

Air Force.

We regard as a minimum the strength already decided for the Royal Air Force at Home, viz.: 123 squadrons (1,512 first-line aircraft) to be completed by April 1937. This figure was based on the assumption that by that date the number of German first-line aircraft will amount to some 1,500. In the absence of any agreement for the limitation of air forces there is, however, no guarantee that she will not build up to an even higher figure of first-line strength. It is therefore vital that the position should be kept under the closest continuous review.

In addition we propose—
(i) Provision of war reserves, without which the Air Force could only fight for a very short time;
(ii) strengthening of the air forces overseas and, in particular, those required to meet the possibility of war with Japan in the Far East;
(iii) additions to the Fleet Air Arm to correspond to the naval programme;
(iv) additions to the Army Co-operation Squadrons (mainly auxiliary squadrons) to provide the requirements of the four contingents of the Field Force.

For all Three Services.

An effective scheme for the expansion of industry in time of war and provision of reserves of war material sufficient to maintain them from the outset of war until industry is able to supply their needs from current output. (Paragraph 34.)

Navy Programme and Requirements.

(9) The naval programme required to carry out the new standard of naval strength proposed above cannot be worked out at present, as it depends upon the programmes of other Powers and upon the information which may be available after the Naval Conference. In any event, it is impossible to increase the Navy to the new standard within the next three years owing to difficulties of material and personnel unless resort is made to extraordinary measures such as those adopted in the case of the Royal Air Force expansion, which, in the opinion of the Admiralty, would prejudice the efficiency of the Service. (Paragraphs 37 to 41.)

We strongly recommend, however, that during the next few years ships should be laid down early in the financial year instead of in the last quarter as at present. (Paragraph 42.)

(10) For the time being we must concentrate on the requirements of the existing approved standard, doing all we can at the same time to prepare for a fresh programme to bring the Navy up to the new standard if it is approved by

the Government. We recommend that the Government should at once approve the new standard in principle and instruct the Admiralty—

    (i) to work out the naval programme required to give effect to it as soon as the necessary data are available; and

    (ii) to make suggestions as to any items in the new programme that can be put in hand before the expiration of the next three years. These will probably be limited by material considerations to the smaller classes of warship.

          (Paragraphs 43 and 44.)

(11) To complete the needs of the existing approved standard the programme we recommend includes:—

    7 capital ships to be laid down in the period 1937—39 (2—3—2). (Paragraphs 46 and 47.)

    4 aircraft carriers (some of a smaller type) to be laid down in the period 1936—42. (Paragraph 48.)

    5 cruisers a year between 1936 and 1939. (Paragraph 49.)

    1 destroyer flotilla in 1936—37 and thereafter 1 flotilla in alternate years up to 1942. (Paragraph 50.)

    Submarines, sloops, other small craft and auxiliaries at the same rate as in the past, that is to say about 3 submarines and 5 or 6 sloops a year. (Paragraph 51.)

(12) The cost of the above construction programme is approximately £ $19^1/_4$ million in 1936, rising to £ $36^1/_2$ million in 1939. Thereafter it should fall, but only if the quantitative restrictions of the Naval Treaties are renewed. Otherwise it may increase. If the new standard of naval strength is adopted an increased programme will be required involving additional expenditure not yet calculable. (Paragraphs 52 and 53.)

(13) The naval deficiency programme includes:—

    Complete modernisation for 3 capital ships.

    Partial modernisation for 4 capital ships.

    (Further modernisation if quantitative restrictions are not renewed and other nations retain their older capital ships.)

    Construction of a further Boys Training Establishment.

    35,600 increase in personnel between 1936 and 1942.

    Fleet Air Arm increase from 190 (the present figure) to 504 by 1942. (Paragraphs 55 to 64.)

Army Programme and Requirements.

(14) The Army Programmes and requirements include:—

Field Force: First Contingent (Regular Army).

    4 Divisions.

    1 Mobile Division (6 mechanised Cavalry Regiments and a Tank Brigade with supporting arms and services).

    3 new Army Tank Battalions (making, with the existing Battalion, one for each division).

    Speeding up mobilisation arrangements to enable the Mobile Division and Air Defence Brigades to be disembarked on the Continent in a week, and the remainder of the first contingent a week later. (Paragraphs 65 to 67.)

Second, Third and Fourth Contingents (Territorial Army).

Second Contingent of 4 Divisions at 4 months after the outbreak of war.
Third Contingent of 4 Divisions at 6 months after the outbreak of war.
Fourth Contingent of 4 Divisions at 8 months after the outbreak of war.
(Paragraph 68.)

Modernisation of the Territorial Army at a cost of £26,000,000, the previous suggested allotment of £ 250,000 a year being retained for improvement of training and efficiency. (Paragraph 69.)

Ammunition reserves for the earlier contingents. (Paragraph 70.)
Coast Defence Modernisation at home and abroad. (Paragraph 71.)
Air Defence of Great Britain to be within sight of completion in five years. (Paragraphs 72 and 73.)

An increase of 4 infantry battalions as an instalment of a possible eventual increase of 12 (or 14) battalions. (Paragraph 74.)

Re-equipment of the Field Artillery by converting the 18-pdr. gun to take a 25-lb. shell (with increase of range to 12,000 yards), which will replace both the 18-pounder field gun (range 9,000 yards) and 4.5-inch howitzer (range 6,500 yards).

Ammunition for the above. (Paragraphs 75 to 77.)
Improvement in Housing conditions. (Paragraph 78.)

Air Force Programme and Requirements.

(15) The Air Force Programme and Requirements include (paragraph 80):—
  (i) Completion of the expansion programme as at present approved so as to increase our metropolitan first-line air strength to 123 squadrons (1,512 aircraft) by April 1937.
 (ii) Army Co-operation squadrons to accompany the field forces on the following scale:—
First Contingent (regular), 7 squadrons (each of 12 aircraft), together with one squadron for communication purposes.
Second Contingent (territorial) (after 4 months), 4 or 5 squadrons;
Third Contingent (territorial) (after 6 months), 4 or 5 squadrons;
Fourth Contingent (territorial) (after 8 months), to be raised on mobilisation.
The above involves raising 4 new regular bomber squadrons and 4 new auxiliary squadrons, and possibly 2 additional Territorial squadrons later.
(iii) A first-line strength of 504 aircraft for the Fleet Air Arm and further shore accommodation at home and abroad.
(iv) Additional aircraft at overseas stations amounting to 13 squadrons and 2 or more Spotter Flights, viz.:—
Singapore.—An extra land-plane squadron and 2 additional landing grounds.
Penang, Ceylon and Aden.—One land-plane squadron apiece to co-operate with and assist the Navy.
Hong Kong.—3 squadrons, 1 spotter flight, 1 repair unit and an additional aerodrome.

Middle East.—An addition of 1 General Purpose Squadron.

Malta.—2 squadrons and 1 spotter flight as the ultimate strength, subject to later consideration as proposed in paragraph 29.

West Africa.—1 General Purpose Squadron and an aerodrome.

East Africa.—1 General Purpose Squadron.

West Indies.—1 reconnaissance (flying boat or land-plane) squadron.

Gibraltar.—An aerodrome to provide an intermediate air base on an "All British" air route to Malta and the Far East.

Certain of the above proposals must be regarded as provisional since they are dependent on the outcome of the international situation (Paragraphs 80 to 82.)

(v) *War Reserves.*—In order to bridge the gap between the outbreak of war and the time at which industry can meet wastage—

A war reserve of aircraft (amounting to 150 per cent. of first-line strength);

Four months' supply, additional to the above, of airframes and engines for additional flying training schools to be established on the outbreak of war to maintain the supply of pilots;

A reserve of six months' supply of bombs, small arm ammunition and pyrotechnics;

For motor transport—initial requirements with reserve of technical vehicles not readily obtainable from civilian sources (Paragraphs 83 to 86.)

(vi) Storage for reserves and the provision of jigs and tools for manufacture of aircraft. (Paragraph 87.)

(vii) *Personnel.*—A further entry to the Royal Air Force Reserve of 600 Pilots a year for the next three years, additional to the 200 a year to which the Air Ministry are now working. (Paragraph 88.)

Industrial Production.

(16) The only method by which very large deficiencies in war material can be supplied and an adequate "war potential" built up is by the creation of a "Shadow Armament Industry" (paragraph 91), which will demand an approved long-term programme of rearmament, continuity of orders, Government assistance and greater recourse to non-competitive contracts (paragraph 92). In this connection certain problems will arise, notably—

the provision of additional machinery, methods of collaboration with the industry, provision of labour, the prevention of profiteering and the allocation of firms to defence departments (paragraph 93), and the extension of Government factories (paragraph 94).

(17) The cost of the industrial measures recommended is necessarily conjectural; the suggested figure for the War Office is £ 16,000,000, for the Air Ministry £ 10,100,000, but these figures are dependent on the success attending the policy of expanding industry. (Paragraph 95.)

(18) The state of preparedness which would be achieved by the end of 1938—39 if *no* special measures are instituted for increasing factory output are dealt with in paragraphs 96—98. The Army would be the most adversely affected since the first contingent of the Field Force would still be short by 50

per cent. of its present deficiencies and also have no "war potential" behind it. In the absence of this "war potential," stocks would have to be built up gradually to a value of £150—£200 million. (Paragraph 97.) For the Royal Air Force the enlargement of the sources of production which is necessary to carry out by 1937 the expansion programme already authorised will (it is anticipated) substantially provide by 1939 the further numbers of aircraft and engines required to build up war reserves. The £10,100,000 referred to in (17) above is required to enable sources of production not employed in satisfying Air Force requirements in peace to turn over to war production without delay in an emergency. (Paragraph 98.)

(19) In the most favourable conditions it will be impossible to carry out the full programme of supply for the emergency of war by the 31st March, 1939. (Paragraph 100.)

Miscellaneous Requirements.

(20) In Section VIII of this Report we have drawn attention to developments which will require attention in the near future, of which the most important are—

(i) Provision of requirements for Air Raid Precautions, e.g., gas masks for the civilian population and other anti-gas equipment. (Paragraphs 102 and 103.)

(ii) Dangers to which our vital industries are liable from air attack, and notably the importance of Woolwich, Billingham and Ardeer in this connection. (Paragraphs 104 and 105.)

(iii) Increased provision for the Secret Service. (Paragraph 106.)

(iv) Armed merchant cruisers and defensively equipped merchant ships. Certain limitations are at present imposed by the Washington Naval Treaty. If these limitations are not repeated in any future Treaty the position will need reconsideration. (Paragraph 107.)

(v) The desirability of encouraging commercial air enterprises. (Paragraph 108.)

(vi) The importance of maintaining at the highest state of efficiency the Regular and Auxiliary forces in the Colonies, Mandated Territories, &c. (Paragraph 109.)

(vii) The need for drawing the attention of the Dominions to the measures to be undertaken in this country and for inviting their co-operation. (Paragraph 110.)

(viii) The need for remedying deficiencies in India. (Paragraph 111.)

Costs and Finance.

(21) The proposals of this Report would result in an increased annual expenditure over the £124 million (original Estimates) voted for the defence services in 1935 of the order of:—

1936	...	...	...	...	...	49,650,000
1937	...	...	...	...	...	86,750,000
1938	...	...	...	...	...	102,400,000
1939	...	...	...	...	...	88,450,000
1940	...	...	...	...	...	90,050,000

A total of £417¹/₂ million over the five-year period, of which £239 million is in the next 3 years. All figures are, however, necessarily speculative, and are merely an attempt to indicate the order of magnitude of the expenditure. (Paragraphs 112—114.)

(22) In addition are the costs for air raids precautions equipment, approximately £5 million (paragraph 115), an increase to £¹/₂ million per annum for the Secret Service (paragraph 116) and a number of outstanding matters on which it is not possible to make recommendations or frame costs at the present time (paragraph 117).

General.

(23) We recommend in general that every possible step should be taken to bring home to the people of this country an understanding of the international situation and the need for sacrifices, both personal and financial, in order to provide the defence forces and defences essential to security. In particular we recommend—

(a) that the importance of defence should be emphasised in our educational system at least to the same extent as, and as an integral element in the propaganda for peace and the League of Nations, that is carried on to-day in our schools. (Paragraph 135.)

(b) that civilian Departments of the Government should render all the assistance within their power to the Defence Departments, *e.g.*, in the expansion of industry and recruitment for the forces. (Paragraph 136.)

(c) That the attention of the Departments concerned should be drawn to the vital importance to Imperial Defence of an improved physical standard in the population. (Paragraph 137.)

(24) Our Report is based on a reasonable estimate of what is required to meet our responsibilities in respect of the security of the Empire, and does not provide a margin for every conceivable danger, such as an unexpectedly rapid increase in the naval strength of Japan or the air strength of Germany; a sudden attack in time of normal diplomatic relations such as was deemed possible before the war. (Section X.)

(Signed)

M. P. A. HANKEY *(Chairman)*.
ERNLE CHATFIELD.
E. L. ELLINGTON.
N. F. WARREN FISHER.
A. A. MONTGOMERY-MASSINGBERD.
ROBERT VANSITTART.

(Signed)   H. R. POWNALL *(Secretary)*.
A. W. CLARKE *(Assistant Secretary)*.

2 Whitehall Gardens, S.W.1,
November 21, 1935.

PRO. Cab. 24/259

228

APPENDIX VIII

Fair play or false play? Doubts about the fairness of the German Government during the negotiation of the Anglo-German Naval Treaty. The British Naval Attaché's report from Berlin to the Director of Naval Intelligence; a secret memorandum by R. F. Wigram, with R. L. Craigie's letter and T. S. Phillips' note.

A copy of our Naval Attaché's report (N.I.D. 327/36) has been inserted.

As recently as 1st February, 1936, Admiral Raeder categorically denied reports to the effect that Germany is violating the Anglo-German Naval Agreement, and he has given his personal assurance, to our Naval Attaché, that the terms of the agreement were being closely adhered to; and that nothing was being built, or would be built, which was not allowed to Germany under the agreement (M. 01536/36).

In view of Admiral Raeder's emphatic assurances, the present report is discredited, and it seems improbable that Admiral Raeder will permit the desire for secrecy to override Germany's obligations in regard to the interchange of Naval information with ourselves (P.D. 04992/35).

Our Naval Attaché has since reported that he has reason to believe the information furnished by the Italian Naval Attaché was absolutely false.

(Illegible signature)
D. N. I.

From: Naval Attaché, Berlin.
To: Director of Naval Intelligence.
Date: 18th February, 1936.

German Naval Construction.

My R/S G. 20/36 of to-day's date.

The Italian Naval Attaché informed me that he had seen in the Germania Yard, Kiel, the keels of two Aircraft Carriers and a 10,000 ton cruiser, the third of the series.

2. He is quite positive about this, and told me that 12 La Mont or Benson boilers had been ordered for the two cruisers (one also building at Deutsche Werke) and 14 Wagner boilers for the 2 aircraft carriers.

3. Four destroyers building at Deutsche Werke are now in the water, and their completion will be hastened. The delay in construction has been caused by uncertainty in boiler policy. It was originally intended to fit Benson boilers,

229

but these boilers in the "Grille" have been giving trouble, and the work of installing the boilers was suspended for some time. See also para. 4 of my R/S G(T)1/36 dated 6.1.36.

4. Although he did not know whether construction had commenced, Captain de Courten said definitely that ten 550-ton submarines would be built in the next programme.

5. I have for some time past been suggesting to the Liaison Officer at the Marineleitung that I should like to go to Kiel to see some ships and establishments, but he has always asked me to put my request in writing and to state exactly what ships I want to see.

This I have now done, and on the 13th instand, I asked if I might visit Kiel from 24th to 29th February, and suggested visiting "Admiral Scheer", "Nürnberg", "Tsingtau", a "Flottenbegleiter" and a "Schnellboot". If my visit is permitted I may be able to obtain some further information about ships building.

6. May I be informed please whether the fact of these ships (2 aircraft carriers and a third 10,000 ton cruiser) being ordered has been notified to the Admiralty in accordance with the terms of the Naval Agreement?

(Sd.) G. C. MUIRHEAD GOULD.
Captain, R. N.
Naval Attaché.

Memorandum by Mr. Wigram.

Anglo-German Naval Treaty.

I was informed two days ago by a diplomatist here, who asked that his name might not be mentioned, that he had been shown by a friend in the German diplomatic service a circular to German Embassies abroad explaining the circumstances in which the Anglo-German Naval Treaty had been concluded.

The circular was dated about 10 days after the conclusion of the Treaty in the summer of 1935; and it emphasised that one of the motives directing the German Government's attitude was that Germany was not, at the time of the signature of the Treaty, in a position to build more than one-third of the British Fleet. The circular continued that as soon as the German yards were able to build a larger fleet, the whole situation would be reviewed.

(Sgd) R. F. WIGRAM
November 20th, 1936

FOREIGN OFFICE, S W. 1.
3rd December, 1936.
(A 9482/4671/45)

Private and Confidential

My dear Phillips,

I enclose a copy of a memorandum which has been sent to me by Wigram, Head of the Central Department of the Foreign Office, recording a statement made to him by a diplomatist here in regard to the German attitude towards the Anglo-German Naval Treaty.

230

While I do not personally believe that a circular could in fact have been sent out in terms suggested by Wigram's informant, I think that the Admiralty ought to be aware of this report. It seems to me most improbable that, even had the German Government intended from the first to play us false, they would, at the very moment when they were insisting in the agreement itself on its permanent nature, have taken the risk of circulating to all their Missions abroad a written acknowledgment of their own bad faith. Even, however, had they been guilty of such a gaffe, it is unlikely that any German diplomatist would have communicated to a foreign colleague information of so secret a character. What has probably happened is that some relatively harmless passage in the circular, if circular there was, has been twisted into the present story.

There is much that happened during the negotiation of the Anglo-German Naval Treaty and much that has happened during our recent discussions with the Germans which leads me to doubt very seriously whether Germany had in 1935, or has today, any deliberate intention of going back on this Agreement. Assuming no serious deterioration in Anglo-German relations, my personal estimate of the probable course of events is that the German Government will be as little desirous of entering into a naval race with us after they have reached their 35% strength as they are at the present time. That they are contemplating the possibility of an eventual appeal to us under Article 2 (c) of the Agreement for the purpose of increasing Germany's naval strength vis-à-vis of France and Soviet Russia, I have no doubt. If, however, we proceed with our present rearmament programme, the resulting increase in our own naval strength will in any case give Germany extra elbow-room and place us in a better position for refusing any German request for an increase in the ratio.

Yours sincerely,

R. L. Craigie

The attached letter and report received from Sir R. Craigie refer to an alleged circular note sent by the German Government to German Embassies abroad in July, 1935, implying a complete lack of good faith on the part of the Germans in negotiating the 35% Anglo-German Agreement of 1935.

Up to date we have had no cause to doubt Germany's good faith in the carrying out of this Agreement, and the consultations which have taken place with them seem to show that they attach importance to its exact observance. If they intended to throw the agreement over when it best suited them, it is difficult to believe that they would insist in the meticulous regulation of such matters as overage tonnage, transfer and adjustment.

I concur with Sir R. Craigie that little credence should be given to this report of German bad faith.

(T. S. Phillips)

PRO. Adm. 116/3377

APPENDIX IX

British and German comment on the Anglo-Soviet Naval Discussions of July 29, 1936. Excerpts from a German memorandum (Jan. 23rd 1937) and from the records of a British-German meeting held at the F. O. on 13th Febr. 1937.

Copy
(A 8350/4/45)
TRANSLATION.

The German Government have taken note of the following memoranda of His Majesty's Government and have examined them in detail.

Summary of the results of the Anglo-Soviet naval discussions of July 29, 1936;

British memorandum of July 22, 1936, with documents A, B and C.

The information which His Britannic Majesty's Government have communicated to the German Government relating to certain building intentions of the U.S.S.R. have evoked acute apprehensions on the part of the German Government. It must give rise to the gravest fears regarding the national safety of Germany. The German Government hope that His Britannic Majesty's Government will make every endeavour to induce the U.S.S.R. to renounce their far-reaching demands which, moreover, are not in accordance with the provisions of the London Treaty of 1936. The German Government are of the opinion that should this building plan of the U.S.S.R. be carried out, the result will be a violent and menacing disturbance of the naval equilibrium, which would compel the German Government to consider the possibilities contemplated in regard to such cases.

The German Government are sincerely desirous of continuing to make a positive contribution to the pacification of Europe in that they are prepared to conclude a bilateral *qualitative* agreement even in the particularly unfavourable naval situation in which Germany is placed by reason of the course of action intended by the U.S.S.R. They must, however, make their participation dependent upon the acceptance of the reservations proposed in section I g, Nos. 1—4, which are requisite for ensuring the threatened national security.

I. *Influence of the Anglo-Soviet naval agreement on Germany's naval situation.*

The Soviet Union fleet in the Far East — an integral part of the Soviet Navy — has not been placed under any qualitative obligation. The German Government have repeatedly stated that an engagement of the same nature applying to the U.S.S.R. is a preliminary condition for the conclusion of a qualitative agreement with His Britannic Majesty's Government on the basis of the London Treaty of 1936. This similarity of obligation is traversed by the U.S.S.R.'s reservations. If the Anglo-Soviet naval agreement is concluded in the form of the existing draft, the German naval situation will deteriorate to a considerable extent.

(a) *Concentration of the several Portions of the Soviet Fleet in European waters.*

A close connexion exists between the several parts of the Soviet fleet. It must be regarded as one single whole. Moreover the German Government regret that after the conclusion of the Franco-Soviet military alliance they must also regard the French and Soviet navies as one unit in the event of war.

The Soviet Union can at any time concentrate the various parts of their fleet. The Far Eastern fleet or parts thereof can be detached to European waters without special difficulties in times of political tension. This transfer is the more easy to effect when, in virtue of the Franco-Soviet military alliance, the French bases in Indo-China, the Red Sea and the Mediterranean are available to the Soviet fleet. The provisions dealing with the exchange of information in relation to "vessels" which are *transferred* from the Far Eastern fleet to the European fleet prove that a *transfer* of parts of the Far Eastern fleet is contemplated by the Soviet Union as well.

Moreover, consequent on the fortification of the Dardanelles the Black Sea fleet is no longer confined to the Black Sea, in view of the Turkish–Soviet pact of friendship of 1925 and the Franco-Soviet military alliance. Hitherto it has been needed in the Black Sea for the protection of Soviet interests and to guard the coast. *Now* Turkey can close the Dardanelles for the benefit of the Soviet Union. In that case the Black Sea fleet is free and can be moved to other localities in the Soviet Union without any military disadvantages necessarily arising in the Black Sea.

The new transit provisions also tend in the same direction in the event of war — viz. they signify a closing of the Dardanelles to non-riparian States.

It is also to be counted on that parts of the Soviet Far Eastern or Black Sea fleet will be placed at the disposal of France in the Mediterranean, so that French forces in corresponding strength are set free for the northern theatre of war.

His Britannic Majesty's Government could with equal right and on the same grounds as the U.S.S.R. exclude from qualitative limitation their naval forces in the Far East. They have however regarded the safety clauses as sufficient to meet a threat to their national security.

The German Government are unable to admit that this solution for the safeguarding of national security, which satisfies all the other contracting parties, is insufficient for the U.S.S.R., and they must therefore draw the corresponding conclusions.

(b) *New Constructions for the Far Eastern fleet.*

The shipyards of the U.S.S.R. in the Far East only permit the construction of smaller craft. Fighting units for the Far East will consequently be built mainly in the Soviet Union's dockyards in the Baltic Sea or in other European waters until they are finally taken over and all their trial voyages are completed. The trial voyages can be delayed at will, so that the Soviet Union has the possibility of retaining in European waters for a considerable time, but especially

234

when the situation is politically uncertain, vessels which are constructed for the Far East.

(c) *Equipment of the U.S.S.R. at Sea.*

Within a short period and with an enormous outlay in staff and material the Soviet Union have built up their army and air arm. The building up of the Soviet fleet has been taken in hand with a tremendous utilisation of labour. In the course of the negotiations His Britannic Majesty's Government have several times stated that the building up of the Soviet fleet would not proceed particularly fast. According to the view of the German Government this opinion is not well-founded. The efforts of the U.S.S.R. to improve their naval armaments have achieved noticeable succes in a short time. Thus for example the Soviet Union already possess 120 submarines ready for action and a number of further submarines are under construction. Similar results must be expected as regards the construction of other classes of vessels. According to reliable reports warships are being built for the U.S.S.R. not only in dockyards of the Union but also in those of other European countries.

In this connexion it may be pointed out that according to the reservation in section I of the summary of the results of the Anglo-Soviet naval discussions, the U.S.S.R. have even the right to construct in Europe (Baltic dockyards) for the Far East any type of vessel *without* qualitative restrictions.

(d) *Armament of Soviet Union Battleships.*

In virtue of the Franco-Soviet military alliance, Germany must in the event of war count upon the U.S.S.R. *and* France being her opponents. Consequently Germany, on the basis of the building intentions of France and the U.S.S.R. which have so far become known, must reckon in future with at least 4 modern French battleships and an undetermined number of modern Soviet battleships, of which two are armed with 15-inch or 16-inch guns. The German Government would regard it as an unjustified limitation if in addition to the quantitative restriction there should also apply a restriction in regard to the armament of German battleships. Should the U.S.S.R. obtain the right to arm their new battleships about to be built with guns of higher calibre than 14-inches, Germany must deduce corresponding conclusions in respect of the armament of her battleships.

If all the signatories of the Washington Treaty of 1922 accede to the provisions of article 4 (2) of the London Agreement ot 1936, and the said provisions thereby acquire validity, the German Government must insist on a reduction of the armaments of the Soviet Union's battleships from 16-inch to 15-inch guns, if there is no success in inducing the U.S.S.R. to accept a calibre of 14 inches.

COPY.
(A 1322/54/45)

RECORD OF MEETING BETWEEN UNITED KINGDOM AND
GERMAN DELEGATIONS HELD AT THE FOREIGN
OFFICE AT 11 A.M. ON SATURDAY, 13TH FEBRUARY, 1937.

PRESENT:

Dr. Ernst Woermann . . . Counsellor at German Embassy.
Rear-Admiral Wassner . . . Naval Attaché
Dr. Erich Kordt . . . First Secretary at German Embassy.
Captain Phillips ⎫ . . . ADMIRALTY.
Commander Bell ⎭
Sir Robert Craigie ⎫
Mr. Holman ⎬ . . . FOREIGN OFFICE.
Mr. Fitzmaurice ⎭

SIR ROBERT CRAIGIE stated that, before considering the draft documents
for discussion by the meeting, he desired to make certain brief oral comments
on the observation made in paragraph 2, page 2 of the German Memorandum
of January 23rd in connexion with the Soviet shipbuilding programme. He
pointed out that His Majesty's Government were unable to regard the existing
Soviet programme of naval construction as far as it was known to us as upsetting the maritime equilibrium of Europe. It was true that the Soviet Government were intending to construct two capital ships, 7 sub-category (a) cruisers
instead of the original 10 and had already a considerable submarine force,
but on the other hand the German Government would realise that at the time
of the signature of the Anglo-German Naval Agreement of 1935, the Soviet
Navy was, apart from submarines, almost non-existent. Since the War, Soviet
Russia had taken no steps to reconstruct her fleet, and it would have been
taking an optimistic view to have assumed at the time Anglo-German agreement was concluded that Soviet naval forces were likely to remain at zero.
In the past, Soviet Russia had always maintained a certain level of naval
strength, which appeared commensurate with her needs. A normal and reasonable naval reconstruction must therefore be anticipated and should not be
regarded as carrying with it the consequences referred to in the German Memorandum. In view of the close relations existing between His Majesty's
Government and the German Government in regard to naval matters, he knew
that he could speak with complete frankness and he wished therefore to take
the opportunity of placing on record the views of His Majesty's Government
on the point at issue, although he did not think that any detailed discussion of
the question at the present time would serve a useful purpose.

DR. WOERMANN replied that there was nothing new in what had been
said in the German Memorandum. In any case it was not stated therein that
a situation had arisen in which Germany would be obliged to claim her rights
under the Anglo-German Naval Agreement of 1935.

236

ADMIRAL WASSNER observed that at the time of the conclusion of the Anglo-German Agreement practically no Soviet submarines existed, whilst today the submarine fleet amounts to about 180 vessels. That state of affairs could not have been foreseen.

SIR R. CRAIGIE replied that in 1935 it was known that the Soviet Government were building a considerable submarine fleet, probably in view of the situation in the Far East, and, it was now hoped that the German Government would take a reasonable view as to what was to be regarded as abnormal.

PRO. Adm. 116/3378

APPENDIX X

Hitler and the British Navy.
(I.K.'s note. June 30th, 1937)

Colonel Bodenschatz, who is liaison officer between Göring and Hitler and sees a lot of the latter, told me *that one of Herr Hitler's favourite hobbies was the study of marine construction of warships*. He was fully informed not only in regard to all details affecting the German fleet but also foreign fleets as well. He took a particular interest in the British fleet and was able at a moment's notice to give full details in regard to the class, tonnage, armament and equipment of any ship in the British Navy. For example, he knew exactly where the gun turrets in H.M.S. "Hood" were placed, the calibre and situation of her anti-aircraft guns, maximum speed. thickness of armour plating, etc., etc.

Colonel Bodenschatz emphasised two or three times that naval matters interested Herr Hitler quite particularly and that he was a careful student of British naval matters in particular. He added that the Chancellor's fondness for the Navy was proved by the fact that he never missed an opportunity of attending the launch of a German warship and that he was never in better form than when inspecting German naval units in the yacht "Grille". German naval officers had frequently been caught out by the Chancellor on purely technical matters.

I remarked that it was curious that a man born in Austria, who had until recently never seen the sea and who in his book condemned the German naval policy before the War, should be so enthusiastic about marine matters. Colonel Bodenschatz replied that it was indeed remarkable, but that it was nonetheless a fact.

(Intd.) I. K.
June 30th, 1937.

PRO. Adm. 116/3378

APPENDIX XI

Nevile Henderson's uneasiness about Hitler's aim to denounce
the Naval Agreement (to A. Eden), and F. O. information to the Admiralty
on the matter (W. Strang to Capt. T. S. V. Phillips)

BRITISH EMBASSY
BERLIN.
July 1st. 1937,

Personal

Dear Secretary of State,

In a recent private letter (June 22nd) I mentioned an impression I had got
in regard to Hitler's restiveness on the subject of the Anglo-German Naval
Agreement.

General Göring came to lunch here the other day with his chief A. D. C.,
Colonel Bodenschatz. The accompanying interesting account of a conversation
which the latter had on that occasion with Kirkpatrick lends point to the above
impression.

The German controlled Press constantly refers to that agreement as the
definite proof of Germany's good-will and good intentions, and is always
asking when Great Britain is going to respond to that gesture.

I doubt whether Hitler would go so far as to denounce the agreement today
or tomorrow on the ground that it had been made as a basis for an understanding which Great Britain refuses to implement. Germany is too busy with land
rearmament (and is handicapped even in that by shortage of raw material)
to make an empty threat of that kind at the moment. It would be materially
impossible for her to begin now on a big shipbuilding programme. Even to
keep up with a third of our new programme will tax her present resources.
Nevertheless I have an uneasy feeling that Hitler often feels like denouncing
the agreement.

Possibly *I am unduly uneasy for the very reason that I regard the Anglo-
German Naval Agreement as the foundation and test stone of any present and
future understanding with Germany.* I am quite alive to the arguments about
the air being as or more important than the sea, but, even so, it is the two
together which would make the menace doubly formidable. Whether Spain
has strengthened the argument that a war can be definitely won in the air
alone or not is an open question and I fancy the Germans are just as uncertain
about this as we probably are.

On the other hand, I am very disinclined to believe in the reality of Germany's aggressive intentions against Great Britain unless and until she goes back on the Naval Agreement. If she does, either before or after an understanding, it will then, but in my opinion only then, be quite certain what her ultimate intentions are. Otherwise, risk though there be, it has got to be faced and we have got to trust her.

All this is by the way. The point I want to make is that Hitler regards the Anglo-German Naval Agreement as a real sacrifice and contribution on the part of Germany. It is a sacrifice which touches him personally. If we attach value to the agreement, we must be on the watch and do our best to avoid giving him any excuse to scrap it.

Yours ever,

(Sd.) NEVILE HENDERSON.

He feels, I think for instance, that the upshot of the Leipzig incident indicates that G. B. is not prepared to cooperate in defending German naval interests.

(Intld.) N. H.

FOREIGN OFFICE, S. W. 1
20th July, 1937.

Secret.

Dear Phillips,

It may interest to you to know that in a letter to the Secretary of State dated 22nd June the Ambassador in Berlin wrote as follows about an interview he had had with the Chancellor: —

"There was just one other disturbing impression, though quite vague and undefined, which I got from this interview. It was that Hitler was feeling a little sore that the German naval forces should be so inferior to the British. He compared, for instance, the "Leipzig" to the "Hood" from the point of view of the naval ratio, etc. It made one wonder if he had not got at the back of his mind the thought that if the British Navy, with its great superiority over the German, did not keep the peace on the High Seas, then he would have to think about revising the Naval Agreement."

On 1st July the Ambassador wrote a further personal letter on the same subject, a copy of which is enclosed, together with a copy of the record of the conversation with General Göring's Aide-de-Camp which is referred to in it.

Yours sincerely

W. Strang

PRO. Adm. 116/3378

APPENDIX XII

Henderson's letter to Viscount Halifax about Field-Marshal Göring's view of the Naval Agreement

CONFIDENTAL.

Copy No. 142

[C 3325/132/18]

Sir N. Henderson to Viscount Halifax.— (Received April 22.)

(No. 381.)

Berlin, April 20, 1938

My Lord,

I have given elsewhere an account of a conversation which I had with Field-Marshal Göring on the 16th instant in regard to Herr von Schuschnigg and other Austrians at present under arrest.

2. At the end of my visit, when I was preparing to leave, the conversation turned to more general subjects. The field-marshal, speaking very bitterly, said that he could not understand the mentality of the British and felt sometimes mad with rage against them. They had, he said, lost all sense of fairmindedness and were merely influenced by emotions of fear and prejudice. The only country which had justifiably a right to object to the union of Austria with Germany was Italy. Yet it was Britain which had protested, whereas Signor Mussolini and the Italians had been wise enough to accept with good grace what they could not prevent. The Germans were grateful for this and to-day, in consequence, even the people, who would far prefer to be friends with England and had never trusted the Italians, had changed their views and now thought really well of the Italians. The field-marshal seemed genuinely disappointed at our having missed what seemed to him a golden opportunity to prove for once that England did not always stand everywhere in Germany's path.

3. I told Field-Marshal Göring that the Italian censorship was doubtless responsible for the absence of criticism in Italy and that, in any case, it was probably true to say that we were more disinterestedly sincere and honest in our opinions. We might misunderstand the Germans, but they certainly misunderstood us if they imagined that we would sit by and approve the forcible entry of a hundred thousand troops and police into Austria. Public opinion in England had been outraged at what had all the appearance of a rape. We might not have objected to seduction, whereas now the British public was more than ever convinced that the only policy which counted for Germany was one of brute force. Austria had stimulated recruiting in England, but had, on the other hand, given rise to much unfortunate talk as to further German aggression. Nor was it surprising that people asked where the limit was and did not believe that Germany would ever settle down peacefully as a satisfied country.

4. Field-Marshal Göring replied that he appreciated the fact that England

was rearming. He never allowed any of his officers to speak disparagingly of Britain or to underrate her strength. He added that incidentally one of the surest ways to win a war was to appreciate justly the capacities of one's adversary! He hated, however, the idea of what he called the two great Germanic peoples fighting each other again. Before 1914 it was Germany who always talked of "The Day" and regarded war with England as inevitable and so brought it on. Now it was the other way round. It was England which regarded war as inevitable and there was a real danger of its resulting once again in consequence of that very mentality. It was a curious fact that England, which had understood better than anyone else and sympathised so actively with the process of Italian unification in the last century, was blinder than anyone else to the process of German unity in this century. (This is a favourite subject of comparison just now in the German press.)

5. Germany, he continued, would finally become a territorially satisfied nation as soon as the Sudeten question was settled. He had, he said, recently seen Herr Henlein, who had not been hopeful as to the possibility of coming to an arrangement with Dr. Beneš. If the latter proved unreasonable, then anything might happen, and be described the fate of the Czechs in violent terms. But, apart from the Sudeten, everything else was of minor importance: Danzig was already practically German again; the problem of the corridor could be solved possibly by a corridor across a corridor; Memel would also have to come back to Germany, but these were all matters of comparatively easy adjustment. (Please see in this connexion my despatch No. 324 of the 1st April.) Germany, he added, was not going to worry about 40,000 Germans in Eupen, and it was utter nonsense to talk about the half-million Germans in Hungary or the three-quarter million in Yugoslavia. The former had settled there of their own free will and were perfectly happy. As for Yugoslavia, Germany wanted her to be as strong as possible and regarded her as a possible future ally ("Bündnismacht"). Economically, Germany wanted, of course, her place in the world, but there was room for both England and Germany, and the latter was only too willing to come to any agreement that England liked about spheres of influence for trade. He wished, he said, that he could speak to Mr. Chamberlain himself about all this, although he supposed that he would merely talk about peace. Well, if he wanted peace and peaceful solutions, the best thing that His Majesty's Government could do would be to let Dr. Beneš know that he must come to an agreement direct with Germany. Finally, as a sort of afterthought, he mentioned, colonies, which he said Germany must have to be really satisfied.

6. When the field-marshal began to talk wildly about dividing the appendix (which is his favourite term for Czechoslovakia) between Poland, Hungary and Germany, I warned him that aggression there was likely to have far more serious consequences than in the case of Austria; but otherwise I did not interrupt this monologue, nor did I express any views at all myself as to a solution of the Sudeten. At the same time I could not but reflect that Field-Marshal Göring's language, intemperate though it often is and was on this occasion as regards the Czechs, reflects the ideas of the great proportion of this people as well as of the Sudeten themselves. It is eleventh hour so far as Czechoslovakia is concerned, and if she takes the wrong turning now she may well lose everything. It is not arguments about historical or natural frontiers, or considerations about strategical or economic factors, which will count to-day but facts of nationality

244

and geography, however unpleasant they may be to others. Unless Dr. Beneš, relying on British support, is determined like Herr von Schuschnigg to risk not only the entire independence of his country but another world war as well, he will be well-advised now to make the best bargain that he can with Herr Hitler himself before the twelfth hour strikes. However distasteful it is to me to express such a categorical opinion, I would not be justified in giving any other. I believe that it is open to us to try, probably with success for a while, to impose another solution, particularly if we were to announce our determination to intervene in the event of aggression, however engineered. But, sooner or later, there is not a hope of the Sudeten remaining citizens of Czechoslovakia unless they do so willingly.

7. Nor did I make any comment to Field-Marshal Göring on the colonial question except to observe firstly that, whereas on the 3rd March His Majesty's Government was prepared to discuss that question, the events of the 12th and 13th March had caused the possibilities in that respect to recede into the background, and secondly to remark that no understanding between countries or individuals was possible without reciprocity. I quoted Herr Hitler's own words in *Mein Kampf* in this connexion, and said that if Germany could not agree with us about Central Europe, I did not see whence reciprocity was to be found.

8. Field-Marshal Göring's reply to this was "limitation of armaments". Once the Sudeten question was out of the way Germany would be quite willing to discuss this. Moreover there was already the Naval Agreement. It had never been valued in England, and he himself bitterly regretted that Herr Hitler had ever consented to it at the time without getting anything in exchange. It had been a mistake, but Germany was nevertheless not going to remain in a state of inferiority in this respect *vis-à-vis* a hostile Britain, and would build up once more to a 100 per cent. basis. Then, I said, you will certainly have war. Field-Marshal Göring argued that naval equality did not necessarily mean an unfriendly Germany. I replied that Herr Hitler was wiser than he was. We would always go to war with a country which threatened us on the sea. Germany was a continental Power and we might not be justified in seeking to restrict her land forces, but Britain was an island and her whole existence rested on air and sea power. If Germany wanted war, naval competition was the surest way to bring it about. Field-Marshal Göring appeared reluctantly to agree, and remarked that while Herr Hitler did not regard himself as bound by the treaties which the previous régime has signed he would always respect his own signature. Nevertheless, I would draw your Lordships' attention to the fact that this is the first time that a German has even hinted to me of the possibility of going back on the Naval Agreement.

9. At one moment in the course of this conversation Field-Marshal Göring asked me rather uneasily what we sought to get out of our agreement with Italy, and observed that if we hoped to weaken the Berlin—Rome axis we would not succeed in doing so. I told him that such was not the object of His Majesty's Government, though I hoped that a friendly Signor Mussolini might help even with Berlin. But the whole aim of our negotiations with Italy were, I said, to restore peace and confidence in the world in general and in the Mediterranean in particular. I had every hope that this end would be ensured by their successful conclusion. That was something, possibly a great deal. Nor,

indeed, had we even begun negotiations with Italy to the exclusion of Germany
If it had not been for the internal crisis here, we would have commenced
discussions with the German Government at the same time as with Rome. As
it was I had seen Herr Hitler on the 3rd March, but events in Austria had inter-
vened and put the clock back. Field-Marshal Göring retorted that Austria
has simplified matters and was a step towards peace just as much as our
agreement with Italy. Perhaps, I replied, but the whole difference lay in the
methods employed.

I have, &c.
NEVILE HENDERSON.

PRO. Adm. 116/3378

APPENDIX XIII

Admiralty and F.O approve the language Henderson held to Göring
(V.H. Danckwerts to W. Strang and F.O. to Henderson)

Plans Division,
Naval Staff
Admiralty, S.W. 1
18th May, 1938.

Dear,

Thank you for the copy of a despatch recording a conversation between our Ambassador in Berlin and Field Marshal Göring on 16th April, in which the Field Marshal referred to the 1935 Naval Agreement.

2. We fully concur with the language used by the Ambassador in reply to Göring's remarks. The only additional point to which attention might be drawn is Göring's statement that the Naval agreement had never been valued in England. That is certainly not the case; as you know the Admiralty attach the greatest importance to this agreement, a feeling which is shared by the Government and has been frequently expressed in Parliament, and occasionally in the Press.

3. In this connection one might refer to an article by Hector Bywater in the "Daily Telegraph" of 6th December, 1937, which gives a very fair picture of the value attached to this agreement. To give only one quotation from this article — "In British naval circles, at least, this agreement is held to be one of the greatest and most beneficial diplomatic achievements of the post-war era."

Strang, (To) Esq., CMG.,   Yours
Foreign Office.   (Capt. V.H. Danckwerts, C.M.G.)

(F.O. comment on the margin: "Slight exaggeration".)

(To) Sir N. Henderson,   July, 1938.
Berlin.

Sir,

With reference to the final paragraph of my despatch No. 1092 of July 6th I have to inform you that the observations of Field Marshal Göring referred to in paragraph 8 of your despatch No. 381 of April 20th have, in view of the important issues involved, been given further serious consideration in consultation with the Admiralty. The views expressed however in the following paragraphs should be treated as confidential and are for your own guidance in the event of the Anglo-German Naval Agreement of 1935 being raised again in conversation with you by Field Marshal Göring or other German statesmen.

2. The continued existence of the Anglo-German Naval Agreement of 1935 is naturally of great importance to us from the point of view of our future naval policy and construction, inasmuch as it eliminates rivalry and introduces a factor of certainty in the European situation as far as our security is concerned. The value to be attached to this Agreement was, as you will have observed, stressed by the Prime Minister in his speech in the House of Commons on the 26th instant.

3. On the other hand it must not be assumed that the German Government obtained no advantage by subscribing to it and that they are still entitled to a further *quid pro quo* from us. At the time of the conclusion of the Agreement the German Government were well aware that 35% of our navy was probably the most that they could hope to achieve for a considerable period of years. This was their chief concern. *The Agreement as far as they were concerned was valuable because it was a means of obtaining from His Majesty's Government (alone of the ex-Allied Powers) a formal acceptance of the German thesis that the naval provisions of the Treaty of Versailles had ceased to exist and because it enabled them to forestall the juridical objections of other signatories of the Treaty and to build with the approval of* His Majesty's Government as much as they were likely to be able to build within the next few years. They did not concern themselves about the ultimate future because they no doubt reckoned, if the necessity should ever arise, on being able to free themselves from the Agreement by finding some plausible excuse.

4. Field Marshal Göring's threat that in certain circumstances Germany might, presumably after denouncing the Anglo-German Naval Agreement of 1935, proceed to build up to 100% of the British fleet *is clearly bluff.* In view of the great existing disparity in the size of the two navies this threat could only be executed if British construction were to remain stationary over a considerable period of years whilst German tonnage was being built up to it. This would not occur. *Although Germany is doubtless capable of realizing the 35% figure by 1942 if she so desires,* or even appreciably earlier, it seems unlikely (considering her difficulties in connection with raw material, foreign exchange and the necessity of giving priority to her vast rearmament on land and in the air, and considering our own big programme) that she would appreciably exceed that figure during the course of the next few years. This is not to say that we have not every interest in avoiding a denunciation of the Anglo-German Agreement of 1935, which would create a present state of uncertainty as to Germany's intentions and the ultimate threat of an attempt at parity with our Navy, which must be regarded as potentially dangerous given that Germany has been credited with a capacity for naval construction little inferior to our own. Indeed, so important is the Naval Agreement to His Majesty's Government that it is difficult to conceive that any general understanding between Great Britain and Germany, such as General Göring is believed to desire, would any longer be possible were the German Government to denounce the Naval Agreement. *In fact, a reaffirmation of the latter*

would in all probability have to figure as part of such a general understanding.

5. From the political aspect, the German navy has we think been to Germany mainly an instrument for putting political pressure on this country. Before the war, Germany would have been willing to cease, or greatly moderate, her naval competition with this country, but only in return for a promise of our neutrality in any European conflict. Hitler has attempted the same thing by different methods, but he has seen one side of the picture, as all German politicians have only seen one side of the picture. It is clear from his writings that he was enormously impressed with the part played by the pre-war naval rivalry in creating bad relations between the two countries. From this he argued that the removal of this rivalry was all that was necessary to obtain good relations. By making us a free gift of an absence of naval competition he hoped that relations between the two countries would be so improved that we should not, in fact, find it necessary to interfere with Germany's continental policy. He overlooked, as all German politicians have overlooked for many years past, that this country is bound to react, not only against danger from any purely naval rival, but also against the dominance of Europe by any aggressive military Power, particularly if in a position to threaten the Low Countries and the channel ports. British complaisance can never be purchased by trading one of these factors against the other and any country that attempts it is bound to create for itself disappointment and disillusion as Germany is doing.

PRO. Adm. 118/3378

APPENDIX XIV

"The situation has arisen." Germany builds up to 100%
of the British submarine tonnage. Von Dirksen's letter to Viscount Halifax

German Emb. London, 10th Dec., 1938.
Secret.
Received in F. O. 13th Dec.
Translation.

My Lord,
I have the honour in the name and under the instructions of my Government to inform Your Excellency as follows:

1. The Development of the situation in the recent months of this year has led the German Government to realise the necessity of paying increased attention to the protection of their maritime communications in the event of warlike complications. They therefore feel compelled all within the limits of the possibilities of the naval agreements concluded with H.M.G. in the U.K. in 1935 and 1937, to take into consideration the improvement of the protection of these maritime communications. The German Government have furthermore decided to make the fullest use of the possibilities arising out of the agreements.

2. In the agreement concluded on June 18th 1935 between H.M.'s G. in the U.K. and the German Government regarding the ratio of strength between the British and the German Fleets it is laid down in par 2(f) that Germany has the right to possess a submarine tonnage equal to that of the total submarine tonnage of the members of the British Commonwealth. In the same paragraph the German Government undertook not to exercise this right to the full extent, but promised that their submarine tonnage should not exceed 45% of the total submarine tonnage of the members of the British Commonwealth unless a situation should arise which makes it necessary, in the opinion of the German Government to avail themselves of their right to a percentage exceeding the 45 per cent above mentioned.

3. The German Government are of the opinion that such a situation has arisen. They accordingly intend to revert to the right laid down in the abovementioned agreement enabling them to build up to 100 per cent of the British submarine tonnage. According to the procedure contemplated in the agreement, they thereby inform H.M.G. in the U.K. of this decision.

4. At the same time, the German Government inform H.M.G. in the U.K., that they have determined, in view of the above mentioned consideration and the information in their possession regarding the extent of the construction

of heavy cruisers by the USSR, to give to the 2 cruisers "K" and "L" now under construction a different armament to that hitherto contemplated. In fulfilment of article 20 of the Anglo-German Naval Agreement of 1937 the particulars in respect of these cruisers were communicated in Dec. 1937 to H.M.G. in the U.K. and 12, 15 cm guns were stated as being the chief armament. The German Government refer in this connexion to the exchange of notes of July 17, 1937.

To Viscount Halifax   I have etc. von Dirksen.

PRO. Adm. 116/3369

LIST OF ABBREVIATIONS

AMZV P. Z.: Archív Ministerstva Zahraničních Věci. Polítícké Zprávy.

DBFP: Documents on British Foreign Policy (2nd Series: 1929—38; 3rd Series: 1938—39.)

TWC: Trials of War Criminals.

DGFP: Documents on German Foreign Policy. (Series G: 1933—37, Series D: 1936/37—40.)

FRUSDP: Foreign Relations of the United States. Diplomatic Papers.

IMT: Tribunal Militaire International. Procès des Grands Criminels de Guerre.

MTI Magyar Távirati Iroda (Hungarian Telegraphic Agency).

OL: Országos Levéltár (National Archives).

PRO: Public Record Office.

(Less often used abbreviations are given in full wherever they come up in the text.)

BIBLIOGRAPHY

[Informative and revealing for the period and subject dealt with by the author. |

GUIDES

The Annual Register
British Museum Catalogue of Printed Books and Subject Index
British National Bibliography [since 1950]
Butler, D.—Freeman, J. *British Political Facts* 1900—1967 [1968]
Concise Dictionary, 1901—50
Dictionary of National Biography [from 1921 a volume for each decade]
Government information and the Research Worker [London, 1952]
Guide to Parliamentary Papers [1956]
A Breviate of Parliamentary Papers, 1917—1939 [1951]
A Breviate of British Diplomatic Blue Books, 1919—39 [1963]
Keesing's Contemporary Archives [since 1931]
Mitchell, B. R.—Deane, Ph. *Abstract of British Historical Statistics* [1962]
The Statesman's Yearbook
Survey of International Affairs [yearly since 1925]
Who was who [four volumes covering 1897 to 1950]
Bajkova, A. N. *Istoriya Anglii.* Moscow, 1963 [covering books and articles
    edited in the Soviet Union]
Watt, D. C. United States Documentary Resources for the Study of British Foreign
    Policy, 1919—1939 in *International Affairs.* 38[62] pp. 63 ff.

SOURCES [UNPUBLISHED]

Archív Ministerstva Zahraničních věcí [AMZV] Prague
    Kabinet Ministra
    Trezorove Spisy
    Kroftovy výklady na poradách
    Politické zprávy [PZ]
Baldwin, S. Papers. Cambridge University Library
Captured Enemy Documents [American Historical Association.]
    1. Selection Series I. 1920—1938. 52 reels
    2. University of Michigan Selection. German Naval Archives. Project I. 2.
Chamberlain Archives. Birmingham University Library.
Chatfield Papers. Privately owned by the 2nd Lord Chatfield

H. Dalton's Diary, 1937—40. London School of Economics' Library.
Deutsches Zentralarchiv Potsdam [DZA] 60975—78 [Ribbentrop] Febr. 1934—
    1937.
Fisher, Sir Warren, Papers. LSE Library.
Hoare, S. Papers. Cambridge University Library
Lloyd George Papers. Beaverbrook Library
Lothian Papers. Scottish Record Office, Edinburgh
Militärgeschichtliches Forschungsamt [Freiburg] [MGFA]
    II. M 1, 9, 10, 11, 13, 15/1, 14/2, 17/1, 34/1, 34/2, 34/3, 34/4, 34/5, 34/6,
    44, 48, 52, 58/3. III. M 96, 502/2, 503/2, 511/2.
Országos Levéltár [National Archives], Budapest
    Kabinetiroda iratai [K. 58] (Cabinet Papers)
    Külügyminisztérium. Politikai Iratok [K. 63] (Foreign Ministry. Political
    Papers)
    Külügyminisztérium. Reservált Politikai Iratok [K. 64] (Foreign Ministry.
    Reserved Political Papers)
    Külügyminisztérium. Számjeltáviratok. [K. 74] (Foreign Ministry. Cipher
    Telegrams)
Politisches Archiv des Auswärtigen Amtes [Bonn] [Pa.]
    Büro des Reichsministers. K. 15. Armee, Marine, Luftwaffe. Bd. 1. 6. England
    Bd. 12.
    Abteilung II. F. — Abrüstung. 7. No. 2. Deutsche Panzerschiffbauten. Bd. 1.
    Abrüst. Marine Konferenz, 1935 Bd. 1. 2.
    Abteilung II. F—M [Militär und Marine]
    F. 18. Flottenauslandsreisen 1933 Bd. Berichte. Bd. 1.
    F. 19. Flottenauslandsreisen 1934 Bd. 1. Berichte. Bd. 1.
Geheimakten 1920—1936.
    II. FM / Militär- und Marineattachés. Allgemein, Bd. 5.
    England. Marine-Attaché. London. Bd. 1—4
    England. Marine-Attaché / Deutsch—englisches Flottenabkommen und
    Marinekonferenzen 1935/36. II. F. M. 16.
    Länder III.
    England. Pol. 2. Politische Beziehungen Englands zu Deutschland. Bd. 6.
    Politische Abteilung III.
    England. Pol. 10. Nr. 2. Deutsche Marineattachés in England. Bd. 1.
    Dienststelle Ribbentrop.
    1/1 Teil 1. Vertrauliche Berichte 1935—1939
    1/1 Teil 2. Vertrauliche Berichte 1935—1939
Public Record Office [London]
    Cabinet Papers.
    Admiralty Papers.
The Papers of Lord Vansittart [Private Collection]

SOURCES [PUBLISHED]

Allianz Hitler, Horthy, Mussolini. Ed. L. Kerekes. Budapest, 1965.
Bruns—Gretschaninow *Politische Verträge.* Berlin, 1936, 1940. I—III.
Degras, J. *Soviet Documents on Foreign Policy.* 1953 et sequ. I—III. V.
Deutschland—England 1933—1939. Hrsg. v. F. Berber; Berlin, 1940.
Diplomáciai iratok Magyarország külpolitikájához 1936—1945 (Diplomatic Docu-
    ments on Hungary's Foreign Policy. 1936—1945) I—IV. V. Ed. L. Zsigmond,
L. Kerekes, M. Ádám, Gy. Juhász; Budapest, 1962, 1965, 1969.
Documents diplomatiques français 1932—1939. IIᵉ Série [1936—1939] Tome 1.
    Paris, 1963.

Documents on British Foreign Policy 1919—1939. Second Series [1930—1937] Vol. I—VI. London, 1950 . . .

Documents on German Foreign Policy 1918—1945. Series C. Vol. I—V. London, 1957—66.

Documents on International Affairs, 1933—1934. Ed. J. W. Wheeler-Bennett, London, 1934.

The Führer Conferences on Naval Affairs in Brassey's Naval Annual for 1948.

Halmosy, D. Nemzetközi szerződések, 1918—1945. (International Treaties 1918—1945) Budapest, 1966.

Hansard's Parliamentary Debates [since 1908].

The Speeches of Adolf Hitler, 1922—39. Ed. N. H. Baynes. Vols. I—II. Oxford, 1942.

Domarus, M. Hitler, Reden und Proklamationen 1932—1945. Bd. I.: Triumph [1932—38] Würzburg, 1962. München, 1962/63.

The Confidential Papers of Admiral Horthy. Ed. M. Szinnai—L. Szücs. Budapest, 1965.

Károlyi Mihály válogatott írásai. (Selected Writings of Mihály Károlyi) I—II. Vols Budapest, 1964.

The Collected Writings of J. M. Keynes. London, 1971. . .

Les Lettres secrètes échangées par Hitler et Mussolini. Paris, 1946.

Martens Nouveau Recueil Général de Traités, 28, 30 vols.

Papers relating to the Foreign Relations of the United States [Annually. Two supplements for the period 1931—1939].

Roosevelt and Frankfurter. Their Correspondence, 1928—45. London, 1968.

The Trial of the Major War Criminals before the International Military Tribunal. Proceedings, Vols. I—XXIII, Nuremberg, 1947—49. Documents in Evidence, Vols. XXIV—XLII. Nuremberg, 1947—49.

Statement Relating to Defence issued in Connection with the House of Commons Debate on March 11, 1935. London, 1935.

A Wilhelmstrasse és Magyarország. Német diplomáciai iratok Magyarországról, 1933—1944. (Wilhelmstrasse and Hungary. German Diplomatic Documents on Hungary, 1933—1944) Ed. Gy. Ránki, E. Pamlényi, L. Tilkovszky, Gy. Juhász. Budapest, 1968.

SECONDARY WORKS [GENERAL ACCOUNTS]

Chabod, F. L'Italia contemporanea (1918—48). Torino, 1961.

Chastenet, J. Histoire de la Troisième République. Vol. VI—VII. Paris, 1962/63.

Cole, G. D. H.—Postgate, R. W. The Common People. London, rev. ed. 1946.

Havighurst, A. F. Twentieth Century Britain, London, 1962.

Hoensch, J. K. Geschichte der Tschechoslowakischen Republik 1918—1965. Stuttgart, 1966.

Hubatsch, W. Die Weltgeschichtliche Entwicklung zwischen 1920 und 1945. In: Die grosse illustrierte Weltgeschichte. Hrsg. von H. Michaelis. Bd. II. Gütersloh, 1964.

Kerekes, L. Ausztria története 1918—1955 (The History of Austria 1918—1955). Budapest, 1966.

Mackiewiecz, S. Histoire Polski 1918—1939. London, 1941.

Macartney, C. A. Hungary and Her Successors, The Treaty of Trianon and its Consequences 1917—1937. N. Y.—Toronto, 1937.

Macartney, C. A. A History of Hungary 1929—1945. N. Y. 1956.

Marlow, J. Anglo—Egyptian relations 1800—1953. London, n. d.

Mowat, C. L. British History since 1926. London 1960.

Olivova, V. *The Doomed Democracy—Czechoslovakia in a disrupted Europe 1914—*
38. London, 1971.
Parker, R. A. C. *Das zwanzigste Jahrhundert.* I. 1918—1945. Frankfurt, 1967.
Miller, A. F. *Ocherki noveishei istorii Turtsii.* Moscow, 1948.
Rauch, G. von *Geschichte der Sovietunion.* Stuttgart, 1969.
Patyomkin, V. P. ed. *Istoriya diplomatii.* Moscow, 1945.
Seaman, L. C. B. *Post Victorian Britain, 1902—51.* London, 1966.
Smellie, K. B. *Great Britain since 1688.* London, 1962.
Taylor, A. J. P. *English History 1914—1945.* London, 1965.
Trukhanovsky, V. G. *Noveishaya Istoriya Anglii.* Moscow, 1958.
Volkov, F. D. *Angliya 1924—1945.* Moscow, 1964.
Walters, F. P. *A History of the League of Nations.* I—II. Vols. London, 1958.

SECONDARY WORKS [POLITICAL]

Ádám, M. *Magyarország és a kisantant a harmincas években.* (Hungary and the
Little Entente in the Thirties) Budapest, 1968.
Aigner, D. *Das Ringen um England. Das deutsch-britische Verhältnis. Die öffentliche*
Meinung. 1933—1939. 1969.
Amery, L. S. *The German Colonial Claim.* London, 1939.
Amery, L. S. *Thoughts on the Constitution.* London, 1947.
Barker, A. J. *The Civilizing Mission: A History of the Italo-Ethiopian War of*
1935—1936. N. Y. 1968.
Batowszki, H. *Srodhowoeuropejska polityka Polski w latach 1932—39.* Warszawa,
1960.
Baumont, M. Hrsg. *The Third Reich.* N. Y. 1955.
Lord Beaverbrook *The Abdication of King Edward* VIII. Ed. A. J. P. Taylor,
London, 1966.
Beloff, M. *The Foreign Policy of Soviet Russia 1929—1941.* I—II. Vols. London—
N. Y. Oxford, 1947—49.
Berend T. I.—Ránki Gy. *Magyarország a fasiszta Németország „életterében."*
1933—1939 (Hungary in the "Lebensraum" of Fascist Germany. 1933—1939),
Budapest, 1960.
Bergamini, D. *Japan's Imperial Conspiracy.* London, 1971.
Bracher, K. D. *The German dictatorship—the origins, structure and consequences*
of national socialism. Trans. J. Steinberg. London, 1971.
Brand, C. F. *The British Labour Party. A Short History.* Stanford, 1964.
Breyer. R. *Das deutsche Reich und Polen 1932—37. Aussenpolitik und Volksgruppen-*
fragen. Würzburg, 1955.
Bromhead, P. A. *The House of Lords and Contemporary Politics 1911—1957.*
London, 1958.
Broszat, M. *200 Jahre deutsche Polenpolitik.* München, 1962.
Butler, D. E. *The Electoral System 1918—1962.* London, 1963.
Campion, Sir Gilbert *British Government since 1918.* London, 1950.
Carr, E. H. *International Relations between the Two World Wars.* London, 1947.
Carr, E. H. *The Twenty Years' Crisis.* London, 1938.
Carr, E. H. *German—Soviet Relations between the Two World Wars.* London, 1952.
Cato [M. Foot, F. Owen, P. Howard] *Guilty Men.* London, 1940.
Chester, D. N. ed.—Wilson, F. M. G. written by: *The Organisation of British*
Central Government 1914—1956. London, 1956.
Churchill, W. S. *The Gathering Storm.* London, 1948.
Coates, W. P.—Zelde, K. *A History of Anglo—Soviet Relations.* London, 1943.
Cole, G. D. H.—Cole, M. I. *The Condition of Britain.* London, 1937.
Cole, G. D. H. *The History of the British Labour Party.* London, 1948.

Connell, G. *The Office: A study of British Foreign Policy and its Makers.* London, 1958.

Craig, G. A.—Gilbert, F. *The Diplomats, 1919—1939.* I—II. Vols. Princeton, New Yersey, 1953.

Cross, C. *The Fascists in Britain.* London, 1961.

Deakin, F. W. *The Brutal Friendship.* London, 1962.

Deakin, F. W. *The Embattled Mountain.* Oxford, 1971.

Debicki, R. *Foreign Policy of Poland 1919—39. From the Rebirth of the Polish Republic to World War II.* N. Y. 1962.

Denne, L. *Das Danzig-Problem in der deutschen Aussenpolitik, 1934—39.* Bonn, 1959.

Deutschland—England 1933—1939. Die Dokumente des deutschen Friedenswillens. Berlin, 1940.

Drechsler, K. *Deutschland—China—Japan 1933—1939.* Berlin [Ost], 1964.

Dzelepy, E. N. *Franco, Hitler et les alliés* Bruxelles, 1961.

Duroselle, J. B. *De Wilson à Roosevelt.* Paris, 1960.

Duroselle, J. B. *Histoire diplomatique de 1919 à nos jours.* Paris, 1953.

Eden, A. *Foreign Affairs.* London, 1939.

Ehrman, J. *Cabinet Government and War 1890—1940.* London, 1958.

Flandin, P. E. *Politique Française, 1919—1940.* London, 1947.

Fleming, D. F. *The Cold War and its origins. 1917—1960.* Vol. I. London, 1961.

Fomin, V. T. *Aggresiya fashistkoi Germanii v Evrope 1933—1939.* Moscow, 1963.

Freytagh-Loringhoven, A. Freiherr von. *Deutschlands Aussenpolitik, 1933—1940.* Hamburg, 1941.

Furnia, A. H. *The Diplomacy of Appeasement. Anglo-French Relations and the Prelude to World War II. 1931—1938.* Washington, 1960.

Gannon, F. R. *The British Press and Germany, 1936—39.* London, 1971.

Gathorne—Hardy, A. M. *Short History of International Affairs, 1920—1939.* London, 1950.

Gilbert, G. M. *Nuremberg Diary.* N. Y. 1947.

Gilbert, M. *Britain and Germany between the Wars.* London, 1964.

Gilbert, M.—Gott, R. *The Appeasers.* London, 1963.

Gilbert, M. *The Roots of Appeasement.* London, 1966.

Gollancz, V. *Is Mr. Chamberlain saving Peace?* London, 1939.

Lord Hailey *African Survey.* London, 1938.

Hancock, W. K. *The Survey of British Commonwealth Affairs.* Vol. I. 1937. Vol. II/1. 1940. Vol. II./2. London, 1952.

Hannington, W. *Unemployed Struggles, 1919—1936.* London, 1936.

Hilger, G.—Meyer, A. G. *The Incompatible Allies. A memoir-history of the German—Soviet Relations 1918—1941.* N. Y. 1953.

Hinsley, F. H. *Power and the Pursuit of Peace, Theory and Practice in the History of Relations between States.* Cambridge, 1963.

Hoggan, D. V. *Der erzwungene Krieg.* Tübingen, 1962. [7. Aufl.]

Lord Allen of Hurtwood *Peace in our Time.* London, 1936.

Hutt, G. A. *Post-War History of the British Working Class.* London, 1937.

Iklé, F. Ch. *German—Japanese Relations, 1936—1940.* N. Y. 1956.

Jacobsen, H. A. *Nationalsozialistische Aussenpolitik, 1933—38.* Frankfurt am Main, 1968.

Jennings, W. I. *Cabinet Government.* London, 1959 [3rd ed.]

Jennings, W. I. *Parliament.* London, 1957 [2nd ed.]

Jordan, W. M. *Great Britain, France and the German Problem 1919—39.* London, 1943.

Juhász Gy. *Magyarország külpolitikája 1919—1945* (Hungary's Foreign Policy 1919—1945). Budapest, 1969.

Jurkiewicz, J. *Pakt wschodni. Z historii stusonkow miedzynarodovych w latach 1934—35*. Warszawa, 1963.

Kelley, D. M. *22 cells in Nüremberg*. London, 1947.

Kelsall, R. K. *Higher Civil Servants*. London, 1955.

Kennedy, J. F. *Why England sleeps*. London, 1940.

Kogan, N. *Italy and Allies*. Cambridge, Mass. 1956.

Kordt, E. *Wahn und Wirklichkeit. Die Aussenpolitik des Dritten Reiches*. Stuttgart, 1948.

Kovács, E. *Magyar-lengyel kapcsolatok a két világháború között* (Hungarian-Polish Relations between the two World Wars) Budapest, 1971.

Kuzminski, T. *Polska, Francja, Niemcy, 1933—35*. Warszawa, 1966.

Kvaček, R. *Nad Evropou zataženo. Československo a Evropa 1933—1937*. Praha, 1967.

Langer, W. L.—Gleason, S. E. *The Challenge to Isolation*. London, 1952.

Lapter, K. *Pakt Pilsudski—Hitler*. Warszawa, 1962.

Laqueur, W. *Deutschland und Russland*. Berlin, 1965.

Launay, J. de *Histoire Contemporaine de la Diplomatie secrète* [1914—1945]. Bruxelles, 1965.

Liddell Hart, B. H. *The other side of the Hill*. London, 1951.

Lord Londonderry *Ourselves and Germany*. London, 1938.

Louis, R. *Great Britain and Germany's Lost Colonies*. London, 1967.

Mackiewicz, S. *Colonel Beck and his Policy*. London, 1944.

Mackintosh, J. P. *The British Cabinet*. London, 1962.

Mahaney, W. L. *The Soviet Union, the League of Nations and Disarmament 1917—1935*. Pha. 1940.

Maisky, J. M. *Who helped Hitler?* London, 1964.

Mansergh, N. *Survey of British Commonwealth Affairs. Problems of External Policy*. London, 1952.

Marwick, A. *War, Peace and Social Change, 1900—1967*. London, 1968.

McCallum, R. B. *Public Opinion and the Last Peace*. London, 1944.

McElwee, W. *Britain's Locust Years, 1918—40*. London, 1962.

McKenzie, R. T. *British Political Parties*. London, 1963.

Medlicott, W N. *Contemporary England, 1914—1964*. London, 1967.

Medlicott, W. N. *British Foreign Policy since Versailles*. London, 1940.

Mielcke, K. *Nationalsozialistische Aussenpolitik, 1933—1939*. Hannover, n. d.

Miller, I. K. *Belgian Foreign Policy between two Wars. 1919—1940*. N. Y. 1951.

Miloukov, P. N. *La Politique Extérieure des Soviets*. Paris, 1936.

Morrison, H. *Government and Parliament. London*, 1954.

Mowat, C. L. *Britain between the Wars, 1918—40*. London, 1955.

Muggeridge, M. *The Thirties*. London, 1940.

Nagle, Th. W. *A study of British Public Opinion and the European Appeasement Policy 1933—1939*. Genf, 1951. [Sten. MS.]

Namier, L. B. *Diplomatic Prelude*. London, 1947.

Naylor, J. F. *Labour's International Policy*. London, 1969.

Niclauss, K. *Die Sowjetunion und Hitlers Machtergreifung. Eine Studie über die deutsch—russischen Beziehungen der Jahre 1929 bis 1935*. Bonn, 1966.

Niekrich, A. M. *Vneshnaya politika Anglii 1939—1941 gg*. Moscow, 1963.

Noël, L. *L'Agression allemande contre la Pologne*. Paris, 1946.

Northedge, F. S. *The Troubled Giant. Britain among the Great Powers 1916—1939*. London, 1966.

Ormos M. *Franciaország és a keleti biztonság, 1931—36*. (France and Eastern Security, 1931—36), Budapest, 1969.

Petrie, Sir Charles *The Powers behind the Prime Ministers*. London, 1959.

Pohle, H. *Der Rundfunk als Instrument der Politik, zur Geschichte des deutschen Rundfunks von 1923—1938.* Hamburg. 1955.
Popov, V. I. *Diplomaticheskie otnosheniya mezhdu SSSR i Anglii* [1929—39.] Moscow, 1965.
Presseisen, E. L. *Germany and Japan. A Study in totalitarian diplomacy 1933—1941.* The Hague, 1958.
Pritt, D.—Smith, E. *They helped Hitler.* London, 1936.
Renouvin, P. *Les crises du XXᵉ siècle. II. De. 1929 à 1945.* In *Histoire des relations internationales.* Vol. 8. Paris, 1958.
Reynolds, P. A. *British Foreign Policy in the Interwar Years.* London, 1954.
Rintelen, Enno *Mussolini als Bundesgenosse.* Tübingen, 1953.
Roos, H. *Polen und Europa. Studien zur polnischen Aussenpolitik, 1931—1939.* Tübingen, 1957, 1962.
Ross, J. F. S. *Parliamentary Representation.* London, 1948, 2nd ed.
Rothstein, A. *British Foreign Policy and its Critics.* London, 1969.
Rowse, A. L. *All Souls and Appeasement* . London, 1961.
Salvemini, G. *Prelude to World War II.* London, 1953.
Sasse, H. G. *100 Jahre Botschaft in London.* Bonn, 1963.
Schmokel, W. W. *Dream of Empire, German Colonialism, 1919—1945.* New Haven—London, 1964.
Schoenbaum, D. *Hitler's Social Revolution. Class and Status in Nazi Germany, 1933—1939.* N. Y. 1966.
Scott, W. E. *Alliance against Hitler. The Origins of the Franco-Soviet Pact.* Duke, 1962.
Seabury, P. *The Wilhelmstrasse. A Study of the German Diplomats under the Nazi Regime.* London, 1955.
Shirer, W. S. *The Rise and Fall of the Third Reich.* London, 1961.
Smellie, K. B. *A Hundred Years of English Government.* London, 1950.
Soják, V. ed. *O Československé zahranicni politice, 1918—1939.* Praha, 1956.
Sommer, Th. *Deutschland und Japan zwischen den Mächten 1935—1940.* Tübingen, 1962.
Strachey, J. *The Coming Struggle for Power.* London, 1932.
Taylor, A. J. P. *The Origins of the Second World War.* N. Y. 1962.
Taylor, A. J. P. *The Troublemakers.* London, 1957.
Thomas, H. *The Establishment.* London, 1959.
Thompson, N. *The Anti-Appeasers. Conservative opposition to appeasement in the 1930's.* London, 1971.
Truchanowski, W. G. Hrsg. *Geschichte der internationalen Beziehungen 1917—1939.* Berlin [Ost], 1963. In English: Moscow, 1967.
Ushakov, B. *Vneshnaya politika gitlerovskoi Germanii.* Moscow, 1961.
Vere-Hodge, E. *Turkish Foreign Policy, 1918—1950.* London, 1951.
Villari, L. *Italian Foreign Policy under Mussolini.* N. Y. 1956.
Watt, D. C. *Personalities and Policies.* London, 1965.
Weinberg, G. L. *The Foreign Policy of Hitler's Germany—the Diplomatic Revolution in Europe, 1933—36.* London, 1971.
Wheeler-Bennett, J. W. *The Nemesis of Power, the German Army in Politics, 1918—1945.* London, 1953.
Wiskemann, E. *The Rome—Berlin Axis.* N. Y.—London, 1949.
Wiskemann, E. *Europe of the Dictators 1919—1945.* London, 1966.
Wojciechowski, M. *Stosunki polsko—niemieckie 1933—1938.* Poznan, 1965.
Wolfers. A. *Britain and France between two Wars.* London, 1940.
Wrench, E. *Geoffrey Dawson and our Times.* London, 1940.
Zeman, Z. A. B. *Nazi Propaganda.* London, 1964.

SECONDARY WORKS [MILITARY AND NAVAL]

Acworth, Captain B. *Britain in Danger: An Examination of our Own New Navy.* London, 1937.

Acworth, Captain B. *The Restoration of England's Sea Power being a Second Edition of the Navy and the Next War with four New Chapters,* including "Collective Security," "Air Power and Sea Power" and "The Anglo-German Naval Treaty." London, 1935.

Benoist-Méchin, J. *Histoire de l'armée allemande depuis l'armistice.* Paris, 1964. I—III.

Bensel, R. *Die deutsche Flottenpolitik von 1933—1939. Eine Studie über die Rolle des Flottenbaues in Hitlers Aussenpolitik.* Berlin, Frankfurt/M. 1958.

Bildingmaier, G. *Seegeltung in der deutschen Geschichte.* Darmstadt, 1967.

Butler, W. E. *The Soviet Union and the Law of the Sea.* London, 1971.

Castellan, G. *Le Réarmament clandestin du Reich, 1930—1935.* Paris, 1954.

Lord Chatfield *The Navy and Defence.* London, 1942.

Clark, R. *Tizard.* London, 1965.

Csürös, L. *Tengerek, hajók, háborúk.* (Seas, Ships, Wars), Budapest, 1942.

Deutsche Seestrategie in zwei Weltkriegen/Die Wehrmacht im Kampf. Bd. 12/1957.

Dreyer, Sir Frederick *Sea Heritage.* London, 1956.

Earle, E. M. ed. *The Makers of Modern Strategy.* Princeton, 1943.

Edwards, K, Lt. C. R. N. *Uneasy Oceans.* London, 1939.

Erfurth, W. *Die Geschichte des deutschen Generalstabs von 1918—1945.* Göttingen, 1957.

Fairhall, D. *Russia looks to the Sea.* London, 1971.

Forrest, D. *The Atlantic System. The story of Anglo-American control of the Seas.* N.Y. 1941.

Fuller, J. F. C. *The Conduct of War, 1789—1961: A Study of the Impact of the French, Industrial and Russian Revolutions on War and its Conduct.* London, 1961.

Fuller, J. F. C. *A Military History of the Western World.* 3 Vols. London, 1954. 1955, 1956.

Gemzell, C. A. *Raeder, Hitler und Skandinavien.* 1965.

Giese, F. E. *Kleine Geschichte der deutschen Flotte.* 1966.

Gladisch, W. *Geschichtliche und militärpolitische Betrachtungen zum deutsch—englischen Flottenabkommen von 1935.* Berlin, 1936.

Grenfell, R. *The Art of the Admiral.* London, 1937.

Grenfell, R. *Main Fleet to Singapore.* London, 1951.

Grőner, E. *Die deutschen Kriegsschiffe,* 1915—1945. 2 vols. 1966—67.

Gretton, Sir Peter W. *Churchill and the Royal Navy.* London, 1968.

Guinn, P. *British Strategy and Politics.* London, 1965.

Hallgarten, G. W. F. *Hitler, Reichswehr und Industrie. Zur Geschichte der Jahre 1918—1933.* Frankfurt, 1955. 4. Aufl. 1965.

Herzog, B. *60 Jahre deutsche U-Boote, 1906—1966.* 1968.

Higham, R. *Armed Forces in peace time: Britain 1918—1939.* London, 1963.

Hossbach, F. *Zwischen Wehrmacht und Hitler.* 1965.

Howard, M. *The Theory and Practice of War: Fifteen Essays presented to Captain B. H. Liddell Hart on his Seventieth Birthday.* London, 1965.

Hubatsch, W. *Der Admiralstab und die obersten Marinebehörden in Deutschland 1848—1945.* Frankfurt/M. 1958.

Ingrim, R. *Hitlers glücklichster Tag, London am 18 Juni, 1935.* Stuttgart, 1962.

Ivanov, L. N. *Morskaya politika i diplomatiya imperialisticheskikh derzhav.* Moscow, 1964.

Johnson, F. A. *Defence by Committee* [CID]. 1960.

Kimminich, O. *Rüstung und politische Spannung. Studien zum Problem der internationalen Sicherheit*. Gütersloh, 1964.

Lewis, M. *The History of the British Navy*. London, 1957.

Liddell Hart, B. H. *The Defence of Britain*. London, 1939.

Liddell Hart, B. H. *Jetzt dürfen sie reden, Hitlers Generale berichten*. Stuttgart—Hamburg, 1950.

Louis, W. R. *British Strategy in the Far East, 1919—39*. London, 1971.

Macintyre, D. *The Naval War against Hitler* [British Battles Series]. London, 1971.

Marder, A. *The Anatomy of British Sea Power*. N. Y. 1940.

Marder, A. *From the Dreadnought to Scapa Flow*. London, 1961—70.

Masanori Ito *The End of the Imperial Japanese Navy*. N. Y. 1965.

Meinck, G. *Hitler und die deutsche Aufrüstung, 1933—1937*. Wiesbaden, 1959.

Miles, G. A. A. *Navies, 1900—1945. The New Cambridge Modern History*. Vol. 12. Cambridge, 1960.

Morgan, J. H. *Assize of Arms. The Disarmament of Germany and her Rearmament, 1919—1939*. N. Y. 1946.

Mueller-Hillebrand, B. *Das Heer, 1933—1945. Entwicklung des organisatorischen Aufbaus*. 3 Bde. Darmstadt, 1954.

Noel-Baker, Ph. *The Private Manufacturers of Armaments*. London, 1937.

Pack, S. W. C. *Sea Power in the Mediterranean*. London, 1971.

Nicoll, P. H. *Englands Krieg gegen Deutschland. Die Ursachen, Methoden und Folgen des Zweiten Weltkrieges*. Tübingen, 1963.

Postan, M. M.—Hay D.—Scott J. D. *Design and Development of Weapons*. London, 1964.

Richmond, Sir Herbert *Statesmen and Sea Power*. [Ford Lectures at Oxford in 1943].

Robertson, E. M. *Hitler's Pre-War Policy and Military Plans, 1933—1939*. London, 1963.

Roskill, S. W. *The Art of Leadership*. London, 1963.

Roskill, S. W. *British Naval Policy between the Wars*. Vol. I. 1919—29. London, 1968.

Roskill, S. W. *The Navy at War, 1939—1945*. London, 1964.

Roskill, S. W. *The Strategy of Sea Power*. London, 1962.

Russell, Sir Herbert. *Sea Warfare today*. London, 1940.

Salewski, M. *Entwaffnung und Militärkontrolle in Deutschland*. München, 1966.

Salewski, M. *Die deutsche Seekriegsleitung 1935—1945*. Band I. 1935—1941. Frankfurt/M, 1970.

Schurman, D. M. *The Education of a Navy*. London, 1965.

Snyder, W. *Politics of British Defence Policy*. Columbus, Ohio, 1965.

Talbot-Booth, E. C. *All the World's Fighting Fleets*. London, n.d.

Tansill, Ch. C. *Back Door to War. The Roosevelt Foreign Policy, 1933—41*. Chicago, 1952.

Thomas, G. *Geschichte der deutschen Wehr-und Rüstungswirtschaft* [1918—1943/45] Hrsg. W. Birkenfeld. Boppard, 1966.

Völker, K. H. *Die deutsche Luftwaffe, 1933—1939*. Stuttgart, 1967.

Walter, B. *Die deutsche Aufrüstung 1934—1939. Militärische und politische Konzeptionen*. 1969.

Watts, A. J.—Gordon, B. G. *The Imperial Japanese Navy*. London, 1971.

Wheeler-Bennett, J. W. *The Nemesis of Power. The German Army in Politics, 1918—1945*. London, 1953.

Zakharov, S. E. *Istoriya voenno-morskogo iskustva*. Moscow, 1970.

SECONDARY WORKS [ECONOMIC]

Ashworth, W. *An Economic History of England 1870—1939*, London, 1960.

Berend, T. I.—Ránki, Gy. *Közép-Keleteurópa gazdasági fejlődése a 19—20 században* (The Economic Development of Central Eastern Europe in the 19th and 20th Centuries), Budapest, 1969.

Deane, Ph.—Cole, W. A. *British Economic Growth, 1688—1959*. Cambridge, 1962.

Einhorn, M. *Die ökonomischen Hintergründe der faschistischen deutschen Intervention in Spanien, 1936—1939*. Berlin, 1962.

Fischer, W. *Die Wirtschaftspolitik Deutschlands, 1918—1945*. Lüneburg, 1961. 2. Aufl. 1968.

Francis, E. V. *Britain's Economic Strategy*. London. 1939.

Kahn, A. F. *Great Britain in the World Economy*. N. Y. 1946.

Keynes, J. M. *The Economic Consequences of the Peace*. London, 1919.

Klein, B. *Germany's Economic Preparations for War*. London, 1959.

Lochner, L. P. *Die Mächtigen and der Tyrann. Die deutsche Industrie von Hitler bis Adenauer*. Darmstadt, 1955.

Richardson, H. W. *Economic Recovery in Britain*. London, 1967.

Peacock, A. T.—Wiseman, J. *The Growth of Public Expenditure in the United Kingdom*. London, 1961.

SECONDARY WORKS [BIOGRAPHIES]

Baldwin, A. W. *My Father*. London, 1955.

Boyle, A. *Montague Norman*. London, 1967.

Bullock, A. *Ernest Bevin*. Vol. I. 1960.

Bullock, A. *Hitler, a Study in Tyranny*. London, 1962.

Butler, J. R. M. *Lord Lothian* [Philip Kerr] London, 1960.

Chatterton, E. K. *Leaders of Britain*. London, n. d.

Churchill, R. *The Rise and Fall of Sir Anthony Eden*. London, 1959.

Churchill, W. S. *Great Contemporaries*. London, 1937.

Clay, H. *Lord Norman* [Montague Norman]. London, 1957.

Colvin, I. *Vansittart in Office*. London, 1965.

Feiling, K. *The Life of Neville Chamberlain*. London, 1946.

Foerster, W. *General Oberst Ludwig Beck, Sein Kampf gegen den Krieg, aus den nachgelassenen Papieren des Generalstabschefs*. München, 1953.

Gretton, Sir Peter *Former Naval Person*. London, 1968.

Hancock, W. K. *Smuts: the Field of Force*. London, 1968.

Harrod, R. F. *John Maynard Keynes* [Lord Keynes]. London, 1951.

Higham, R. *The Military Intellectuals in Britain: 1918—1939*. New Brunswick, 1966.

Kirkpatrick, Sir I. *Mussolini, Study of a Demagogue*. London, 1964.

Krebs, A. *Fritz Dietlof Graf von der Schulenburg. Zwischen Staatsraison und Hochverrat*. Hamburg, 1964.

Macleod, J. N. *Chamberlain*. London, 1961.

Martienssen, A. K. *Hitler and his Admirals*. London, 1948.

Martin, K. *Harold Laski*. London, 1953.

Marwick, A. *Clifford Allen*. London, 1964.

McLachlan, D. *In the Chair: Barrington-Ward of The Times*. London, 1971.

Middlemas, K—Barnes, J. *Baldwin: A Biography*. London, 1969.

Nicolson, Sir Harold *King George the Fifth: Life and Reign*. London, 1952.

Postgate, R. *George Lansbury*. London, 1951.

Schwarz, P. *This Man Ribbentrop, His Life and Times.* N. Y. 1934.
Strawson, J. *Hitler as Military Commander* [Military commanders series] London, 1971.
Taylor, A. J. P. *Beaverbrook.* London, 1972.
Teslar, J. A. *Edward Śmigły-Rydz Marszałek Polski.* Zyciorys. Warszawa, 1937.
Wedgwood, C. V. *The Last of the Radicals.* London, 1951.
Young, G. M. *Stanley Baldwin* London, 1951.

MEMOIRS AND DIARIES

Abetz, O. *Das offene Problem. Ein Rückblick auf zwei Jahrzehnte deutscher Frankreichpolitik.* Cologne, 1951.
Aloisi, P. *Journal* [25 July 1932 to 14 June, 1936.] Paris, 1957.
Amery, L. S. *My Political Life.* Vol. II. *The Unforgiving Years,* 1929—40. London, 1955.
Beck, J. *Le dernier rapport. Politique polonaise, 1926—1939.* Neuchâtel, 1951.
Beneš, Dr. E. *Memoirs of . . .* London, 1954.
Blücher, W. von *Gesandter zwischen Diktatur und Demokratie. Erinnerungen aus den Jahren 1935—1944.* Wiesbaden, 1951.
Bonnet, G. *Défense de la Paix, 1936—40.* Vol. I. De Washington au Quai d'Orsay. 1946. Vol II. *Fin d'une Europe.* 1948.
Boothby, R. *I fight to live.* London, 1947.
Brandt, W. *In exile, Essays, reflections, letters, 1933 17.* London, 1971.
Brockway, A. Fenner: *Inside the Left.* London, 1942.
Channon, Sir Henry, Chips *The Diaries of. .* Ed. R. R. James. London, 1967.
Lord Chatfield *It might happen again.* London, 1947.
Churchill W. S. *The Second World War.* Vol. I. *The Gathering Storm.* London, 1948.
Ciano, G. *Diario 1937—1938.* Roma, 1948; *Diario 1939—40.* Milano, 1949.
Ciano, G. *Diplomatic Papers.* London, 1948.
Cockburn, P. *The Years of the Week.* London, 1968.
Cockburn, C. *In Time of Trouble.* London, 1956.
Cockburn, C. *Crossing the Line.* London, 1958.
Comnen, N. P. *Luce e ombre sull'Europa 1914—1950.* Milan, 1957.
Cooper, Duff [Lord Norwich] *Old Men Forget.* London, 1953.
Coulondre, R. *De Staline à Hitler.* Paris, 1950.
Lord Cunningham of Hyndhope *A sailor's Odyssey.* London, 1951.
Dahlerus, B. *The last Attempt.* London, 1947.
Dalton, H. *Memoirs.* Vol. I. *Call back Yesterday.* London, 1953. Vol. II. *The Fateful Years.* London, 1957
Dirksen, H. von *Moskau, Tokio, London. Erinnerungen und Betrachtungen zu 20 Jahren deutscher Aussenpolitik 1919—1939.* Stuttgart, 1949.
Dodd, W. E.—Dodd, M. *Ambassador Dodd's Diary, 1933—1938.* London, N. Y. 1941.
Dönitz, K. *Zehn Jahre und Zwanzig Tage.* Bonn, 1958. In English: N. Y. 1959.
The Eden Memoirs [Lord Avon, Anthony Eden]. *Facing the Dictators.* London, 1962.
Einzig, P. *In the Centre of Things.* London, 1960.
Fisher, H. A. L. *An Unfinished Autobiography.* London, 1940.
François-Poncet, A. *Von Versailles bis Potsdam, 1919—45.* Mainz—Berlin, 1949
François-Poncet, A. *Souvenirs d'une Ambassade à Berlin.* Paris, 1946. In English: London, 1949.
Fromm, B. *Blood and Banquets. A Berlin Social Diary.* N. Y.—London, 1942.
Gallacher, W. *Revolt on the Clyde.* London, 1936

Gallacher, W. *The Rolling of the Thunder*. London, 1947.
Gafencu, G. *Last Days of Europe*. London, 1948.
Gamelin, M. G. *Servir*. Vol. II. Le prologue du drame. Paris, 1946.
Gilbert, M. *Plough my own Furrow*. London, 1965.
Grigg, P. J. *Prejudice and Judgment*. London, 1948.
Grew, J. C. *Ten Years in Japan*. N.Y. 1944.
Guariglia, R. *Ricordi, 1922—46*. Roma, 1950.
Lord Halifax *Speeches on Foreign Policy*. London, 1940.
Lord Halifax [originally E. Wood, then Lord Irwin] *Fullness of Days*. London, 1957.
Hamilton, M. A. *Remembering My Good Friends*. London, 1944.
Harvey, John ed. *The Diplomatic Diaries of Oliver Harvey 1937—1940*. London, 1971.
Herriot, E. *Jadis*. I—II. Paris, 1948—52.
Henderson, N. *Failure of a Mission*. Berlin, 1937—1939. N Y. 1940.
Hossbach, F. *Zwischen Wehrmacht und Hitler 1934—1938*. Wolfenbüttel—Hannover, 1949.
Hull, C. *Memoirs*. I—II. Vols. London, 1948.
Jones, Th. *A Diary with Letters, 1931—1950*. London, 1969.
Jones, Th. *Whitehall Diaries, 1916—25*. London, 1969.
King-Hall. S. *My Naval Life*. London, 1951.
Kirkpatrick, I. *The Inner Circle. Memoirs*. London, 1959.
Kordt, E. *Nicht aus den Akten*. Stuttgart, 1950.
Laroche, J. *La Pologne de Pilsudski. Souvenirs d'une ambassade, 1926—1935*. Paris, 1953.
Laval, P. *The unpublished Diary*. London, 1948.
Liddell Hart, B. H. *The Memoirs of*. Vol. I—II. London, 1965.
Lipski, J. *Diplomat in Berlin, 1933—1939*. Ed. W. Jedrzejewicz. N.Y.—London, 1968.
Lady Lloyd George *The Years that are Past*. London, 1967.
Lloyd George, D. *A Diary by Frances Stevenson*. Ed. A.J.P. Taylor. London, 1971.
MacMillan, H. *Winds of Change, 1914—1939*. London, 1966.
    The Blast of War, 1939—45. London, 1967.
Maisky, J. M. *Who helped Hitler?* London, 1964.
Martin, K. *Editor*. London, 1968.
Morrison, H. *An Autobiography*. London, 1961.
Mosley, Sir Oswald *My Life*. London, 1968.
Mussolini, B. *Memoirs, 1942—43*. London, 1943.
Nicolson, H. *Diaries and Letters*, 1930—9. London, 1966.
    1939—45. London, 1967.
Noël, L. *L'agression allemande contre la Pologne. Une ambassade à Varsovie, 1935—39*. Paris, 1946.
Papen, Franz von *Der Wahrheit eine Gasse*. München, Köln. 1952.
    In English: London, 1952.
Paul-Boncour, J. *Entre deux guerres*. I—III. Paris, 1945—46.
Percy, Lord Eustace [Lord Percy of Newcastle] *Some Memories*. London, 1958.
Pollitt, H. *Serving my Time*. London, 1940.
Putlitz, W. G. Edler Herr zu *Unterwegs nach Deutschland*. Berlin, 1972.
Raeder, E. *Mein Leben*. I. B. *Bis zum Flottenabkommen mit England, 1935*. Tübingen, 1956. II. B. *Von 1935 bis Spandau 1955*. Tübingen, 1957.
Rauschning, H. *Gespräche mit Hitler*. Zürich—Wien—N.Y. 1940.
Ribbentrop, J. von *Zwischen London und Moskau. Erinnerungen und letzte Aufzeichnungen*. Leoni/Starnberger See, 1954, 1960. In English: 1954.

Rosenberg, A. *Das politische Tagebuch Alfred Rosenbergs aus den Jahren 1934—35 und 1939—1940.* Göttingen, 1056.

Salter, J. A. [Lord Salter] *Memoirs of a Public Servant.* London, 1961.

Samuel, Sir Herbert *Memoirs.* London, 1945.

Schacht, H. *76 Jahre meines Lebens.* Bad Wörishofen, 1953.

Schacht, H. *Account settled.* London, 1948.

Schellenberg, W. *The Labyrinth, Memoirs.* N. Y. 1956.

Schmidt, P. *Statist auf diplomatischer Bühne. 1923—1945.* Bonn, 1951.

Schweppenburg, Geyr von, L. Freiherr *Erinnerungen eines Militärattachés.* Stuttgart, 1949. In English: London, 1952.

Shirer, W. L. *Berlin Diary. The Journal of a Foreign Correspondent, 1934—1941.* London, 1941.

Simon, Sir John *Retrospect.* The Memoirs. London, 1952.

Lord Strang *Home and Abroad.* London, 1956.

Szembek, J. *Diariusz. Teki Jana Szembeka, 1933—1945.* I—II. Oprac. T. Komarnicki. London, 1964.

Szembek, J. *Journal, 1933—1939.* Paris, 1952.

Lord Swinton *I remember.* London, 1948.

Tabouis, G. *Blackmail or War.* London, 1938.

Tabouis, G. *Ils l'ont appelée Cassandre.* N. Y. 1942.

Tabouis, G. *Vingt ans de suspense diplomatique.* Paris, 1958.

Lord Templewood [Sir Samuel Hoare] *Nine Troubled Years.* London, 1954.

Lord Templewood [Sir Samuel Hoare] *Empire of the Air.* London, 1957.

Thomas, J. H. *My Story.* London, 1937.

Weizsäcker, E. von *Erinnerungen.* München—Leipzig—Freiburg, 1950. In English: London, 1951

Wiskemann, E. *The Europe I saw.* London, 1968.

Weygand, M. *Mémoires.* Paris, 1950—56. I—III. B.

Vansittart, Sir Robert *Lessons of My Life.* London, 1943.

Vansittart, Sir Robert *The Mist Procession.* London, 1955.

Zhukov, Marshal G. K. *The Memoirs.* London, 1971.

ARTICLES

Bensel, R. "Die Deutsche Flottenpolitik von 1933—1939. Eine Studie über die Rolle des Flottenbaus in Hitlers Aussenpolitik." *Marine Rundschau.* Beih. . 3. Berlin/Frankfurt, 1958.

Bloch, Ch. "Les relations anglo—allemandes de l'accord de Munich à la denonciation du traité naval de 1935." *Revue d'Histoire de la deuxième Guerre Mondiale.* 1955.5.

Borisov, D. "Anglo—Germanskie otnosheniya." *Mirovoe Khazyaistvo i Mirovaya Politika.* 1936. 8.

Burdick, Ch. B. "German Military Planning and France, 1930—38." *World Affairs Quarterly.* 1959/60. 30.

Crowther, G. "The Finance of Military Adventures." *The Spectator.* 1935. 7. 19.

Eichholtz, D.—Hass, G. "Zu den Ursachen des zweiten Weltkrieges und den Kriegszielen des deutschen Imperialismus." *Zeitschrift für Geschichtswissenschaft.* Berlin. 1967. 7.

Fisher, Sir, W. "The Beginnings of Civil Defence." *Public Administration.* 1948. Winter.

Freyberg—Eisenberg, Frh. von "Das deutsch—englische Flottenabkommen vom 18. Juni 1935." *Zeitschrift für ausländisches öffentliches Recht.* 1936. Bd. 6.

Géraud, A. (Pertinax) "France and the Anglo-German Naval Treaty." *Foreign Affairs*. 1935. 10.

Germains, V. W. (The Rifleman) "Some Problems of Imperial Strategy." *The National Review*. 1938. 6.

Gooch, G. P. "The Grouping of the Powers." *The Hungarian Quarterly*. Vol. 3. 1.

Haraszti, É. H. "Anglia és a német kérdés 1935 elején" (Britain and the German Problem at the Beginning of 1935). *Századok*. 1970. 3.

Haraszti, É. H. "Békéltetők" (Appeasers). *Történelmi Szemle*. 1969. 3—4.

Haraszti, É. H. "Az 1930-as évek és az 1935 júniusi angol—német flottaegyezmény" (The 1930s and the Anglo-German Naval Agreement of June 1935). *Századok*. 1971. 3—4.

Haraszti, É. H. "Two Secret Reports from the Hungarian Archives." *New Hungarian Quarterly*. 1967. 27.

Hattori, T. "Japans Operationsplan für den Beginn des Pazifischen Krieges." *Wehrwissenschaftliche Rundschau*. 1957. 5.

Ivanov, L. "Razriv londonskih pirigovorov i morskaya politika ih uchastnikov." *Tikhii Okean*. 1935. 1.

Jacobsen, H. A. "Zur Programmatik und Struktur der Nationalsozialistischen Aussenpolitik 1919—1939." Beilage zur Wochenschrift *Das Parlament*. 1967/50.

Jerukhamovich, I. "Anglo—germanskoe morskoe soglashchenia i ugroza novoi voiny." *Morskoi Sbornik*. 1935. 8.

Kornev, N. "Tvortsy Anglo—Germanskogo morskogo soglashcheniya." *Novii Mir*. 1935. 7.

Kühne, H. "Zur Kolonialpolitik des faschistischen deutschen Imperialismus, 1933—39." *Zeitschrift für Geschichtswissenschaft*. 1961. 9.

Lévay, G. "A haditechnika a tengereken" (The Technique of War on the Seas). *Hadtudományi Közlöny*. 1967. 3.

MacDonald, R. "Peace, Germany and Stresa." *The Times*. 1935. 4. 26.

Malanowski, W. "Das deutsch—englische Flottenabkommen von 18. Juni 1935 als Ausgangspunkt für Hitlers doktrinäre Bündnispolitik." *Wehrwissenschaftliche Rundschau*. 1955. 5.

Major, M. "Az angol fegyverkezés gazdasági vonatkozásai" (Economic Aspects of British Rearmament). *Magyar Katonai Szemle*. 1938. 10.

Marder, A. „The Royal Navy and the Ethiopian Crisis of 1935—36." *The American Historical Review*. 1970. 6.

Martin, Lawrence, W. "The Market for Strategic Ideas in Britain." *The American Political Science Review*. 1962. 3.

v. Németh, L. "A világ fegyverkezési versenye." (The World's Armament Race), *Külügyi Szemle*. 1937. 7.

Olivová, V. "Československo—sovětská smlouva z roku 1935." *Československý časopis historický*. 1964.

Ohmae, Toshikazu "Die strategischen Konzeptionen der japanischen Marine im zweiten Weltkrieg." *Marine Rundschau*. 1956. 5.

Ormos, M. "Sur les causes de l'échec du pacte danubien [1934—35]." *Acta Historica*. 1968. 1—2.

Ormos, Sz. M. "A fegyverkezés kérdése az európai diplomáciában Hitler hatalomra jutása után, 1933—34." (The Armaments Issue in European Diplomacy after Hitler's Access to Power) *Századok*. 1966. 2—3.

Petsi, M. A. "Ob Anglo—germanskom sgovore po voprosy o Baltistkam More." *Izv. An. Eston. SSR*. Tallin. 1955. 4. v. 1. [Eesti NSV Teaduste Akadeemia Toimetised.]

Popov, V. I. "Konferentsiya v Montreux 1936 goda." *Voprosy Istorii*. 1963. 11.

Popov, V. "Rasplata za nedalnovidnuyu politiku" *Mezdunarodnaya zhizn*. 1963. 11.

Réczey F. "Fegyverkezés a tengeren." (Rearmament on Sea), *Külügyi Szemle*. 1936.

Rhode, G. "Aussenminister Josef Beck und Staatssekretär Graf Szembek." *Vierteljahrshefte für Zeitgeschichte*. 1954.

Richmond, Sir Herbert [Adm.] "Naval Rearmament." *The Ninteenth Century and After*. 1936. 1.

Richmond, Sir Herbert [Adm.] "The case against Big Battleships. *The Nineteenth Century and After*. 1934. 8.

Richmond, Sir Herbert [Adm.] "The Battleship, Tonnage and Guns."*The Spectator*, 1935. 6.

Seabury, P. "Ribbentrop and the German Foreign Office." *Political Science Quarterly*. 1951. 66.

Soloveytchik, G. "Baltic Problems." *The Spectator*. 1936. 8.

Toscano, M. "Eden at Rome in the Eve of the Italo-Ethiopian Conflict." *Nuova Antologia*. 1960. 1.

Trevor-Roper, H. R. "Hitlers Kriegsziele." *Vierteljahrshefte für Zeitgeschichte*. 1960. 8.

Vilunaz, Iu. G. "Angliya i pakt chityriokh gerzhav v 1933 godi." *Vestnik Leningrad Univerziteta*. 1966. 2.

Wandycz, P. S. "Beneš and Beck." *The Central European Federalist*. 1961. 1.

Watt, D. C. "The German Diplomats and the Nazi Leaders, 1933—1939." *Journal of Central European Affairs*. 1955/56. 15.

Watt, D. C."The Anglo-German Naval Agreement of 1935: An interim Judgment" *The Journal of Modern History*. 1956. 6.

Watt, D. C. "Anglo-German Naval Negotiations on the Eve of the Second World War." *Journal of Royal United Service Institution*. 1958.

Weber, dr. T. "Az angol külpolitika irányvonalai." (Guidelines of British Foreign Policy), *Külügyi Szemle*. 1935.

Whealey, J. "Mussolini's Ideological Diplomacy: An unpublished Document." *The Journal of Modern History*. 1967. 12.

Wirth, F. "Und London schweigt. Aus den Geheimpapieren des Foreign Office." *Die Welt*. 1968. 1.

DISSERTATIONS

Gotlieb, H. B. *England and the Nature of the Nazi Regime. A Critical Assessment of British Opinion, 1933—39*. Oxford, 1953.

Heineman, J. L. *Constantin Freiherr von Neurath and the Conservative Influence on German Foreign Policy*. Cornell Univ. 1964.

Kieser, R. *Englands Appeasement-Politik und der Aufstieg des Dritten Reiches im Spiegel der britischen Presse, 1933—1939*. Winterthur, 1964.

Korusiewiecz, L. *Polish-German Diplomatic Relations, 1934—1939*. Berkeley, 1953.

Malanowski, W. *Der Widerstreit von Tradition und Doktrin in der deutschen Aussenpolitik von der Revisionspolitik zur einseitigen Liquidation des Vertrages von Versailles 1932—1936*. Hamburg, 1955.

Wiggershaus, N. *England und die deutsche Aufrüstung, 1933—35*. Bonn.

INDEX*

* Footnotes and Appendices are not included.

271

bour Party, 18—19, 85, 107; Navy, 62, 66—67, 71, 73, 75, 88; Peace Ballot, 27, 107; Public opinion, 13, 17—18, 43, 85—87, 98, 107, 110; R. A. F., 30, 34, 36, 72; (policy and) Soviet-Union, 32, 40—45, 148; trade, 60, transport, 60

Budapesti Hírlap, 17

Bullitt, W. C., 149—150

Bülow, B. W. von, 18, 20, 32, 34, 36, 94, 96

Bürkner, L., 81—84

Canaris, W., 54

Canary Islands, 68

Cape of Good Hope, 75

Cerruti, É. 95

Cerruti, V., 54

Chamberlain, Austen, 96

Chamberlain, Neville, 45, 73—74. 86, 116, 125, 153, 156, 158

Chatfield, Admiral Lord, 71—72, 79, 115—116, 153

Chambrun, Ch. de, 146

Chatham, 72

Chequers, 114

Chicago Daily News, The, 152

Chicago Tribune, 87

Chilston, Lord, 41, 150

China, 130, 149

Churchill, W., on Empire, 60, 136; on Germany, 13, 35—36, 45, 57, 108; on Naval Agreement, 9, 128—129; on Naval Strategy, 72—75, 107, 124, 155

Cincinnati Enquirer, 151

Clifford Allen (Lord Allen of Hurtwood), 18

Cliveden set, 9, 20

Collective Security, 15, 22, 44, 115, 124, 126, 143

Committee of Imperial Defence, 28, 76, 78, 80, 116, 153

Cocks, Mr., 120

Cooper, Duff, 136

Corbin, Ch., 33, 139

Craigie, Sir R., 85, 91—92, 97—98, 100—101, 110, 113—114

Cranborne, Lord, 46

Czechoslovakia, 14, 25, 45—46, 47; Eden's visit to 47—48; Frick's Protectorate of Bohemia and Moravia, 19, and France, 55; and Germany, 69

Cuxhaven, 58

Cyprus, 60

D'Abernon, Lord, 18

Daily Herald, 98, 117

Daily Mail, 118

Daily Telegraph, 19, 34, 83, 118

Dalton, H., 149

Danckwerts, W. H., 98, 106

Danubian Pact, 14, 25, 38, 40, 126, 141, 145, 147

Dardanelles, 158

Dawson, G., 114

Denmark, 70

Des Moines Register, 151

Deutsche Allgemeine Zeitung, 134

Dieckhoff, H. H., 91

Dill, J., 31—32

Dirksen, H. von, 156

Docteur, Adm., 139

Dodd, W. E. 152

Doenitz, K. Adm., 155

Dolobrand, Lord, 121—122

Drummond, Sir E., 51, 145—146

Eastern Europe, 21—22, 24—25, 30, 38, 47, 52, 68, 88, 126, 131

Eastern Pact, 15—16, 22—23, 25, 38, 40, 42, 44—46, 47, 53, 89, 115, 126, 141, 145, 147

Ebbutt, N., 89

Echo de Paris, 138—139

Eden, A., on Anglo—German Naval Agreement, 9, 82, 121, 127—128, 158; Character, 25, 78, 107, 113; and France, 16, 33, 140—141, 143; and Germany, 25, 35, 38, 40—41, 49, 84, 154; and Poland, 46—48; and Rome, 146—148, and Stresa, 50—51, 54; and Soviet Union, 32, 40—45, 149

Egypt, 146

Elbe, 97

Ellington, Sir E., 29, 153

Emden, 58

Engels, F., 10

Eritrea, 51

Ethiopia, 14, 16, 49—52, 54, 76—77, 117, 139, 141—142, 145—148

Europe, 59, 115, 130, 137, 143, 150, 159

Excelsior, 138

Eyres-Monsell, Sir B., 71, 92, 106, 110, 119—120, 124—125